# MEXICAN CINEMA

# MEXICAN CINEMA
## Reflections of a Society

REVISED EDITION

## Carl J. Mora

UNIVERSITY OF CALIFORNIA PRESS

BERKELEY · LOS ANGELES · LONDON

University of California Press
Berkeley and Los Angeles, California
University of California Press, Ltd.
London, England
© 1982 by
The Regents of the University of California
Revised edition © 1989
Printed in the United States of America

2   3   4   5   6   7   8   9

First Paperback Printing 1989

**Library of Congress Cataloging in Publication Data**

Mora, Carl J.
Mexican cinema: reflections of a society / Carl J. Mora—Rev. ed.

p. cm.
Includes bibliographical references.
1. Motion-pictures—Mexico—History.     I. Title.
PN 1993.5.M4M6     1989     791.43'0972—dc20     89-5205
ISBN 0-520-04304-9

To the memory of my parents

To Gigi

# Contents

Preface to the Revised Edition                                          xvii

Preface                                                                   xi

Introduction                                                              1

CHAPTER 1.   The Silent Film Era:   1896–1929                             5

CHAPTER 2.   The Coming of Sound:   1930–1939                            28

CHAPTER 3.   War and Growth of a Major Film Industry:
             1940–1946                                                   52

CHAPTER 4.   "Golden Age," Crisis, and Retrenchment:
             1947–1959                                                   75

CHAPTER 5.   Decline, Renovation, and the Return of
             Commercialism:   1960–1980                                 101

CHAPTER 6.   "...To Rebuild a Ruined Cinema in a
             Ruined Country":   1981–1989                               149

APPENDIX 1.   Selected Filmographies                                    187

APPENDIX 2.   Useful Addresses                                          191

Notes                                                                   193

A Note on Sources                                                       219

Bibliography                                                            223

Index                                                                   245

# Tables

1. Number of Films Premiered in the Federal District, 1953–1958     98

2. Mexican Film Production, 1958–1963     104

3. Mexican Film Production, 1971–1976     118

# Preface

A few years ago when I was an editor for an academic publisher, I tried to find someone to write a book on Latin American cinema. I had taken note of the scholarly attention being given to films and the concomitant increase in books on the subject. There were serious—and not so serious—books on Hollywood of course, but much was also being published on international cinema: the motion pictures of Britain, France, Italy, Japan, Germany, Eastern Europe, China, even India and Nigeria. However, there was practically nothing available in English on Latin American films.

My inquiries produced no results. Most American film scholars who were at all aware of Latin American filmmaking thought only of the work of Luis Buñuel, Cuban filmmakers, or a handful of independent Marxist cineasts in various countries. Many were unaware of any large-scale commercial filmmaking below the Rio Grande; others were derisive of "mariachi and melodrama" potboilers or "white telephone" filmic soap operas (such as Argentine middle-class melodramas of the 1940s and 1950s in which a white telephone was a prominent feature). A few expressed genuine interest in the idea and agreed with me that there was indeed a need for such a book, but unfortunately they were either unqualified or could not spare the time to do it.

It was at this point that I decided to write a history of the Mexican cinema—the largest and most important in the Spanish-speaking world—as I realized that by chance I seemed to be one of the very few people in the United States in a position to carry out such a study. Serendipitously, I was able to draw upon my own childhood experiences for the initial inspiration to write on Mexican films. I belong to the last pretelevision generation, one still molded by the movies. In addition to the regular fare of Hollywood films on which I was raised, I was fortunate to have attended concurrently, on a regular basis, the Hispanic movie houses of New York. In these, over a number of years, I viewed a multitude of Mexican, Argentine, Spanish, and occasionally other Spanish-language films. The names of Dolores del Río, Pedro Armendáriz, and María Félix were as familiar to me as were those of Humphrey Bogart, Katharine Hepburn, or Gary Cooper. I might even say that I experienced a "bicultural" (since that term is so popular nowadays) moviegoing youth.

I remember attending, in 1939 or 1940, the Belmont Theater somewhere near Times Square, which was the first movie house in New York to show Spanish-language films exclusively. In the next decade and a half, responding to the steadily increasing Puerto Rican influx, such specialized movie houses proliferated: the Hispano Theater on 110th Street and Lenox Avenue was one of the first to follow the Belmont's lead. At the height of their popularity, there must have been at least a dozen—mostly in Manhattan, but a few in the Bronx, Brooklyn, and more recently, Queens. The three I usually attended were the Del-Mar on 137th Street and Broadway, the San Juan on 168th Street and Broadway, and the Costello on Fort Washington Avenue near Broadway. I might justify the inclusion of these reminiscences by truthfully claiming that some of my earliest research for this book was done in these locales. Such an assertion is merited because even if I cannot remember more than a few of the hundreds of films that I saw, I did gain a "feel" for Mexican cinema, and for the movies of Argentina and Spain as well.

My first recognition of the cultural and linguistic variations among Hispanic peoples was obtained from Mexican and other Latin American movies. More important, from these Latin American films I became aware of the multileveled, complex cultural and social nature of Latin American societies. This, I realize, goes against detractors' comments on the "old" Latin American cinema, which dismiss it as some kind of cultural-imperialistic tool designed to deaden the progressive political instincts of the people with an unending cycle of tacky melodramas. In part, it is to contest such ideas that I have written this study.

My main reason for writing this book, however, is simply to provide an introduction to the Mexican commercial cinema for American and other English-speaking readers. Although the United States has been, and continues to be, a major foreign market for Mexican movies, the overwhelming majority of Americans are unaware of them. Mexican films are restricted to the Hispanic theater circuits and shown without English subtitles; therefore anyone wishing to see a Mexican movie would have to be fairly fluent in Spanish. Such a requisite effectively eliminates almost the entire general audience in the United States from exposure to Mexican cinema.

Very few Mexican films have been provided with English subtitles and distributed to general audiences here. A spate of coproducing between Mexico and Hollywood in the 1940s and 1950s resulted in a few films made both in Spanish and English versions. This activity led also to a number of Mexican performers establishing themselves in American and European cinema; among these were Pedro Armendáriz, Ricardo Montalbán, Katy Jurado, Rodolfo Acosta, and Alfonso Bedoya. But Mexican motion pictures themselves received scant notice, the exceptions being a handful of Luis Buñuel films such as *Los olvidados* (1950) (*The Young and the Damned*), *Subida al cielo* (1951) (*Mexican Bus Ride*), and *Adventures of Robinson Crusoe* (1952).

Undeniably, there are culturally determined differences in taste and subject matter between American and Latin American audiences. Most Mexican films, as is true of the films of any country, are made with specific home audiences in mind and as such may be unappealing to foreign audiences. For instance, Mexican filmmakers of the 1940s and 1950s responded to their mainly middle-class movie-goers' liking for melodrama and turned out great numbers of such movies. To a trained observer familiar with the Mexican milieu, such motion pictures can provide a wealth of insights into bourgeois mores; to someone lacking sufficient background in the evolution of Mexican melodrama and its roots in Spanish, French, and Italian nineteenth-century theater, it is perhaps easy to say, as a prominent critic did in a review of Buñuel's Mexican films, that the "acting is broad by any standards except Latin American."[1]

The great majority of European and Japanese films are produced for home markets and may also be considered too "broadly" acted for American audiences. Yet the many Mexican films that through the years have attempted to rise above the level of popular melodrama have also been ignored in this country. Interestingly, these films found a reception in Europe, especially France. After World War II, the work of such major Mexican directors as Alejandro Galindo and Emilio "El Indio" Fernández were screened regularly and reviewed by leading film critics.

Our lack of knowledge and/or interest in Latin American films is really only one aspect of the traditional disdain with which most Americans, intellectuals as well as the average person, have regarded Latin America. Although in recent years this unfortunate attitude has been rectified somewhat with regard to Latin American literature, there is still too much of an unwillingness to try to communicate with Latin America even if only for our own ultimate benefit. Not only are relations between the United States and the Iberoamerican republics strained and interlaced with conflict, but immigration, both legal and illegal, from these countries is reaching all-time highs. The growing and increasingly important political and cultural impact of the variegated Hispanic population in the United States, both native and immigrant, is causing fear and resentment among many non-Hispanic Americans, a state of affairs fueled by our traditional ignorance of Latin America and its peoples.

Having more Americans see Mexican and other Latin American movies is certainly not going to resolve serious long-standing international and domestic problems. But films are a potentially useful source for international and intercultural understanding; they are the quickest and cheapest way of traveling to another country for an hour or two and thoroughly immersing oneself in that society. There are, of course, pitfalls in this approach; a director can distort (or present his or her own very personal view of) a country's "reality" just as can a relatively uninformed foreigner. Yet since films are for the most part a collective economic activity, responsive to the mood of the public, the cumulative effect of seeing a number of movies of different themes and genres made by a variety of directors can be to offer some insights into the various ways in which that society sees itself as well as to its tensions and biases.

The above, simply, is what I hope this book will suggest to some readers. A more immediate hope specifically concerns the United States and Mexico. The two countries share a long border and a troubled history. The future promises to exacerbate rather than ease the problems. Yet in the United States media traditionally there has been a dearth of information and interest concerning Mexico. The average American knows precious little about the government, economy, culture, and society of our southern neighbor, in spite of the fact that Mexico's burgeoning population, its growing yet troubled economy, and, more recently, its emergence as a major oil-exporting nation increasingly are having a direct bearing on the domestic situation in the United States.

A greater exposure to Mexican films might make a small contribution toward changing the average American's stereotype of Mexicans and other Latin Americans as exotic, unpredictable, and perhaps rather primitive beings. After all, this is the view that has been fostered in innumerable Hollywood movies—an example of the power of films to reflect and propagate cultural attitudes.

The leftist Latin American filmmakers and their admirers in this country often decry the "imperialistic" preponderance of Hollywood films in Latin America and other foreign markets. Yet one possibly fortuitous effect of this cultural imperialism can be that many foreigners know us better than we know them. A Latin American moviegoer after years of watching American films without ever having been in this country might have a fairly good, albeit unstructured, idea of American society and its problems as well as its blessings. For instance, a study of the relationship between American films and immigration from Latin America would probably demonstrate Hollywood's important role in enthusing foreigners to want to enjoy American consumer society. In other words, American films have most certainly fueled the "revolution of rising expectations." The effects of motion pictures upon society are extremely complex and are a subject whose importance has just recently been recognized. The movies we see reflect our own attitudes; they are what we are and what our dreams and fears are. By taking them seriously, we might better understand ourselves as well as others.

The support, interest, and cooperation of many people have contributed to the writing of this book. To my deep sorrow, my father did not live to see its completion. Without the many years of weekly family excursions that he enthusiastically led to the Spanish-language theaters, I never would have been able to even conceive of this study. Because of his love for the *cine cristiano*, as he jokingly referred to it, my father was the person ultimately responsible for this book.

Edward H. Moseley, my dissertation advisor and good friend, made it possible for me to write my dissertation on the Mexican cinema, which was the basis for this book. Others who encouraged me in the initial stages of this work and who read earlier drafts were E. Bradford Burns, Julianne Burton, Lawrence A. Clayton, Carlos E. Cortés, Helen Delpar, Martin Taylor, and Paul Vanderwood. My appreciation also to Ernest Callenbach, editor at the University of California Press, who offered many helpful suggestions, and to Mary Lamprech for her careful editing. Although all of the abovementioned persons have been of inestimable help to me, responsibility for any and all errors lies entirely with me.

A very special expression of gratitude is due Alejandro Galindo, with whom I spent a delightful afternoon in Mexico City during my stay there in July 1977. Over many cups of coffee, first at the Wings Restaurant in the Cineteca Nacional and then at Sanborn's, he shared with me his vast knowledge of Mexico's cinema. And thanks are also due to Sigifredo García Sanz who found time in an extremely busy schedule to discuss the film industry with me, and for his subsequent help in obtaining stills and additional data.

I am eternally indebted to my cousin Arturo Mora and his wife Carmela whose spontaneous and warm hospitality helped make my brief stay in Mexico City an exceedingly productive one. Arturo's help at that time and since in opening bureaucratic doors and helping me obtain movie stills is deserving of more than mere thanks. Fernando del Moral of the Cineteca Nacional and José Olivarez of Azteca Films in Los Angeles were also most cooperative in supplying me with stills and additional information.

My love and warmest thanks go to my wife, Gigi, who has always been supportive through the many months of research and writing that went into this book; and to my children, Valerie and Vincent, who usually were understanding as to why I was unable to spend more weekends with them.

# Preface to the Revised Edition

The original edition of this book terminated somewhat abruptly with the administration of José López Portillo (1976–1982). This new edition carries the narrative forward to encompass the *sexenio* of Miguel de la Madrid (1982–1988) and the recently initiated one of Carlos Salinas de Gortari (1988–1994). The original edition included an extensive appendix listing most Mexican films made between 1896 and 1980. It has been replaced by much briefer filmographies of the work of some of the leading Mexican directors: Fernando de Fuentes, Emilio Fernández, Alejandro Galindo, Luis Buñuel (his Mexican films only), Luis Alcoriza, Felipe Cazals, Alberto Isaac, and Arturo Ripstein. However, for those readers who would find information of value in the film lists of the original appendix, I direct them to consult the 1982 edition of this book.

Let the reader be forewarned that this revised edition does not convey news of a dramatic rebirth of Mexican cinema—no repeat thus far of the "golden age" of the 1940s and early 1950s burst upon the world cinematic scene, nor was there a "new wave" comparable to that of 1970–76. This is not to say that no films of interest were produced in the 1980s. There were indeed a number of worthwhile films which are discussed in the new Chapter 6, films that in one way or another reflected the rapidly changing social, political, economic, and cultural milieux of 1980s Mexico. The main purpose of this new edition remains unchanged from that of the original version: to inform a wider audience outside of Latin America about the Mexican film industry and the wide cultural impact it had, both domestically and internationally, in the 1940s and 1950s and again in the early 1970s. And if a Mexican *nouvelle vague* did not arise in the 1980s perhaps one will in the 1990s, especially in view of what at this writing seems to be an enthusiastic outburst of democracy in Mexico complete with a raucous opposition to rattle the composure of the PRI-dominated bureaucracy under which the film industry has both prospered and languished.

Since the original edition of this book was published in 1982, I have been gratified to see an increased recognition of Mexican cinema among American and British film scholars. Whereas prior to the appearance of my book the English-speaking researchers who delved into Latin American films tended to overlook our southern neighbor's important movie industry, over the last few years I have noticed fuller accounts of filmmaking in Mexico and increased citations of this book as well as of Mexican sources in film publications.

A number of people were most helpful in facilitating my way through the research for this edition. Dana Evans Balibrera was invaluable in putting me in contact with Dr. Carlos Yates and Juan López Moctezuma of Azteca Films and Mario Bracamonte of VideoVisa in Los Angeles. I want to thank Dr. Yates and Mr. López Moctezuma for sharing their ideas and concerns with me, and for arranging screenings. Thanks also to Mr. Bracamonte for describing the rapidly expanding video industry.

In Mexico, I'm very grateful to Mercedes Certucha, director of the Cineteca Nacional, for receiving me on short notice and putting me in the capable hands of Cristián González, who arranged screenings and shared his thoughts about Mexico and its cinema. Cristián and his charming wife, Pía Ana Corti Velázquez, in addition to providing a valuable overview of the frustrations and joys of filmmaking, were most hospitable and gracious during my stay in Mexico City. Special thanks also to Antonio Bautista, head of Documentación e Investigación, who provided valuable data for this book. Others who provided information and help were Mario Aguiñada, Héctor Palacios, Salvador Alvarez, and Esperanza Guerra. At IMCINE I had the pleasure of meeting its new director, Ignacio Durán, recently arrived from his previous assignment as cultural attaché at the Mexican Embassy in Washington, D.C. to assume his new duties. At CONACINE, my gratitude to Fernando Macotela and his assistant Lic. Cortés for their help in the midst of busy schedules. And I wish to thank Felipe Cazals and Alejandro Pelayo for sharing their somewhat contrasting views of their country's problematic cinema. Thanks also to Theo Crevenna of the University of New Mexico who made it possible for me to meet his brother, Alfredo Crevenna, a distinguished veteran director, who gave me further insights into Mexican cinema. Lourdes Ramírez of Continental Films was most helpful in arranging for screenings. My thanks also to Alejandro Vergara and his capable projectionists at Churubusco studios. My appreciation to Manuel Barbachano Ponce of Clasa Films Mundiales and Carlos Bender Guevara and María Cruz Mora Arjona of Pel-Mex for providing stills.

Finally, my appreciation overflows for my indefatigable cousin Arturo Mora and his wife Carmela who were always on call to help us with the logistics of getting into, around, and out of the urban madness of Mexico City. Sigifredo García Sanz was extremely helpful in putting me in touch with useful sources. Marta Berlanga of Ciudad Juárez was most kind and patient in dealing with the bureaucracy of the Mexican National Railways. Dan Sheldon read the new text and offered valuable suggestions. Ernest Callenbach encouraged and guided me through the preparation of this new edition, and edited the manuscript. And thanks to my wife Gigi for braving Mexico City's pollution and for her (usually) unfailing good humor and adaptability to some Mexican public transportation systems.

Carl J. Mora
Cedar Crest, N.M.
May 6, 1989

# Introduction

In the 1960s, an exciting alternate cinema developed in Latin America—a politically oriented, largely Marxist movement that sought to project the truth, as its cineasts saw it, of the neocolonial, exploited condition of their part of the continent. The first manifestation of this urge to break with the commercial and cultural strictures of the past is generally recognized to have occurred in Brazil in the late 1950s. There an innovative group of young, committed directors, led by Glauber Rocha, launched the "Cinema Novo" which, simply stated, sought to portray the grim realities of Brazilian life—the poverty, the underdevelopment, the gulf between classes—in sum, the essence of the national experience. This movement arose and ran its course, however, within a long-established commercial movie industry. Brazilian cinema had existed for years; it did not begin or end with Cinema Novo.

Another cinematic movement of "social realism" began in Chile in the 1960s. It was given full government backing under the Allende administration after 1970 and then cut short in the bloody coup in 1973 that toppled the Marxist president. The principal figure of this Chilean cinema is Miguel Littín who made *El chacal de Nahueltoro* (*The Jackal of Nahueltoro*) (1969) and *La tierra prometida* (*The Promised Land*) (1973); after the coup he fled Chile and has since been making films in Mexico and Europe.

In Bolivia there was also a nascent cinema created by Jorge Sanjines and Antonio Eguino. Their UKAMAU group made *Ukamau* (1966), *Yawar Mallku* (*Blood of the Condor*) (1969), and *El coraje del pueblo* (*The Courage of the People*) (1971)—stark, intense films dealing with Bolivia's neocolonialist status, underdevelopment, and social and racial conflicts.[1]

Cuba, after the triumph of the Revolution in 1959, set out to create a new film industry with the full backing of the Fidel Castro regime. Although many people outside Cuba expected that the output of ICAIC (Instituto Nacional de Artes e Industrias Cinematográficas) would adhere to a doctrinaire Marxist-Leninist line, Cuban cineasts surprised their potential critics by creating such frank and insightful films as the magnificent *Lucía* (1968) and *Memories of Underdevelopment* (1968), along with a host of well-made albeit more frankly political features and documentaries. In December 1979, ICAIC hosted the First International Festival

1

of New Latin American Cinema with about five hundred invited filmmakers and cinema scholars attending from Latin America and the United States.[2] Cuba's prerevolutionary filmmaking was limited to a few ill-fated efforts resulting in low-quality commercial movies, and to being used as a tropical set for Mexican productions.

Besides Brazil, Argentina was the only other major filmmaking Latin American country to have developed an alternate, leftist cinema. It arose largely under the auspices of radical Peronists like Fernando Solanas and Octavio Getino with their epic albeit wearisome two-part exposé of imperialism and dependency, *La hora de los hornos* (*The Hour of the Furnaces*) (1968).[3]

This "new" Latin American cinema deservedly has attracted international praise and has even created a small following in the United States where Latin American films traditionally have been ignored. However, much of the New Latin American Cinema is not only not new, it is largely nonexistent. Conservative and right-wing governments in many Latin American countries have virtually ended the work of independent, leftist filmmakers through imprisonment, exile, or by just making it too difficult for these cineasts to make motion pictures.[4]

The adherents of this revolutionary cinema have often made the mistake of dismissing Latin America's commercial cinema as being uniformly of extremely bad quality, a poor carbon copy of Hollywood. Well-intentioned as these critics might be, their opinions are based upon, first, unfamiliarity with the commercial cinema and, second, an ideological identification with the Marxist Latin American cineasts who have created the revolutionary cinema.

The controversy between commercial entertainment, art, and political objectives in cinema (i.e., propaganda) is at least as old as films themselves. Originally an outgrowth of photographic time and motion studies, cinema was at first strictly commercial entertainment. Early cineast/entrepreneurs, like Louis and Auguste Lumière in France, produced short films of everyday scenes for showing to audiences fascinated with the novelty. These and other filmmakers soon graduated to recording important public events—funerals, coronations, wars—and gave birth to the newsreel which by its very nature is political propaganda. Soon the fiction film came along, combining elements of commercialism, art, and propaganda. By World War I, all the belligerent nations were producing fiction films. which exploited such topics as class, ethnic, racial and nationalistic prejudices.

For a committed Marxist (or National Socialist, Christian Fundamentalist, or whatever), it is quite natural that the only proper role of film should be to mobilize people toward a specific political goal. This goal, in the case of Latin American leftists, is a "cinema . . . that is antioligarchical and antibourgeois on the national level and anticolonial and antiimperialist on the international level."[5]

Such an interpretation of the role of cinema is perfectly satisfactory for politically motivated film, but motion pictures that fall into other categories (and there are many) should not be judged by these standards. Primarily, films have been and are still made for entertainment—in fact cinema is the first mass entertainment medium in history. But in the process of entertaining, films have, at times unwittingly, served educational ends and have been instrumental in reflecting, if not forming, cultural attitudes.

Many students of film have written extensively on the historical and sociological value of commercial films. Thus Siegfried Kracauer, the well-known German film scholar, has stated: "The films of a nation reflect its mentality in a more direct way than other artistic media for two reasons: first, films are never the product of an individual . . . second, films address themselves, and appeal to, the anonymous multitude. Popular films—or, to be more precise, popular screen motifs—can therefore be supposed to satisfy existing mass desires." He goes on to say: "What films reflect are not so much explicit credos as psychological dispositions—those deep layers of collective mentality which extend more or less below the dimension of consciousness."[6] The British historian Paul Smith has written: "The film records the outlook, intentions and capacities of those who made it; it illustrates in some way the character of the society in which it was produced and for which it was designed; it is the most perfect record of one factor operating within and upon that society—itself."[7]

The idea that often is found in writings on the New Latin American Cinema— that militant or revolutionary filmmaking owes nothing to the commercial cinema of Mexico, Argentina, and Brazil—is belied by the frequent denunciations of this "old" cinema by proponents of the new. Most of the "new" cineasts, from the Bolivian Antonio Eguino to the Mexican Alfonso Arau, grew up with the commercial Latin American cinema or even, as in Arau's case, earned their living in it.[8] Thus the militant cineasts are reacting not only against all the perceived evils and injustices of their societies but also to both the Latin American and Hollywood movies they saw in their youth. The New Latin American cinema has its inspirational roots in the commercial Latin American movie industries, especially Mexico's, even if only as a rejection of the latter.

This book will show the development of commercial filmmaking in Mexico. But the effects of the success of the Mexican movie industry from the 1940s to the 1960s had repercussions on the popular culture of all Latin America and Spain. Mexican films served as a conduit for a complex of ideas and influences: Mexican music, slang, performers, and folklore were popularized throughout the Hispanic world; on another level, the ideology and social views of the Mexican bourgeoisie were disseminated throughout Latin American society. In other words, Mexican cinema has practiced "cultural imperialism" just as Hollywood is so often accused of doing.[9]

Today Mexico is emerging as an important influence in both Latin American and world affairs. True, its oil wealth is the single most important factor for this new status, but Mexico's role is being made easier because it has enjoyed the respect of its Latin American neighbors for many years. The programs arising from the Mexican Revolution have served as models for land reform, labor legislation, and nationalization of foreign-owned enterprises for subsequent political and social movements in other Latin American countries. Mexico has also long been recognized as a cultural center, both of the fine arts and, as this book will show, of the popular culture of the mass entertainment media. Having established itself as an important shaper of mass culture in the hemisphere, Mexico can look to its cinema as the principal means used to achieve its present position of leadership.

# 1

# The Silent Film Era
# 1896–1929

Mexico in the 1890s was one of the *belle époque*'s success stories. Buoyed by his country's economic progress, progress at least by the standards of Positivism and the prevailing wisdom of the era's liberal tenets, the old authoritarian president, *don* Porfirio Díaz, presided over a nation whose future, like that of all Western civilization, was perceived to be bright indeed. Mexico's international credit standing, then as now, was excellent; British, American, Spanish, French, and other European firms, along with a number of native entrepreneurs and ranchers, built and operated the country's railroads, extracted its mineral wealth, cultivated its fields, herded its cattle, and managed its factories. Progress was being achieved by taking the only effective course, that of entrusting the economy—and the political system—to an elite of Mexican and foreign capitalists. To this end the resources of Mexico, along with its laws and government, had in effect been put at the disposal of entrepreneurs who were willing to invest in the country's development—upon the guarantee of favored treatment and assured profits.

Since Mexico was prosperous, politically stable, and a member in good standing of progressive European civilization, it was not surprising that the projectors and films developed and produced by Louis and Auguste Lumière should appear in Mexico almost immediately after their popularization in Europe. Mexican audiences flocked to the *cinematográficos* as enthusiastically as did their European and North American counterparts. Elsewhere in Latin America, newly opened theaters in Buenos Aires,[1] Rio de Janeiro,[2] and Havana[3] were also hard put to keep up with the crowds that flocked to be enraptured by these early flickering films.

The silent film era in Mexico has not been well documented and can only be pieced together from scattered journalistic sources of the time. Emilio García Riera, Mexico's leading film historian, decries the lack of sources necessary to form a comprehensive picture of his country's early filmmaking, since most of the movies made between 1897 and up to the 1920s have been lost.[4] The most complete reconstruction of the silent film era has been accomplished by Luis Reyes de la Maza who, culling accounts from Mexican newspapers and popular magazines of the time, put together a tantalizing glimpse of the social milieu of those bygone times. The following account is based largely on his book.[5]

The very first "moving pictures" in Mexico were provided by Thomas A. Edison's kinetoscope in January 1895; a certain John R. Roslyn invited the press to witness the novelty prior to initiating public showings. The kinetoscope, or nickelodeon, did not prove to be very popular since it was subject to frequent breakdowns, and the viewer had to watch the brief show through an eyepiece. The effort to provide musical accompaniment by means of a pair of headphones through which the faint melodies of a scratchy recording could be heard was also unsuccessful. The pictures themselves seemed to be largely restricted to "the contortions of a clown or the somersaults of an acrobat."[6]

In August 1896, however, the newspapers announced the arrival of Louis and Auguste Lumière's famous invention, the *cinématographe*. Reportedly it was a Frenchman, Gabriel Vayre, who obtained authorization to set up the first projector in Mexico, at number 9 Plateros Street, today Madero Avenue, and called the location "Cinematógrafo Lumière."[7] The Lumière projector caused an immediate sensation in the capital, and the city's residents lined up in Mexico's first movie queues to see such one-minute films as *The Card Players*, *Arrival of a Train*, *The Magic Hat*, and other such brief performances that had premiered in Paris as recently as December 1895 and were already being shown around the world.

Luis G. Urbina attended the performances at the Cinematógrafo Lumière and wrote an article about the experience, making him, in effect, Mexico's first film critic:

> The cinema is the fashion in Mexico. Its appearance has excited the capital, if the capital is considered to be limited between Peter Gay's Bar Rhum on Plateros Street, and the Escandón Palace on San Francisco Street. The new contraption has triumphed here over the kinetoscope. . . . For the moment all eyes are on the cinema.
>
> This new contraption which tries, as do its rivals, to entertain us by reproducing life, also lacks something: it lacks color. Perhaps with time it will acquire sound. . . . When fantasy, that curious dreamer, recovers from its amazement it gives thanks to Science, so abused, which Spencer has characterized as Cinderella. And there are those who still maintain that science is arid![8]

By December 1896 a more varied and attractive program was being offered the enthusiastic public by Vayre. The following is a typical program as advertised in the newspapers:

> Cinematógrafo Lumière. No. 9 Plateros Street. Program for Monday, December 14, 1896. 1st. Military parade in front of the Royal Palace in Madrid. 2nd. Women of the island of Tenerife supplying coal to ships of the squadron. 3rd. Parade of the Queen's Lancers. 4th. A Spanish engineer regiment en route to Cádiz to embark for the Cuban campaign. 5th. Spanish artillery in combat. 6th. Spanish infantrymen on bivouac. 7th. View of Berlin. 8th. Two Bengal tigers in the Paris zoo.[9]

These brief views of the colonial war raging in neighboring Cuba, along with those of the Parisian tigers, bore no comparison with the newsreels that in later years were to become part and parcel of every moviegoer's experience. But such films, though intended primarily to entertain with their novelty rather than inform, pointed up the immense importance of the new medium of cinematography: Distant events in faraway countries could be captured on celluloid and reproduced on a white screen in a darkened salon. No longer would the conflict in Cuba, or the Kaiser reviewing his troops in Berlin, or the crowded streets of New York be items solely to be read about, or frozen in photographs—such events from the world's vast panorama could now be magically brought to life anywhere. These first films, obtained from the Lumière firm, brought Europe to life before Mexican audiences, but it would not be long before these audiences would see *actualidades* of their own country. The early cinema not only enabled audiences to see real-life views of foreign countries, but it also better acquainted them with their own societies.

The origins of filmmaking in Mexico are immediately associated with the name of Salvador Toscano Barragán (1872–1947), a young engineering student who was the first Mexican to open a movie salon, make films of real-life events, and create in 1898 the first of his country's "fiction films", *Don Juan Tenorio*, a one-reeler starring the popular actor Paco Gavilanes.[10] During the Revolution, Toscano was to record extensively many of the historic events that shaped modern Mexico, footage that years later would be compiled by his daughter, Carmen Toscano, into a full-length documentary, *Memorias de un mexicano* (1950).

In 1897 Toscano ordered a projector and camera, a *toma vistas* (view taker), from the Lumière brothers. Opening a salon at number 17 Jesús María Street, he began to show Lumière films with musical accompaniment provided by an Edison phonograph.[11] At around midyear, Toscano transferred his salon to a larger, more comfortable site at the corner of Plateros and Espíritu Santo (today Madero Avenue and Isabel la Católica). It is misleading to think of Vayre's Cinematógrafo Lumière and Toscano's unnamed salon as true movie houses; they were simply large rooms into which these early entrepreneurs crowded as many chairs as they could for their brief shows. However, in March 1898 a projector of United States manufacture was set up in the Grand National Theater; this was a "veriscope," touted as being superior to the Lumière projector but in reality the same apparatus. It was simply an early instance of misleading advertising in the cinema industry, designed to fool the patent office as much as the spectators. The program was the Fitzsimmons-Corbett fight, the first American film shown in Mexico.[12]

By 1900 the cinema's popularity was solidly established and it enjoyed the loyal following of thousands. The programs still consisted of short comedy routines and acrobatics, in addition to the varied scenes of dignitaries and events in foreign countries. Thus the cinematic novelty had not yet encroached on the popularity of the traditional theater, but in the same year the latter's first real challenge arrived in the capital: the first "full-length" feature to be shown in Mexico, a French import called *The Passion of Jesus Christ*, in three reels.[13]

In 1901, Salvador Toscano returned from Paris bringing with him a load of brand-new films and the latest Lumière projector, the *biograph*. He rented the

Orrin Circus Theater and there screened his new movies, among which was probably the first bullfight ever shown on a Mexican screen, although it was either a French or Spanish *corrida*.[14]

Between 1901 and 1904, many new cinematic salons opened throughout Mexico City. The largest cigarette manufacturer of the time, El Buen Tono, opened its own salon on the top floor of the building which housed the company offices, just across the street from the site on which the Palace of Fine Arts would shortly be erected (Juárez Avenue and San Juan de Letrán). Instead of charging admission, El Buen Tono would simply accept a certain number of its empty cigarette boxes. In January 1904, it premiered the first version, probably of French origin, of *Don Quijote de la Mancha*. It was also one of the longest films seen in Mexico up to that time, being more than 450 meters in length and lasting about forty-one minutes.[15]

In 1905 another name famous in the early annals of film in Mexico made its appearance: Enrique Rosas introduced the new Pathé projector, setting it up in the Orrin Circus Theater. Soon his performances gained greater popularity than Toscano's. Rosas presented such talked-about films as the farce *Un carbonero en el baño* (*A Coal-Man in the Bath*) and the dramatic *Un drama en los aires* (*A Drama in the Skies*). Like Toscano, he had his own camera and soon was able to announce the showing of Mexican-made films. Every week he would offer highlights of the previous Sunday's bullfights; on June 25 Rosas announced film of the funeral procession of don Manuel Azpiroz, Mexico's ambassador to Washington, who had died in that city and whose remains had recently been brought back for burial. The audiences flocked to these and other programs principally to see the familiar streets of Mexico City on the screen and to catch glimpses of familiar faces. So successful were Rosas's programs that he moved to the more comfortable Riva Palacio Theater on Ayuntamiento; here he initiated such innovations as special children's admission prices on Thursdays and free admission for ladies on Mondays.[16]

The competition between Toscano and Rosas continued unabated through 1905, a year that saw more than two hundred short films screened in the capital's two or three salons. On October 29, Toscano showed *The Great Train Robbery* (1902); another landmark film projected in Mexico City that year was G. Méliès's *A Trip to the Moon* (1902). Toscano again showed his 1898 one-reel effort, *Don Juan Tenorio*. In addition he screened his current films such as *Guanajuato Destroyed*, showing the effects of a disastrous flood on that picturesque city; *Horse Races*, showing President Porfirio Díaz at the Hipódromo de la Condesa; *Automobile Races; Bullfight by Fuentes; Jota Danced by the Beautiful Romero; The Villa of Guadalupe* and other such movies. Somewhat out-of-date films from abroad were shown, such as *Alfonso XIII in Paris, Great Fire in Denver, The Workers' Strike in Russia, The Revolution in Russia, The Portsmouth Peace Conference,* and *The War in the Transvaal*.[17]

The year 1906 began with the premiere of the first "cops and robbers" serial—Pathé Frères's *Los rateros de París* (*Thieves of Paris*). In February a new salon, La Boite, was opened on San Juan de Letrán, using the latest 1906

Lumière-Pathé projector. Faced with the increased competition of an additional moviehouse, Toscano announced his acquisition of a brand-new 80-ampere Pathé "Lantern."[18] Not to be left behind, Enrique Rosas advertised in March the following program for his Riva Palacio Theater:

The management announces for today two shows in which will be screened the highly interesting views of the presidential visit to Yucatán. . . . 1st. Departure from Mexico of General Díaz. 2nd. Bay of Veracruz. 3rd. The Wharf. 4th. The gunboat Bravo. 5th. The port of Progreso. 6th. General Díaz disembarks in Progreso. 7th. The president in Mérida. 8th. Panoramic view of Mérida. 9th. General Díaz visits the Institute. 10th. Mrs. Romero Rubio de Díaz visits the Cathedral and the Bishopric. 11th. The lake of the San Cosme suburb. 12th. General Díaz leaves Mérida. 13th. The president makes his farewell to Yucatán.[19]

In addition to closely covering the old dictator's ceremonial visit to that distant corner of the republic, this program afforded the first close look at Yucatán for the great majority of the capital city's moviegoers.

Although the greatest cinematic activity was to be expected in Mexico City, provincial audiences in the other states of the extensive country were also being drawn into the new medium. Jorge Stahl (b. 1880), one of the true pioneers of the Mexican film industry, was one of the early entrepreneur showmen. His father had a hat factory in Guadalajara and young Jorge, at the age of fifteen, began a photography business. He sold it so as to acquire an Edison Kinetoscope at the St. Louis Exposition of 1904. With this machine he traveled all over the country— Guanajuato, San Luis Potosí, Chihuahua—renting theaters in these cities for one peso. Stahl recounts the following experience:

In 1906 something curious happened to me. I opened a projection salon in Guadalajara and called it Cine Verde, with four hundred chairs and a pianola. It was a small area, but since it was the first cinema, it was the gathering place for Guadalajara society. At that time the governor was Mr. Miguel Ahumada; he sent for me a few times to tell me that that was a very dangerous locality because, in the event of a fire, a real disaster could take place. For this reason he passed various ordinances: for more doors, an evacuation route. . . . All of these things we carried out. Since the salon was always filled and people were always waiting for the second or third show . . . he says to me one day: "Listen friend Stahl, you get that cinema out of there . . . because with that nonsense you're making more money than I do as governor." He did not at all appreciate our success. And it wasn't at all difficult to fill a little locality of four hundred capacity, at twenty-five *centavos* per show. Everyone in Guadalajara was always there.[20]

The popularity of the cinema, and consequently the demand for films, increased markedly in 1906: whereas at the beginning of the year there had been just three movie salons in Mexico City, by the end there were sixteen.[21] Luis G. Urbina, writing in the December 9, 1906 issue of *El Mundo Ilustrado*, commented on the increased traffic and crowds in that part of the city where the movie salons were concentrated:

They go to . . . cinema because it fills and entertains them with a pacifying, child-like innocence, and later upon returning to their bare and melancholy abode, their fantasy, like an Aladdin's lamp, continues decorating with ephemeral delights the sadnesses of existence.[22]

It was natural that the disadvantaged sectors of society, in Mexico and else-where, should respond with enthusiasm to the cinema. The developmental policies of the Díaz régime transformed Mexican society by creating the industrial infrastructure that was to make possible Mexico's economic advances after the 1940s; in the process of creating an industrial proletariat, however, a great many people were uprooted from their rural homes (now increasingly being taken over by large landholders and speculators) and forced to seek livelihood in the factories of the cities, or, starting at this early date, in the southwestern United States. Between 1810 and 1910, the population of Mexico increased 148 percent from six to fifteen million inhabitants—and the greater part of this increase was registered during the Díaz dictatorship from 1876 to 1910. This largely urban demographic growth has been generally attributed to the improvement of communications, industrialization, and the era's peace and stability.[23] Mexico's internal and exter-nal migration prior to 1910, though significant in itself, was dwarfed by unprece-dented population growth in the following decades, a growth greatly accelerated by the Revolution, and by developments in our own day. The increasingly greater visibility of the "underclasses" was already evident by 1906, and Urbina was moved to observe:

The popular masses, uncouth and infantile, experience while sitting in front of the screen the enchantment of the child to whom the grandmother has recounted a fairy tale; but I fail to understand how, night after night, a group of people who have the obligation of being civilized can idiotize themselves at the Salón Rojo, or in the Pathé, or the Monte Carlo, with the incessant reproduction of scenes in which the aberration, anachronisms, inverisimili-tudes, are made *ad hoc* for a public of the lowest mental level, ignorant of the most elementary educational notions.[24]

Although the above may be interpreted as a "Positivist" view of the cinema's social effects, there is no evidence that the authorities felt that the burgeoning number of movie salons and the intermingling of classes within them posed any great threat to the existing social order. On the contrary, and no doubt contributing to Urbina's consternation, hundreds of individuals fanned out across Mexico armed with projectors rented from firms like E. Moulinié or J. D. Tippett. Just as Jorge Stahl described, they carried a few films with them and set up mobile salons in even the tiniest of villages. Nevertheless these showmen realized tidy profits. Some of them eventually became distributors, as did Stahl, who came to acquire a stock of seven thousand films.[25]

The major French and American producers also sought to sell their films to the proliferating number of exhibitors. One of the first advertisements to this effect appeared in 1906:

Mexican National Phonograph Co. No. 77, 5 de Mayo extension. Three Edison films of the San Francisco earthquake are offered for sale.[26]

The Pathé Frères company soon opened its own offices in Mexico City for the sale of the parent firm's products: the Spanish titles of some typical films and their prices were *El cofrecito del Rajá (The Rajah's Small Trunk)*, 660 meters, 123 pesos; *Romeo cogido en la trampa (Romeo Caught in the Trap)*, 60 meters, 36 pesos; and *Los hermanos rivales (The Rival Brothers)*, 145 meters, 87 pesos.[27]

However, an ambitious distributor by the name of Jorge A. Alcalde placed his orders directly to the United States and France. Strangely, the parent companies, Pathé in particular, felt no compunction about bypassing their authorized representatives in Mexico and selling films to Alcalde. When he placed an advertisement in the paper listing a large number of new acquisitions, the Pathé Frères office in turn announced that all other film vendors were its branch offices. Alcalde was so incensed by being referred to as a "branch office" that he countered with an advertisement in which he indignantly asserted his autonomy at the same time naming all the firms in the United States, France, and England with which he did business.[28]

The Mexican Pathé office countered by reducing the price of all their films to sixty centavos a meter (heretofore prices had ranged between 1.70 pesos and 75 centavos per meter). This led to an all-out price war between Pathé and Alcalde which the latter won, in a manner of speaking, by offering all his films at one centavo per meter. Pathé of course retreated and priced their films at the standard rates; in a few months the Paris office realized its unethical conduct and dealt only through its representative office in Mexico City. This curious episode, according to Reyes de la Maza, is an example "of the astute and determined businessman in the first years of the cinema in Mexico, when this was an open business and did not see itself suffocated by official agencies or powerful unions."[29]

While Mexicans from a wide social spectrum were increasingly spending more of their leisure time at the cinema, momentous events were in the offing. The country was approaching the centennial of Father Miguel Hidalgo y Costilla's 1810 uprising which eventually led to independence from Spain. The year 1910, however, was to bring much more to Mexico than just a grand nationwide celebration, but the citizenry was of course unaware of the portentous events in its future.

Meanwhile, Mexicans went to the movies. Anticipating the upcoming centennial celebrations, the country's first major film made from a script[30] was premiered at the Salón Vista Alegre; this was Felipe de Jesús Haro's production of *El grito de Dolores (The Shout of Dolores)* (1908)[31] which attempted to recreate the events surrounding Father Hidalgo's (played by Haro) abortive 1810 uprising. This movie also set a significant precedent for many subsequent Mexican films in that it was the first to be panned by the critics, in this case the reviewer for *El Imparcial*:

In one of the capital's salons we were surprised a few nights ago to see a movie . . . which should have deserved its audience's applause. What we saw was nothing less than the conferences that the priest Hidalgo had with his allies a few hours before uttering his famous *grito*. This was followed by Hidalgo's arrival at the atrium of the temple of Dolores, the gathering of the people who, summoned by the bell, slowly began arriving until there was a very large number of insurgents . . . right there he was given the standard with the Virgin of Guadalupe. The old man, in spite of his age, bounded rapidly, flag in hand, onto the saddle (which was of the type used nowadays). He rode off like lightning and the mob followed him. . . . After what seemed to be endless running around over a vertiginous road without any kind of rhyme or reason that the public could discern, that phalanx of patriots arrived at the town of San Miguel el Grande—of this we were assured by the more alert viewers—and as it seemed they were going to stop there for awhile, the disorder grew and about a dozen gendarmes appeared, but not just in any old way but . . . with their Colt pistols. The insurgent mob, determined as it had been to crush whatever enemy stood in its path, fell in with the orders of the police of a hundred years later . . . and from that point the hero took off for parts unknown, since he was not seen again until the apotheosis, in which he appeared reclining over a tricolor flag, which Iturbide had undoubtedly lent him.

And so it occurred to me, as I think it would have to any person of average intelligence: why were not the gendarmes eliminated, or the conference with the Corregidora in Dolores, the contemporary saddle, the transfer of the standard at the time of the *grito*, and so many anachronisms that even children could notice? So many errors can be excused only if this is seen as the initiation of one of the most useful applications that the cinema will shortly have: to provide history lessons for schoolchildren, but in the meantime it is ludicrous to see the picture presented by Hidalgo and his army running around the mountains aimlessly on a brute horse, and obeying the orders of the police of San Miguel el Grande.[32]

It is quite possible that Haro's apparent *faux pas* in showing the revolutionary throngs meekly responding to the fictitious gendarmes' orders was not entirely an innocent blooper; given the Díaz regime's obsession with law and order it conceivably would not have looked with favor on scenes in which unruly mobs defied the established authorities, even if these happened to be Spanish colonial authorities. Whether any censorship was exercised on Haro's film, or whether he prudently wrote the scene into his script, is impossible to document.

Since Mexican cinema was to all intents and purposes nonexistent before 1910, moviegoers flocked to see principally American and French productions, but especially the latter. Toward the end of the nineteenth century the influence of France in literature, painting, and the theater had become predominant in Mexico, at least among the educated classes. This "detestable end-of-the-century taste . . . takes possession of architecture and the great lesser arts such as fashion and jewelry."[33] The theater, notwithstanding the apparent competition of the film salons, was to enjoy a revival thanks to the work of Virginia Fábregas, "the first modern actress in Mexico."[34] Born María Barragán in Yautepec, Morelos, she debuted in the 1890s with a popular Spanish actor, Leopoldo Burón. In 1904 she acquired the Renacimiento Theater and renamed it the Virginia Fábregas Theater; here she presented the latest works of the Paris stage, which were very popular with society under Díaz, as well as recent productions from Spain.[35]

Concurrent with the urbane, cosmopolitan theatrical trend personified by Virginia Fábregas, another quite different one was germinating among the lower classes. This *género chico* (short plays based on folklore, popular themes, and with certain political overtones) of popular culture was not to come into full flower until after the initiation of the Revolution when "beginning in 1911 we find the panorama of a nation which, complacent and between belly-laughs, approaches the humorous reduction of its own existence. The repertory: gendarmes with hanging mustaches, pulque parlor drunks, unrequited lovers, clownish ranchers. Spanish tavern owners, *peladitos*, Indians from Xochimilco, 'outsiders.' "[36] The *carpa*, or tent show, was the medium in which these popular genres flourished; it was also the training ground for many of the performers who would later graduate to the *revistas*, or music halls, of the cities, and finally to films. The quintessential *peladito*—a picaresque "wise guy" from the slums of Mexico City—is Mario

Moreno "Cantinflas" who got his start in a carpa in Jalapa; other early Mexican comics who were the creators of a distinctly national style of humor were Roberto Soto, Leopoldo Beristain, and don Catarino whose costume was a forerunner of Cantinflas's.[37] The legitimate theater and the *género chico* were to have a strong effect on the later cinema, both in subject matter and acting styles.

But it would still be some time before such popular expressions of the national culture were to reach Mexican screens. Meanwhile, in 1909 the "pax Romana that the dictator Porfirio Díaz imposed on Mexico did not encourage a popular brand of laughter, even though the people did not appear to be suffering. If their ruler did not distribute bread equitably, at least he kept them entertained with the circus of his court. They enjoyed his parades and the idea that they were governed by yesterday's hero."[38] In this enterprise, the cinema was admirably suited to advance the interests of the *porfiriato*; that year a filmic record was made of the president's visit to Manzanillo in December 1908 to inaugurate the opening of the railroad between that port and Mexico City. The Ministry of Public Education hired Gustavo Silva to photograph the entire journey and the final result was announced in the following glowing terms:

THE PRESIDENT'S JOURNEY TO MANZANILLO FILMED! Last night the rushes of the motion picture taken during the presidential trip to Manzanillo . . . were shown at the hall of the Superior Council of Education. The rushes were seen by the Minister of Public Instruction and Fine Arts, *Licenciado don* Justo Sierra; by the subsecretary Lic. Ezequiel A. Chávez; by Lt. Colonel Porfirio Díaz, Jr.; by Lic. *don* Pablo Macedo and by Mr. *don* Luis G. Urbina. The film in question has a length of more than 500 meters and reproduces the most interesting details of the trip. . . . It commences with the departure of the presidential party from the Buenavista station in this city, and the dirigible El Buen Tono, which escorted the train in which the president was riding, could be clearly seen. The most attractive parts of the route to Colima can be admired, and the reception for the presidential train in that city, as well as in Manzanillo and Guadalajara. The precision of all the most important details reproduced by the film is notable: the cruise around the bay aboard the "Ramón Corral," the presentation of the "Catinat's" commander, the reception in Colima, the parade and reception in Guadalajara, and the banquets in Manzanillo; everything can be seen with clarity and exactness."[39]

It was reported that *don* Porfirio watched the movie a few days later and expressed satisfaction with the new invention and the cameraman's work. Soon after, the Ministry of Public Instruction and Fine Arts released the movie to a distributor who either sold or rented it to exhibitors around the country.[40] In October 1909 Enrique Rosas filmed the meeting in Ciudad Juárez between Díaz and President William Howard Taft; the documentary was announced with great fanfare and screened exclusively at the Academia Metropolitana.[41]

Clearly, Mexican filmmaking was limited in the prerevolutionary period to what we would now call "propagandistic" features designed to enhance the glory of the dictatorship. "Popular" culture was still excluded from the better urban stages and had not made its appearance on film if one excludes from this category the first screening of the bullfights in the El Toreo Plaza of Mexico City.[42] In such features, the weekly bullfights and the eulogistic recordings of the chief executive's official peregrinations, it can be said that a style had already been established that succeeding generations of Mexican newsreels would faithfully follow up to the present day.

Since Mexican humor was absent from the screens, as it also was from the legitimate stage, audiences laughed at French slapstick shorts, especially those featuring the great comic Max Linder.[43] In the pre-1914 period, French film studios practically monopolized the world market and, in the silent film era, comedy, being entirely visual, was instantly communicable to audiences of any national or cultural background. Even in Italy, which had a well-established comic tradition in the *commedia dell'arte*, the influence of French comedy was all-pervading in this early period.[44] It is apparent that conventions in comedy, as in melodrama, were quite universal, at least in societies sharing Western cultural traditions. Virginia Fábregas was most instrumental in breathing new life into the Mexican theater. But also in the prerevolutionary period, the best French, Spanish, and Italian companies regularly toured the country, and some of the major international artists appeared there.[45] Such already strong cultural ties were strengthened by the popularity of the cinema before the regular tours of foreign and domestic actors were interrupted by years of civil war.

The year 1909 also marked a tragic event in Mexican cinema history: the first major fire in a crowded movie salon, at the Flores Cinema in Acapulco. When it was over, two hundred persons had been burned or suffocated to death. The early phosphate film was extremely flammable and the merest spark from the projector might ignite the film being run; this is what happened in the Acapulco salon. The rest of the four hundred meters of film in the projector quickly caught fire and the conflagration immediately spread to other film stock in the wooden projection shed.

The disaster in Acapulco shocked the entire country and for a few days following the tragedy, the capital's movie salons were practically empty.[46] The Salón Rojo, which came under the management of Jacobo Granat in June, boasted of its four fire exits. The suppliers of projectors took advantage of the disaster to hawk their wares: "The terrible fire in Acapulco and the enormous loss of life would not have occurred if an Edison cinematograph had been used."[47]

Nineteen hundred and ten, the centennial year, arrived and Mexico proceeded to grandly celebrate its first one hundred years of independent existence.[48] Military parades, official ceremonies, foreign delegations, balls, all testified to the prosperity and respect that Mexico enjoyed in the international community. Mexican cinematographers, especially Salvador Toscano and Enrique Rosas, dedicated themselves to capturing on celluloid the highlights of this important occasion. Many of these have been preserved in *Memorias de un mexicano*, splendorous scenes which form an ironic backdrop to the disaster that was shortly to overtake the *porfiriato*. In addition to the documentaries, the country's second commercial film was produced in honor of the centennial: *El suplicio de Cuauhtémoc (The Torture of Cuauhtémoc)* by Unión Cinematográfica, S.A., the second, albeit short-lived, Mexican movie company (the Alva Brothers' was the first, producing *El grito de Dolores* in 1908). Although no written sources seem to be available regarding the film itself, its subject matter is significant in that it "reflected the revived interest in Mexico's Indian past, also notable in music, literature, dance, and art,"[49] prior to the Revolution.

In 1910 Francisco Madero, a wealthy Chihuahua rancher and opponent of Díaz, issued his "Plan of San Luis Potosí," a manifesto that ignited the widespread resentment against the government. He set November 20 as the day on which the people should revolt against the tyrant Díaz. Even though scattered, tiny bands of revolutionaries did launch attacks against government installations on November 18–20, "the inability of the Díaz government to quell these small revolutionary brush fires revealed the hollowness behind its impressive facade."[50] The situation steadily worsened for the government and finally, on May 25, 1911, Díaz resigned: Madero's call for a revolt,"essentially a colossal bluff,"[51] had succeeded.

The year 1911 was therefore rather devoid in movie news since the public and the newspapers naturally enough had much more serious matters to contend with. But it was not long before Mexican cinematographers were to begin bringing to the public views of the fratricidal struggle that was shaking the country. In 1912 the first newsreel of which there is any record curiously seemed to be reflecting a peaceful Porfirian society:

Salón Allende. Today we inaugurate the film series entitled *Revista Nacional*, produced by the firm Navascue's y Camus. This bimonthly newsreel will show local and national events of palpitating actuality. The first film to be exhibited today shows the following events: Exhumation of the journalist *don* Trinidad Sánchez Santos, Olympic games, September 16th parade, Triumphal arches on San Francisco Avenue, Festivals of Covadonga, Disturbances in the Chamber of Deputies, Regattas in Xochimilco.[52]

European newsreels remained very popular as Mexican audiences learned, perhaps with a sense of morbid fascination, that in the Old World the primary concern seemed to be "enlisting troops."[53] Escapist films also increased in appeal, including the showing at the Salón Rojo of Sarah Bernhardt's *Camille*; other major films shown on capital screens in 1912 were, from Italy, *The Divine Comedy*, from France, Victor Hugo's *Les Misérables*, and in a neighborhood theater, *The Adventures of Sherlock Holmes*, which the copywriter for the advertisement, after repeatedly gallant efforts, still could not get quite right. The film's title appeared on different occasions as *Las aventuras de Charley Colms* and *Las aventuras de Shaley Colmmes*.[54] Another odd exercise in publicity was Jacobo Granat's advertisement for films of "the centennial of Independence, in which appears the illustrious figure of General *don* Porfirio Díaz, which is enthusiastically applauded even by the ladies."[55] The Revolution, however, was not entirely ignored on the Salón Rojo's screen: *La revolución en Chihuahua (The Revolution in Chihuahua)* aroused great interest since it showed scenes of the Madero government's military campaign against the rebel forces of Pascual Orozco in the north; musical accompaniment was provided by a military band. The Hidalgo Theater showed *La revolución en Veracruz (The Revolution in Veracruz)* which also helped to make audiences realize "the sadness of a war between brothers and the cost in lives."[56]

The cinema was accused of fostering immorality almost from its inception and there are reports of the Federal District authorities prohibiting showings of "por-

nographic'' films exhibiting ''secrets of the *boudoir* and spasms of the bedroom.''
It was even said that the Pathé cinema in Irapuato, not content with projecting
''immoral'' films, also passed out ''pornographic pamphlets.''[57] In both the
capital and the provinces moralists decried the fact that on Sunday afternoons
children gazed at '' 'scenes of adultery, of crude lasciviousness, of brutal revenge,
of horrifying cynicism, all skillfully projected.' They saw rapine, assassinations,
robberies, and suicides.''[58] The guardians of the public morality agonized over the
temptations that middle-class Mexican youth might encounter in darkened screening halls, even if properly chaperoned:

| | |
|---|---|
| Vamos al cine, mamá | (Let's go to the cinema, Mama |
| Mamá . . . matógrafo, | Mama . . . matograph |
| que eso de la ''oscuridá'' | Because I like the darkness |
| me gusta una atrocidá[59] | very much) |

The perils were not only moral but physical as well; in 1918 a certain
Dr. Chacón gave a learned discourse in the Medical Academy to ophthalmologists
regarding the ill effects that the cinema could cause to eyesight.[60] Such concerns
reflected an ever-growing awareness of the social impact that this new form of
entertainment could have. Thus regulation came early: in 1913 the first ordinances
governing the licensing and operation of movie salons in the Federal District were
published. These also included safety measures designed to avoid disasters like the
Acapulco fire in 1909. In addition, the regulations stipulated that all descriptive
subtitles were to be written in ''correct Spanish,'' those in any other language
being prohibited unless a corresponding translation was also provided.[61]

It was during the waning days of Madero's provisional regime that the first
Italian costume drama played in Mexico. *Quo Vadis*, ''indubitably the first great
hit of the new form of entertainment,''[62] enjoyed a worldwide success and directed
Italian filmmaking toward the lavish historical spectacular. It premiered at the
Arbeu Theater in July 1913 and was billed as ''the biggest event in the history of
Mexico!''[63] In November the Salón Rojo followed suit with the second Italian
''superproduction,'' *Marc Antony and Cleopatra*, with music provided by an
orchestra ''formed by professors of the National Conservatory of Music.''[64]

But the make-believe carnage of ancient Rome that Mexican moviegoers
enjoyed on the screen was soon to be supplanted by agonizingly authentic blood-
shed in the very heart of the capital. *Porfirista* (pro-Díaz) elements in combination
with some foreign business interests had been planning to topple the well-meaning
but largely ineffectual Madero almost from the time he arrived in Mexico City.

On February 9, 1913, Bernardo Reyes, a Díaz supporter still smarting over the
old caudillo's overthrow, and Félix Díaz, nephew of the deposed dictator, initiated
a coup attempt designed to terminate the provisional government. This led to an
artillery duel in the middle of Mexico City between Díaz and General Victoriano
Huerta whom Madero had ordered to put down the still-unimportant flareup. The
fighting lasted from February 9 to 17 (''La Decena Trágica'' or the ''Tragic Ten'')
in which hundreds of innocent bystanders were slaughtered.

The result was that Huerta himself toppled Madero and probably arranged his
assassination. Huerta's bloody assumption of power caused widespread repercus-

sions: immediately Emiliano Zapata in Morelos and Francisco "Pancho" Villa in Chihuahua rallied to Venustiano Carranza's call for a drive to unseat the "usurper" from the presidency. In this effort, the "Constitutionalists," as the Carranza-Villa-Zapata coalition was called, had the support of the new American president, Woodrow Wilson, who could not abide Huerta. This all led to years of bloody civil war and complex political maneuverings involving principally the various Mexican factions and the United States, but also, at various times, Germany, Britain, and Japan. Meanwhile, the so-called epic Revolution forged ahead with Zapata's movement encompassing the more radical elements and Carranza's the bourgeois, reform-minded groups. Francisco Villa's host composed of northern cowboys, railroad workers, and farmers was a populist surge lacking any well-defined political or ideological thrust.

Movies of this epochal, fratricidal struggle were in great demand, and an enterprising producer sent his cameramen to film the *zapatistas* in Morelos. The result was a three-thousand-meter documentary, *Sangre hermana (Blood of Brothers),* in which "the public could see with clarity the horrors of *zapatismo.*" This film was premiered at the Lírico on February 14, 1914, and reportedly was very well attended. The advertising for it, as the above example illustrates, had to be couched in terms acceptable to Huerta's censors, but the film itself apparently displayed considerable sympathy for the revolutionary cause, and the capital's citizens through it could vent some of their hatred of the government.[65]

In May 1914 the Salón Rojo presented a film of the "terrifying April 10 battle at San Pedro de las Colonias":

The formidable encounter between the federal forces commanded by the heroic generals J. Refugio Velasco, De Moure, Maas, Romero, Ruiz, Jaso López, García Hidalgo, Almazán, Alvarez, Monasterio and others, with the revolutionary forces. A realistic, effective movie, without artifice, taken on the battlefield at great personal danger by an expert cinematographist of the Pathé Frères firm of Paris. The most definitive and truthful demonstration of the cruel fratricidal struggle that has caused a sea of blood to run across the soil of the tormented Mexican nation. All of the scenes are authentic, exact, as can be confirmed by the above-cited heroic generals. The heroism of the combatants and the bitterness of the struggle will accentuate in the spirit of all Mexicans the desire for unity so as to calm the anguish of our shattered nation.[66]

Jacobo Granat's injection into his advertising of a plea for reconciliation among his countrymen seems to have gone unnoticed by the *huertistas* who, in any event, had much more serious problems on their hands than movie publicity. The basic antagonism between Wilson and Huerta had, through an involved series of events, resulted in the bombardment of Veracruz on April 21 by the United States fleet and that city's occupation by American troops.

By June, film of the event was being shown on the capital screens. The following advertisement for the Trianon Palace gives an indication of the contents of the movie along with widely shared Mexican sentiments:

The very interesting motion picture, *The North American Invasion*, will be exhibited. Events in Veracruz. A film of actuality which reveals the iniquitous deed committed by the *yanqui* invader. The interesting scenes reproduced by the cinematographer already indicate the contrast between the active Veracruz of yesterday, of the free and sovereign Veracruz, with today's Veracruz, trampled upon by our eternal enemy. On the screen you will see all the port's social classes attending the funeral of the heroic captain Benjamín Gutiérrez, giving the lie with this act to that segment of the capitaline press that has placed in doubt the conduct of this noble city. Among the diverse scenes reproduced by this interesting movie, we will cite the following: Panoramic view of the Bay of Veracruz. San Juan de Ulúa. Mexican artillerymen. The North American squadron in combat formation facing the heroic port on the morning of April 21. The Ipiranga. The *Prairie* bombarding the Naval School. The streets of Veracruz after the combat. The neutral White Cross volunteers its service. . . . Damages caused by the bombardment . . . the invaders' camp. . . . What the *yanquis* mean by equality. Seaplanes maneuvering.[67]

War had broken out in Europe in August 1914 and by November the first films of that conflict were shown in Mexico at the Salón Rojo, which announced that the latest views from the fighting fronts would be shown weekly. The domestic civil war continued to receive good coverage as well as sympathetic treatment for Huerta's enemies if one is to judge by some of the copy in one of Granat's advertisements for a program featuring scenes of Villa's attack on Nuevo Laredo followed by the "triumphal" entry to that border city of the "Supreme Chief of the Constitutionalist Army," Venustiano Carranza. It was described as a "national motion picture which reproduces a great historical event."[68] Such films, which were also being shown throughout the cities and hamlets of Mexico, must have played an important role in familiarizing the citizenry with the leaders of the factions contending for power at that time. In fact, the cinemas of the republic became lively centers of political commentary as these well-known figures— Huerta, Carranza, Alvaro Obregón, Villa, Zapata, and many others—were jeered[69] or applauded according to the public's preferences. Sometimes the audience's reaction was a good deal more volatile as in Martín Luis Guzmán's following description of movie-going Conventionists, as the supporters of Villa and Zapata were known, in Aguascalientes in 1916 watching a newsreel:

We, nonetheless, did not see the end of the movie because something happened unexpectedly that obliged us to flee the spot we occupied just behind the screen. Don Venustiano of course was the personage who most often appeared on the screen. His appearances, increasingly more frequent, had been becoming, as was to be expected, more and more unappreciated by the Conventionist audience. From the hissing mixed with applause on the first occasions he was seen, it progressed to frank hissing; then to hissing bordering on whistling; to open hooting, and finally to bedlam. And in that way, by stages, it finally resulted, when Carranza was seen entering Mexico City on horseback, in a hellish uproar culminating in two gunshots.

Both projectiles punctured the screen in the exact spot on which was outlined the First Chief's chest, and they struck the wall, one, half a meter above Lucio Blanco: the other, closer even, between Domínguez's head and mine.[70]

The years between 1916 and 1920 were tumultuous ones for Mexico, but in spite of grave domestic and international problems the epic phase of the Revolution was winding down. Venustiano Carranza's provisional administration was able, through the military prowess of Obregón, to eliminate the threats from Villa and Zapata. War with the United States was narrowly averted and a new constitution promulgated in 1917, a document that in its labor, land tenure, and social welfare provisions was the most radical in the world at that time. It provided the political and juridical infrastructure that guides the country to this day, the "institutionalized Revolution," as Mexican politicians have been fond of saying these many years.

The Mexican film industry was born in the midst of this profound transformation of the nation's society and it was to grow with the rest of the economy, as the latter became more diversified and acquired more complex technologies through the subsequent decades. In purely economic terms, films were to become an important export and thus a source of badly needed foreign exchange; by 1961 they were in sixteenth place among Mexico's export commodities. In that year films brought in 100 million pesos in revenues from foreign markets, greater than such important export items as henequen and tomatoes.[71] The cinematic medium's great propaganda value had already been recognized by the political authorities:

The government quickly appreciated the ability of films to speak to mass audiences. The Ministry of War, as one example, expressed a lively interest in filmic interpretations of the Revolution which kept Mexico in chaos throughout much of the 1910-1920 decade, and financed such films as *Juan Soldado, El precio de la gloria [The Price of Glory]* and *Honor militar [Military Honor].*[72]

In spite of war and uncertainty—or perhaps because of it—the movies thrived. The great Italian spectacle film, *Cabiria*, opened to enthusiastic audiences in 1916. General Pablo González, the man who was to bring about Zapata's assassination in 1919,[73] was quoted as saying that *Cabiria* was "the most gorgeous work I have seen in my life."[74] Foreign serials were introduced, including the famous Pearl White adventures, and Charlie Chaplin made his first appearance on Mexican screens. The popularization of "police" films brought forth a denunciation of "*Sherlockholmismo cinematográfico*" by the editors of *El Tiempo*. They were concerned lest the showing of such movies, especially in lower-class theaters, serve as training if not inspiration for criminal elements, a concern that continues to our own day. The alarm that *El Tiempo* expressed over the mixture of classes in neighborhood salons—bourgeois, workers, foreigners, soldiers, ruffians, respectable women, secretaries, maids, and prostitutes—would indicate just as well the democratizing influence of the cinema, whether it itself was a factor in this process or simply reflecting the changes that were occurring in the larger society as a result of the Revolution.[75]

More important, however, was the vigor displayed by Mexican cineasts at this time. On September 15, 1916, the first full-length film made in the country was premiered at the Hidalgo Theater. This was *1810 o los libertadores de México (1810 or the Liberators of Mexico)*, produced in Mérida, Yucatán, by the firm Cimar. The screenplay was written by the Yucatecan poet, Arturo Peón Contreras.[76]

Manuel de la Bandera, an actor and founder of the México-Lux production company, attempted to establish a school to train performers for the cinema. His first effort in September 1916 came to naught, but by 1917 Mexican filmmaking was promising enough to come to the attention of President Carranza who ordered that a cinematic school to be headed by the same Bandera be formed as part of the National School for Theatrical Music and Art.[77]

Mimí Derba, a popular stage actress, is an important name in the nascent film industry; with Enrique Rosas she cofounded Azteca Films which produced *En defensa propia (In Self Defense)* in 1917. The first full-length (one-hour) film to be made in the Federal District was, however, *La luz (The Light)*, produced by Bandera's company, México-Lux. Starring Emma Padilla and Ernesto Agüeros, it was directed by Ezequiel Carrasco, a photographer at the National Observatory. It had its premiere at the Salón Rojo in June, a gala event attended by Venustiano Carranza. It was the first Mexican film to employ such cinematic techniques as closeups and tracking shots.[78] It was based on a 1915 Italian film, *Il Fuoco (The Light)*, starring the *diva* Pina Menichelli,[79] but transplanted to a Mexican setting, shot on location in Chapultepec, Xochimilco, and Viveros de Coyoacán.

Azteca Films's *En defensa propia*, starring Mimí Derba, was released in July. According to *El Pueblo*, which termed it the "first artistic nationally made film," it was a great success (the same newspaper had severely criticized *La luz* which in turn had been well received by all other writers). It would be of interest to briefly outline the plot here in order to get an idea of the stories favored by the Mexican public at the inception of the national movie industry. *En defensa propia* tells of Enriqueta, recently orphaned, who is obliged to work and finds employment as a governess for the widower Julio Mancera's small daughter. In time Enriqueta and Julio fall in love and marry, but it is not long before a cousin of Julio's, Eva, arrives from Europe. The unscrupulous woman, obviously a typical vamp, sets about to break up Enriqueta and Julio's idyllic marriage. Eva is close to succeeding but she is foiled at a party that she has insisted on giving for all of Julio's friends; at an unguarded moment she is surprised in the garden by Julio, Enriqueta, and all the guests in a compromising situation with Mauricio, Julio's best friend.[80]

Except for the backgrounds, it is evident that this plot outline was not terribly unique to the Mexican ambience. The story was most probably inspired by a European model in much the same way that *La luz* was. Since Italian cinema was at its peak at this time it seems likely that *En defensa propia* was, like *La luz,* adapted from one of Italy's upper-class dramas, a form already in decline.[81] Mimí Derba's second effort for Azteca Films was *La soñadora (The Dreamer)* (1917). Writing of this movie, an anonymous reviewer for *El Pueblo* expressed his misgivings over the already evident tendency of his country's filmmakers to portray a nonexistent, artificial Mexico. In one party scene the guests, "dressed in Louis XV style" dance a "clumsily executed" minuet which has no relation to "these violent times, of the danzón and fox-trot. . . . How much better it would have been if Mimí's 'national beauty' had been presented clad in the typical Mexican dress tracing out the steps of a daring and gay *jarabe*."[82]

The years between 1915 and 1923 have been termed the "Golden Age"[83] of the Mexican silent cinema, although production was extremely modest, especially if compared with the output of the major filmmaking countries, but still impressive according to Latin American standards.[84] In this period new production companies were organized in Guanajuato[85] and Mazatlán as well as in Mexico City, but, unlike Brazil, in which a regional filmmaking pattern was to arise,[86] the Mexican cinema industry, like the Argentine, was soon to be centered in the capital city's environs. By 1919 Enrique Rosas had left Azteca Films and with the Alva brothers formed Rosas, Alva, y Cía, which produced the most distinguished Mexican film of the silent era, *La banda del automóvil gris (The Grey Car Gang)*.

After 1917 the main studio facilities were those belonging to Azteca Films (on the corner of Balderas and Juárez) and the ones belonging to Manuel de la Bandera's company, México-Lux or Productora Quetzal.[87] Since they were located within the city they cannot have been very extensive. Jorge Stahl recalls that in Mexico City "there was no studio adequate for the achievement of a better-quality film," and opened one in the Condesa suburb, on no. 117 Montes de Oca Street. He does not mention what year he did this but refers to "more than two hundred and fifty films made in ten years," and states that *Tiburón*, starring Joaquín Coss, was the first one produced there.[88] It must have been around 1919, since it is in that year that the Stahl name first appears as a movie producer (Jorge's brother, Carlos, directed a good many of the Stahl studio productions). The figure he quotes of 250 films would seem to indicate that Mexican film production was more significant than the extant sources show; however, Stahl says that these were all very brief, amateurish efforts, and of them no trace or memory remains.

The upswing in film production from 1917 reflects the return to Mexico of at least the beginnings of political if not economic stability. On February 5 the Constitution of Querétaro became the new law of the land, replacing the Constitution of 1857. On that day, too, the last American troops of Pershing's "punitive expedition" quietly retreated across the border. On March 11 elections were held and Venustiano Carranza emerged victorious.

Mexico managed to stay clear of the European conflict and most people in the country were undoubtedly relieved to see American troops in the trenches of France instead of galloping around the Chihuahua deserts. Tensions with the United States flared up again after the end of the World War, mostly over the touchy subject of American properties in Mexico, especially oil. In 1919 revolts against the Carranza administration broke out: Félix Díaz again trying his luck in Oaxaca, and Pancho Villa initiating anew his nuisance raids. In October an anti-Carranza band captured the United States consul in Puebla, William O. Jenkins, and held him for ransom. Carranza was either unable or unwilling to obtain his release and Jenkins finally had to ransom himself. As soon as he was free, however, federal authorities arrested the American consul on the rather doubtful charge that he had arranged his own abduction. The affair caused excitable elements in both countries to talk of war for awhile. The strongly anti-Carranza Jenkins remained in Mexico and went on to become an important figure in the film industry.[89]

Carranza, by contrast, was the victim of Mexico's last successful military coup. Alvaro Obregón unseated him in May 1920 and Carranza was machine-gunned while trying to flee with a good part of the Treasury. The 1920s were the period of the "Northern Dynasty," called thus because Mexico's leaders were from the northern states, principally Coahuila, Sonora, and Chihuahua (Carranza had been governor of Coahuila when the Revolution began in 1910). Howard Cline has summarized Obregón's administration in the following manner:

His court was composed of an interlocking directorate of military men, intellectuals, labor leaders, and agrarians. From 1920 through 1933 these leaders hacked away at the roots of Mexican difficulties; slowly and painfully they wrestled with the undramatic chores of reconstruction and rehabilitation. By historical accident national leadership for the Revolution had come primarily from the North; this circumstance goes far to explain the peculiar cast, the emphasis, and the goals of their programs. The general tone of the golden twenties everywhere in the world provided the atmosphere in which they toiled.[90]

The apparent vigor of the fledgling film industry seemed to reflect the Obregón presidency's business-like approach to the rebuilding of Mexico. By the early 1920s, however, film production was falling off in spite of the construction of new facilities like Jesús Abitia's Chapultepec studios.[91] Mexican films at this time had no foreign markets and their hold on the domestic one was precarious indeed. Silent films moreover were almost strictly visual, and the plots could easily be followed without much recourse to the brief descriptive titles. Mexican movie-makers generally attempted to copy European, especially Italian, cinema: the stories, the acting styles, and even the institution of the *diva*, in the persons of Mimí Derba, Emma Padilla, and Elena Sánchez Valenzuela, were adopted by Mexican filmmakers. An exception was the previously mentioned *La banda del automóvil gris* (1919). Produced and tautly directed by Enrique Rosas, it was patterned after the highly popular serials from France and the United States. The film related the exploits of an actual criminal gang that had operated in Mexico City—a gang, it was rumored, with political connections. The criminals utilized a grey automobile for their capers, hence the film's title. Rosas was inspired to make the movie when he photographed the execution of the real gang. Joaquín Coss played the leading role and assisted with the direction. The movie debuted on December 12, 1919, in twenty-eight Mexico City theaters. Of it García Riera has remarked, "*El automóvil gris* conserves its flavor and freshness. Efficiently realized and with a good rhythm, the film constitutes a magnificent testimony of its time, of the revolutionary epoch."[92]

From a peak production in 1919 of fourteen films, including a newsreel series that reached seventy editions, Mexican filmmakers' output gradually declined until in 1923 only two films were made, and in 1924 apparently none. Production increased to about seven movies in 1925 but the popularity of Hollywood films was a challenge that the undercapitalized and largely unoriginal national companies were unable to overcome. The United States was producing between five hundred and seven hundred features a year by the early 1920s, a gargantuan industry that was backed by an aggressive marketing organization throughout the world. In 1923, for instance, First National Pictures opened its own distribution offices in Mexico City and not long afterwards Universal, Paramount, and Fox followed suit.[93]

While Mexican filmmakers in the silent film era seemed little preoccupied with depicting, either negatively or positively, their neighbors to the north, Mexico was becoming an important thematic component of early American cineasts. The great

Scenes from *La banda del automóvil gris* (1919). (Pelmex)

majority of representations of Mexicans or Mexico on American screens were
distinctly negative and almost entirely within the "Western" genre. It must be
remembered that this was a period in which racist attitudes were freely expressed
in the media, not only in the United States but throughout most of the world. The
most famous example of this in the film is probably D. W. Griffith's *Birth of a
Nation* (1915)—an undeniably great film, it nonetheless represented blacks in a
highly offensive manner, but the portrayal was undoubtedly concurrent with the
image of blacks held by the great majority of white Americans at the time.[94]

The traditional enmity toward Mexicans in the southwestern United States,
extant even before the two nations warred in 1848, had generated a legacy of
hatred, suspicion, and bigotry. These attitudes were exacerbated by the Mexican
Revolution, whose social effects spilled over the border into the United States. The
sporadic official hostility between Washington and Mexico throughout the
1910s–1930s did little to uplift the Mexican image in American films. Although
Westerns were the principal genre to draw upon both then-current attitudes and
literary stereotypes to depict Mexicans as "conniving, untrustworthy persons,
who usually operate outside of the law,"[95] other films addressed themselves to
contemporary problems. For instance, in 1915 William Randolph Hearst helped to
finance a fifteen-part serial entitled *Patria* starring Irene Castle. The film depicted
a Japanese-Mexican invasion of the United States and clearly was designed to
capitalize on the nervousness many Americans felt over revolution in Mexico,
Japanese involvement south of the Rio Grande, and United States-Japanese
tensions. The serial was vastly popular but so offensive to the Japanese ambassador that President Wilson asked the film company to withdraw *Patria* from
public exhibition.[96]

It seems likely that such American films, for obvious reasons, were not
exported to Mexico. Thus moviegoers in the Mexican capital were for the most
part unfamiliar with the Hollywood Western's portrayal of the "Mexican
greasers" so familiar to American Western folklore. More concern was expressed
over American films made in Mexico and the image they presented of the country.
The pilgrimage of American filmmakers to Mexico is as old as the cinema industry
itself: in 1898 the Edison Company sent photographers south of the border to make
such brief films as *Mexican Rurales Charge*, *Mexico Street Scene*, and *Train Hour
in Durango, Mexico*.[97] One of the first complaints against the "distortion" of
Mexico on American screens appeared in 1920. An unidentified American offered
to make films in Mexico so as to familiarize foreign audiences with the country—
an offer that apparently elicited a subsidy from the Mexican government. The
movie later appeared in the United States under the title, *The Real Mexico*,
including scenes of "the Texcoco market with a couple dozen seminaked Indians
selling firewood with an explanatory title stating 'Productive transactions.'" The
commentator reserves his most indignant reaction for a shot of Madero Avenue
with the title, "The capital's most aristocratic avenue"; it was shown almost
deserted, but at the moment the camera was filming, two or three burros loaded
with coal passed by.[98]

In spite of the many troubles between Mexico and the United States, the Salón

Rojo saw fit to celebrate the American independence day in 1918 with a "solemn commemoration . . . program dedicated to the honorable and dignified American colony and its allies."[99] This was the introduction to a showing of the latest newsreels from the European battlefields. It seems strange that the Salón Rojo's management, whose business depended on the public's good will, would refer to the United States in a manner that must certainly have been anathema to a good number of Mexicans. Perhaps it can most readily be explained as still another manifestation of the peculiar love-hate relationship that has always existed between the two countries—that perplexing blend of mutual attraction and antipathy that many Mexicans and Americans feel toward each other.

The decade of the twenties witnessed the emergence of a fabulous movie industry in Hollywood and, as a consequence, a decline in production in Mexico. The highly professional American films offered their audiences fantasy and glamor, and this was the period of the great "stars": Rudolph Valentino, Douglas Fairbanks, Theda Bara, Charles Chaplin, and many others. The industries of Western Europe, especially Italy and France, failed to recover their prewar vigor. Only in Germany, traumatized by defeat and narrowly avoiding a Marxist revolution, did directors such as Fritz Lang attempt to interpret and explain the anxieties of German society, and through their efforts German expressionism made a deep impression on cineasts throughout the world. The Bolshevik government of Russia was among the first to realize the enormous propaganda potential of the cinema and directors like Sergei Eisenstein raised "expressive realism" to an art.[100]

In view of such developments in Europe it is somewhat puzzling that the revolutionary government of Mexico did not place more emphasis on the utilization of film as an educational and propagandistic tool. Under the dynamic leadership of the enigmatic José Vasconcelos, Minister of Education under Obregón from 1921 to 1924, a great cultural, educational, and artistic movement got underway.[101] Artistic and musical festivals were organized among schoolchildren in which native traditions were revived and glorified; painters like Diego Rivera, José Clemente Orozco, and David Alfaro Siqueiros resurrected and gave new significance to an ancient tradition of mural art—"the message was Marxian, the technique Mexican."[102]

Clearly Mexico in the 1920s had a monumental task of reconstruction before it, and perhaps its disorganized, suffering, and poverty-stricken society was not in a position to respond to a government educational program in which film would play a major role. The problem was basic education—the need to eliminate widespread illiteracy and to raise the self-esteem of the Mexican masses. This is what Vasconcelos's programs attempted to do and evidently he did not recognize the part that films could play in the process. Even if Vasconcelos had realized the potentialities of motion pictures, it is doubtful that his Ministry of Education with its painfully inadequate budgets could have subsidized much filmmaking.[103] The troubled Mexican film industry, such as it was, remained solidly in private hands.

If Mexican films per se had not made a particularly strong impression on the world cinema, Mexican performers were achieving international stardom. Antonio Moreno was the first, appearing in a 1920 American production released in Mexico under the title of *Los peligros de la montaña del trueno o Aventuras de Moreno (The Dangers of Thunder Mountain or Adventures of Moreno)*. It was made by the Vitagraph Company and was reportedly premiered in Mexico even before it was shown in the United States.[104] Ramón Novarro was another transplanted Mexican who became an established figure in American films.[105] But far and away the most successful performer, and the one who achieved true stardom, was Dolores del Río, born Dolores Asúnsolo y López Negrete in Durango in 1906.

The Revolution forced Dolores's father, who was director of the Bank of Durango, to seek refuge in the United States. In the meantime, the mother and her four-year-old daughter sought a measure of peace in Mexico City. There Dolores attended an exclusive French private school and, as was proper for a well-bred young lady of the Porfirian aristocracy, she studied Spanish dancing. In 1921, at the age of fifteen, she married Jaime Martínez del Río, a wealthy lawyer and *hacendado*, eighteen years her senior. After a two-year honeymoon in Europe, during which on one occasion she volunteered to dance for Spanish soldiers wounded in the Moroccan war and drew plaudits from Alfonso XIII, the happy couple returned to a comfortable yet uneventful life in Mexico City. Their placid existence was radically changed by a chance visit from their friend, the painter Adolfo Best Maugard, who brought some American friends with him—the film actors Claire Windsor and Bert Lytell, and the director, Edwin Carewe.

The American filmmaker was highly impressed with Dolores and asked her if she would be interested in working in a movie. The idea excited both Dolores and Jaime, both of whom longed for a change as well as a chance to get away from the insecurities of Mexico. By August 1925, they were in Hollywood and Dolores del Río's international film career, spanning almost fifty years, had started, beginning innocuously enough with a bit part in United Artists's *Joanne* (1925). In keeping with a long-established American tradition by which any Latin American, and especially Mexican, with positive personal attributes was perceived as being "Spanish," so too did Dolores's billing tout her as a "Spanish actress." Quite possibly also, the continuing uneasy relations with Mexico might have persuaded studio publicists that it would not do for them to go out of their way to inform the moviegoing public that their newest glamorous property hailed from that troublesome neighbor full of rampaging Indian bandits.

In rapid order, Dolores del Río appeared in *All the Town is Talking* (1925) with Edward Everett Horton, and *Upstream* (1926) with Walter Pidgeon. When she appeared in Raoul Walsh's *What Price Glory?* (1926) as Charmaine, the French peasant girl pursued by Victor McLaglen and Edmund Lowe, Dolores was established as a star. She starred in *Resurrection* (1927) directed once again by Carewe, this time playing a Russian peasant. Other notable silent films that Dolores made were *Ramona* (1928) and *Evangeline* (1929); she made fifteen in all, including the films already mentioned.

Dolores del Río had not yet learned English (she was directed through interpreters), a not insurmountable problem in silent films. She made the difficult and surprising transition to sound, having learned English, and went on to an equally successful career in the "talkies."[106] She was not to make a Mexican film until 1943.[107]

While Dolores del Río was achieving international stardom and other Mexican performers, most notably Ramón Novarro, Lupita Tovar, Raquel Torres, Lupe Vélez, and Gilbert Roland, were establishing careers in Hollywood, the Mexican silent film industry languished, unable to offer even token competition to American products. Even though Mexican production could be characterized as flourishing when compared to that of Argentina and other Latin American countries,[108] this was small consolation to the country's filmmakers. In the late 1920s, however, some names appeared that were to become important in the 1930s and 1940s and to contribute to the Mexican film industry's commercial, if not artistic, success in ensuing years. Among these were the Stahl brothers, Jorge and Carlos, who produced *La linterna de Diógenes (The Lantern of Diogenes)* (1925), and especially Miguel Contreras Torres, a revolutionary officer-turned-filmmaker, who made *El sueño del caporal (The Corporal's Dream)* (1922), *De raza azteca (Of Aztec Race)* (1922), *El hombre sin patria (The Man Without a Country)* (1922), *Fulguración de la raza (Resplendence of the Race)* (1922), *Almas tropicales (Tropical Souls)* (1923), *Atavismo (Atavism)* (1923), and *Oro, sangre y sol (Gold, Blood, and Sun)* (1925). According to García Riera, Contreras Torres's work is "without doubt the most important of the twenties." His films were "imbued with a patriotic spirit similar to that which animates commemorative political speeches."[109]

The advent of sound was to cause profound changes in the international cinema. The popularity of Hollywood films was not to diminish by any means, but forces would be brought into play that were to revitalize or initiate the movie industries of many countries. Mexican reality would begin to find its voice, however fitfully, in the films of the 1930s.

# 2

# The Coming of Sound
# 1930–1939

From the very inception of the cinema, the synchronization of sound with the screen image had been a cherished dream. We need only recall Luis G. Urbina's musings on the subject after attending a performance at the Cinematógrafo Lumière in the late 1890s: "It . . . lacks something . . . . Perhaps with time it will acquire sound."[1] Experimentation with sound had started early although such attempts invariably failed. In Mexico the first public demonstration of synchronization of sound with film occurred at the Colón Theater in June 1912, an experiment mounted by one of M. León Gaumont's assistants—or at least it was thus reported. The French filmmaker had preferred not to display his untried *chronophone* in Paris just yet and supposedly arranged to have it tested in Mexico instead. It was no more than a phonograph record synchronized with the film and it was a complete failure, not only because the supposed Gaumont assistant was not really what he pretended to be but also because he was inept at operating the equipment. He was incapable of correctly synchronizing the record with the screen images and only succeeded in eliciting some "frightful noises which had nothing in common with what was being seen on the screen." The *cronófono*, as it was called in Mexico, was kept in the Colón's storage room until 1927 when a second unsuccessful attempt was made to work it.[2]

The coming of sound, in Eric Rhode's telling words, was to release "energies that had long been suppressed."[3] As this chapter will describe, the energies generated by the Mexican Revolution sought expression through the new medium of sound films and resulted, toward the end of the decade, in the establishment of a sophisticated industry. The movies produced by Mexican studios in these years reflected a variety of societal, cultural, and political concerns. They also provided an outlet for the ambitions of some members of the new entrepreneurial class created by the Revolution. A number of producers were revolutionary officers or cronies of influential politicos. Foreign influences also played a major role in the development of the Mexican film industry and the two major sources will be discussed: the artistic and intellectual ferment of interwar Europe, and the techniques and styles of Hollywood. The latter's ill-fated attempt to make "Hispanic" films for the international Spanish-speaking market was especially important, providing a training ground for directors and performers who later went to Mexico. Although Mexico was in the process of recovering from a destructive civil war and developing ways of continuing and institutionalizing its revolution, it was also caught up in the complexities of the postwar world.

The intellectual and political reactions to the revolutionary changes taking place both in the Old and New Worlds were reflected in the new art of the cinema. The "talkies" were to acquire great importance in many countries as a medium for expressing vague national anxieties. The world was in turmoil, and social and political change was occurring faster than most people could come to terms with it. The *Belle Époque* of prewar days had signified the end of an era of smug self-complacency in Western and Western-affiliated cultures. The World War shattered the security of the middle classes and tragically demonstrated the fatal flaws in the sacred double pillars of European claims to superiority: capitalism and nationalism. Imperialism, the manifestation of this system in Asia and Africa, had also been dealt a death blow although its weakened structure was not to collapse completely until after 1945.

The "roaring twenties" exemplified the general rejection of traditional social restraints in the West. What was known in the Anglo-Saxon countries as Victorian morality had been rent asunder by the brutal stresses of total war. The rejection of prewar ethical and sexual standards resulted in a more or less "liberated" class, among the elites at least. Another kind of liberation—and much more ominous to many—was represented by the Bolshevik triumph in Russia and the founding of Comintern-affiliated Communist parties throughout the world. The middle and upper classes in capitalist countries lived in fear of what they considered a proletariat subverted by Bolshevik agents.

Perhaps the cinema could be ideally adapted to further the interaction of social change and art. Working from this premise, Lev Kuleshov, at the Moscow State School of Cinematography, came to believe that editing was the basic tool for adapting the cinema to artistic or social purposes. He worked out a theory of montage which a short time later would be taken up by Sergei Eisenstein, a filmmaker who was to have a profound effect on the Mexican cinema.

The struggle to understand and express the social and technological changes which were taking place assumed many forms. The Futurist movement, for example, attempted to find artistic inspiration in the industrialized urbanism of the twentieth century and its influence soon spread to film. This group of artists was the first willing to cooperate with the Bolsheviks, who accepted for a time the Futurists' views as official policy.[4]

The Futurists' restlessness and preference for the bizarre was one attempt aesthetically to come to terms with and respond to the multifaceted uncertainties of postwar life. In painting, surrealism and cubism reflected this intellectual restlessness. These forms found their way into the cinema in such films as *The Cabinet of Dr. Caligari* (1920), for which the presurrealist Alfred Kubin, "who . . . made eerie phantoms invade harmless scenery and visions of torture emerge from the subconscious,"[5] designed the sets. The Futurist style was also incorporated in the work of French avant-garde filmmakers: in Louis Feuillade's *Fantômas* (1913) the main character "pierces a white wall and blood gushes out of it . . . and five men in identical masks and black tights pursue each other at a ball."[6] Louis Delluc, in his use of objects to convey his central characters' mental states, especially in the lost film *Le Silence* (1920), strongly influenced both Jean Epstein and the Spaniard Luis Buñuel. In fact, Delluc's techniques can be said to have reached their fullest expression in the 1960s, in Alain Resnais's *Last Year at Marienbad* (1961) and Buñuel's *Belle de jour* (1966).[7] Buñuel, along with his fellow Spaniards Pablo Picasso and Salvador Dalí, was intimately associated with prewar and postwar Parisian artistic circles. Buñuel and Dalí collaborated in the classic but bizarre surrealist experiment *Un Chien andalou (The Andalusian Dog)* (1928). Its imagery "includes hands and armpits covered by ants, soiled bodies, an emphasis on buttocks and the usual apparatus of sadistic practice."[8] In *L'Age d'or (The Golden Age)* (1930) Buñuel developed further these symbols:

Less brittle and more wide-ranging than its predecessor, *L'Age d'or* brings this anality even more into the open: lovers roll ecstatically in mud beneath the shocked gaze of some dignitaries: later the woman dreams about her lover as she sits on the lavatory. From its opening sequence—a documentary in the manner of Painlevé about the death rites of scorpions—to its concluding quotation from de Sade's *140 Days in Sodom*, in which various noblemen dressed in robes imitative of figures from the past, including Christ, totter from their debauchery into the snow, *L'Age d'or* extends caustically over many notions of civilization and style, including the manners of polite society, the corruption and suicide of a minister and even the founding of Rome.[9]

Diego Rivera, who along with David Alfaro Siqueiros and José Clemente Orozco was to found the Mexican muralist movement under the sponsorship of Vasconcelos, was also a part of this European artistic and intellectual maelstrom. He was in Europe during the war and in the immediate postwar years "joined the Cubist movement, became a friend of Picasso ('I have never believed in God,' he said, 'but in Picasso, yes.'), fraternized with Apollinaire, quarreled with and made up with Modigliani. . . . He stayed a long time in Italy studying the frescoes of the Renaissance. He glowed with enthusiasm for the new Russia that was emerging from the revolution."[10]

Rivera participated in and absorbed the intellectual excitement of the European avant-garde and returned to his native Mexico to create a muralist genre that received inspiration from both pre-Columbian fresco painting and Old World traditional and revolutionary concepts. Simultaneously, Luis Buñuel was developing his unorthodox film techniques and antibourgeois posture in silent films—a style he was to bring to fruition in Mexico during the 1940s and 1950s.

Nationalists in Mexico and elsewhere in Latin America were concerned that the advent of sound films represented "the most powerful weapon" in the American "peaceful invasion" of their countries. If all films henceforth were to be made in the English language, they worried, the Latin American publics would "by force have to learn that tongue if they wished to be entertained and after a few years Castilian would be forgotten, passing into the category of dead languages."[11] The newspaper *El Universal* launched a campaign to convince all Latin American governments to prohibit the showing of English-language films, an objective which most other Mexican newspapers and magazines enthusiastically supported. One exception was the monthly magazine *Continental* which attacked *El Universal*'s position and defended the screening of movies in any language, especially English, since it would help "Mexicans learn that language which was indispensable in the business world." The magazine's spirited defense of foreign-made "talkies" (as they were also called in Mexico at this time) might very well have been based on the fact that foreign film distributors regularly bought twelve pages of advertising in *Continental*; in addition, the editors displayed rather bad timing in publishing, in the very same issue in which they stated their pro-English-language "talkies" position, a letter from Paramount Films de México, S.A. congratulating them on the editorial.[12]

Sound films were not greeted with enthusiasm elsewhere in the world either: Chaplin felt they were unsuitable to his sophisticated comedy style of mime and characterization; and the Soviet directors, Eisenstein among them, felt that sound introduced additional technical and marketing difficulties.[13] The advent of sound ended the careers of some boxoffice idols, notably Douglas Fairbanks and Mary Pickford. Many foreign artists in Hollywood were unable to handle dialogue adequately, although, as has been seen, Dolores del Río, whose English was certainly almost nonexistent in the 1920s, did make the transition quite successfully to the talkies, as did Greta Garbo. However, other performers, such as Emil Jannings, Pola Negri, and Conrad Veidt, returned to Europe.

As pointed out in chapter 1, Mexican filmmaking was practically at a standstill by the end of the silent film era. The only moviemakers of any consequence were the ex-revolutionary fighter, Miguel Contreras Torres, who cultivated a super-patriotic genre, and Jorge Stahl, who had run the gamut from pioneer cameraman *à la* Toscano to distributor and studio owner. Both Contreras Torres and Stahl were to achieve greater prominence after the production of Mexican sound films began. Other directors, producers, and performers of the early 1930s were to arrive in Mexico by way of Hollywood's Spanish-language film production. The major American companies, in an effort to retain and widen their lucrative Latin American markets, and undoubtedly concerned about the implications of campaigns against English-language films such as the one waged by *El Universal*, imported stage actors and directors from Spain and Latin America. Initially, the films were simply Spanish-language versions of English-dialogue originals or sound remakes of silent originals. Toward the end of Hispanic movie production, especially at Fox, some films were produced in Spanish only.[14]

By 1929 all of Hollywood's production facilities had converted to sound but American films could obviously only be marketed in English-speaking countries. Therefore the large studios began simultaneously to produce silent versions of their films for foreign consumption. This ploy was a resounding failure in countries like France, Germany, and the Soviet Union that were already making their own sound films. Movie production in Spain and Latin America, on the other hand, was incapable of supplying a market of one hundred million people who demanded films in Spanish. Movies with Spanish subtitles were unsatisfactory because of the high illiteracy rate generally throughout Latin America.[15] In addition, the Mexican government, as did others in Latin America, demanded "absolute Castilian purity in the subtitles of foreign films."[16] Hollywood thus began the production of features in Spanish, French, and German but soon found that European audiences much preferred seeing the original versions starring popular American stars.

Only film production in Spanish, however, became established in Hollywood. In spite of these "Hispanic" pictures' general unpopularity with Latin American audiences, more than 113 were made between 1930 and 1938.[17] Strangely enough, Hollywood never utilized its best-known Latin American stars, Dolores del Río and Lupe Vélez, in Spanish-language films, although Ramón Novarro did appear in a few. Marlene Dietrich and Emil Jannings also never made Hollywood films in their native tongue, while Greta Garbo and Maurice Chevalier did.[18]

There seem to have been two principal reasons for the nonacceptance by the Latin American publics of these Hollywood Spanish-language films. First, there was the jumble of accents—Spanish, Cuban, Mexican, Argentine, Chilean, and others—which imbued these movies with an air of unreality. For the first time, through the medium of sound films, the average person of one country came to realize how his language was spoken in another. Though Spanish theatrical companies had for generations been touring throughout Spanish America, the legitimate theater was usually restricted to a relatively well-educated elite who expected national and regional variances in the spoken language. But the cinema exposed mass audiences to a sort of collective culture shock; they heard their own language emerging from the screen images' lips, but a language that sounded bizarre and alien—even if understandable. Part of the problem was the American producers' assumptions—even if they knew a little Spanish—that the so-called Castilian Spanish, the language as spoken in the central plain of Spain, was acceptable everywhere in the Western Hemisphere. The immediate result of this linguistic confusion was that Argentina declared that she would not permit the importation of the multiaccented films or those in "Castilian."[19] Spain, for its part, stated that its moviegoers "could not bear to listen to the irritating Latin American accents" and that if the "c" or "z" were not "orthographically pronounced," the American studios "need not bother" sending their films.[20] Lest it be assumed that all of this bickering over language was simply an isolated case of Hispanic xenophobia, it should be pointed out that in Britain at this time, movie audiences began to complain of pictures in "American" and that there were demands that actors should speak English "correctly."[21]

The second factor that rendered Hollywood Hispanic films unacceptable to their intended audiences was the same one that doomed the making of American pictures in French, German, or Italian: the Latin American audiences enjoyed seeing American stars and "would not easily accept their substitution by José Crespo or Luana Alcañiz."[22] On the surface, the two factors would seem to contradict each other since the linguistic dispute was ultimately an expression of a particularly strident nationalism that was emerging throughout the world in the

1930s. Yet this xenophobia was transcended by Hollywood's "dream factories" which had already established the American movie as the favorite entertainment of millions throughout the world irrespective of nationality or ideology.[23]

A rather interesting film that was made after the regular production of Hispanic films ended was Columbia's *Verbena trágica (Tragic Festivity)* (1938).[24] It starred the eminent Mexican actor, Fernando Soler, playing the role of Mateo Vargas, a Spanish immigrant in New York. As the film begins, we are shown a, or perhaps *the*, Hispanic neighborhood in Manhattan, whose multinational residents are making preparations to celebrate *El día de la raza*—Columbus Day. This small, improbable neighborhood is a paean to Pan-Americanism since the inhabitants seem to represent every Latin American country. However, the principal characters are Spaniards and as the fiesta celebrations—more reminiscent of a typical Little Italy street *festa*—proceed, we see Mateo just released from a short stint in jail for hitting a policeman. Mateo is a boxer and neighborhood hero and his return is eagerly awaited by everyone except his wife Blanca (Luana de Alcañiz). This is because she happens to be a couple of months pregnant, and since Mateo has been in prison for eight months it does not take him long to realize that something has been going on in his absence. Blanca's lover is Claudio (Juan Torena), Mateo's best friend and fiancé of Blanca's half-sister, Lola (Cecilia Callejo).

It is soon evident that the basic problem with all these emigré Spaniards (they are not refugees from the Civil War raging at that time; in fact references to Spain make the country appear completely normal) is their difficulty in adapting to life in New York. Claudio is disgusted because he cannot find a job and has no money to marry Lola; Mateo's problems, as reflected in his unexplained act of hitting a policeman, stem from his homesickness and his unhappiness with American ways—the "noise," the "bluff," the "hypocrisy." The rest of the film is a melodramatic account of Mateo's finally realizing that it is Claudio who is Blanca's lover; with the street festivities as a backdrop, Mateo pursues Claudio, catches up with him on a fire escape, and punches him, causing Claudio to fall to his death in the street below. This time Mateo's temper and his exaggerated sense of honor have brought him serious trouble.

*Verbena trágica* is interesting in that it seems to be a last-ditch attempt by Hollywood to find some formula that would appeal to Latin American audiences. Although it is difficult to know what kind of distribution the film had in Latin America, it probably was not extensive. By 1938–1939, Mexican filmmaking was well established and expanding rapidly;[25] it was well on its way toward exploiting the Latin American markets that Hollywood had failed to reach with its Spanish-language productions. It is difficult to tell whether *Verbena trágica* was designed to utilize Columbia's remaining Spanish production facilities in an attempt to find a market among Hispanics in the United States. Employing an already-familiar actor like Fernando Soler with a back-up cast of leftovers from Hollywood's Hispanic heyday would seem to indicate some such intent. In the late 1930s, the major Hispanic group would have been the Mexican-Americans of the Southwest. This was before the great Puerto Rican influx of the late 1940s and

1950s that was to make New York City a major foreign market for the Mexican film industry;[26] it also predated the much larger immigration, both legal and illegal (of Mexicans, Dominicans, South Americans), of recent decades. The Cuban population of Florida, centered at this time in the Tampa area, was minimal and unimportant as a motion picture market. In any event, Fernando Soler recalls that when he went to Hollywood in 1938 to make *La verbena trágica* and *El caudal de los hijos (The Fortune of Children)* he was "unimpressed" with either film; the experience served only to corroborate his opinion that in Mexico they "performed technical miracles."[27] Yet, whether the Columbia studio executives' intention was to appeal to Latin American audiences or United States Hispanic audiences, their choice of an aggressively Spanish group of principal characters in *Verbena trágica* seems to betray a basic misconception of their market. The imagined problems of Spanish immigrants in New York would presumably hold little interest for movie audiences in Bogotá or Lima and perhaps even less for a Mexican-American public in Los Angeles or San Antonio, even if one ignores the fact that Spanish immigration to the United States has always been statistically insignificant. It is true that throughout the film other obvious national types make brief appearances—Argentines, Mexicans, and a black man who is supposed to be either Cuban or Puerto Rican. Yet such obvious contrivances imbue the entire film with an air of unreality, and *Verbena trágica* serves as a fitting epitaph to Hollywood's ill-conceived and ill-fated attempt to make movies in Spanish for Latin America.

The sound era in Mexico began on July 6, 1929, when *The Jazz Singer* starring Al Jolson was premiered at the Olimpia Theater. It was the first film with a complete sound track although for some years incidental sound effects or background music had been included in some movies,[28] one of numerous examples being the metallic sound of gold coins being dropped on a table in the scene where Judas is being induced to betray Jesus in Cecil B. DeMille's otherwise silent *King of Kings* (1927). It is also at this time that Luz Alba (pseudonym of the journalist Cube Bonifant) began writing her highly regarded film reviews in *El Universal Ilustrado*. Jorge Ayala Blanco considers her, along with Xavier Villaurrutia, the only writer in this period who foresaw and sensed the rudiments of a specifically cinematic culture. In her reviews Luz Alba was one of the first in Mexico to take always into account the "decisive participation" of the director.[29] Fittingly, the premiere of *The Jazz Singer* was favorably chronicled in Luz Alba's movie column.[30]

The excitement caused by the novelty of sound soon led to the various international controversies already described and Hollywood's failed venture into foreign-language motion picture production, especially in Spanish. The way was now clear for the rebirth of a Mexican film industry which was symbolized by the 1931 production of *Santa*, a remake of the 1918 silent film based on the Federico Gamboa novel. The Compañía Nacional Productora de Películas was formed on the initiative of a wealthy film distributor and ex-revolutionary associate of Madero, Juan de la Cruz Alarcón, the journalist Carlos Noriega Hope, and the veteran cineast Gustavo Sáenz de Sicilia. Antonio Moreno was brought from Hollywood to direct Mexico's first sound movie. From the United States also came Lupita Tovar (to play the title role), Donald Reed (professional name of Ernesto Guillén), and Alex Phillips to supervise the filming. Among other significant names associated with *Santa* were: Roberto and Joselito Rodríguez who devised an original sound system for the film; Agustín Lara, who wrote the music; and Miguel Lerdo de Tejada, musical director.[31] Shooting began on November 3, 1931, in the Nacional Productora studios; on March 30, 1932, *Santa* was premiered at the Palacio Theater. It cost 45,000 pesos to make and ran for eighty-one minutes.

Santa is a humble country girl who lives happily with her family in Chimalistac until she is seduced and abandoned by the army officer Marcelino (Donald Reed). Her brothers, learning of the dishonor she has brought on the family, cast her out. Santa makes her way to Mexico City where she finds work at a brothel run by doña Elvira (Mimí Derba) and where Hipólito (Carlos Orellana), a blind piano-player, is also employed. Both Hipólito and the bullfighter El Jarameño (Juan José Martínez Casado) fall in love with Santa who has by this time become quite renowned in her trade. She goes to live with El Jarameño but when he surprises her one day with Marcelino he throws her out of his house. Santa sinks to the lowest depths and develops cancer; Hipólito arranges for an operation but she dies during surgery. He has her buried in Chimalistac.

García Riera says that *Santa* is "mysteriously lacking in the poetry that time tends to attach to even the worst of films."[32] Yet, as Salvador Elizondo comments, the film represents a "peculiar condition" that occupies a "preeminent place in the Mexican soul; the idealization, through moralizing, of the prostitute, that irresistibly attractive yet veiled being. . . . Terror of the mother [the opposing and

Donald Reed and
Lupita Tovar in *Santa*
(1931). (Cineteca)

Lupita Tovar and Juan José
Martínez Casado in
another scene from *Santa*.
(Cineteca)

Santa and her brothers, right to left—Lupita Tovar, Antonio R. Frausto, and an unidentified actor. (Cineteca)

equally prevailing symbol of Mexican popular culture] drives us with ever-increasing fury into the arms of the prostitute.''[33]

Another significant event for the future of Mexican cinema was the arrival in the country in late 1930 of Sergei Eisenstein, the eminent Soviet director, accompanied by his collaborators Grigori Alexandrov and the cameraman Eduard Tissé. Eisenstein had been traveling through Western Europe and the United States studying the latest cinematic technology, especially that of sound. He was under contract to Paramount to film Theodore Dreiser's *An American Tragedy*, but the restrictions placed upon him by the studio executives prompted him to leave in disgust. Eisenstein had already agreed to carry out a filmmaking assignment for the Japanese government when he met Upton Sinclair and Diego Rivera. The latter tempted the Russian with beguiling descriptions of the stark beauty of Mexico and Sinclair assured him of financial backing if he would undertake a film project in that country.

Eisenstein and his crew traveled throughout Mexico filming the land and the people, and most of his actors were picked from the peasants and average villagers—a technique that was to be adopted by the postwar Italian neorealists. The Russian cineast immersed himself in the culture and life of revolutionary

Mexico; he sought out the country's most remote corners and assiduously studied Mexican history and customs. Eisenstein also made contact with the young artists and writers of Mexico and benefited from their advice and help. Among these were the artist and poet Isabel Villaseñor who played the role of María in the second episode, "Apotheosis of the Magüey," of Eisenstein's projected epic which he was going to call *¡Que viva México!* There were also Agustín Aragón Leiva, and the painter Adolfo Best Maugard, who had been instrumental in starting Dolores del Río on her Hollywood career.

Difficulties, however, soon emerged. A manager, Sinclair's relative, was imposed on Eisenstein and he proceeded to hinder and delay the filming. After thirteen months of work, the Russian cineast left Mexico with eighty thousand meters of unedited film; at Laredo, Texas, he was obliged to wait almost two months for authorization to reenter the United States and then, because of contractual commitments, he had to go directly from there to the Soviet Union.

*¡Que viva México!* was never released in any form approved by Eisenstein. Sinclair sold Sol Lesser (producer of the Tarzan pictures) the authorization to use whatever stock he needed for his feature, *Thunder Over Mexico*. Somewhat later, Marie Seton, Eisenstein's biographer, utilized some of this film for her picture, *Time in the Sun*. All this resulted in a good deal of controversy in the United States, but the most tragic aspect of the affair was that Eisenstein himself was never given the opportunity to fashion the film on Mexico that he had originally envisioned.[34]

Still, his unrealized film was to have an important influence, even if indirect, on subsequent Mexican filmmakers who were to develop a "national" style of cinema, especially Emilio "El Indio" Fernández.[35] García Riera comments that Eisenstein's work in Mexico

permitted various Mexican cineasts more or less solidarized with populist currents to create a style which would be characterized by meticulous camerawork (concentrating on clouds and magüey plants) and would gratuitously pay tribute to a hieratism by which they pretended to attain a national essence.[36]

Although 1932, the year in which *Santa* was released, saw only six films produced, it was significant in that it witnessed the debut of two directors who would soon make valuable contributions to their country's cinema. These were Fernando de Fuentes[37] who made *El anónimo (The Anonymous One)* and Arcady Boytler, a pre-Bolshevik Russian filmmaker who had studied under Stanislavsky and, in Mexico, met Eisenstein.[38] He directed *Mano a mano (Hand to Hand)*, the first *charro* sound film. Boytler's cameraman was Alex Phillips, a Canadian who had met Mary Pickford in Europe while he was serving in his Canadian unit in World War I; she later helped him get a start in Hollywood from where he went to Mexico to photograph *Santa*. Phillips made Mexico his home and was to become one of the industry's leading cameramen.[39]

In 1933 Mexican film production was at the forefront of Spanish-language moviemaking with twenty-one feature films, among them these important works: Fernando de Fuentes's *El compadre Mendoza (Godfather Mendoza)* and *El prisionero trece (Prisoner Number Thirteen)* and Arcady Boytler's *La mujer del puerto (The Woman of the Port)*. The industrial infrastructure behind this spurt in production consisted of two studios: those of Nacional Productora with three sound stages, and Jorge Stahl's México-Films studios with three sound stages. By the end of the year, the Industrial Cinematográfica, S.A. studios were also in operation. The average cost of making a film at this time was between twenty thousand and thirty thousand pesos (between $5,700 and $8,500 in 1933 dollars); the director usually earned fifteen hundred pesos ($425) and the ''star'' between five hundred and a thousand (between $140 and $285). The total number of personnel in the industry came to somewhere between two hundred and three hundred, none as yet unionized.[40]

Arcady Boytler's *La mujer del puerto* was described by Luz Alba as ''the first national movie which truly deserves the qualification of excellent.'' An uneven film, it did not elicit unqualified praise from all critics when it first appeared. Yet, later students of the film have continued to find merit in it: according to Carlos Monsiváis, ''Boytler realizes the first singular Mexican film, absolutely personal . . . [it] possesses atmosphere and personages, it is endowed with a certain unusual intensity.'' Tomás Pérez Turrent, a contemporary Mexican critic and cineast, says of it: ''Much has been said of the influence of German expressionism on Boytler. In effect, it exists, but it is not the only influence; present also are Jacques Feyder . . . Lacombe . . . except that Boytler surpasses them all.'' And Georges Sadoul thought it had a ''captivating and sensitive atmosphere.''[41]

The story of *La mujer del puerto*, based on a short story by Guy de Maupassant, was a sordid one of betrayal, prostitution, and incest. In Veracruz, Rosario (Andrea Palma) cares for her gravely ill father. She learns that her fiancé is having an affair with another woman; when her father confronts the fiancé with this, the latter hurls the old man down a flight of stairs, killing him. Rosario buries her father while the joyous sounds of the carnival reverberate in the background. Time passes and she has become a prostitute. Alberto (Domingo Soler), a sailor on a Honduran freighter, visits the cabaret in which she works. Rosario takes Alberto to

Domingo Soler and Andrea Palma in Arcady Boytler's *La mujer del puerto* (1933). (Cineteca)

her room where they have sex. Afterwards, as they talk, they realize that they are brother and sister, having lost contact long before (although this is never fully explained). Rosario, horror-stricken, hurls herself from the sea-wall and drowns in spite of Alberto's efforts to stop her.[42]

Another significant film is Fernando de Fuentes's *El compadre Mendoza*, adapted by De Fuentes from an idea by Mauricio Magdaleno and Juan Bustillo Oro. During the Revolution, the landowner Mendoza (Alfredo del Diestro) works out a modus vivendi with both the *zapatistas* and the *huertistas*. When one or another band rides up to his hacienda, he displays pictures of either Huerta or Zapata, as appropriate, and throws a party for his guests. On one of his trips Mendoza marries Dolores (Carmen Guerrero). While he is away, the *zapatistas* surprise a band of federal troops partying in Mendoza's house; on his return they detain and are going to shoot him but General Felipe Nieto (Antonio R. Frausto) spares Mendoza's life. In gratitude, he asks Nieto to be his son's godfather and makes him his *compadre*. Nieto, on his frequent visits to the hacienda, falls in love with Dolores and grows very fond of her son. Meanwhile, after the revolutionaries capture a wheatladen train that Mendoza was sending to the capital, he finds himself in severe economic difficulties. He is forced to accept a deal from the *huertistas* to betray Nieto. While his *compadre* is being assassinated, Mendoza hurries from the hacienda with his wife and child.[43]

*El compadre Mendoza* is a film of rare sensitivity, insight, and dramatic power. It has and continues to draw praise from Mexican critics like García Riera, Ayala Blanco, and Tomás Pérez Turrent, who tend to be hypercritical of their country's cinema. Georges Sadoul, who was largely responsible for the rediscovery of De Fuentes by young Mexican critics, says of the film in his *Dictionnaire des Films* that *El compadre Mendoza* "is one of the great accomplishments of the Mexican cinema during the rich 1932–1952 period. The satire is carried along with enthusiasm, good humor, a vivid sense of observation, and the memories of the

Fernando de Fuentes's *El compadre Mendoza* (1934) with Luis G. Barreiro (left) and Alfredo del Diestro. (Cineteca)

Mexican Revolution (still quite recent) contribute to make of the 'compadre' a true social type.''[44]

*El compadre Mendoza* is an important film that escaped international notice when it was released in 1933. The reason for this is clear enough: Mexico, with the rest of Latin America, was outside the mainstream of Western culture—and so it remains today. Western intellectuals, and by ''Western'' here is meant the United States, Britain, France, Italy, and Germany, had tended to dismiss, if not disparage, the culture of Latin America by characterizing it as simply an ''extension'' of Spain and Portugal. For many years Latin American literature was unknown to Western audiences, until critics and publishers in first Europe and then the United States ''discovered'' Jorge Luis Borges, Pablo Neruda, Gabriela Mistral, and more recently Gabriel García Márquez, Carlos Fuentes, and Manuel Puig, among others. It must be said, however, that French and Italian intellectuals tended more than the Anglo-Saxons to follow and appreciate the literature of Latin America. To a lesser extent the same is true of Latin American films. The French especially have generally been more aware of them perhaps as a result of the Cannes Film Festival. Since World War II, Mexicans and other Latin Americans have always participated at Cannes, and at Venice as well. This being the case, a good many French film critics and scholars have tended to be more aware of Latin American cinema than have their American or British counterparts. Mexico's past isolation from world film audiences explains why *El compadre Mendoza* originally passed unnoticed by international cineasts and why in more recent years both the film and its director have begun to receive the credit due them.

Like the contemporaneous literary movement referred to as the ''Novel of the Mexican Revolution,'' the significance of *El compadre Mendoza* lies in its expression of a feeling of disillusionment at the corrupted ideals of the Revolution. The *hacendado* Mendoza, in his cynical manipulation of both sides, represents the newly emerging postrevolutionary bourgeoisie that replaced the Porfirian aristocracy but which in its principles differed little from the deposed elite.

The following year, 1934, marked the inauguration of President Lázaro Cárdenas who was to usher in the most radical political climate that Mexico had experienced since the epic phase of the Revolution. During his six-year administration, the distribution of land was to be dramatically stepped up and Communist influence in labor and education circles was to reach its peak; however, the dramatic highlight of the Cárdenas years was the expropriation of the American and British oil fields in 1938, which many Mexicans came to look upon as the ''economic emancipation'' of their country. As if auguring *cardenismo*, there was in 1934 briefly a cinema of *''contenido social*,'' as García Riera terms it, expressed through two films, *Redes (Nets)* and *Janitzio*.

*Redes* was produced by the Ministry of Education (Secretaría de Educación Pública), the first time since before 1920 that the government had financed a full-length feature film. The project had its origins in 1932 when the New York photographer, Paul Strand, arrived in Mexico with the intention of putting together a book of photographs on the country. In this he was supported by the distinguished conductor and composer, Carlos Chávez, and a prominent Marxist,

Narciso Bassols, who was then Minister of Education. The three concocted an idea to make government-financed films "with the people and for the people." The critic and art historian, Agustín Velázquez, joined the group and they soon had a script for a full-length film and a director in the person of a young Austrian, Fred Zinnemann.

The story of *Redes* concerns a young fisherman, Miro (Silvio Hernández), who organizes his fellow workers against the monopolist (David Valle González) who buys their catch at very low prices. The monopolist bribes a local politician to seed discord among the fishermen who then quarrel among themselves; when the police are called in to quell the disturbance, the politician takes advantage of the confusion to shoot Miro. His death, however, serves to unite the fishermen and they carry Miro's corpse to the city in a demonstration of labor solidarity.

*Redes* expressed for the first time the elements considered by the country's intellectuals as "ideal for a good national cinema":

a combative social content, good photography that reveals the beauty of native faces and the on-location filming, an accomplishment and montage inspired by Eisenstein's example. With all this, a linkage was attempted with the themes and forms of the most advanced currents of plasticity, music, and the other Mexican arts which came together in a necessity to revindicate and uplift the Indian in the picture of national culture.[45]

Continuing in this short-lived vein of "social content" cinema was *Janitzio* directed by Carlos Navarro and written by Luis Márquez who based the story on an Indian legend from the Pátzcuaro area. The plot was based on a true incident that transpired on the island of Janitzio: an Indian girl had become the mistress of an outsider—a Spaniard who lived in Pátzcuaro and who was already resented by the Indians because he bought their fish catch at a low price and sold it at a large profit. The girl, on her return to Janitzio, was stoned by the islanders and banished from the community. The cast included Emilio "El Indio" Fernández who was to enjoy a long career as performer and director. He later wrote and directed two films based on *Janitzio*: the famous *María Candelaria* (1943) and *Maclovia* (1948).

According to Ayala Blanco, the "fundamental influences" on Navarro and cameraman Jack Draper were the photography of *Thunder Over Mexico* (Eisenstein's cannibalized footage from his projected *¡Que viva México!*), Robert Flaherty's *Moana* (1928), and F. W. Murnau's *Tabu* (1929–1931). Of *Janitzio* he says: "By means of elaborate images and a very slow interior rhythm, we come into contact with the primitive paradise of the Rousseauan savage who lives in harmony with nature, but an imperfect paradise since tabus exist and the white man mars it."[46] In the screenplay for *Janitzio*, the story of the Indian girl who was disgraced for loving a white man is essentially retained. Her lover is not a Spanish buyer but an engineer (Gilberto González) who arranges to imprison the fisherman Zirahuén (Emilio Fernández) so he may seduce his fiancé Eréndira (María Teresa Orozco). Ayala Blanco considers the film's principal attributes to be the images of the "fishermen's butterfly-like nets floating over the lake and the innocence of the native characters."[47]

*Redes* and *Janitzio* can be considered as superior films that served to initiate an

Emilio "El Indio"
Fernández in Carlos
Navarro's *Janitzio*
(1934). (Cineteca)

"Eisenstinian" current of "Indianist" films that were to be a distinguishing feature of the Mexican cinema for the next twenty years. Romanticized, and often melodramatic, such films, along with those dealing with the theme of the Revolution as in De Fuentes's *El compadre Mendoza*, were to constitute a "national" style of cinema and stand in counterpoint to the horde of melodramas based mostly on French and Spanish theater pieces that Mexican filmmakers were to churn out in the following decades. An example of this attachment to nineteenth-century European models, so typical of the Porfirian middle class and emulated by the postrevolutionary elite, was *Bohemios (Bohemians)* (1934). Instead of drawing on the vigorous contemporary artistic and literary life of Mexico, the film based itself upon the outmoded theme of the penniless artist enamored of a sickly girl.[48]

Other films made in 1934 and meriting special mention are Fernando de Fuentes's *El fantasma del convento (The Phantom of the Convent)*, an effective horror story that takes place in an abandoned colonial monastery; *Chucho el Roto*, set in the late nineteenth century and the most expensive film made in Mexico up to that time, costing 100,000 pesos; De Fuentes's *Cruz Diablo*, an adventure with sixteenth-century New Spain as a background; and Juan Bustillo Oro's *Dos monjes (Two Monks)*, an expressionist experiment in the style of Robert Wiene's *The Cabinet of Dr. Caligari*.

The first year of the Cárdenas presidency was marked by increased labor-management frictions culminating in a great number of government-backed strikes. This was reflected in the growing film industry by the creation of the UTECM (Unión de Trabajadores de Estudios Cinematográficos de México), with Enrique Solís being named as General Secretary. The UTECM was affiliated with the Communist-run labor union, the CTM (Confederación de Trabajadores Mexicanos), founded in 1936 by Vicente Lombardo Toledano.[49]

The government of Lázaro Cárdenas, buoyed by the commercial and artistic success of *Janitzio, Redes*, and *El compadre Mendoza*, took the first steps signaling active official participation in the movie industry and, as some feared, its possible nationalization. Certainly there was sufficient precedence for such a step, at least in the minds of the independent producers. In Germany from the time of World War I, the government had exercised control over filmmaking by buying out the largest private producers and acquiring ownership over all studio facilities; now, under Adolf Hitler, German filmmakers were totally at the disposal of the State. In Italy also the Fascist regime of Benito Mussolini had stepped in to build Cinecitta, the great studio complex outside of Rome and thereby to take a commanding role in film production. In the Soviet Union the process had been completed even earlier. Another leading film producer, Japan, was experiencing a similar evolution under the increasing political power of the militarists.[50]

The Mexican government largely subsidized the construction of the new CLASA (Cinematográfica Latino Americana, S.A.) studios which were equipped with the latest equipment and were as up to date as any Hollywood or European facility. For the first time in Mexico, a movie studio was supplied with Mitchell cameras, re-recording (or synchronization) equipment, a "gamma" processing laboratory, and "back-projection" equipment, among other of the latest advances. The first film to be made at these studios was Fernando de Fuentes's *Vámonos con Pancho Villa (Let's Go with Pancho Villa)* (1935); the government was generous with assistance to the similarly named production company, CLASA Films. It made available a complete military train, a regiment of regular army troops, ordnance, artillery, uniforms, horses, and assorted military equipment. When CLASA, after the film was completed, declared bankruptcy (the movie had cost one million pesos), the government subsidized it for the same amount thus saving the company. However, in spite of these developments which seemed to presage a state cinema industry, filming was to remain a private enterprise preserve in which investors placed their money in order to realize a profit in the shortest time possible. Without a rational system of financing and credit, lacking an effective distribution system, and with no foreign markets to speak of, Mexican production went from crisis to crisis. In 1935 twenty-two films were produced, one fewer than the year before. By contrast, Spain almost doubled its production over the previous year's to forty-four thus placing her first among Spanish-speaking countries. Argentina slowly expanded its film industry by releasing thirteen full-length features. In the same year, Hollywood produced eight Hispanic movies, the most important of which were Paramount's *El día que me quieras (The Day That You Love Me)* and *Tango Bar* with Carlos Gardel, the Argentine singing idol who was to perish that same year in a tragic plane crash in Medellín, Colombia while on a tour of Latin America.[51]

The second of Fernando de Fuentes's great "trilogy"[52] of films, *Vámonos con Pancho Villa*, was completed in 1935, although because of CLASA's financial difficulties its premiere was delayed until 1936, after Fuentes' third and most popular picture, *Allá en el Rancho Grande (Out at Big Ranch)*, had been released. In *Vámonos con Pancho Villa*, De Fuentes views the Revolution as a cataclysmic event that sweeps away its uncomprehending participants; he portrays the disillusionment that arises from the dichotomy "between the Revolution understood as an ideal and the Revolution itself, chaotic, contradictory, and relentless."[53]

The time is 1914. Miguel Angel (Ramón Vallarino), a deserter from the federal army, rejoins his friends Tiburcio (Antonio R. Frausto), Melitón (Manuel Tamés), Martín (Rafael F. Muñoz), and the Perea brothers, Máximo (Raúl de Anda) and Rodrigo (Carlos López "Chaflán"), a group of adventuresome ranchers who dub themselves "los leones de San Pablo." They decide to join the forces of Pancho Villa (Domingo Soler) whom they find distributing corn to the troops from a train. The film consists of a series of episodes in which either one of the *leones* or another individual is killed. Miguel Angel and Tiburcio, the only survivors of the group, are en route to Zacatecas on a *villista* train when a cholera epidemic breaks out. When Miguel Angel falls ill, Tiburcio is forced to kill him and cremate the body. In the face of Villa's fear of the epidemic, Tiburcio leaves the train and returns, disillusioned, to his village.

*Vámonos con Pancho Villa* is a remarkable film which looks back on the still-recent events that constituted a traumatic part of the lives of most Mexicans of the time, and coldly demythologizes them, revealing the Revolution for what it was in a multitude of major and minor details. That this could have come about in a time of renewed radical activity, and that the government, while heavily supporting the film, made no attempt to influence the theme, speaks highly of the open

De Fuentes's *¡Vámonos con Pancho Villa!* (1935) with (left to right) Rafael F. Muñoz, Antonio R. Frausto, Ramon Vallarino, and Manuel Tamés. (Cineteca)

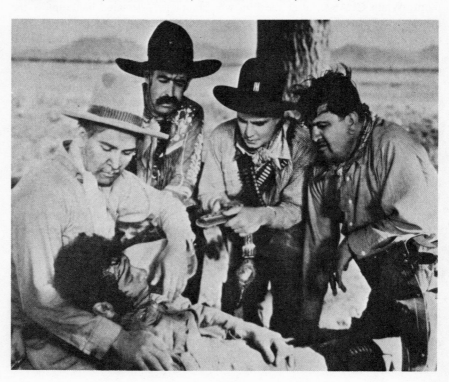

political climate of the time.[54] *Vámonos con Pancho Villa* was the last Mexican motion picture to deal honestly with the country's recent past. What seemed to be the auspicious beginnings of a serious national cinema, however, were soon to be overwhelmed by a commercialist trend given impetus by events in the world beyond Mexico's borders.[55] Ironically, it was Fernando de Fuentes himself who was to powerfully influence this development of the cinema with his next film.

*Allá en el Rancho Grande* (1936) "opened to Mexico all of the markets of Latin America and changed the course of the industry."[56] It demonstrated to Mexican filmmakers that the Latin American publics expected of them "Mexican" movies—that is, "films that would be vehicles for the unique 'national color' of Mexico."[57] They were not interested in Mexican movies that were simply duplications of Hollywood Hispanic films. The majority of the country's production had been "family melodramas" such as the Spaniard Juan Orol's *Madre querida* (1935), a tear-jerking, shamelessly sentimental paean to motherhood which was rushed through production so as to be premiered on Mother's Day. It was a great hit at the boxoffice in Mexico and its success inspired other producers to emulate it—a phenomenon of the mass entertainment business with which we are quite familiar in the United States. Outside of the country, however, such films were not popular enough to establish a firm foothold for the Mexican cinema.

From left to right, Lorenzo Barcelata, Esther Fernández, and Tito Guízar in Fernando de Fuentes's *Allá en el Rancho Grande* (1936). (Azteca Films, Los Angeles)

Tito Guízar (center) in a scene from *Allá en el Rancho Grande*. (Azteca Films)

The success of the *comedia ranchera* was not simply a case of adapting the internationally popular Hollywood Western to a Mexican setting. The American cowboy picture was a popularization of the Turner thesis of the expansion and conquest of the frontier: the rugged individualist confronting a hostile and primitive environment and overcoming it through sheer will power, thus ensuring the extension of democratic institutions. In innumerable Westerns the theme is repeated again and again wherein the hero, on behalf of the "little people," confronts the local tyrant (usually the owner of a big cattle spread who is headquartered in the local saloon) who aspires to reduce the entire region and its people to the status of a fiefdom. This is contrary of course to the American democratic ideal and the petty bourgeoisie (small farmer, sheepman, shopkeeper, newspaper publisher, town officials), inspired by the hero's example of personal courage and moral integrity, rather than being "led," are galvanized into corrective action.

There is no comparable universe in the Mexican experience; a similar myth of the frontier did not develop in the popular consciousness. The *charro* might ride a horse like his American counterpart and be dressed in what appears to resemble the cowboy's dress but there the similarity ends. The Yankee cowboy costume is that of a working man—plain, homespun with no fancy frills (with the possible exception of the costumes that Gene Autry and, particularly, Roy Rogers wore). The charro is magnificently attired in an embroidered riding suit that bespeaks a hoary tradition of rural aristocracy. His environment is not a wild frontier area but a minutely ordered feudal society in which the *hacendado* presides with paternalistic yet firm authority over his socioeconomic inferiors—the hacienda's employees, tenants, and, of course, women. The charro glories in his masculinity and he exercises it not so much to right a wrong but rather to enhance his male self-esteem and social prerogatives. It is the idealization of an attitude firmly rooted not only in the Porfirian past but in Mexico's colonial tradition and can be said to reflect a powerful conservative tendency in the society. In other words, the charro or *ranchero* was generally not trying to initiate social change but rather to maintain the status quo. He came to represent the traditional and Catholic values in defiance of the leftist, modernizing tendencies emanating from the cities.[58]

*Allá en el Rancho Grande* brought to life just such a traditional society but tellingly placed it in contemporary Mexico at a time when the Cárdenas government was making it very clear that its objective was to extirpate all traces of prerevolutionary institutions and create a "classless" society. Fernando de Fuentes rejected such "socialistic" pretensions by exalting the traditional *patrón-peón* and male-female relationships, and by so doing he struck a responsive chord in the Mexican middle class which was fearful of the "spread" of communism under the leftist Cárdenas. The Mexican film industry in fact reflected the conservative forces that were gaining in power and influence and which were to displace the left-wing reformists in 1940 with the inauguration of President Manuel Avila Camacho (1940–1946). De Fuentes, who had himself given strong impetus to the development of a political "message" cinema with *El compadre Mendoza* and *Vámonos con Pancho Villa*, reversed the trend (and in the process rejected his own incisive probings into the Mexican condition as epitomized in these two films) and put Mexican cinema on a solidly commercial, *petit bourgeois* track. In *El compadre Mendoza*, De Fuentes was first critical of the apolitical, opportunistic class that went along with the Revolution as long as its interests were not threatened, yet readily turned against it to maintain its economic position. In *Vámonos con Pancho Villa* he then examined the Revolution and saw it as a cataclysm which sucked in helpless individuals and destroyed them, and which in the end did not really improve conditions. Finally, in *Allá en el Rancho Grande*, he rejected the uncertainties and perils of revolutionary change and opted for an idealized prerevolutionary social order in which individuals of different classes each knew their place and were the happier for it.[59]

On a less socially symbolic level, *Allá en el Rancho Grande* was the prototype for the most enduring genre of the Mexican cinema—the musical *comedia ranchera*. It established its star, Tito Guízar, as a favorite of millions throughout the hemisphere; he eventually became quite well known in the United States and for a number of years was to be the "typical" Latin American in a number of American films.[60] *Allá en el Rancho Grande* made music de rigueur for all subsequent ranch comedies and it helped to establish the *mariachis*, those stringed instrument and vocal groups originally from the state of Jalisco, as what in effect have become the national musical ensemble.[61] In fact the latter is a good example of what Carlos Monsiváis describes as the development by the Mexican establishment of an "official" yet spurious folklore which has been useful not only in attracting tourism but, much more importantly, in blurring regional differences so as to create a more integrated society.[62]

The resounding success of *Allá en el Rancho Grande* inspired the "entire Mexican cinema to move to that very productive *Rancho* which had also given it its first figure of international prestige, Tito Guízar."[63] Of the thirty-eight films made in 1937, more than half were based on folkloric or nationalistic themes. The civil war in Spain reduced that country's production to only ten motion pictures while Argentina's output rose to twenty-eight.[64] Some details of interest in an otherwise undistinguished roster of films that year were: the first Mexican color film was made, Roberto A. Morales's production of *Novillero (Novice Bullfighter)* directed by Boris Maicon and photographed by Ross Fisher (the color process used was "cine-color");[65] the debut of Alejandro Galindo, who was to become one of the most important and prolific of his country's filmmakers, directing *Almas rebeldes (Rebel Souls)* which was produced by Raúl de Anda;[66] the inauspicious debut of Jorge Negrete, the future box-office idol and singing charro par excellence, in *La madrina del diablo (The Devil's Godmother)*;[67] and the first Mexican film directed by a woman (there were to be precious few), *La mujer de nadie (Nobody's Woman)* directed by Adela Sequeyro.[68] This year also saw the film debut of Mario Moreno "Cantinflas" in a minor supporting role in Miguel Contreras Torres's *No te engañes corazón (Don't Deceive Yourself, My Heart)*.[69] Fernando de Fuentes enticed Lupe Vélez from Hollywood to appear in *La Zandunga*, a folkloric comedy set in the Isthmus of Tehuantepec. In spite of her participation, the film was a commercial and artistic failure.[70] The reluctance of the other Mexican Hollywood star, Dolores del Río, to appear in one of her own country's films did not endear her to many of her countrymen; she justified her absence from Mexican screens by arguing that the national industry was not as yet "of sufficient solidity."[71]

Dolores del Río was certainly accurate in her assessment of Mexico's film industry, especially since she was viewing it from the standpoint of the huge American industry—huge not only physically but in capitalization, investment, distribution, and profits. Put in the simplest terms, the moguls of Hollywood were not only hard-nosed businessmen but also dedicated filmmakers; they plowed their profits back into the movie business. In Mexico, on the other hand, producers were often businessmen out to make a quick profit who had little interest in building a solidly based production company.[72] Thus directors were hampered in their efforts to make quality films by a strong commercialist imperative: the producers were reluctant to invest large sums of money in an industry in which they had little faith, and when they did they expected monetary returns as quickly as possible.[73] Thus shooting schedules were impossibly short—two to three weeks on the average—

and budgets as restricted as could be gotten away with. The possibilities of a state cinema were demonstrated by the success of De Fuentes's *Vámonos con Pancho Villa* which had enjoyed the Cárdenas government's generous support and was produced in the modern and largely officially financed CLASA studios. Yet the specter of "socialism" thoroughly frightened both petty bourgeois investors and filmmakers even though the administration's measures stopped far short of nationalization. The most radical actions taken by the government were in its encouragement of unionization in the film industry as well as in other Mexican industries. Another measure taken by Cárdenas was the requirement that all theaters show a minimum number of Mexican films, a reflection of the difficulty of competing with Hollywood and its well-organized distribution systems. Another unsettling development was the entrance of American capital into Mexican filmmaking as exemplified by RKO's direct participation in the production of national films.

When compared with the problems that, say, French and Italian cinema had experienced after World War I, the organization, or rather lack of it, that characterized the Mexican industry was far from unique.[74] Most film production was carried out by small companies, some of which were formed solely for the purpose of making one film and then dissolved; studios, like those of CLASA and Estudios Azteca, were privately owned and the facilities rented to filmmakers. The movie industry was indeed on a shaky footing in spite of the 1936 success of *Allá en el Rancho Grande*; the popularity of that film demonstrated the potential, and the need for, international markets. Unfortunately, in 1937 the commercialism and lack of creativity of most producers led them to try to capitalize on De Fuentes's triumph by churning out more than twenty *"Rancho Grandes,"* that is, musical melodramas based on folkloric or nationalistic themes. During 1939 only thirty-seven films were made, twenty less than the previous year, even though the membership of UTECM had grown steadily every year since its founding until it numbered over 410.[75] Another indication of the "crisis" was Argentina's production, surpassing Mexico's for the first time with fifty films in 1939, making it the largest producer in the world of Spanish-language movies.

The last years of the decade of the 1930s were tumultuous and significant ones for Mexico. Lazaro Cárdenas had injected a new vitality into the Revolution, an energy that was to be quickly dissipated after 1940. Mexico had defied the great capitalist powers—the United States and Great Britain—by expropriating their oil properties in 1938 after a prolonged and bitter labor dispute. In addition, the Cárdenas government had extended open and full support (as far as Mexico's limited means allowed it) to the beleaguered Spanish Republic. After Franco's victory in 1939, Mexico opened its doors to thousands of Spanish refugees. This sudden inflow of immigrants constituted in its majority an elite of Spanish society—writers, artists, intellectuals, political activists. Among this number were many filmmakers and performers whose names in a few years were to become standards of the Mexican movie industry:[76] Angel Garasa,[77] José Baviera, Emilio Tuero, Emilia Guiú,[78] and Luis Alcoriza.[79]

Yet these dramatic events were not reflected at all in the Mexican cinema of the period—it was the beginning of the "detachment from reality" that was to characterize the greater part of the filmmaking of the 1940–1965 era.[80] For instance, Alejandro Galindo's *Refugiados en Madrid (Refugees in Madrid)* (1938), although set in the Spain of the Civil War and concerning a group of presumably anti-Franco Spaniards taking refuge in a Latin American embassy in Madrid, managed to avoid all reference to the contending factions and convert the subject into a stock melodrama.[81] *El indio (The Indian)*, made that same year, was based on the prize-winning novel of the same name by Gregorio López y Fuentes. Obviously a cinematic effort to parallel the "Indianist" literary genre, it instead presented an idealized and exotic view of the Mexican Indian.[82] Alejandro Galindo, although blatantly inspired by the Hollywood gangster film, made a technically competent movie, *Mientras México duerme (While Mexico Sleeps)* (1938), which established him as one of the more talented Mexican directors working at the time. It starred Arturo de Córdova and was photographed by Gabriel Figueroa.[83]

As if to symbolize the declining days of the Cárdenas regime and the desire of the country's bourgeoisie for "normalcy," Juan Bustillo Oro's 1939 production of *En tiempos de don Porfirio (In the Times of Don Porfirio)* was that year's most successful film at the box-office. The nostalgia it evoked of a simpler and more peaceful epoch could also be interpreted as a rejection by the middle class of the more socialistic aspects of the Revolution. The appearance in the film of such popular actors as Fernando Soler, the Spanish immigrant Emilio Tuero, and the fine comic actor Joaquín Pardavé were also potent factors in the movie's success.[84] Another historical note of importance is the formation of Posa Films which featured the popular *carpa* (tent show) comic, Cantinflas, in two short features, *Siempre listo en las tinieblas (Always Ready in the Darkness)* and *Jengibre contra dinamita (Ginger versus Dynamite)*.[85]

Just as 1939 signified the end of the civil war in Spain, this fateful year was to see the long-awaited and feared outbreak of war in Europe. The effects of the world conflict on Mexico—not only on its film industry but in almost all aspects of the economy—were to be fortuitous indeed. The ambitious rising entrepreneurial class, anxiously awaiting the welcome end of Lazaro Cárdenas's presidential term, looked forward to a regime that would place its greatest priority on the expansion of the Mexican economy rather than on unsettling and even dangerous notions of "social justice" and "class struggle." It was the attitudes of this *nouveau riche* petty bourgeoisie, ambitious yet unsure of itself and identifying somewhat with Porfirismo, that were to set the tone for Mexican movie production of the following decades. With the official denouement of *cardenismo*, the danger (if ever it existed) of a nationalized film industry was safely past; the cinema was firmly in private hands and was to remain so during the boom years of the 1940s and 1950s, and well into the crisis-ridden 1960s.

Bolstering the Mexican middle class' identification with international democracy (and the business opportunities inherent in such an alignment), Franklin Delano Roosevelt's "Good Neighbor" policy sought to emphasize to Latin America that the nations of the area were full and equal partners in the struggle against fascism. An important part of this campaign was the effort to ''improve'' the Latin image in Hollywood films. To the United States's favorite Latin American, Tito Guízar,[86] was now added Arturo de Córdova who appeared in an English-language film, *Miracle on Main Street* as well as in the Hispanic feature, *El caudal de los hijos*. Even Miguel Contreras Torres wrote, produced, and directed an English-language feature, *The Mad Empress*, for Vitagraph.[87] However, the principal example of Hollywood's response to Washington's new Latin American policy was Warner Brothers' major production of *Juárez* with Paul Muni in the title role. Bette Davis played Carlotta, Briane Aherne was Maximilian, and John Garfield—of all people—portrayed the young Porfirio Díaz. Perhaps one of the most incongruous scenes in all film history (and there are many) is the sight of Díaz (Garfield) kneeling at Juárez's feet (Muni) and asking the deliberately Lincolnesque president to explain democracy to him. The movie never went on to reassure its viewers as to how well Juárez's definition of this elusive political art had been absorbed by his eager protegé. *Juárez* nonetheless was given first-class treatment in Mexico, being premiered at the Palace of Fine Arts by decree of Lázaro Cárdenas himself.[88]

Such an auspicious event was a fitting demonstration of the increased respect in which the Latin American ''partners'' were to be held, even though some cynics might have pointed out that the formerly scoffed-at nations south of the Rio Grande were practically the only friends the United States had left in the world who were not directly threatened by Axis military might. Whatever Hollywood did or did not do to bolster the Good Neighbor policy, events beyond its control were to facilitate the growth of a major and competing movie industry right on its doorstep.

# 3

# War and Growth
# of a Major Film Industry
# 1940–1946

Replying to a reporter's query on his attitude toward the Catholic Church, the new president of Mexico, Miguel Avila Camacho, answered, "*Soy creyente*" ("I am a believer").[1] In the context of Mexican politics since the Revolution, which had been stoutly anticlerical, this was tantamount to an American chief executive refusing to attend the church of his choice on Sunday. Although the Mexican left was disconcerted, it was exactly the message that the country's fretful middle classes had been hoping for. As if to symbolize the transition from Cárdenas's activist administration to a more conservative regime, the last film produced in 1940 bore the title, *Creo en Dios*—coincidentally it was also the last motion picture made under the Cárdenas presidency.[2]

During the administration of Avila Camacho (1940–1946), the Mexican film industry was put on a commercial footing through state support to private producers. In one sense this official interest in the cinema was a very real indication of the importance in which it was held; but the other side of the coin demonstrated a voracious acquisitiveness typical of all areas of Mexican economic life in which fortunes were waiting to be made by those individuals aggressive (and unscrupulous) enough to take advantage of the opportunities presented by World War II.

The war raging in Europe and Asia proved a windfall for Latin America whose raw materials were in great demand by the Allies. The curtailment of imported manufactured goods from the United States and Europe also was a significant impetus to industrialization in the major countries of the area like Argentina, Brazil, and Mexico. The Mexican and Argentine film industries reflected this industrializing process as they stepped in to supply national and foreign Spanish-speaking markets with a commodity formerly supplied by Hollywood and, to a lesser extent, European producers. Portuguese-speaking Brazil, being practically a continent unto itself, did not require foreign markets for its films. The war did create a demand within Brazil for national films and the 1940s saw its studios produce up to one hundred movies a year.[3] Argentina in the late 1930s and early 1940s was Mexico's strongest competitor and its production was still ahead of the latter's in 1941—forty-seven films[4] to thirty-seven for Mexico.[5] One of the more significant commercial and artistic successes of the Argentine cinema at this time was Lucas Demare's *La guerra gaucha (The Gaucho War)*, which dealt with the struggle for independence against Spain. The film "employed the sun as a major symbol, implicitly linking it to the Inca past as well as to the new Argentine nationality."[6] The popularity of this movie clearly indicated, as *Allá en el Rancho Grande* had a few years before, that Latin American audiences responded to and enjoyed seeing Latin American themes on the screen, even if the settings were not in their own particular countries.

The Mexican cinema of 1941 sought to tap this current of Pan-Americanism with *Simón Bolívar*, produced, written, and directed by Miguel Contreras Torres. However, that year's most popular and profitable film was Julio Bracho's initial directorial effort, *¡Ay, qué tiempos, señor don Simón! (Oh, What Times, Mr*. don *Simón!)*—an appealing and lively musical exercise in Porfirian nostalgia starring Joaquín Pardavé, Arturo de Córdova, and Mapy Cortés. It took in just over 137,000 pesos at the box-office in its first three weeks of exhibition, a record for the time.[7] The film's success also indicated that Mexican middle-class audiences were still much more attracted to the *belle époque* than to Pan-Americanism.

In 1940, Mario Moreno "Cantinflas" had scored an international success with *Ahí está el detalle (There is the Detail)*, his first full-length feature. The former *carpa* comic transcended the conventional theatrical humor of Juan Bustillo Oro's direction "with the effect of a bomb."[8] His irreverent, street-wise language was the perfect counterpoint to Joaquín Pardavé's polished but superficial phrases—in other words, the *pelado* (lit. "hairless"—a penniless nobody) meets the hypocritical creole and shows him up. The film's high point, which created a following for Cantinflas throughout the Spanish-speaking world, was the final courtroom scene in which he delightfully flouts social and legalistic conventions and succeeds in so confusing the arrogant judge and attorneys that they end up talking in *cantinflismos*.[9]

Cantinflas's second full-length feature in 1941 was *Ni sangre ni arena (Neither Blood nor Sand)*, a parody of Vicente Blasco Ibáñez's bullfight novel *Sangre y arena*, which had recently been filmed in Hollywood (*Blood and Sand*) starring Tyrone Power, Rita Hayworth, and Linda Darnell. Hoping to capitalize on the American motion picture's popularity, Posa Films, hereafter to be Cantinflas's exclusive producer, signed Alejandro Galindo to direct the popular comic. The association was reportedly not a happy one and the two were never to work together again; however, Galindo's assistant, Miguel M. Delgado, hit it off much better with Cantinflas and became his favorite director.[10] *Ni sangre ni arena* was vastly popular and took in 54,000 pesos in four days at the Alameda Theater, another box-office record.[11] This success was followed in short order by *El gendarme desconocido (The Unknown Policeman)*, with Mapy Cortés and Gloria Marín, considered by many to be among Cantinflas's best movies. Commenting on the reasons for Cantinflas's popularity and of this film in particular, García Riera writes:

No other Spanish-speaking actor has enjoyed *Cantinflas's* popularity, and this can perhaps be readily explained by the fact that, apart from a great personal charm, this actor does not employ any dramatic artifice. In other words, *Cantinflas* is the first *real and living* personage in a cinema characterized by its attachment to cheap histrionics. Such an accomplishment favors the unsophisticated spectator's identification with the character, something which has rarely occurred in any other case.

The ridiculization [in *El gendarme desconocido*] of the police, generally detested by the public, is established from the first moment in which *Cantinflas* appears in his uniform. Seeing "one of their own" converted into a guardian of law and order gives the spectator a sensation of freedom. The public solidarizes itself with *Cantinflas* for the very reason that the character's ridiculousness and his encyclopedic ignorance place him at a disadvantage in relation to any spectator. Thus, the weapons employed by *Cantinflas* (the weapons of a picaresque character) to flout authority are within reach of the most humble and ignorant of men.[12]

A classic of the "family drama" genre was *Cuando los hijos se van (When the Children Leave)* directed by Juan Bustillo Oro, now more in his element. It starred Fernando Soler, Joaquín Pardavé, and—Latin America's favorite self-sacrificing mother figure—Sara García. This film attests perhaps to the Mexican public's capacity for self-punishment since for four weeks it kept drawing crowds eager to sit through its 139 minutes of unrelenting melodrama and nostalgia. Directed in a strictly theatrical style by Bustillo Oro with a seemingly immobile camera, the film tells in excruciating detail the story of a staunchly *petit bourgeois* Córdoba family. The complicated plot essentially concerns the father Pepe Rosales's (Fernando Soler) misjudging of his "good" son Raimundo (Emilio Tuero). The young man is falsely incriminated by the ne'er-do-well son José (Carlos López Moctezuma), whom the father considers a model of filiality. The mother, Lupe (Sara García), with her unerring maternal instinct, never doubts for a moment the innocence of the disgraced Raimundo who later proves his devotion by returning from Mexico City, where he has triumphed as a singer, to save his parents from bankruptcy

Mario Moreno "Cantinflas" (right) with Joaquín Pardavé in *Ahí está el detalle* (1940). (Azteca Films)

*El gendarme desconocido* (1941) with (left to right) Carlos López Moctezuma, Mapy Cortés, and Cantinflas. (Cineteca)

Cantinflas in *El extra* (1962). (Azteca Films)

brought about by José's dishonesty. Raimundo is shot to death by the usurer Patricio Gómez (Miguel Inclán, at his most deliciously villainous), but before dying Raimundo manages to destroy the falsified note that Patricio held on the Rosales house. With the entire family gathered at Christmas eve dinner, José confesses his guilt and is dutifully forgiven by Pepe who finally recognizes the moral superiority of the departed Raimundo, whose empty chair forms part of the family gathering.[13]

In Bustillo Oro's universe, the family, "autonomous, victorious, omnivorous,"[14] stands coldly aloof from the world around it. The Rosales household seems to be suspended in time with its walls effectively keeping out the disturbing society outside. Disaster invariably comes to any of its members who seek to break their bonds with the sacrosanct family and it is only when they have rejected the world outside and all personal ambition that they find security, a security disconcertingly based on their individual failure and dependent on a stultifying submersion within the family. Such a regressive idealization of traditional values was an effective way, if only for 139 minutes, of shutting out not only the changes that Mexico was undergoing but the unsettling Axis victories and the radically altered world order that they portended.

Another type of retreat from reality, yet a considerably more entertaining one, was represented by the box-office success of Joselito Rodríguez's ¡Ay Jalisco no te rajes! (Oh Jalisco, Don't Back Down!), which was Jorge Negrete's first great triumph and definitely established him as the quintessential Mexican singing charro.[15] In Alejandro Galindo's words, Negrete was the most faithful representative of the Mexican ideal: "dark-complexioned, tall, proud, romantic, pistol-packing, and who sings his sorrows as readily as his joys."[16] Finally, 1941 saw also the directorial debut of Emilio "El Indio" Fernández who had been involved in films for some years in Hollywood and Mexico—he was the male dancer in the jarabe tapatío sequence in the cockfighting arena in Allá en el Rancho Grande. His La isla de la pasión (The Island of Passion) concerned a group of Mexican soldiers stranded on Clipperton Island off the coast of Central America.[17]

Thus Mexican film production in 1941, as exemplified by Simón Bolívar, Ni sangre ni arena, El gendarme desconocido, ¡Ay, qué tiempos señor don Simón!, Cuando los hijos se van, and ¡Ay Jalisco no te rajes!, demonstrated several of the basic formulas that were to find favor with Latin American audiences. First was the historical/patriotic epic, by no means new to Mexican filmmaking. However, such productions, because of the necessarily limited budgets and consequently short shooting schedules, suffered in comparison with Hollywood films on which millions of dollars were spent.[18] Of course, it should be kept in mind that Hollywood rarely filmed Latin American themes and when it did, the results were as often as not offensive to the sensitivities of the country concerned.[19] The second formula, and commercially a resoundingly more successful one, was the Cantinflas movies. It was enough simply to have the enormously popular comic on the screen for the film to make money. This success, unsurprisingly, tended to fossilize Cantinflas's performances and, according to some observers, he continued making essentially the same film for the next three decades.[20]

The melodrama based on attachment to traditional values—"God, Nation, and Home"[21]—was already an important component of the Mexican cinema as exemplified by *Cuando los hijos se van*. In the next decade there were to be variations on this theme; for example, the sacrosanct family is threatened by carnal or material temptation from the outside world, whether it be a cabaret girl as in Alberto Gout's *Sensualidad (Sensuality)* (1950) or a vacuum-cleaner salesman as in Alejandro Galindo's *Una familia de tantas (An Ordinary Family)* (1948).[22]

The continued utilization of a limited number of themes within a handful of well-defined genres would quickly have bored audiences were it not for a corresponding "star system" as the key element in marketing the product. Thus certain performers specialized in defined roles and the films being discussed here provide outstanding examples of actors already established in their particular genres.

Among the "star" fixtures of the cinema was "the mother of Mexico," Sara García. Born in Orizaba, Veracruz on September 8, 1895, of immigrant Spanish parents, she began her distinguished acting career before 1910 in silent films. Sara García then acted in the theater, principally doing Spanish plays. Her first sound film was *El pulpo humano (The Human Octopus)* (1933), but the role that made her a star was *No basta ser madre (It's Not Enough to be a Mother)* (1937). Of *Cuando los hijos se van* she recently said:

it is an immortal motion picture, no matter what is said against it. The cinema might end, but *Cuando los hijos se van* will go on, because in every home the children eventually leave: or they become monks or nuns, or they elope, or they go to work in a foreign country, or they marry, or whatever. In effect, life itself is contained in the title. . . . The public goes to see it, they feel it, they cry. . . . Because of all this . . . it is a classic film.[23]

Sara García. (Cineteca)

Sara Garcia in scenes from various films. On lower right, she is shown in *Papacito lindo* (1939) (Cinetecca).

The other enduring cinematic formula, the *comedia ranchera*, was represented by *¡Ay, Jalisco no te rajes!* The predictable succession of love affairs, personal misunderstandings, conflicts, and spurious folklore—all liberally garnished with ranchera music—could not have retained the public's interest without the appearance of a "superstar" such as Jorge Negrete. Soon Pedro Infante was also to achieve star status in this genre, although his signal triumph was in *Nosotros los pobres (We the Poor)* (1947), a melodrama of the urban poor that was to be the greatest box-office hit in the history of Mexican cinema.

The debut of Emilio "El Indio" Fernández was, in hindsight, perhaps the most significant event of this year. A man of complex personality, withdrawn, and occasionally violent, Fernández was to be the founder of a "Mexican school" that achieved international recognition in the late 1940s and 1950s. His work, at its best, is intensely nationalistic and overly sympathetic to the Indian whose culture has been under relentless attack from the mestizo and creole sectors of Mexican society. Fernández, in close collaboration with the renowned cameraman Gabriel Figueroa, was to glorify Mexico's landscapes, dramatic, cloud-laced skies, and, more importantly, its stoic, beautiful Indian faces. And of the latter, he utilized two of the most magnificent: Dolores del Río and Pedro Armendáriz. It has often been said of Fernández (and, of course, Figueroa) that he is the principal Mexican exponent of the "Eisenstinian" style as embodied in the never-completed *¡Que viva México!* Whatever inspiration Fernández received from Eisenstein was apparently far from direct, and the photographic techniques were most probably passed on to "El Indio" (as to many others) through Fred Zinnemann's *Redes*.[24] Whatever the processes through which Fernández developed his style, his name was to become synonymous with "quality" Mexican cinema, especially in Europe, and he would be the only Mexican director whose work was to become somewhat known in the United States, principally through *The Pearl* (1945) and *The Torch* (1947), both starring Pedro Armendáriz.[25]

In order to begin organizing the film industry on a more rational financial basis, the Banco Cinematográfico was founded on April 14, 1942, "on the initiative of the Banco Nacional de México and with the moral support of President Avila Camacho."[26] The Banco began as a private institution although the government's interest in this new credit agency was no secret; Avila Camacho "did not think it opportune to give the Banco an official subsidy because it was his wish that private enterprise develop by its own efforts."[27] Nonetheless, the Banco Cinematográfico was backed by official agencies like the Banco de México and the Nacional Financiera which held 10 percent of its stock.[28] The board of directors was made up of six bankers and industrialists and two cineasts. Mauricio de la Serna and Jesús Grovas.[29]

The creation of the Banco Cinematográfico was a solid indication of the importance in which the national film industry was held in high official circles. In an effort to centralize the sporadic activities of small, undercapitalized producers, the Banco in its first year extended credits of 5 million pesos to nine production companies (out of a total of about thirty): Grovas, S.A., Films Mundiales, América Films, Ixtla Films, CLASA, Juan Bustillo Oro, Cinematografía Miguel Zacarías, Vicente S. Piques, and Producciones Fernando de Fuentes.[30] Of these, the largest firms were Grovas, which produced eight films in 1942, and Films Mundiales with six motion pictures.[31]

Partly as a result of the creation of a centralized credit institution for production and distribution, the following year, 1943, saw the Mexican cinema show promise of fulfilling its potential and becoming a true industry. Seventy films were produced in "the great year,"[32] while Argentina's output declined sharply to thirty-six and Spanish studios made only fifty-three.

A number of factors contributed to this impressive performance. First, because of a common language and similar cultural background, Mexican movies undoubtedly appealed to the tastes of the mass Latin American audience;[33] second, and closely connected with the first factor, Hollywood production, at this time entirely given over to supporting the war effort, held little appeal for Latin Americans. In addition, the pro-Axis inclinations of various Argentine governments during the war years motivated the United States to apply certain sanctions against that country, and among these was the cutting off of raw film to Argentine producers. Fortunately for Mexican producers, their government's declaration of war on Germany, Japan, and Italy and its subsequent support of the Allied cause led to reciprocal actions on Washington's part. Most important for Mexico's film production was the allocation by the United States of raw film and cinematic equipment to bolster its movie industry. Now that Hollywood had to resign itself to the temporary loss of its Latin American market, it was quite willing to support the Mexican film industry.[34]

A number of creditable films were produced in 1943. Emilio Fernández achieved his greatest artistic triumphs with *Flor silvestre (Wild Flower)* and, especially, *María Candelaria*. Julio Bracho's *Distinto amanecer (A Different Sunrise)* suggested the possibility of a sophisticated, urban-oriented cinema in the *film noir* vein. There was also Fernando de Fuentes's *Doña Bárbara*, based on the novel by Rómulo Gallegos and starring María Félix, an actress of great beauty who was to be one of the leading box-office attractions of the Mexican cinema. The influence of Orson Welles was evident in Alejandro Galindo's *Tribunal de justicia (Tribunal of Justice)* and Norman Foster's *La fuga (The Escape)*. The latter also made the best version of *Santa* to date.[35] Miguel Contreras Torres directed the interesting *La vida inútil de Pito Pérez (The Useless Life of Pito Pérez)* based on the novel by José Rubén Romero, and Bustillo Oro made *México de mis recuerdos (Mexico of my Memories)*, perhaps his best film.[36]

The chaos of war had its disrupting effect on such matters as copyright conventions, and Mexican producers took advantage of the situation to adapt for

Fernando de Fuentes's *Doña Bárbara* (1943) with María Félix (left) and Maria Elena Marqués. (Cineteca)

María Félix in *Doña Bárbara*. (Azteca Films)

Emilio Fernández's *Flor silvestre* (1943) with Pedro Armendáriz (left) and Hernán Vera. (Cineteca)

Emilio Fernández and Dolores del Río in *Flor silvestre*. (Azteca Films)

the screen the works of more than twenty foreign authors. This tendency was denounced by some as a perpetuation of a "Porfirian inferiority complex" in which "culture, good taste, and intelligence were [considered to be] European specialties which America should import without taking the trouble to comprehend."[37] Whatever the merits of this argument, the inevitable reaction was a nationalist cinema which the Banco Cinematográfico encouraged by granting more generous credits to those producers making such films. Agustín J. Fink, president of Films Mundiales, backed Fernández and Bracho in their efforts to reflect the contemporary Mexican reality on the screen.[38]

*Flor silvestre* and *María Candelaria* were Fernández's two great triumphs of 1943. The latter won international renown for its creators when it was entered in the first postwar international film festivals at Cannes (1946) and Locarno (1947). The film won several important prizes at both festivals and helped to establish a European market for the Mexican cinema. Fernández's choice of Dolores del Río to star in both films was also an effective way of assuring that international film circles would focus some attention on his work.

*María Candelaria* was loosely based on *Janitzio* (1934). The setting is shifted from the island of Janitzio to Xochimilco. As the film begins, a group of journalists

Pedro Armendáriz and Dolores del Río in *Flor silvestre*. (Azteca Films)

are interviewing a world-famous artist (Alberto Galán). A young woman reporter asks him about a painting of a nude Indian girl he had done years before and which he never revealed. The painter replies that it was the cause of a tragedy and proceeds to tell its story.

It is Xochimilco in 1909. María Candelaria (Dolores del Río) earns her living by gathering flowers and selling them at the market. She is in love with Lorenzo (Pedro Armendáriz) and they plan to marry. However, the villagers resent María because her mother was a prostitute and at one point Lorenzo has to intercede when the Indians threateningly block María's way. She owes a small sum of money to don Damián (Miguel Inclán), a villainous mestizo who owns Xochimilco's only general store and ruthlessly exploits the Indians. Don Damián demands that María pay the money she owes him or he will take her little pig with which she hopes to raise money so she and Lorenzo can get married.

Lorenzo and María are at the market. The artist is painting in the street when he notices María. Struck by her beauty, he buys all her flowers and asks her to pose for him but Lorenzo won't allow it. Undaunted, the artist sends an Indian to follow María and find out where she lives. Meanwhile, don Damián is determined to take María's pig, having been frustrated once in the attempt at the blessing of the

Dolores del Río and Pedro Armendáriz in Emilio Fernández's *María Candelaria* (1943).
(Azteca Films)

animals ceremony at the village church. He paddles up to María's shack and just misses getting a shot at Lorenzo. In a rage, he then kills the little pig. Shortly after, María falls ill with malaria; Lorenzo, in desperation, brings the dead pig to don Damián and asks him for quinine tablets (since he is the only one in the village authorized by the government to distribute them). Don Damián refuses to hand over the tablets and holds Lorenzo at bay with a rifle. After Lorenzo leaves, Damián decides to close the store and get away for a few days because he fears "these Indians' treachery."

The artist, however, had learned of María's illness and sends a doctor to tend her, although too late to prevent Lorenzo from breaking into don Damián's store where he takes not only the malaria tablets but also a dress. A few days later, don Damián has Lorenzo arrested in the middle of the wedding ceremony in which María is wearing the stolen dress. Lorenzo is sentenced to one year in prison. María seeks help from the artist and the priest (Rafael Icardo), but they can do nothing to help Lorenzo. The artist tells the priest that he considers María to be the "essence of Mexican beauty"; the priest then assures María that there is nothing wrong in her posing for the artist. However, she refuses to pose in the nude, leaving the painting unfinished. The artist completes it by using another model.

The villagers, however, are scandalized when they learn of the painting, thinking that María posed in the nude for it. Egged on by don Damián, a mob gathers and goes in search of María. Terrified, she flees back to the village with the mob in pursuit; she attempts to reach the jail and Lorenzo but is cornered by the villagers and stoned to death. Lorenzo hears the commotion and breaks down the cell door but too late to save María. In the film's final scene, he has placed María's body in a dugout canoe and surrounded it with flowers as he sadly takes it to be buried.

In spite of the criticism leveled at *María Candelaria*, it remains a classic of the Mexican cinema and the work that created an international following for "El Indio." The film has been criticized for presenting a "tourist's" Mexico, an image of stoic, attractive Indians patiently paddling their flower-laden dugouts along the scenic canals of Xochimilco, and for creating a stereotype of them that subsequent cineasts would perpetuate.[39] Yet the film retains a simplicity and lyrical beauty that can still be appreciated over thirty-five years later. Moreover, false idealiza-

Pedro Armendáriz and Dolores del Río in *María Candelaria*. (Cineteca)

tion or not, Fernández presented a positive view of Indians—a group that more often than not had been the butt of music-hall jokes. Not everyone was happy with *María Candelaria* for this reason. As Fernández himself comments:

We filmed *María Candelaria* in Xochimilco, with many problems caused by the weather and many personal differences. A few good people couldn't go along with the film. It seemed to them—imagine!—exotic and also depressing. They were scandalized and ousted me from the production company . . . because I had made "such shit about Indians." I had to resolve to starve to death.[40]

The film was boycotted by Emilio Azcárraga who refused to run it in his Alameda Theater. Agustín J. Fink then stepped in and rented the Palacio Theater where it was premiered to a full house, which included the Soviet ambassador, Constantin Oumansky, who was enthusiastic about the film.[41]

Julio Bracho's *Distinto amanecer* was another of 1943's distinguished films. Set in a realistic yet threatening urban setting, *film noir* style,[42] it tells the story of an idealistic labor leader, Octavio (Pedro Armendáriz), fleeing the gunmen of a

Andrea Palma in Julio Bracho's *Distinto amanecer* (1943). (Cineteca)

corrupt state governor because he has evidence that the functionary suppressed a strike at the bidding of foreign interests. The incriminating documents are in a box at the post office which Octavio is trying to reach. He is being tailed by one of the governor's men; to elude him Octavio slips into a theater where a lively musical number from ¡Ay, qué tiempos señor don Simón! is in progress on the screen. Octavio sits next to Julieta (Andrea Palma). When she starts to light a cigarette he blows out her match and tells her to obey the no-smoking sign. Julieta answers that she obeys cigarette advertisements instead and gets up to go to the ladies' room. Octavio follows her right in after he notices the governor's man in the theater. Once inside the ladies' room, Julieta and Octavio discover they know each other; they had been politically active university students years before. She tells him that she married the third member of the group, Ignacio (Alberto Galán), now an unemployed diplomat. Julieta lets Octavio out a side door from the ladies' room and she takes him home to a run-down building to meet Ignacio.

Thus a sequence of events is set in motion in which the personal relationships among Julieta, Octavio, and Ignacio are subsumed by their social obligations. Julieta and Octavio have always loved each other and his reappearance is a troubling experience for her. Their emotional problems are intertwined with the danger that now faces all three, and Julieta and Ignacio decide to help Octavio obtain the evidence that will expose the corrupt governor. The entire action of *Distinto amanecer* transpires in the course of one night. During that time Julieta is forced to kill the governor's henchman, and she and Octavio have to get rid of the body. In the meantime, Ignacio obtains the critical document from the post office box. He is aware of Julieta's love for Octavio and is prepared to step out of the way so they can be together. At the last moment, in the railroad station, she changes her mind and stays with Ignacio. Octavio leaves on the train for the south with the valuable evidence safely in his possession.

*Distinto amanecer* was a laudable attempt to interpret the tensions of contemporary Mexican society. Of the three once-idealistic university companions, only Octavio has continued the struggle as an activist labor leader. Julieta and especially Ignacio are disillusioned by the increasing materialism of Mexican life—he comments bitterly about "a country in which politics drags everything with it, and a time in which a chauffeur earns more than a teacher." Yet Octavio is still fighting the good fight, and he enthusiastically tells Julieta that the scandal will cause high government officials to fall and that his group will then demand radical changes. The film was criticized in some quarters for Julieta's "melodramatic" decision to stay with Ignacio,[43] but Salvador Elizondo says of *Distinto amanecer* that it

well deserves the place of honor that New York's Museum of Modern Art has conferred upon it. It was the first Mexican motion picture to focus upon life as a phenomenon in which two forces come together: love and solidarity. Unfortunately, timidity, or perhaps caution, prevented the very interesting problems set forth there of being resolved with frankness. To *Distinto amanecer* belongs the honor of being one of the very few Mexican movies that does not moralize. It would have been enough for the characters to succumb to the amorous passion set forth from the beginning for this to undoubtedly have been one of the more formidable films made in this country.[44]

Pedro Armendáriz and Alberto Galán in *Distinto amanecer*. (Cineteca)

The three existing studios—CLASA, Azteca, and México-Films (Stahl)—
were hard put at this time to keep up with the increased production. Many
producers had to wait weeks before sound stages were available.[45] An American
industrialist, Harry Wright, began construction of extensive new studio facilities
on a ninety-two-thousand-square-meter area between the Azteca and CLASA
studios in the Churubusco suburb.[46] All this activity attracted the attention of
N. Peter Rathvon and Phil Reisman, president and vice-president respectively of
RKO Radio Pictures which had been involved in movie production in Mexico
since the late 1930s. Reisman was also a member of Nelson D. Rockefeller's
Office for Coordination of Inter-American Affairs, the agency through which the
Mexican film industry was receiving so much valuable assistance. Rathvon and
Reisman arrived in Mexico City in September 1943 with the intention of investing
heavily in the increasingly lucrative Mexican movie business. They offered to
distribute worldwide the entire production of CLASA Films and Films Mundiales;
they tried to buy 51 percent of Posa Films's shares and proposed that Cantinflas,
their exclusive artist, make several films in Hollywood. The RKO executives also
tried to share equally with Harry Wright a controlling interest in the company that
was building the new Churubusco studios. Even though most of these grandiose
projects failed to materialize,[47] they caused concern among many Mexican film

executives who feared the ''Americanization'' of the industry. Already there was consternation at Wright's construction of new studios since it was feared that production capabilities were not yet broad enough to justify the extensive new facilities.[48]

Still, in 1944 the industry produced an unprecedented seventy-five films, and witnessed the debut of fourteen new directors, the most significant being Roberto Gavaldón with his splendid motion picture, *La barraca (The Cottage)*. Just as this increased output signified that filmmaking in Mexico was now indeed on an industrial footing, the outbreak of serious intra-union disputes could be taken as another indication of the industry's growing pains. Other observers look upon this unionization as an attempt by the film industry's skilled workers to protect their own jobs by systematically excluding new blood. In spite of the industry's impressive growth, everyone concerned fully realized that such expansion had its limits—each had to retain his slice of a limited pie. This ''closed door'' policy was evident in the formation in 1944 of a Director's Guild of which Alejandro Galindo was named secretary-general; whereas in 1944 fourteen new directors made their appearance, only one director was admitted into the organization in each of the following two years.[49]

By 1944 all film workers—from performers, directors, cameramen, and technicians right down to ticket-sellers and popcorn salespeople in movie theaters—were represented by the Sindicato de Trabajadores de la Industria Cinematográfica (STIC), founded in 1919 as the Unión de Empleados Confederados del Cinematógrafo.[50] The actors were grouped in Section 2 of STIC, along with technicians and lesser-skilled studio employees—in effect putting internationally known performers at the same level as a carpenter. Objecting to this categorization, the actors, led by Jorge Negrete and Mario Moreno, led a movement to form their own section. STIC's chief, Enrique Solís, opposed such an action, citing what some newspapermen characterized as ''socialist'' reasons; however, ''the times had changed: Avila Camacho and not Cárdenas was president . . . and Fidel Velázquez had substituted Lombardo Toledano at the head of the CTM.''[51] The National Committee of the CTM supported the actors' secession and authorized their formation of a section 7. The workers then went on strike halting filming during all of April.[52]

In 1943 the STIC had seven thousand members organized in forty-seven sections with three thousand workers in the Federal District.[53] But dissatisfaction with Solís's stand on separate sections for actors, cameramen, and directors had already led to a dispute between him, his secretary-general Salvador Carrillo and Gabriel Figueroa, the head of section 2, Técnicos y Manuales (cameramen and technicians' section).[54] The motive for this splitting off of the artists and skilled workers—the actors, cameramen, and directors—from the STIC was that the industry's growth was greater in distribution and exhibition than in production. Thus, these members of the union felt threatened; ''they felt that the industrial union did not take into account their needs and, if matters continued thus, that soon they would have neither voice nor vote in union matters.''[55] Thus, after a great deal of bitter recriminations and some threat of violence, the Sindicato de Trabajadores de la Producción Cinematográfica (STPC), incorporating the seceding sections from the STIC, was officially recognized by the CTM on March 14, 1945, as the official bargaining agent for its members, an action bitterly protested by the STIC.[56] A projected strike against the studios by STIC personnel was to be met by armed actors led by Mario Moreno, Jorge Negrete, and Arturo de Córdova. Their militancy had its effect and the STIC called off the work stoppage. Finally, on September 3, 1945, Avila Camacho issued an executive order delimiting the areas of responsibility of the two contending unions: STIC over the distribution, exhibition, and production of newsreels and short films, and STPC over the production of feature-length films. In effect two competing unions were now in existence, each with a full complement of performers, directors, and technicians. The STPC, of course, had the "name" personnel authorized to make profitable full-length features. STIC-affiliated directors, that is, those who made short features, were barred from the STPC's Directors' Guild because they lacked "experience" in directing full-length movies. However, it was obvious that the only way to obtain this experience was in the STPC. It was simply a way for the established directors to keep out new blood and assure themselves work. The creation of the STPC and the division of responsibilities between it and the parent STIC resulted in much bitterness and incessant conflict. In the 1960s and 1970s, rising production costs led many producers to work illegally with the STIC to produce full-length features thus reversing the situation for the STPC-affiliated Churubusco-Azteca studios who now saw their own production drastically curtailed and many of their workers unemployed.

The presidential support for the STPC was dramatically symbolized by the appearance of Mario Moreno, Jorge Negrete, María Félix, and other film luminaries on the presidential balcony alongside Avila Camacho on the occasion of a parade organized by the STPC to show its gratitude to the president. In the face of such massive official opposition, the STIC had no other choice but to accept the situation.[57]

In spite of the complicated union problems, production continued. One film, *La barraca*, stood out in 1944, outshining by far the other mostly mediocre seventy-four motion pictures. Among the latter, to be sure, were a number of interesting productions. Fernández directed *Las abandonadas (The Abandoned Ones)* and *Bugambilia*, both starring Dolores del Río and Pedro Armendáriz. Norman Foster made a creditable bullfight movie, *La hora de la verdad (The Hour of Truth)* with Ricardo Montalbán; and María Félix continued establishing herself as the "*devoradora de hombres*" ("devourer of men") in such films as *Amok* and *La monja alférez (The Ensign Nun)*.

Roberto Gavaldón's *La barraca*, based on the novel by Vicente Blasco Ibáñez, was a paean to a lost Spain, that is, to the pre-Franco era. With the screenplay written by Blasco Ibáñez's daughter, Libertad, and the participation of more than sixteen Spaniards in the production, the film was "much more Spanish than anything else."[58] Set in Valencia in the 1880s, *La barraca* faithfully reproduced

Luana Alcañiz and José Baviera in Roberto Gavaldón's *La barraca* (1944). (Cineteca)

the Valencian countryside and folkways. The story of Batiste and his ill-fated struggle against intolerance and superstition can be seen as an allegory of the dark night which Spain had been enduring since 1939, at least in the view of Spanish republican exiles and their many sympathizers in Mexico and throughout Latin America. But now with the end of the war clearly approaching, hopes were being raised that Franco's fascist regime would soon go the way of those of Hitler and Mussolini. Thus, *La barraca*, recreating in loving detail the rural Valencian society of a bygone era, paid tribute also to the enduring values of the "eternal" Spain.[59]

It is Valencia in 1880. Barret (Pascual Guillot), a bankrupt farmer, has been driven off his land. He gets drunk and kills the usurer responsible for his ruin. Barret dies in prison, his wife expires in the hospital, and his four daughters become prostitutes. His friends and neighbors, led by Pimentó (José Baviera) and his wife Pepeta (Luana Alcañiz), vow that no one will ever work the lands that once belonged to *tío* Barret.

Ten years later, however, Batiste (Domingo Soler), his wife Teresa (Anita Blanch), and their five children move into the abandoned farmhouse as tenants. Even though they work hard to improve the property, they have to cope with the hostility of their neighbors. This culminates in a fight between Batiste's sons and a group of boys during which Pascualet, the youngest, is thrown into a stagnant pond. He becomes seriously ill.

In the meantime, Pimentón accuses Batiste of irrigating out of turn. Batiste has to appear before the Tribunal of the Waters, an ancient body dating back to pre-Visigothic times. He cannot prove that Pimentón is lying, and is found guilty and fined five pesetas. Soon after, Pascualet dies almost at the instant that Batiste's horse is killed. Grief-stricken and furious, Batiste challenges Pimentón to face him man to man, but Pimentón cowers in his darkened house.

After the tragedy of Pascualet's death, the villagers make amends and welcome Batiste and his family into the community. Things seem to improve for awhile until Pimentón is chastised by the landowner for always being late with his rent; she taunts him by saying "*Muchos recuerdos a Batiste*" as he is ordered from her house. At the cantina, a drunken Pimentón complains that the landlord "is not afraid of us anymore" because Batiste defied the community and got away with it. Batiste arrives at this point; he is attacked by Pimentón but breaks a chair over his assailant's head. The old hostility reemerges and Batiste and his family find themselves once again isolated. While hunting in the swamp, Batiste is shot and wounded. He pursues his attacker and kills him. It is Pimentón. Batiste and his family are burned out of their house. Resigned to defeat, they sadly pack up their meager belongings and leave, joined by Tonet (Manolo Fábregas) who has fallen in love with Batiste's daughter Roseta (Amparo Morillo).

*La barraca* is a story of irrational intolerance and the inability of a good man to cope with it. An allegory, certainly, of the Spanish Republic, but an allegory submerged in nostalgia and folklore. Gavaldón went to great pains to reproduce as realistically as possible a nineteenth-century Valencian *huerta*; an elaborate outdoor set was constructed that portrayed a Spanish farming community down to the smallest detail. The same care was lavished on the actors' dress, the dialogue, and the customs of Valencia, the Tribunal of the Waters scene being an especially noteworthy instance. Aside from its many artistic and technical merits, the significance of *La barraca*, according to Ayala Blanco, is:

The phenomenon of Spanish emigration following the republican collapse and the numerous Hispanic population that refuses to assimilate form perhaps the principal motor nerve of the film. A work of collective inspiration, *La barraca* departs from (and directs itself to) a specific audience of refugees and residents, a restricted audience but one which counts for much and predominates in the Mexican cultural order.[60]

As Avila Camacho's presidential term was drawing to a close, so too was the war. For Mexico the bloody struggles on far-flung battlefields had meant prosperity for many areas of economic activity besides the film industry. The conflict had also attracted a host of foreigners to Mexico's peaceful and profitable shores, King Carol of Rumania among them. Mexico City was now more cosmopolitan and sophisticated than it had been in the halcyon days of the Porfiriato. The nouveau riche, both Mexican and foreign, required smart activities on which to spend ostentatiously—night clubs, restaurants, horse racing, and other patrician pastimes.[61] While the wealthy were converting the capital into a mild Latin

American version of prewar Paris, the Bracero Program sent thousands of humbler Mexicans to toil in the fields of the southwestern United States, an arrangement that enabled additional millions of dollars to flow into Mexico in the form of remittances from its temporarily expatriated farmworkers. And since the war had closed off overseas travel, American tourists discovered Mexico and found to their delight that it was no longer populated by bandelier-clad revolutionary *bandidos* (or Marxist presidents that expropriated American properties). Quite the contrary, Americans could run down to Mexico and be free of ration books and other wartime exigencies.

A marked change had taken place in relations between Mexico and the United States in just a few short years. Mexico's adoption of a more conservative stance and its support of the Allied cause (war had been declared against the Axis powers on May 30, 1942) certainly softened some previously strong anti-Mexican attitudes in the United States. It is fascinating to reflect also on the role that Hollywood might have had in this process of implementing the Good Neighbor policy at the urging of the Roosevelt administration. For instance, Nelson D. Rockefeller's Office for Coordination of Inter-American Affairs asked Walt Disney to make a goodwill tour of Latin America, an area where he enjoyed great popularity.[62] The result was two films, *Saludos Amigos* (1943) and *The Three Caballeros* (1945). In *Saludos Amigos*, Donald Duck met the parrot José Carioca, the feathery incarnation of Brazil, an important South American ally. It was a musical romp combining animation and live action that had the effect of showing to American audiences that South America was a magic land full of color, vivacity, and appealing people, not to mention animals. Then the United States's other important Latin American ally, Mexico, received its turn in *The Three Caballeros* in the person of Panchito, a sombrero-wearing, charro-clad, pistol-packing rooster. True, a bit of the old stereotype remained in Panchito but he was a thoroughly likable, fun-loving albeit assertive type who showed "*el pato Pascual*" and José Carioca the wondrous beauties of Mexico: piñata parties, the *jarocho* dances of Veracruz, a charro-clad girl dancing with enormous animated cacti to the tune of "Jesusita en Chihuahua," posadas, and other celebrations of Mexican folklore. Mexico had never been given such a benign and positive image by Hollywood, and *The Three Caballeros* undoubtedly aided tourism to that country if not necessarily contributing to greater international understanding. At least the theme of Pan-Americanism was sounded in the film's title song (set to the music of the popular *ranchera* "Ay Jalisco no te rajes"):

> Oh, we're three caballeros
> Three gay caballeros
> They say we are birds of a feather . . .

Thus in the persons of Donald, José, and Panchito, the United States, Brazil, and Mexico were three pals, none more equal than the others. Latin American audiences were enchanted with both *Saludos Amigos* and *The Three Caballeros* since never before had a *yanqui* filmmaker presented their countries in such a favorable and appealing way. Disney's attention to accuracy was also a major factor in his films' popularity in Latin America; the music, dances, and costumes were authentic and properly placed. No *chinas poblanas* dancing flamenco or gauchos doing rhumbas, as most Hollywood films had for years freely lumped together without regard for what musical style or mode of dress was typical of a particular country.[63]

As to the war itself, very little of it was reflected in Mexican films. A projected movie on the sinking of the *Potrero del Llano*, a Mexican freighter torpedoed by a German submarine off the Florida coast on May 14, 1942, and which was the *casus belli* for Mexico's declaration of war, was never realized.[64] A number of low-budget, uninspired efforts usually dealt with very *macho* charros besting Axis saboteurs and spies who were in Mexico obviously up to no good, as in *Soy puro mexicano (I'm Pure Mexican)* (1942).[65] One film, *Tres hermanos (Three Brothers)* (1943), told of three brothers in the American army. But then the Mexican film industry's specialty was not combat films, a topic that in any event reflected very little of the Mexican experience.[66] If anyone in Mexico or the rest of Latin America wanted to see war movies, Hollywood was supplying plenty of those. Mexican films appealed generally to lower-class audiences who were by and large uninvolved in the global struggle.

The war years were a crucial period for the Mexican movie industry. Vital foreign markets were carved out by producers and distributors quick to take advantage of the effect of the war on Hollywood and other foreign producers. Genres—the *comedia ranchera*, the urban melodrama, the musical comedy— were refined and linked to a star system for maximum exploitation. This formula proved a great success with most Latin American audiences, who were generally uninterested in the war propaganda movies emanating from Hollywood and Great Britain. Quality cinema was also created, that is, films that attempted to portray the realities of Mexican society. Thus Fernández made his compatriots deal with the problems of Indians in *María Candelaria*, and with the meaning of the Revolution in *Flor silvestre*. Julio Bracho with *Distinto amanecer* explored the relevance of old values in the face of a changing, ever more materialistic social and political order. Gavaldón's *La barraca*, although dealing allegorically with the anguish of Spain, dramatized universal problems applicable to Mexico as well as to any other society.

# 4

# "Golden Age," Crisis, and Retrenchment: 1947–1959

With the war over, Mexico entered a "boom" period of unprecedented economic expansion and prosperity under the administration of Miguel Alemán (1946–1952). These years also constitute the film industry's "Golden Age," at least in production and profits. Yet even though filmmaking in this era was at its peak and a number of significant films were made, the outlines of a crisis were there for all to see. The main problem was the very success the industry had been enjoying—producers became wedded to audience-tested genre pictures not only because such movies were popular with the public but also because the Banco Cinematográfico would only back projects with the greatest possibility of commercial success.

The unionization of the industry's workers also contributed to the general artistic stagnation. This was perhaps most serious in the Directors' Guild, which zealously limited the number of new directors so as to protect the livelihoods of the older members. Another flaw inherent in such a closed system was that many of the directors prized by producers were those who could crank out formula movies as quickly and cheaply as possible.

The major factor sustaining such a movie industry was the "star system." Mexican producers and directors were indeed fortunate in that during the 1940s and 1950s a fortuitous confluence of talented, charismatic, and attractive performers appeared who could assure commercial success for even the worst of films. The problem with this was that a motion picture became a vehicle for the star and consequently the director and the script became of secondary concern. This was the situation faced by Luis Buñuel when he arrived in Mexico in 1946 to work for Oscar Dancigers.

Buñuel, the renowned creator of *Un Chien Andalou*, *L'Age d'or*, and *Las Hurdes—Tierra sin pan* (*Las Hurdes—Land Without Bread*), had been in the United States since 1938 working at various times for the Museum of Modern Art in New York, for Hollywood's Hispanic productions, and in the making of military training films.[1] His first film in Mexico was *En el viejo Tampico* (*In Old*

*Tampico*), later renamed *Gran Casino*, and it starred Jorge Negrete and the great Argentine star, Libertad Lamarque. Negrete, afraid that his career was in the doldrums, was determined to upstage Lamarque who was equally determined to be successful in her first Mexican film and establish herself as the star she had been in Argentina.[2] The result, according to Buñuel, was a ''tourney to see who could sing more tangos, Lamarque or Negrete.''[3] In spite of the two stars' participation, *Gran Casino* was a commercial failure and it would be two years before Buñuel was to make another film.

Under Alemán, steps were taken to assure the government a major role in the film industry, a policy in keeping with the increasing public sector participation in the Mexican economy. The pattern had been well established under Avila Camacho:

Assessing the development of State capitalism during the regime of General Manuel Avila Camacho, we can conclude that if it indeed received a strong impetus with the creation of a series of state-controlled organs and firms and by the widening of governmental faculties and actions in the economy, it also lost much of the nationalist and popular content exhibited during the government of General Cárdenas.[4]

In the film industry, this tendency meant increasing official protectionism in order to safeguard an important national ''cultural'' activity. Thus on February 12, 1946, a law (retroactive to the previous five years) was enacted exempting the movie industry from income taxes. The drafting of a cinematic law was also initiated under Avila Camacho, although the legislation would not be passed until 1949.[5]

The activities of William O. Jenkins, the former United States vice-consul in Puebla who was the central figure in a much-publicized political kidnapping in 1919, serve to illustrate the byzantine workings of the film business in Mexico at this time. Jenkins had settled in Puebla and proceeded to make a fortune in the distribution of alcoholic beverages, medicines, and drugs. His partner, Gabriel

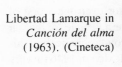

Libertad Lamarque in
*Canción del alma*
(1963). (Cineteca)

Alarcón, built the Reforma Theater in Puebla with financial assistance from the state governor, Maximino Avila Camacho (the president's brother), who also had extensive business dealings with Jenkins. Alarcón and Jenkins then took over ownership of the movie houses in Puebla owned by the Spaniard Jesús Cienfuegos. Alarcón and Jenkins then formed a partnership with the Espinosa Iglesias brothers, the only remaining independent theater operators in the city.

From these modest beginnings, the consortium extended its control to all movie houses in the state of Puebla, forcing out the small, independent operators. Eventually, Jenkins, who functioned as a silent partner, and Manuel Espinosa Iglesias extended their monopoly over a large part of the country: Guadalajara and parts of Jalisco, and the states of Michoacán, Guanajuato, Aguascalientes, Querétaro, Zacatecas, and Durango. Jenkins was also the principal stockholder in the original Banco Cinematográfico which happened to sell its controlling interest in a number of Mexico City theaters to Espinosa Iglesias who formed his exhibition chain, Operadora de Teatros, S.A. Espinosa Iglesias forced Emilio Azcárraga to sell his Alameda Theater and string of movie houses; he accomplished this by informing both Mexican producers and American distributors like 20th Century Fox, Paramount, and Universal that ''if you rent films to the Alameda Theater and its circuit, I will not exhibit any motion picture of yours in our movie houses of Mexico, Puebla, Veracruz, Torreón, and other cities I am beginning to control.''[6] And what Espinosa did not take over, Alarcón, Jenkins's other partner, absorbed into his empire.

Jenkins's financial interests were not limited solely to movie house chains and the Banco Cinematográfico; he was also an important figure in the Nacional Financiera, an official credit agency, where he was in a position to influence contracts and investments ''in almost fabulous amounts.''[7] Jenkins was also an associate of Rómulo O'Farrill in the building of the Packard automobile assembly plant in Puebla and later joined with him in establishing the largest television station in Mexico, now in partnership with Emilio Azcárraga, the displaced owner of Operadora de Teatros and founder of XEW, Mexico's leading radio station.[8]

The multi-faceted operations of Jenkins had to depend on the friendship and protection of powerful politicians. His personal and business relationships with President Avila Camacho's brother, who also happened to be governor of Puebla, make this evident enough. Jenkins's almost total control, through his cohorts, over the country's exhibition houses caused public alarm and resentment during the Alemán presidency. Led by the flamboyant ex-revolutionary officer and producer/director, Miguel Contreras Torres, a group of independent producers protested against the Jenkins monopoly. To counter Jenkins and assist the film industry in the face of foreign competition, President Alemán created the National Cinematic Committee (Comisión Nacional de Cinematografía). The Banco Cinematográfico, heretofore a private firm, was reorganized as the Banco Nacional Cinematográfico with a capitalization of 10 million pesos provided by the federal government on the one hand and the Banco de México, Nacional Financiera, and the Banco Nacional de México on the other.[9] Whether this effectively checked the Jenkins consortium is questionable, given his pervasive influence in Mexican high finance. Despite this move, the Banco Cinematográfico's director in 1953, Eduardo Garduño, publicly attacked Jenkins, saying that "the monopoly hangs heavily over the nation and, in addition, prevents the healthy development of production."[10] A state distributor, Películas Nacionales, S.A., was founded in 1947 presumably to provide an alternative to the Jenkins group; participating in it were: Filmadora Mexicana, CLASA Films Mundiales, Producciones Rosas Priego, and the Banco with a capital of approximately 200,000 pesos.[11]

An outstanding example of official interest in filmmaking was "El Indio" Fernández's *Río Escondido* (*Hidden River*) (1947). Coming on the heels of *Enamorada* (*In Love*) (1946), his successful adaptation of *The Taming of the Shrew* to a revolutionary setting, *Río Escondido* signified a high point in Fernández's career.

*Río Escondido* tells the story of Rosaura Salazar (María Félix), a dedicated and patriotic schoolteacher who is given her assignment personally by the president, Miguel Alemán (playing himself but only shown in silhouetted rear shots). Fernández gives himself over completely to the most blatant and maudlin *patrioterismo* as he shows Rosaura (appropriately wearing a *rebozo*) rushing to her appointment at the Presidential Palace for which she is already late. As she ascends the stairs in front of Diego Rivera's mural, a voice identifies itself as the "bell of Dolores" and sternly recounts for Rosaura's benefit the agonized yet glorious history of Mexico as reflected in the mural; then the voice hurries Rosaura along to her appointment.

Although the president has already seen the large group of schoolteachers, he has Rosaura sent in to him for a private interview, in the process making a group of ministers and doctors wait. Rosaura is on the president's list of "outstanding" teachers and he tells her that this is the reason he has summoned her and her colleagues to personally give them their assignments. He recounts for her Mexico's problems—ignorance, disease, and illiteracy—and ominously refers to "*malos mexicanos*" who oppose the new administration's plans for reform; a tear trickles down Rosaura's cheek. The president assigns her to the town of Río Escondido and instructs her to write to him personally and report on her progress. As she leaves the president's chambers, Rosaura is knocked to the floor by the doctors rushing to get in; she is helped up by her old teacher don Felipe (Arturo Soto Rangel) and Felipe Navarro (Fernando Fernández), a young, just-graduated doctor. Don Felipe, knowing of her heart condition, does not think she is well enough to teach in a rural area, but she convinces him not to inform the authorities.

Rosaura arrives at Río Escondido, a desolate, poverty-stricken community tyrannized by one of the *malos mexicanos* alluded to by the president—the cacique Regino Sandoval (Carlos López Moctezuma), an ex-*villista* gone bad. Rosaura shows her pluck by courageously defying Regino and his murderous henchmen. He is unsuccessful in forcing her to become his mistress, as he had done with the previous schoolteacher. She calls Felipe back from the village to which he had been assigned to combat a smallpox epidemic in Río Escondido. Rosaura and Felipe force Regino to fix up the school and have the townspeople vaccinated in exchange for medical treatment for he has also fallen ill. The village priest

(Domingo Soler), heretofore powerless against the cacique, gains heart from Rosaura and Felipe's courageous example and helps to gather the villagers for vaccination. In the repaired school building, Rosaura exhorts the boys and girls: "Learn so you can regenerate Río Escondido, Mexico, and the world!" She lectures them about "dark forces" in Mexico, especially ignorance; she points to Juárez's picture as an example of Mexico's (and the Indians') ability to reach the heights. "But what am I saying?" she interrupts herself. "We have to start where Juárez did—with the first letter of the alphabet."

Regino feels his power over the villagers slipping away. One night, after drinking heavily, he goes to Rosaura's school where she also sleeps; he attempts to rape her as his men wait outside. A shot rings out from within; Regino staggers from the building with Rosaura following, blasting away at him with a rifle. His men move menacingly toward her but are attacked by torch-wielding Indians and are massacred.

Rosaura, hysterical, collapses. She is seriously ill but insists on dictating her report to the president, which Felipe takes down. Her condition worsens and she is obviously dying; Felipe attempts to teach the village children but concludes that "special ability" is needed for that. A horseman delivers a letter for Rosaura; it is the president's reply: "The *patria* is grateful to you . . . ." She dies just as Felipe finishes reading the letter. The final scene shows Rosaura's tombstone inscribed with a tribute to her.

*Río Escondido*, unsurprisingly, has elicited both condemnation and praise.[12] "At a distance of almost twenty years," says Ayala Blanco, "*Río Escondido*, the film that best reveals the ideals of Emilio Fernández, resembles a sculpture, solitary and unmoving."[13] Gabriel Figueroa's photographic preciosity incorporated all of the Eisensteinian techniques: low-angle long shots in silhouette that emphasize the stark landscape and sky and the smallness of the human figures before them; the closeups of Indian faces and shrouded women; and the "dead tree framing" in which long shots are composed between the gnarled branches of a

María Félix makes a point with the help of Benito Juárez in Emilio Fernández's *Río Escondido* (1947). (Cineteca)

dried-up tree. All of this in addition to the truculent railing against "dark forces" and "bad Mexicans" by the characters—in reality symbols rather than actual people—were sure to cause widespread annoyance as well as admiration. *Río Escondido* received the Ariel in 1949 for the best Mexican film; Fernández and Figueroa were named, respectively, best director and best photographer. Figueroa also received the award for best photography at the Prague Film Festival in 1948 and Fernández received an honorable mention for direction. In that same year, it was awarded the prize for best photography at Madrid.[14]

Another major 1947 film that combined in a disconcerting way elements of musical comedy, melodrama, and stark, brutal realism was Ismael Rodríguez's *Nosotros los pobres* (*We the Poor*). Rodríguez, who had been in films since the 1930s,[15] directed a sprightly and appealing *comedia ranchera* in 1946, *Los tres García* (*The Three Garcias*), and quickly followed it up with a sequel, *Vuelven los García* (*The Garcias Return*). *Nosotros los pobres* was Rodríguez's most popular film. Although it won no prizes, it remains Mexico's all-time leader in box-office receipts and is still seen in neighborhood movie houses as well as on television.

*Nosotros los pobres* is an emotionally drawing experience as it relates the misadventures of Pepe el Toro (Pedro Infante), his sister Chachita (Evita Muñoz), and his sweetheart Celia (Blanca Estela Pavón). The plot is too complex to even attempt to summarize here, but suffice it to say that Rodríguez establishes that poverty is a hellish condition in spite of the nobility of the poor, or at least of some of them. Miguel Inclán as Pilar turns in one of his most hateful roles; not only does his theft of four hundred pesos from Pepe, which is the direct cause of the latter's tragic contretemps, go unpunished, but, dazed by marijuana, he brutally beats Pepe's totally paralyzed mother. Such scenes of violence, another being Pepe's fight in prison with three hoodlums who had framed him and during which he gouges out the eye of one, are skillfully offset by musical numbers or comedy sequences. An additional aspect of *Nosotros los pobres* worth mentioning is that it continued Galindo's innovation from *Campeón sin corona* (*Champion Without a Crown*) of employing authentic street dialogue from the slums of Mexico City.[16] The public's enthusiastic reception of this film encouraged Rodríguez to follow it in 1948 with a sequel, *Ustedes los ricos* (*You the Rich*), in which the fortunes of Pepe el Toro and Celia, now married, are further scrutinized.

The trend toward serious urban drama, however, was best exemplified in the films of Alejandro Galindo. His *Campeón sin corona* (1945) sensitively told the story of Roberto "Kid" Terranova (David Silva), a talented boxer from the slums who lacks the self-confidence to be a champion. Significantly, "Kid" Terranova is cowed psychologically by a Mexican-American boxer, Joe Ronda (Víctor Parra), who spouts English at him during their match. This theme—the inferiority complex of the Mexican—is a favorite of Galindo's and it is a subject he would continue to explore in the years ahead. In 1947 Galindo directed *El muchacho alegre* (*The Cheerful Lad*) for Raúl de Anda; here he took the elements of a standard rural melodrama and transcended its limitations with a superior film.

Returning to his true genre in 1948, Galindo in *¡Esquina bajan!* (*Corner, Getting Off!*) examined the world of unionized workers, in this case, bus drivers.

Alejandro Galindo's *Campeón sin corona* (1945) with (left to right) David Silva, Fernando Soto ''Mantequilla,'' and Conchita Gentil Arcos. (Pelmex)

Comparing Galindo's approach to social problems with that of Rodríguez in *Nosotros los pobres* and *Ustedes los ricos*, García Riera states:

The poor of . . . Rodríguez were condemned to solitary impotence because their idea of solidarity did not go beyond the narrow limits of sentimentalism and because their secret aspiration was to become petty bourgeois; Galindo's poor, on the other hand, recognized their social condition to dignify their humble status. Ismael Rodríguez talked of the poor while Galindo concerned himself with the workers; Karl Marx undoubtedly would have been much more in accord with the latter.[17]

In *Una familia de tantas*, the middle-class father, Rodrigo Cataño (Fernando Soler), seeks by means of an absolute and tyrannical control over his family to shut out society and maintain his home as an oasis of feudal, Porfirian order amid the turmoil of the world beyond. But unlike Bustillo Oro in *Cuando los hijos se van*, Galindo recognizes that Mexico has changed and that the new, unsettling values cannot be kept out. Rodrigo's stern control is disturbed when Roberto del Hierro (David Silva), a vacuum cleaner salesman representing the ''Bright O'Home'' line (and symbolically the encroaching ''American way of life''), aggressively introduces his product into the Castaño home. Fast-talking, intelligent, and ambitious, Roberto represents the upwardly mobile middle-class created by the Revolution and World War II, the very people most despised by a Porfirian gentleman. Yet he is helpless against Roberto who easily convinces him to purchase first the vacuum cleaner and later a refrigerator. Rodrigo's oldest daughter Maru (Martha Roth) is captivated by Roberto and they fall in love. When Roberto announces to Rodrigo that he and Maru want to marry, the old man is furious that they have initiated a relationship without his permission. Maru defies her father and marries Roberto; on her wedding day no one in her family is on hand, having been forbidden by Rodrigo to attend.[18]

The oft-made charge that the Mexican cinema has been largely alienated from reality cannot be made against Galindo. As in *Una familia de tantas*, he has always sought to focus on the underlying tensions of society—to the extent possible, of course, within a capitalistic industrial system. A self-proclaimed "leftist,"[19] Galindo has certainly been much franker than his contemporaries in scrutinizing the contradictions of Mexican life. For instance, his approach to racial tensions in his country is quite unlike that of Fernández who deals with such a complex subject simply by idealizing Indian culture. Galindo takes a much more sophisticated approach in that he is mindful of the subtler tensions between creoles and mestizos in a middle-class ambience. This is a subject that most Mexicans prefer to ignore (or rather sublimate), categorically stating that there is no racial prejudice in their country. Galindo finally made a film in which this problem was the central theme; the picture was *El juicio de Martín Cortés* (*The Trial of Martín Cortés*) (1973) which was almost totally ignored, a snubbing that the director attributes to his countrymen's reluctance to face up to their racial problems.[20] In technique, his camera movements are competent yet unobtrusive, unlike Fernández whose elaborate setups often distract the viewer's attention. Galindo himself dismisses the concern with camera technique as "of no importance."[21]

In the later 1940s the only serious threat to Cantinflas's hegemony appeared. This was the late Germán Valdez "Tin-Tan" (1919—1973), a fresh, imaginative music-hall comic. His humor was quite unlike Cantinflas's, being expressed rather in a spontaneous, often hysterical style; also Tin-Tan was an accomplished song-and-dance man. Born in Mexico City, Tin-Tan moved with his family to Ciudad Juárez in 1931 and from the age of twelve he resided in that border city. He was a radio announcer until he joined the company of the ventriloquist Paco Miller and returned to the capital, where he appeared on the same music-hall programs with Cantinflas. Tin-Tan's specialty at this time was the *pachuco* character he had created, influenced by his proximity to North American culture during his years of residence in Juárez, as well as by the entire milieu of Mexico's border areas. Tin-Tan appeared in the typical pachuco costume, or as it was known in the United States, the "zoot-suit"—wide-brimmed hat with a tremendous feather stuck in the brim, baggy pants, and single-buttoned long jacket.[22]

Tin-Tan also sprinkled English phrases throughout his dialogue in the manner of the Juárez area, but even more so, as Mexican-American pachucos were wont to do. Not that Mexico City audiences were that familiar with the linguistic practices of *pochos* (an Americanized, or "gringoized" Mexican, i.e., a Mexican-American, used in a condescending or derogatory manner), but there does exist a bias of long standing against the northern tier of states—Chihuahua, Sonora, Tamaulipas, Nuevo León, and Baja California. Residents of central Mexico have tended to disdain northerners as being uncultured, boorish, and, perhaps worst of all, semi-Americanized. This attitude increases in intensity when applied to Mexican-Americans. Therefore, although Tin-Tan's pachuco routine was initially accepted for its novelty, he was eventually obliged to change the character, molding it into that of a street-wise native of the Federal District. Yet, Tin-Tan was never a *pelado*, a representative of the lowest class as Cantinflas was; his portrayals were usually of an ambitious, upwardly mobile huckster, as in *Calabacitas tiernas* (*Tender Little Pumpkins*) (1948) and especially *El rey del barrio* (*The King of the Neighborhood*) (1949). Tin-Tan's talent, his art one might safely say, is happily receiving the recognition it has long deserved:

Perhaps it could be said that this comic is superior to ''Cantinflas,'' since in his ''pachuco'' role he reflected an entire phenomenology of transculturation, an entire historical problem based on Mexican-U.S. relations. Tin-Tan's linguistic *pochismo*, his demythicizing character, antisolemn and iconoclastic, place this unforgettable artist as unique in his genre.[23]

Such widely divergent talents as Galindo and Tin-Tan were clearly signs of an exciting and creative vigor in the late 1940s. ''El Indio'' Fernández, although his work was beginning to bog down in clichés, still was capable of lyrical beauty if not dramatic power as in *Enamorada*. Yet even though Mexican cinema was to achieve an almost spectacular success in purely quantitative terms, its aesthetic achievements—those not infrequent moments of true cinematic art it had been able to achieve—were to be suffocated by the commercial demands of a constantly more structured industry. Thus ''formula'' or ''package'' pictures were steadily more in demand—''family'' melodramas, *comedias rancheras*, and comedies, all quite endemic to Mexican cinema since the 1930s. However, *alemanismo* generated something new: the *cabaretera* films.

The prostitute had been an early theme in Mexican films since the silent era and

Germán Valdez ''Tin-Tan'' rhumbas with Tongolele in *El rey del barrio* (1949). (Pelmex)

Tin-Tan in *Hay
muertos que no
hacen ruido*
(1946). (Pelmex)

the early talkies: the three versions of *Santa, La mujer del puerto, La mancha de sangre (The Blood Stain)* (1937), and others. But the excitement and anxieties of the Alemán era injected a new restlessness into Mexican urban society. The emerging new classes of businessmen, technocrats, bureaucrats, and wheeler-dealers sought legitimacy in the traditional middle-class values and thus equity with the remnants of the Porfirian creole elite. The new elites, however, lacked the ingrained conservatism of their forbears and their lack of total commitment to the old ethical and sexual codes is interestingly reflected in the wave of *cabaretera* films of this period. The settings for these motion pictures were the cheap night clubs of the capital and their luckless *ficheras* or B-girls. As representations of a society in the throes of rapid economic and social change, these films often reflected the tensions of postwar Mexico. If the *comedia ranchera* stood for

Tin-Tan in *Tres
lecciones de amor*
(1958). (Azteca
Films)

traditional values, the *cabareteras* dramatized the breakdown of those values. In the first place, the girls found themselves there because of personal or economic adversity. Lacking the skills demanded by an increasingly complex economy and further restrained by a male-dominated society, the girls turned to a traditional profession. In the age-old Hispanic dichotomy, if they could not be "good" women then they must perforce be "bad." But the melodramatic formula (or middle-class ethic) of the prostitute "with the heart of gold" was usually employed in most of these films, to reinforce the underlying moral values.

The urban night spot, in its surrogate role as the city in microcosm, was also a conduit for foreign influences. The music especially symbolized this. Most of it was Afro-Cuban—danzones, rhumbas, congas, mambos, cha-chas—musical forms with a high level of erotic suggestiveness which in turn highlighted the freer sexual standards of postwar urban life.[24] This musical foundation led to the popularization of a number of Cuban performers, the principal ones being Rosa Carmina, María Antonieta Pons, and Ninón Sevilla. The latter was undoubtedly the queen of the *cabareteras*. She was capable of exuding a child-like naïveté as well as cheap eroticism, and her angry outbursts were almost legendary. Ninón Sevilla appeared in many *cabaretera* films in the 1940s and 1950s but her classic pictures are undoubtedly *Sensualidad* (1950) and *Aventurera* (*Adventuress*) (1952). In the former she was a ruthless, amoral B-girl who seduces a repressed, middle-aged husband (Fernando Soler).

*Aventurera* has been lauded as the epitome of the genre, transcending its melodramatic strictures. Directed by Alberto Gout and written by Alvaro Custodio, the film treated middle-class morality as a hypocritical sham and represented Mexican society as being thoroughly corrupt. Elena (Ninón Sevilla), a schoolgirl in Chihuahua City, lives an apparently happy family life in a comfortable bourgeois home. One day she returns home unexpectedly and surprises her mother in a passionate embrace with another man; Elena flees the house in shock and disgust. Returning later she finds her father despondently holding a note from his wife who has run away with the man she "truly loves." Elena's father puts a bullet through his head shortly thereafter.

Elena then goes to Ciudad Juárez to look for a secretarial job. At every job she becomes the object of lustful attentions by her employers, which she virtuously rejects. Jobless and disheartened, she runs into Lucio (Tito Junco), a ne'er-do-well admirer from Chihuahua. He offers to get her a job with a friend of his and takes her to a nightclub where he plies her with champagne. Inebriated, she finally is taken to meet her "employer," Rosaura (Andrea Palma). Elena is given a drugged cup of tea, passes out, and is taken to a bedroom where she is made available while still unconscious to an undetermined number of men. When she wakens, she learns the truth of her situation—that she is bound to Rosaura's employment.

Elena eventually becomes a star of the nightclub (her feature number is a mildly suggestive dance to the music of "In a Persian Market"), although troublesome and subject to furious outbursts. One night she sees her mother's lover and viciously attacks him. Rosaura has had enough and orders her henchman *El Rengo* (Miguel Inclán) to scar Elena's face; Lucio intercedes but Elena stops him from killing *El Rengo*. Elena then becomes a driver for Lucio's gang while they break into a jewelry store; however, the police are waiting for them, having been tipped off by a disgruntled member of Lucio's gang. Lucio is captured but Elena manages to escape. She goes to Mexico City where in no time at all she again becomes a nightclub star. She captivates Mario (Rubén Rojo), a law student and scion of one of Guadalajara's oldest families. Elena accepts his offer of marriage after the same hoodlum that had betrayed Lucio attempts to blackmail her.

Once in Guadalajara, Elena discovers that Mario's "aristocratic" mother is none other than Rosaura, the notorious Juárez madam. From this point on the film becomes progressively more vicious as Elena does her utmost to humiliate and disgrace Rosaura before the cream of Guadalajara society. Mario, of course, has no idea of his mother's secret business activities and is at a loss to explain Elena's behavior and the progressively more open hostility between his mother and his wife. Nonetheless, he faithfully sticks by Elena who has already told Rosaura that she will marry her son to get revenge. One night when Mario is working late, Rosaura surprises Elena attempting to seduce Mario's younger brother; the ensuing argument between the two women results in Rosaura physically attacking Elena. Mario arrives home just in time to catch his mother strangling his wife. Rosaura then leaves on one of her periodic "business" trips.

Elena leaves Mario and also goes to Juárez where her mother is seriously ill in a hospital. Elena coldly refuses to forgive her mother and watches her die. In the meantime, Rosaura has instructed *El Rengo* to kill Elena but he cannot go through with it because he is in love with her. Mario also arrives in Juárez in search of Elena who takes him to Rosaura's brothel-cabaret and leaves the shocked mother and son together. In the meantime, Lucio has escaped from prison and wants Elena to cross the border to the United States with him. Mario appears again and confronts Lucio who beats him up; before Lucio can kill Mario, however, *El Rengo* stabs Lucio to death. Elena and Mario are now free to find happiness together.

Clearly *Aventurera* went far beyond the usual parameters of the *cabaretera* melodrama, allowing its "heroine" to vent her most ruthless instincts freely without eventual punishment. In the course of Elena's misadventures, Mexican middle and upper-class society came in for a severe drubbing. The naïve happiness of Elena with her parents in the opening scenes is soon shattered by her mother's infidelity; but the mother is also a woman trapped in a stifling provincial atmosphere, living with a cloyingly adoring husband for whom she has lost all feeling. In true melodramatic fashion, the mother pays dearly for her reckless grasp at happiness, earning the undying hatred of her daughter and, perhaps worse, unwittingly converting Elena into a cruel, unfeeling person who can look upon others only as objects to be manipulated. And the linking of Juárez's most corrupt underworld activities with Mexico's most conservative, aristocratic, and pro-Catholic elements—Guadalajara's elite—is a shattering commentary on the cynical duality of society, that the most arrogant and privileged groups enjoy their status by the gross exploitation of those less fortunate. In other words, an exclusive, "good" family of Guadalajara, the country's bastion of conservative, traditional moral values, is maintained by the illicit money from a sordid brothel (the oldest and most blatant form of economic exploitation as well as sexism) in a vice center like Juárez, a city that itself lies uncertainly suspended between two antagonistic cultures. In truth, García Riera comments that the Gout-Custodio-Sevilla trio never managed in their other films to attain the ''surprising virulence of *Aventurera*, truly an exceptional achievement of the Mexican cinema.''[25]

Thus if the *cabaretera* film was the ''cinema par excellence'' of *alemanismo*, the genre managed at times to express a devastating indictment of Mexican life.[26] It can even be said that the unabashed greed given free rein by Alemán's ambitious developmentalist regime created severe societal stresses that found expression in some of the most interesting films ever made in Mexico before outright commercial ''packages'' came to predominate in the late 1950s and 1960s. For instance, a minor Fernández/Figueroa vehicle like *Siempre tuya* (*Always Yours*) (1950) made some telling points. The first part of the film has some biting social commentary: tenant farmer Jorge Negrete and his wife Gloria Marín are standing disconsolately in the middle of their barren land: a five-year drought (the same amount of time that Marín has been barren, in a touch of ''El Indio's'' typical symbolism) has ruined them. The dust swirls about the couple as the landlord rides up on a horse and tells them that he too is bankrupt, that they will all have to move on. Negrete considers going to the United States as a bracero but, being a good Mexican, he dismisses the notion. Instead he and Marín move to a shantytown in Mexico City. When the owners decide to raze the shacks, the people, in a display of *lumpen* solidarity, defy the authorities. When they are arrested, a lawyer berates the propertyowners ''for fearing communism but doing more to bring it on than the communists themselves.'' The second half of the film degenerates into musical melodrama: Negrete wins a singing contest on a radio show (interpreting ''México

Alberto Gout's *Aventurera* (1949) with Andrea Palma (right) and Ninón Sevilla. (Cineteca)

lindo y querido''), immediately becomes a star, and is thrust into the hypocrisy and corruption of high society. Gloria Marín, however, knows that her husband will eventually see through the false glamor of his superficial new acquaintances and return to her. He does.[27]

In 1953 Alejandro Galindo filmed one of his most outspoken films, *Espaldas mojadas (Wetbacks)*. Making it to "convince Mexicans not to go to the United States,"[28] Galindo took on the entire gamut of social and economic problems besetting Mexico and even dedicated considerable attention to the status of Mexican-Americans. The realism of the film was heightened by Galindo's use of American actors speaking English dialogue. The problem of Mexican illegal emigration has perhaps never been set forth so well, although at times a mite sensationally, in a commercial film. For instance, Galindo has guard towers on the American side of the Río Grande which scan the water with searchlights. When any individual or group is spotted swimming across, a siren shatters the night silence and the border patrol begins firing, shooting to kill. Although the representation of the United States-Mexico border in *Espaldas mojadas* is more typical of the later Berlin Wall than of anything that ever existed on the border between the two countries, Galindo's intent here was probably not so much anti-American as didactic—to discourage his countrymen from entering the United States illegally. In view of the violence that has periodically flared up along the border, and which continues today, occasionally to an alarming degree, it can be said that in essence Galindo's view is correct: the murderous guardtowers represent the hostility of American society toward the individuals driven away by the poverty and indifference of their own country. Yet there was enough antipathy expressed toward the United States to make the Dirección de Cinematografía fretful and *Espaldas mojadas* was not released until 1955.

The film opens with a view of Ciudad Juárez, here described as a stalwart cultural frontier; a voice-over declares testily that "on this side of the Río Bravo it is *still* Mexico, where Spanish is *still* spoken and songs are sung to the Virgin of Guadalupe . . . on the other side of the Río Grande, as the Americans call it, are skyscrapers and everyone owns a car." A country, continues the narrator, that "forty years of movies have presented as a place where everyone is happy."

After the opening remarks, we see Rafael (David Silva) walking along a Juárez street. At the bracero hiring hall, he explains that he is a heavy equipment operator; the clerk tells him that for Mexicans there is only fieldwork. Rafael has no passport and is turned away. He gets involved with the "coyote" Frank Mendoza (José Elías Moreno) who is illegally contracting workers for Mister Sterling (Víctor Parra). Rafael crosses the Río Grande with a group of braceros that night, managing to survive the fire from the American watchtowers, although a new friend of his is killed.

The rest of the film traces Rafael's life as an illegal alien in the United States, constantly on the move, fearful of being discovered. He is at the mercy of exploiters like Mister Sterling who pay him substandard wages and take out all manner of "deductions." In his odyssey he meets Luis Villarreal alias Louie

Royalville (Oscar Pulido), a picaresque and thoroughly cynical hobo. At one point when Luis has been berating the capitalist system, Rafael remarks that ''you sound like a communist.'' Luis vehemently denies this, saying that under communism everybody is required to work and he could never abide such a system.

Rafael gets work with a railroad gang bossed by Sterling. After an altercation with him—Sterling snarls, in English: ''Don't touch me, you dirty Mexican greaser''—Rafael becomes a fugitive. He arrives at a roadside cafe where María del Consuelo (Martha Valdés) works as a waitress. He had met her briefly earlier in the film just after he crossed over from Mexico. She recognizes Rafael and hides him when a policeman comes in, uttering the classic line: ''You seen a Mexican with a brown leather jacket? Looks more like a wop than a Mexican.'' After the officer leaves, María tells Rafael of her unhappiness: ''I'm not Mexican, I'm a *pocha*. We're worse off than blacks—they stick together and are not pulled toward another country. The Mexicans don't like us and the gringos look down on us.'' Rafael asks her if she'll return to Mexico and marry him. She agrees and they plan to meet in Juárez.

Rafael has to return to Mexico the same way he left it, swimming the river at night. Ironically, he is picked up by a Mexican border patrol the moment he sets foot on the other side. In an uneven scene, made so by Galindo's attempt to pack too much ''message'' into it, Rafael protests to the border patrol officer that he is indeed a Mexican, pointing to his swarthy skin; the officer says that that is no proof, that there are many dark-complexioned people in the world—*pochos*, Greeks, Italians. ''When will you people realize,'' continues the officer, ''the trouble that you cause by crossing illegally? Have you no dignity?'' ''Dignity?'' asks Rafael angrily. ''We're hungry, that's the reason.'' He talks about abuses in Mexico but pleads to be allowed to stay.

Rafael goes to the Juárez cantina where he is to meet María. Coincidentally, he runs into Sterling who had gone there to cancel a contract with Frank Mendoza because the U.S. government was investigating his use of illegal aliens. A fight ensues; the others suggest that instead of killing him there, they take Sterling and dump him in the river. Sterling is shot to death by the American border guards while being forced to swim across. Another man tells Rafael: ''Neither you nor we killed him. It was he who stupidly tried to swim to the other side.''

Not since *El compadre Mendoza* and *Vámonos con Pancho Villa* had a Mexican filmmaker made such an overtly political film and, more importantly, a motion picture that dealt frankly with one of the country's most serious social problems. In spite of certain technical flaws—the clumsy use of back-projections and stock shots, and some uneven direction—*Espaldas mojadas* remains a powerful and generally well-made film.

In 1953 Galindo also made *Los Fernández de Peralvillo (The Fernandezes of Peralvillo)* again starring David Silva and Víctor Parra. Here Galindo takes a hard look at unscrupulous business practices and the class system. This film, too, is an uncompromising look at a slice of Mexican reality. Interestingly, as in *Una familia de tantas*, the principal character played by Víctor Parra is also a door-to-door salesman of American domestic products. Here, though, the salesman is no

Alejandro Galindo's *Espaldas mojadas* (1953). (Azteca Films)

harbinger of change, of the "American Way of Life." He is a bitter, defeated man, humiliated by housewives, building custodians, and his own family. The only way out of his despair is provided by an old friend, David Silva, who brings him into a crooked consortium for the importation and distribution of medicines. Parra, thoroughly corrupted, finally implicates his friend and other associate in a fraudulent business deal. Silva, now a desperate fugitive from the law, shoots Parra down in the middle of the street. Another noteworthy aspect of this film is the acting of Adalberto Martínez "Resortes," a fine comic actor who was to work often with Galindo.

After the fiasco of *Gran Casino*, Luis Buñuel made only one film in the next two-and-a-half years. This was *El gran calavera (The Great Madcap)* (1949), a standard melodramatic vehicle coproduced by Oscar Dancigers and Fernando Soler who also starred in the film. This light comedy concerns Ramiro (Fernando Soler), a dissolute rich widower, who is led to believe by his family that his behavior has ruined them financially; when he learns the truth, Ramiro in turn tricks his family into thinking that they are indeed bankrupt. The result is that all learn to appreciate one another and to value hard, honest work. Buñuel was able to inject his particular brand of humor at the expense of middle-class ideals, but subtly enough so that the general public still enjoyed the movie. Worth noting is that the final scenes in the church in Mike Nichols's *The Graduate* (1967) seem to

Alejandro Galindo's *Los Fernández de Peralvillo* (1953), left to right, Víctor Parra, Andrés Soler, Leonor Llausás, and Sara García. (Cineteca)

be directly inspired by the denouement in *El gran calavera*, where Ramiro disrupts his daughter's wedding by using a large crucifix to ward off the irate guests.[29]

The commercial success of *El gran calavera* enabled Buñuel to make his masterpiece, *Los olvidados* (*The Young and the Damned*) (1950). For almost three years between *Gran Casino* and *El gran calavera*, Buñuel did not work. During that period of forced idleness, he traveled throughout Mexico and was "impressed with the misery of many of its inhabitants." The result was *Los olvidados*, a stark, realistic portrayal of the brutal existence of slum children in Mexico City.[30]

In *Los olvidados*, Buñuel visualized poverty in a radically different way from the traditional forms of Mexican melodrama. Buñuel's street children are not "ennobled" by their desperate struggle for survival; they are in fact ruthless predators who are no better than their equally unromanticized victims. To Mexican audiences, accustomed to the sentimentalized poor of Rodríguez's *Nosotros los pobres*, *Los olvidados* was an unsettling experience and the film initially was not a commercial success, even though its merit was recognized at once.[31]

Buñuel went on to make eighteen more films in Mexico, and to many non-Mexicans, especially in the United States, he was and still is the only name that comes to mind when Mexican filmmaking is mentioned.[32] In spite of his renown, the effect of Buñuel's work on the Mexican film industry was negligible. His only protegé was Luis Alcoriza who collaborated on the script of *Los olvidados* and several other Buñuel films. But few Mexican directors sought to emulate the Buñuel style, although his colleagues have been justifiably proud that the "master's" art matured in Mexico, which made it possible for him to go to Europe and make such celebrated films as *Diary of a Chambermaid* (1964), *Belle de Jour*

Luis Buñuel's *El gran calavera* (1949) with Fernando Soler (middle) (Procinemex)

*(Beauty of the Day)* (1966), *The Milky Way* (1968), *Tristana* (1969), *The Discreet Charm of the Bourgeoisie* (1974), and *That Obscure Object of Desire* (1978). Thus in the years that Buñuel was making films like *Ensayo de un crimen (Rehearsal for a Crime)* (1955), *Nazarín* (1958), *Viridiana* (1961), *El ángel exterminador (Exterminating Angel)* (1962), and *Simón del desierto (Simon of the Desert)* (1965), Mexican filmmaking was falling back more and more on steadily deteriorating melodramatic formula pictures. Undoubtedly it was Buñuel who gave the Mexican cinema whatever vitality it had left in the late 1950s and early 1960s while the creativity of directors like Fernández and Galindo was being suffocated by an increasingly more structured industry. And it was Buñuel's work that managed to keep international attention on Mexican filmmaking.

For instance, *Ensayo de un crimen* (1955) was the first of Buñuel's Mexican films to demonstrate his surrealistic humor toward bourgeois conventions. The character of Archibaldo Cruz (Ernesto Alonso) is quite similar to the bemused aristocrats played years later by Fernando Rey in *The Discreet Charm of the Bourgeoisie* and *That Obscure Object of Desire*. Archibaldo believes that he was responsible when a child for his governess's death. As an adult he is relating the story to a nun in a hospital, and when he appears to threaten her, she rushes out,

Silvia Pinal and Claudio Brook in Buñuel's *Simón del desierto* (1964).

falls down an elevator shaft, and is killed. Archibaldo is convinced that he caused the nun's death and tells the police that it was not his first crime.

Archibaldo relates his plans to murder three women: Patricia (Rita Macedo), Carlota (Ariadna Welter), and Lavinia (Miroslava). In a flashback, the film traces Archibaldo's frustrating relationships with the vulgar yet provocative Patricia, the ''pure'' and religious Carlota whom he intends to marry, and the beautiful model and tourist guide Lavinia. Archibaldo makes elaborate plans to murder Patricia with a razor but his schemes go awry when she commits suicide after a quarrel with her lover. On another occasion his plot to kill Lavinia is foiled when she brings in a group of American tourists to gape at Archibaldo's colonial mansion. Meanwhile Carlota's lover, the architect Alejandro (Rodolfo Landa), desperate at the thought of losing her to Archibaldo, sends him an anonymous note about Carlota's faithlessness. Archibaldo is unfazed since he plans to murder Carlota anyway after they are married. But Alejandro, insane with jealousy, shoots Carlota while she is at a fitting for her wedding dress.

The flashback ends and the police inspector absolves Archibaldo of any respon-

Buñuel's *Ensayo de un crimen* (1955) with Ernesto Alonso and Miroslava. (Pelmex)

Luis Buñuel (seated at left) on the set of *Ensayo de un crimen*. Others are (standing from left to right) an unidentified friend, Jeanne Buñuel, the mannequin, Miroslava, José Ignacio Mantecón, and Rafael Buñuel. Seated at the right is Eduardo Ugarte, who worked on the script with Buñuel. (Pelmex)

sibility for the two women's deaths. The inspector tells Archibaldo that he cannot be prosecuted for just thinking of murdering someone, and advises him to use an electric razor from now on. Later, in Chapultepec Park, Archibaldo hurls a music box into the lake. He had owned it when he was a child but lost the toy when his parents' house was looted during the Revolution. By chance discovering the music box in an antique store, Archibaldo had met Lavinia at the time. By once again owning the music box, his childhood guilt at his governess's death had revived and Archibaldo began to fancy himself a murderer. In casting away the music box, he also frees himself from the psychological fetters that bound him to a guilt-ridden past. Archibaldo then runs into Lavinia who tells him that she has decided not to marry her fiancé, and they walk off happily together.[33]

In the 1950s, Luis Buñuel also made *Subida al cielo (Ascent to Heaven*, released in the U.S. as *Mexican Bus Ride)* (1951); *El bruto (The Brute), Adventures of Robinson Crusoe*, and *El (He)* (all 1952); *Abismos de pasión (Abysses of Passion)* and *La ilusión viaja en tranvía (Illusion Travels on a Streetcar)* (1953). *Subida al cielo* is on the surface a lighthearted tale about a group of bus passengers in the state of Guerrero, but the film is also an allegory of the story of Adam and Eve in which Buñuel aims his customary barbs at religion and society. *El bruto*, starring Pedro Armendáriz and Katy Jurado, is a realistic, violent tale set in an urban slum. Unlike *Los olvidados*, in which Buñuel portrayed the *lumpenproletariat*, *El bruto* deals with workers who exhibit a well-defined class consciousness

Arturo de Córdova in Buñuel's *El* (1952). (Cineteca)

within the melodramatic context of the film. *The Adventures of Robinson Crusoe*, made in English, was the first Mexican film by Buñuel that became an international commercial success. Curiously, it was not premiered in Mexico until three years after it had been seen throughout the world.

*El*, one of the *buñuelistas*' cult films, traces the descent into paranoia and sexual obsession of a devout Catholic aristocrat (Arturo de Córdova). Buñuel humorously examines the shadowy boundaries between madness, sexual desire, and religious fervor, a theme he would return to again years later in *Viridiana*. *Abismos de pasión* was an adaptation of *Wuthering Heights*, and *La ilusión viaja en tranvía* was a "proletarian" comedy of two streetcar conductors who steal a trolley and offer free rides to the public.[34]

Others besides Buñuel occasionally attempted "quality" cinema. A noteworthy effort was *Raíces (Roots)* (1953), a film about Indians that sought to break the Fernández/Eisenstinian mold. Produced by a television executive, Manuel Barbachano Ponce, and directed by Benito Alazraki, *Raíces* was based on four stories: "Las vacas" depicts the struggle for survival of a poverty-stricken Otomí couple. In "Nuestra señora," Jane, an American anthropology student, comes to the conclusion that the Chamulas are savages because one of them baptizes his son

Beatriz Flores and Juan de la Cruz as the Otomí couple in Benito Alazraki's *Raíces* (1953). (Pelmex)

Alicia del Lago in
*Raíces*. (Pelmex)

with the name of the first "animal" to pass in front of his house—Bicicleta ("Bicycle"). She returns to Chiapas some time later and changes her opinion after she finds the Indians worshipping a copy of *La Gioconda* that had been stolen from her. "El tuerto" tells of a one-eyed boy who is tormented by the other children. His mother takes him to a witch-doctor to be cured, but a firecracker accident blinds his other eye. He is now happy because blind people are respected. "La potranca" relates the efforts of a foreign anthropologist in Veracruz to bed a young Indian girl. When he attempts to buy her from her father, the latter agrees as long as the anthropologist gives his own wife in exchange. Although unevenly paced, *Raíces* had enough anthropological and "exotic" value and skillful camerawork to elicit generally favorable comments from European critics.[35]

In December 1952 Adolfo Ruiz Cortines, a scrupulously honest, conservative bureaucrat, was elected president of Mexico. His administration was sure to inspire a less hectic style into Mexican life than that of his flamboyant predecessor. Symbolic of this was the virtual disappearance of *cabaretera* films.[36] The new director of the Banco Cinematográfico, Eduardo Garduño, attempted to reorganize distribution by proposing the creation of six new firms for this purpose to be backed solely by Mexican producers. One goal of this proposed reorganization was to eliminate the problem of *enlatamiento* ("canning" or witholding a new film from circulation); new Mexican films could not be scheduled for public showing soon after completion because of the limited exhibition facilities and the competition of foreign films. The "Garduño Plan" also sought to limit the importation of foreign movies to 150 a year. The exhibitors (who were completely under the Jenkins thumb, especially after ex-president Abelardo Rodríguez sold his chain of movie theaters to the Jenkins group) were opposed to the scheme since it would force them to dedicate more screening time to less profitable Mexican pictures. This controversy, along with a strike against the movie studios and a dispute between Jorge Negrete and Mario Moreno for the leadership of the Asociación

Nacional de Actores (ANDA), paralyzed the industry adding to the traditional uncertainty of business groups toward a new administration.

In 1954, 346 foreign films, mostly American, were shown in Mexico City and only 22 new Mexican films were released, even though national studios had turned out 82 movies in 1953 and 118 in 1954. This, however, was an unusual year and the number of Mexican films released in other years was more typical and in fact showed a very slight increase. But the withholding from commercial release of new movies made it more difficult for producers to recover their investments and consequently the amount of interest paid to the Banco increased, making their dependence on that state agency that much the greater. Finally on January 1, 1954, the Banco announced its reorganization plan by assigning distribution to three large companies it created: Películas Nacionales for distribution in the national territory; Películas Mexicanas for Latin America, Spain, and Portugal; and Cinematográfica Mexicana Exportadora (Cimex) for the rest of the world. Capitalization for these companies was provided in part by the producers themselves who were assessed 8 percent of their gross income to Películas Nacionales and Películas Mexicanas and 2 percent for Cimex.[37]

But growing state intervention simply increased the commercialist nature of the movie industry and production reflected the growing conservatism of the middle class. For instance, more than half of the 1954 films were melodramas dealing with middle-class tribulations[38] and over thirty comedies were based on a new dance craze, the cha-cha. More and costlier movies were made in color and Cinemascope was introduced.[39] There was a greater number of coproductions with other

TABLE 1
Number of Films Premiered in the Federal
District, 1953–1958

| Origin | 1953 | 1954 | 1955 | 1956 | 1957 | 1958 |
|---|---|---|---|---|---|---|
| U.S. | 226 | 251 | 206 | 230 | 188 | 183 |
| Mexican | 87 | 22 | 85 | 84 | 86 | 100 |
| French | 21 | 33 | 39 | 36 | 23 | 33 |
| Spanish | 14 | 13 | 6 | 9 | 12 | 14 |
| Italian | 11 | 28 | 29 | 21 | 8 | 14 |
| British | 9 | 3 | 4 | 1 | – | 10 |
| Argentine | 3 | 2 | 2 | 5 | – | 4 |
| German | 2 | 3 | 2 | 2 | 4 | 9 |
| Soviet | 1 | 11 | – | 6 | 1 | 3 |
| Others | 5 | 2 | 4 | 1 | 9 | 5 |
| TOTAL | 379 | 368 | 377 | 395 | 331 | 375 |

SOURCE: Heuer, *La industria cinematográfica*, p. 63

countries—France, Spain, Cuba, and Venezuela. And Mexican filmmakers, seeking lower costs and more favorable working conditions, filmed outside of the country more than ever before. Even dictator Fulgencio Batista offered Mexican cineasts attractive terms in an effort to lure them to Cuba: 33 percent of the film's cost and generous tax exemptions.[40]

The trend of Mexican cinema in the late 1950s was to make more "spectacular" films in color, to utilize new techniques such as Cinemascope, and to inject a rather hesitant eroticism into standard melodramas by the display of nudity. This policy was designed, on the one hand, to draw domestic audiences away from television and, on the other, to make Mexican movies more competitive on the international scene.[41] The basic problem was that as films became costlier and had to be produced on an assembly-line basis, there was ever-greater reliance on "formulas"—*comedias rancheras*; films based on dance fads—cha-cha, charleston, rock and roll; comedies; lacrimogenic melodramas; horror vehicles à la Hollywood; American-style westerns; and "super-hero" adventures in which masked cowboys or wrestlers took on a variety of evildoers and monsters. Quality plummeted but production increased. With the opening of the América studios in which all personnel belonged to STIC, the production of serials and, illegally, full-length films made originally as serials, increased. Thus "regular" productions were those movies made by STPC personnel at either the Churubusco or San Angel Inn facilities; regular films were also classified into "two-week" and "three-week" productions with restrictions on performers and running time.[42] For instance, the all-time high in production was reached in 1958 with 138 films—116 "regular," 16 episodes, and 6 coproductions filmed outside Mexico. However, the year's only distinguished films were Buñuel's *Nazarín* and, to a much lesser degree, Ismael Rodríguez's "epic" of the Revolution, *La Cucaracha* with Dolores del Río, María Félix, and Emilio Fernández.[43] As if to signal the passing of Mexican cinema's brightest era, Jorge Negrete died of a liver ailment in a Los Angeles hospital on December 5, 1953, Pedro Infante perished in a private airplane accident on April 15, 1957, and Fernando de Fuentes died in July 1958 at the age of sixty-four. Also indicative of the state of the cinema was the suspension of the "Arieles," the annual awards of the Academia Mexicana de Ciencias y Artes Cinematográficas.

The evident qualitative if not yet quantitative crisis of the Mexican movie industry also aroused concern among the country's intelligentsia, especially in the universities. There had existed film clubs in Mexico since 1931 for the dissemination and serious discussion of worthwhile films from all over the world. The Cine Club de México was founded on July 26, 1950, and functioned throughout the decade, including Mexican films in its programs. The Federación Mexicana de Cine Clubs was created in September 1955 by various university-based and independent film clubs. These film clubs' activities were an important factor in the quest for quality filmmaking and in the formation of young cineasts. Although their activities were necessarily restricted to a small minority, the film clubs would make an important contribution to the dialogue that was to emerge in the late 1960s.[44]

From left to right, Jorge Negrete, Carmen González, and Pedro Infante in *Dos tipos de cuidado* (1952). (Azteca Films)

The veteran actors Andrés Soler (left) and Fernando Soler—the film is unidentified. (Azteca Films)

# 5

# Decline, Renovation, and the Return of Commercialism 1960–1980

In 1958 Adolfo López Mateos was designated the PRI (Partido Revolucionario Institucional) candidate for president. During his administration (1958–1964), the film industry was to enter upon its darkest days. The new director of the Banco Cinematográfico, Federico Heuer, in an assessment of the film industry and the Banco's role in it, declared that "had the Banco . . . not existed, the result would have been that all Mexican cinematic production would have fallen into the hands of foreign investors."[1] Although many thought that the Banco's main purpose was to sustain a group of well-connected Mexican capitalists rather than to keep out foreigners from the film industry, it can be argued with equal force that growing state intervention had indeed preserved the industry, even if precariously, and prevented Hollywood producers and distributors from monopolizing filmmaking and exhibition in Mexico and the rest of Latin America. But producers of nonexistent social vision in combination with nervously conservative officials were to render the film industry almost totally unreflective of the problems and tensions of Mexican society. The industry lost its most significant international voice when Luis Buñuel began making more of his pictures outside of the country, mostly in France. Others, like Galindo, were reduced to turning out stock melodramas. Fernández was eventually boycotted by the producers and he lashed out bitterly at the industry, at one point claiming that it was run by Jews.[2] All in all, the outlook for the 1960s was anything but bright.

Under the administrations of López Mateos and Gustavo Díaz Ordaz (1964–1970), Mexico's contradictions reached unprecedented proportions. On the one hand, the continuing developmentalist policies resulted in impressive and continuous economic growth; on the other, this growth was made possible by protectionist measures that rewarded a small class of capitalists and entrepreneurs as well as officials of state enterprises. The result was a small and slowly expanding middle class concentrated largely in Mexico City but also to be found in other industrial urban centers like Querétaro, Guadalajara, Puebla, and Monterrey, and a huge unemployed and underemployed population that flocked to these and other centers in search of scarce jobs. Driven by want from their unproductive land and unable to find employment on vast, irrigated mechanized farms in the north, millions of these people found that the sophisticated, automated industrial technology of the cities could only absorb a small percentage of the jobless rural and urban population. Many of them gravitated to the northern border towns and thence into the United States, as Galindo had already dramatized in *Espaldas mojadas*.[3]

Yet these massive population movements and dislocations and the resultant societal tensions were largely ignored by the film industry which adhered more tenaciously than ever to its timeworn formula movies. Rising costs and collapsing foreign markets made the producers respond to the crisis in simple economic terms. Thus in a memorandum to the Secretary of Gobernación, the Dirección General de Cinematografía, and the STPC on August 17, 1962, the Asociación de Productores denounced the STPC's call for nationalization of the movie industry as a "magic formula to solve any and all problems." The statement went on to say that all that was needed was to cut the artificially high production costs (which were the fault of the STPC) and to maintain and increase the pace of production.[4] The government had previously stated its position, asserting that the "solution did not focus on resolving the problems of the industry, but rather of the producers. . . . We cannot aspire to improve the returns on Mexican films either in the domestic or foreign markets as long as their quality is not improved."[5]

The producers responded to this crisis by increasing production at the América studios which were staffed by STIC personnel and where costs were considerably lower. The films turned out there were ostensibly serials designed for television; however, their marketability on that medium was so restricted that the producers turned to combining the separate serials into one or more full-length features that were released to neighborhood theaters. One of these, which spawned a never-ending series that continues to the present day, was *Santo contra el cerebro diabólico (Santo versus the Diabolic Brain)* (1961) (El Santo was a popular wrestler); it made 125,000 pesos at its premiere in spite of its atrocious quality.[6]

Another gambit of the producers to avoid high costs was to film outside of Mexico where expenses were lower. An additional advantage of foreign filming was that by using those locales and local actors, the movies thus produced might recoup the evanescing Latin American markets. Two examples of these coproductions were *Rumbo a Brasilia (En route to Brasilia)* (1960) and *Los expatriados (The Expatriates)* (1963). In the former, a Mexican engineer (Antonio Aguilar), who is assisting in the construction of the highway to the new Brazilian capital, becomes romantically involved with a Brazilian girl (Angela María da Cunha). Together they help Paulo (Antonio Carlos Pereira), a young black boy, attain his objective of seeing the president to ask for help for his flood-devastated village.[7] *Los expatriados* was made in Puerto Rico and starred Luis Aguilar and Mapy Cortés, the veteran Puerto Rican-born actress. The film related the trials and tribulations of young Puerto Ricans who emigrated to New York. Obviously

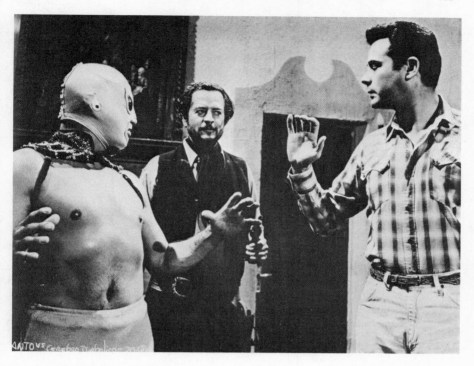

Left to right, "El Santo," Emilio Garibay, and Fernando Casanova in *Santo contra el cerebro diabólico* (1961). (Azteca Films)

inspired by *West Side Story*, it transmitted its message by means of a plenitude of musical numbers.[8]

Mexican filmmakers ranged widely in the effort to find a profitable coproduction formula—they went to Puerto Rico, Colombia, Ecuador, Guatemala, and Venezuela. But such peripatetic recourses could not reverse the painfully clear trend: the markets for Mexican movies in Latin America and the United States were disintegrating. Economic and political problems in the various countries, stricter currency controls, and a general rejection by the publics of the steadily worsening Mexican product took their toll and the results can be seen in table 2.

The revolution in Cuba had eliminated that formerly important market since Fidel Castro's blueprint for a new society hardly included run-of-the-mill Mexican films. However, the new leaders of Cuba well realized the educational and political value of motion pictures and purposefully set out to create a new cinema that shortly would be eliciting the world's plaudits. Interestingly, one of the first efforts of this new Cuban cinema followed in the footsteps of the traditional coproduction relationship with Mexico: this was *Cuba baila (Cuba Dances)* (1959), a joint effort between the newly formed ICAIC (Instituto Cubano de Artes e Industria Cinematográficas) and Manuel Barbachano Ponce, producer of *Raíces*.[9] A member of Barbachano Ponce's team, José Miguel (Jomi) García

Ana Bertha Lepe and an unidentified actor in *Santo contra el cerebro diabólico*. (Azteca Films)

TABLE 2
Mexican Film Production, 1958–1963

| Year | "Regular" (STPC) | Serials (STIC) | Coprods | Indpnt | Total |
|------|------|------|------|------|------|
| 1958[a] | 116 | 16 | 6 | — | 138 |
| 1959[b] | 84 | 21 | 8 | — | 113 |
| 1960[c] | 90 | 22 | 1 | 1 | 114 |
| 1961[d] | 48 | 14 | 6 | 3 | 71 |
| 1962[e] | 56 | 24 | 1 | 1 | 82 |
| 1963[f] | 41 | 30 | 10 | — | 81 |

SOURCE: [a]*Historia,* 7: 8; [b]Ibid., p. 201; [c]Ibid., p. 325; [d]Ibid., 8: 8; [e]Ibid., pp. 210–346; [f]Ibid., p. 348

Toshiro Mifune (right) in Ismael Rodríguez's *Animas Trujano* (1961). (Azteca Films)

Ascot, unable to breach the STPC's Directors' Guild which as always remained shut tight to new talent, returned to Cuba to work on *Cuba 58*, a full-length feature in three segments. García Ascot directed two of them: "Un día de trabajo" and "Los novios."[10]

Jomí García Ascot was a member of the "Nuevo Cine" group, an assemblage of young, generally leftist, critics, scholars, and aspirant cineasts. The group arose from a series of conferences held in 1960 attended by such luminaries as Luis Buñuel, Luis Alcoriza, Carlos Fuentes, and the painter José Luis Cuevas. Although these individuals did not form part of Nuevo Cine, those who did went on to publish a magazine, *Nuevo Cine*, which in its seven issues published (April 1961−August 1962) carried on a lively debate with the "establishment" film-makers and journalists and called for a renovation of Mexican cinema. The editorial board consisted of Emilio García Riera, José de la Colina, Salvador

Elizondo, Jomí García Ascot, and Carlos Monsiváis. Others who became part of Nuevo Cine were: Rafael Corkidi, Paul Leduc, Manuel Michel, Manuel González Casanova, José María Sbert, Tomás Pérez Turrent, Jorge Ayala Blanco, and Salomón Laiter, among a number of other individuals who were to become better known in the coming years.[11]

Even though the movie industry was stagnant and close to bankruptcy, there were hopeful signs in the early 1960s that filmmaking at some time in the future might yet be put on a more rational basis. For instance, ever since a long-forgotten effort during the Carranza presidency there had been no training facilities for young cineasts. The STPC had never attempted to provide such instruction because the Directors' Guild was interested only in protecting the prerogatives of its members. Fernández, Galindo, Gavaldón, Bustillo Oro, and all the others had learned their craft in the early days when the industry was still open to all comers. Some, like Buñuel, received their training in Europe; others, like René Cardona and Tito Davison, in Hollywood's Hispanic movies or elsewhere in Latin America. Aside from the cine-clubs or film societies, there was no place in Mexico where established or would-be directors could study in detail the works of the world's great cineasts. But it was unlikely that a film repository would be established because of official indifference; and most producers cared not a whit for cinema as art or for its social or historical significance. Carmen Toscano, daughter of the pioneer filmmaker, organized a film archive in 1963 wholly on the basis of private contributions. It was called the Cinemateca de México. The organization petitioned President López Mateos for a subsidy and quarters in which to locate the archive. A part of the old Ciudadela building was turned over to Carmen Toscano but due to its decrepit state another location had to be found. The Cinemateca was finally placed on the third floor of the old Palace of Communications. In December 1964, shortly after Gustavo Díaz Ordaz was inaugurated president, the Cinemateca was forced to vacate its premises.[12]

Not all cinematic developments in the first half of the decade were as unpromising. A hopeful sign was the establishment in 1963 of a cinema department at the National Autonomous University of Mexico (UNAM); this department was called the Centro Universitario de Estudios Cinematográficos (CUEC) and was under the direction of Manuel González Casanova, one of the Nuevo Cine group.[13] Another encouraging development was the directorial debut of Buñuel's close associate and friend Luis Alcoriza with Los jóvenes (The Youths) (1960). This film was a cut above the average movie about "rebellious" middle-class youth popular in this period, and Alcoriza in the following years was to turn out a number of well-made and provocative films.

García Ascot made En el balcón vacío (On the Empty Balcony) (1961), an independent production that in spite of being refused distribution by the official channels was a great international success. Collecting money from friends, García Ascot gathered enough funds to buy a 16mm camera. A script was written by Emilio García Riera in three months of "long nocturnal sessions."[14] The filming itself took one year because they could only work on weekends since all the members of the crew had full-time jobs. The film was based on the childhood memories of a woman (García Ascot's wife) wrenched from her native Spain by the Civil War. Even though she has reached adulthood in Mexico, the trauma of flight from her home many years before remains vividly in her consciousness. *El balcón*, as its makers called it, skillfully managed to see such shattering events through the sensitive eyes of a woman projecting herself back to her childhood and recreating the little girl's sense of fear and wonder as she observes the concerned adults about her making secretive preparations for flight. *En el balcón vacío* was invited to be shown at the Locarno Film Festival in 1962 where it was awarded the International Film Critics' Prize and won universal and enthusiastic praise while the official Mexican entries were all but ignored.[15]

Internationally, the best-known Mexican film of this period is Buñuel's *Viridiana* (1961). More accurately it was a Mexican-Spanish production since it was shot entirely in Spain and coproduced by Gustavo Alatriste and Uninci Films of Madrid. It starred the popular Mexican actress Silvia Pinal in the title role of the religion-obsessed girl who thinks she has been raped by her uncle, don Jaime (Fernando Rey, best-known to American audiences as the French drug trafficker in *The French Connection*). In *Viridiana*, Buñuel developed all his favorite anti-Catholic and anti-bourgeois themes within a sombre setting. The film was a huge artistic and economic success, except of course in Spain where it was not unexpectedly banned.[16] In 1962 Buñuel filmed *El ángel exterminador* in Mexico, which concerns a bizarre dinner party in which the guests, for no apparent reason, find themselves unable to leave their host's mansion. Alatriste was the producer and he again backed Buñuel in the latter's last Mexican film, the short feature *Simón del desierto* (1965). In 1965, Buñuel transferred all his filmmaking activities to Europe.

Buñuel's close friend and protegé, Luis Alcoriza, directed *Tlayucan* (1961), a study of small-town life which displayed Buñuelian symbolic techniques, such as the juxtaposing of a young couple with hogs in a comparison of their eating habits. In 1962, Alcoriza made *Tiburoneros (Shark Fishermen)*, the story of Aurelio (Julio Aldama), a businessman who has chosen to forsake urban cares for the simplicity of a shark fisherman's life on the coast of Tabasco. The familiar theme was handled by Alcoriza with sensitivity and realism making the film stand out among the run-of-the-mill products being churned out by Mexican studios.[17] This "new" director gave promise of being a major talent, capable of making distinguished films if given the opportunity.[18]

However, one director like Alcoriza was not about to renovate the film industry. The STPC looked on with increasing frustration as the producers took ever greater advantage of the lower costs of filming at the América studios and the use of STIC personnel. As a consequence, the STPC membership confronted a serious unemployment problem as the production of "regular" films declined steeply. In an effort to break the industry's impasse and influenced by the work of young university-based cineasts, the STPC announced in August 1964 the First Contest of Experimental Cinema. All those aspirant cameramen, scriptwriters, actors, musicians, and directors who would not or could not enter the industry got together and sought financing from friends, their own savings, or independent producers.[19]

Julio Aldama in Luis Alcoriza's *Tiburoneros* (1962). (Azteca Films)

Thirty-two groups signed up when the contest officially opened, but by the time the films were delivered the following year, only twelve groups were represented with an equal number of 35mm full-length motion pictures.[20]

The entries were judged in July 1965 by a jury of thirteen persons representing the industry, various cultural institutions, and critics. First prize was awarded to Rubén Gámez's *La fórmula secreta (The Secret Formula)*, a cruelly humorous probing of the Mexican's "lack of identity with himself."[21] It consists of a series of vignettes, some surrealistic, like the one showing a blood transfusion using Coca-Cola, and others brutally realistic, like the scene of the slaughter of a steer to the strains of spiritually inspiring music.

Second prize was given to *En este pueblo no hay ladrones (In this Town There are no Thieves)* by Alberto Isaac. Adapted by Isaac and García Riera from a story by the famous Colombian writer, Gabriel García Márquez, the film traces the experiences of Dámaso (Julián Pastor), a small-town ne'er-do-well. One night he breaks into the tavern and steals the town's only billiard balls. However, once he has taken them, Dámaso realizes that the tedium of life in the village is completely unbearable without even the opportunity of playing billiards. He returns the balls

Dacia González and Julio Aldama in *Tiburoneros*. (Cineteca)

but is caught. The merit of the film is in the directness of its cinematic language, although its slow pace is at times unnerving. The style is generally well adapted to the subject: the social examination of a small, poverty-stricken town where nothing ever happens. Dámaso is seemingly the only resident who dreams of better things, but is finally overcome by the stultifying inactivity of the town.[22]

The STPC film contest was obviously not a major event in international film history nor even in the Mexican cinematic milieu. It did not cause great excitement among the old-line producers who certainly did not perceive Gámez, Isaac, or any of the other directors as portending any "new wave." But the fact that such a competition took place at all and that it was sponsored by one of the industry's most sacrosanct institutions was significant and it pointed to the possibilities inherent in the future. A number of the individuals participating in the contest were in a few short years to become part of the industry.[23] The competition also symbolized the recognition by the STPC of the growing importance of independent, university-based filmmakers who had heretofore been engaged in literary pursuits, experimental theater, or film criticism, among these being Juan Guerrero, Salomón Laiter, Manuel Michel, Alberto Isaac, and Juan José Gurrola.[24]

The STPC was also no doubt well aware of the struggling independent cinema, especially after the international success of García Ascot's *En el balcón vacío* in

Alberto Isaac's *En este pueblo no hay ladrones* (1965). (Azteca Films)

spite of a boycott of the film by the official distributors and exhibitors. A number of talented people—directors, writers, photographers—were obviously being excluded by the cinematic unions' closed door policies, and the STPC itself was one of the chief culprits in this situation. But now that severe unemployment was widespread in the Mexican film industry, the STPC's voice was added to the many others that for years had been urging reform and renovation. Even though the Banco Cinematográfico in 1960 had bought out the Jenkins group's Operadora de Teatros theater chain, and also become the major stockholder in the Churubusco studios,[25] the same commercialist-minded elements still dominated decision making throughout the official film hierarchy. Thus independent films could not be exhibited in the commercial theater chains but were restricted to the film clubs and private "art" houses, making it impossible for producers of such films to recoup their costs, much less make a profit.[26]

Official protectionist policies failed to satisfy the producers, however. As Tomás Pérez Turrent summarizes the situation in the late 1960s and early 1970s:

Traditionally, these producers operated on credit from the National Cinematographic Bank . . . , inflating their budgets to such an extent that the loan, theoretically designed only to cover a percentage of the total cost, was enough or almost enough to pay for the whole film. To this was added advance royalties for distribution to some South American countries, and thus bad quality cinema became a sure-fire business with few risks.[27]

The tension in Mexican film circles in the late 1960s was generated by the conflict between the entrenched bureaucratic/business groups in the official agencies and the leftist, intellectual, restless "outsiders" being shaped by the universities. Aware of their country's problems and inequities, concerned by the cultural influence being exerted by Hollywood, these young cineasts and scholar-critics longed for a cinema that would deal honestly with Mexican reality. They were familiar with the best of world cinema—Italian neo-realism, the French new wave, the new American filmmakers—and consequently the Mexican "packaged" cinema degenerated in their eyes to an "artistically irrelevant enemy."[28] They looked toward the "new" Latin American cinema, the now quiescent Brazilian Cinema Novo and the exciting and vigorous Cuban filmmakers, as well as to experimentation by such independent cineasts as the Chilean Miguel Littín and the Bolivians Jorge Sanjines and Antonio Eguino.[29]

On a larger scale, a restless resentment was growing among the country's youth, especially in the universities. In 1968 Mexico had been chosen as the site for that year's Summer Olympics, the first Latin American country to be so honored. The country's official and business circles saw it as an international recognition of Mexico's improved status in the Western family of nations, an acknowledgment that the world no longer looked upon Mexico as a "backward" Latin American republic but rather as a progressive, modern state. However, on the eve of the Olympics, massive demonstrations were organized against the administration of Díaz Ordaz. The results led to the greatest tragedy in the history of Mexico since the Revolution and to a bitter schism between the generations that persists to this day.

One of the origins of the student movement was resentment that a quarter-century of rapid economic growth was benefiting only a tiny minority of politicians, bankers and businessmen. There was also growing middle-class irritation over the way the administration of President Gustavo Díaz Ordaz censored movies, books and newspapers, persecuted inde-

Emilio Fernández and Cristina Peñalver in *El silencioso* (1966) (Azteca Films)

pendent intellectuals and summarily jailed outspoken opponents. In the eyes of many Mexicans, the system had become both economically and politically repressive.[30]

The students continued their ever-larger demonstrations, the date for the Olympics drew closer. Díaz Ordaz and his minister of Gobernación, Luis Echeverría Alvarez, seeing Mexico's international prestige on the line, panicked—or perhaps decided to nip this opposition in the bud. The army was sent against the students and many innocent bystanders at the Plaza of the Three Cultures in Tlatelolco. In a night of blood and horror, over three hundred persons were shot down and hundreds more wounded. The carnage was little noted at the Olympic Village and fleetingly reported by the world press,[31] with the honorable exception of the Italian journalist Oriana Fallaci, who was caught in the midst of the massacre.[32]

Nineteen-sixty-eight was a pivotal year in modern Mexican history: the economic, political, and social tensions that had been building up since the 1930s exploded in this bloody confrontation. Many students became radicalized by the experience and whatever guerrilla movement has existed in the country dates from that year. Some Marxist students tried to politicize the peasantry, although perhaps the best-known organizer of the peasants was Lucio Cabañas, a rural schoolteacher. When organizing efforts failed to produce the desired effect among the peasantry, some groups turned to urban terrorism. But more important than such sporadic violence, which has had little direct effect on Mexico's political events, has been an angry undercurrent persisting in Mexican society, especially among the youth.

The events of Tlatelolco gave a greater urgency to the antiestablishment cineasts and, according to Ayala Blanco, a stronger independent cinema "arose on the heels of the politization of certain middle-class nuclei as a consequence of the student movement of 1968."[33] But in the existing political climate, independent filmmakers, even if they could obtain financing from individuals or from university sources, still were up against the stone wall of official distributors and exhibitors. Thus it is not surprising that one of these "new" cineasts, Alberto Isaac, directed the officially sponsored *Olimpiada en México (Olympiad in Mexico)* (1968) and utilized the services of other young filmmakers like Rafael Corkidi, Paul Leduc, and Felipe Cazals who "had no scruples in collaborating" in the project.[34] The film itself, which was the "most favored, best-organized, and costliest made during the presidential term of Díaz Ordaz," was the subject of much controversy.[35]

On the other hand, Centro Universitario de Estudios Cinematográficos (CUEC) at UNAM made its own unique contribution to the student movement of 1968. Being a small, relatively unknown department of the National University and located far from the centers of student activism, CUEC went unnoticed by the authorities. Its members decided to record the student movement on film, utilizing the raw film allocated to the department for its coursework. Leobardo López Aretche directed the project with the assistance of Alfredo Joskowics. So, while other departments and faculties in the institutions of higher learning throughout the Federal District and some of the states were being taken over by student revolutionary committees, the members of CUEC took action in the most effective way they knew: with their cameras. According to Ayala Blanco, *El grito (The Shout)* (1968) is ''the only objective record that exists of any popular movement that occurred in the last thirty years of national life . . . [it] is in the final analysis, the most complete and coherent filmic record that exists of the Movement, seen from the inside and contrary to the calumnies spread by the rest of the mass media.''[36]

The bitterness arising from the bloody events of October 1968 and the subsequent wholesale arrests of student activists and left-wing intellectuals were still widespread when Luis Echeverría Alvarez assumed the presidential office in December 1970. Since he had been head of Gobernación under Díaz Ordaz, many considered him directly responsible for having unleashed the army on the students and their sympathizers. Echeverría was never to overcome this suspicion on the part of the Mexican left, in spite of his openly pro-left and ''Third Worldist'' foreign policy. Although the ideological stance of his administration is beyond the scope of this study, it is necessary to be aware of it when observing the repercussions it had on the film industry. Unlike Díaz Ordaz, Echeverría was quite interested in films.[37] His brother had for many years been a well-known actor as well as Jorge Negrete's successor as head of ANDA.[38] In fact, Echeverría

Rodolfo Landa (center) in *El tesoro de Pancho Villa* (1954); in 1976, under his own name of Rodolfo Echeverría, he was appointed director of the Banco Nacional Cinematográfico. (Azteca Films)

appointed Rodolfo Echeverría to head the Banco Cinematográfico and it was under the latter's direction that the State became directly involved in filmmaking to the almost total exclusion of the private producers.

In its cinematic policies, as well as in all other aspects of its program, the Echeverría administration was highly controversial. The radical left remained skeptical, even hostile, while the business community denounced the president as a Communist. Certainly there had not been a so apparently leftist administration since Cárdenas[39] or such an economically activist one since Alemán.[40]

On January 21, 1971, Rodolfo Echeverría proposed a "Plan for the Restructure of the Mexican Film Industry" in order to "renovate objectives and means during the six-year period so as to change the image of the national cinema, so deteriorated and maligned at the beginning of the decade."[41] In 1971, the State owned outright the Banco Cinematográfico, the theater chain Compañia Operadora de Teatros, and the Churubusco studios; of mixed public and private ownership were the distributors Películas Mexicanas and Cimex, and the promotional firm, Procinemex. Rodolfo Echeverría declared that "although this group of firms seemed to be sufficient to maintain the film industry in a state of equilibrium, their financial status was precarious."[42] Besides, the entire structure was maintained by the government "at high cost" primarily for the benefit of "a group of industrial or private producers—in their majority guided exclusively by the criteria of rapid recuperation and maximum rentability—who produced a commercialist cinema and took advantage of the established mechanisms, from the financing to the exhibition facilities provided by state firms." The result, Echeverría concluded, was a "false product, deformed and rejected by numerous domestic and foreign social sectors."[43]

Some significant accomplishments between 1970 and 1976 were the building of a filmmaking school, the Centro de Capacitación Cinematográfica—a dream of many cineasts since the days of silent movies in Mexico[44]—and nearby, the conversion of two Churubusco sound stages into the Cineteca Nacional, another long-deferred dream finally fulfilled. Here the historically important task of obtaining and preserving prints of commercial Mexican film production was finally undertaken with the full backing and resources of the federal government. In addition, copies of a wide assortment of foreign films were and are being obtained for the benefit of young cineasts and film students, both Mexican and foreign. The Cineteca consists of two theaters open to the public, "Sala Fernando de Fuentes" and "Salón Rojo"; one 35mm private screening room, "Salvador Toscano," for staff use and accredited researchers; and three private 16mm screening rooms.[45] In 1974, the Cineteca's holdings consisted of 1,476 films, including both 35mm and 16mm, full-length and short; by 1976 there were 2,500 films in its archives.[46] By 1976, the State was sole owner of the América studios, Procinemex, Películas Nacionales (which absorbed Cimex), and the only remaining privately owned theater chain, Cadena de Oro, in addition to many other individually owned movie houses as well as a number of new ones built by the Banco.[47]

The most important development of the Echeverrías's *sexenio* was the direct participation of the State in the production of films through three production companies. These were: Corporación Nacional Cinematográfica (CONACINE); Corporación Nacional Cinematográfica de Trabajadores y Estado I (CONA-CITE I); and Corporación Nacional Cinematográfica de Trabajadores y Estado II (CONACITE II). CONACINE was created in October 1974 as a branch of the Banco Cinematográfico and it served as a model for CONACITE I (June 19, 1975) and CONACITE II (May 8, 1975). The Banco had been coproducing films with Churubusco-Azteca studios ever since the latter's nationalization in 1960, but the system was cumbersome and the decision was made to regulate production through these officially created companies. Besides, the almost total suspension of private moviemaking since the Banco's curtailment of credit to the producers necessitated the State's intervention if only to assure work for the thousands of skilled workers in the industry. In fact, thirty-nine films coproduced by the Banco and Churubusco between April 1971 and the time of CONACINE's creation were immediately turned over to the latter.[48] The activities of CONACINE and CONA-CITE I were similar, that is, they both functioned as sole producers or as coproducers with film workers, private investors, and foreign producers. CONACITE II worked exclusively with STIC and América studios.

Total production, both "regular" and "serials," totaled seventy-two films in 1970 (before the inauguration of Luis Echeverría).[49] In 1971, the figure was also seventy-two not including nine independent full-length features and seven films made abroad. However, in comparison to the previous year's output, which was singularly undistinguished, 1971 saw the appearance of a number of interesting films such as Felipe Cazals's El jardín de tía Isabel (The Garden of Aunt Elizabeth), Rafael Corkidi's Angeles y querubines (Angels and Cherubim), Luis Alcoriza's Mecánica nacional (National Mechanics), Juan López Moctezuma's La mansión de la locura (Mansion of Madness), Paul Leduc's Reed: México insurgente (Reed: Insurgent Mexico), Gustavo Alatriste's QRR (Quién resulta responsable) (Who is responsible), and Alfredo Joscowics's Crates and El cambio (The Change). Of course, there were still plenty of "package" films such as Miguel M. Delgado's Santo vs la hija de Frankenstein (Santo versus Frankenstein's Daughter) in addition to the regular fare of comedias rancheras, tearjerking melodramas, and "westerns."[50]

In 1972, the figure rose to seventy-five full-length features in addition to twelve "official" films such as Cartas del Japón (Letters from Japan), about a Mexican engineering student in Japan, Historia del P.R.I. (History of the P.R.I.), Tarahumara—Drama del pueblo (Tarahumara—Drama of the People), and Compañero presidente (Comrade President), a documentary of Echeverría's visit to Chile. Although commercial production included such standbys as Bikinis y rock and Capulina vs las momias (Capulina versus the Mummies), there were also superior films like Arturo Ripstein's El castillo de la pureza (Castle of Purity), Gonzalo Martínez Ortega's El principio (The Beginning), José Estrada's El profeta Mimí (The Prophet Mimi), Alberto Isaac's El rincón de las vírgenes (The Corner of the Virgins), Alejandro Jodorowski's La montaña sagrada (The Sacred Mountain), Mauricio Walerstein's Cuando quiero llorar no lloro (When I Want to

*Cry, I Can't)*, and *Fe, esperanza y caridad (Faith, Hope, and Charity)*, a film in three segments directed respectively by Alberto Bojórquez, Luis Alcoriza, and Jorge Fons.[51] These films were generally well received by the critics and, even if some were flawed, did at least explore new directions previously unsought by Mexican cineasts; more importantly they were made by new directors supported directly by the Banco Cinematográfico through its production companies, an arrangement deeply resented by the old-line producers and directors.[52] Table 3 gives an idea of the scope of state participation in the film industry and the resultant lack of activity on the part of private producers.[53]

The decline in production was a serious matter and was undoubtedly exacerbated by the Echeverría policies. True, better movies were made by young, often leftist directors but this was small comfort to the industry as a whole. Echoing the opinions of his conservative-minded colleagues, one long-time film executive placed the blame entirely on the Echeverría brothers, saying that the Mexican cinema from 1971 to 1976 was "tendentious . . . and up to a certain point, procommunist." He blamed the Banco Cinematográfico for withdrawing credit

From the right, Rita Macedo and Claudio Brook in Arturo Ripstein's *El castillo de la pureza* (1972). (Cineteca)

Claudio Brook and Rita Macedo in *El castillo de la pureza*. (Cineteca)

facilities from the private producers and forcing them to use their own capital or
seek backing from other sources. He concluded that under President Echeverría
and his brother, filmmaking had a "communist slant, totally to please [Echeve-
rría]"; that a film's commercial potential was of "no importance" and public
funds were invested "to line pockets," presumably those of the Echeverrías and
their cronies. As to films with a political or social message, this executive felt that
Mexico's problems "are not political . . . we go to the movies for entertainment. . . . Of what use could a Marxist idea be to the people?"[54]

While many of the preceding remarks are true, others are not entirely accurate.
Production had been falling off since 1960 due to the effects of constantly
diminishing quality and the producers' desire for quick profits on minimal personal
investment.[55] Public monies accomplished this, since films were being financed
up to 80 percent by the Banco Cinematográfico. Inflating the budgets was also
common practice, so that the Banco's "80 percent" share actually paid for the
entire film and left some over for the producer to pocket. This system was leading
the industry from stagnation to ruin, a truth that did not require a great deal of
insight to discern. The Echeverrías recognized the problem and tried to do
something about it by backing new directors, as well as veteran ones, in officially
financed films. Such films as Alcoriza's *Mecánica nacional* (1971), Alfonso
Arau's *Calzonzín inspector* (1973), and Alberto Isaac's *Tívoli* (1974) were also

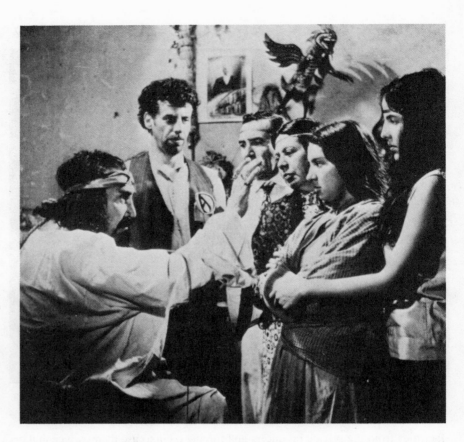

Emilio Fernández (left) and Alfonso Arau in Alberto Isaac's *El rincón de las vírgenes* (1972). (Procinemex)

TABLE 3
Mexican Film Production, 1971–1976

| Year | Banco & private | Private | State prod | Total |
|------|-----------------|---------|------------|-------|
| 1971[a] | 63 | 7 | 5 | 75 |
| 1972[b] | 34 | 8 | 20 | 62 |
| 1973[c] | 26 | 4 | 20 | 50 |
| 1974[d] | 23 | 10 | 21 | 54 |
| 1975[e] | 13 | 7 | 23 | 43 |
| 1976[f] | — | 5 | 37 | 42 |

SOURCES: [a]*Informe general*, p. 46; [b]Ibid., p. 49; [c]Ibid., p. 52; [d]Ibid., p. 55; [e]Ibid., p. 58; [f]Ibid., pp. 59–60 and *Excélsior*, January 19, 1977, Section Cine, Teatro, Radio y TV, p. 5.

more expensive, a fact that fueled the charges of massive corruption in the official film establishment. Such charges might very well have been true, since the system of official corruption was nothing new in Mexico. However, the money spent on these and other films was evident in their superior production values. The infusion of new blood in the directorial ranks was discernible from the controversial themes that these films took on and presented in a realistic, often raw, manner.

A precursor of such films was Alejandro Jodorowski's *El topo* (1970) (*The Mole*), a confused, occasionally brilliant mélange of Eastern metaphysics and satire of the western genre. It also incorporated surrealist techniques borrowed from Buñuel and Fellini but lacked their humanism. Jodorowski's satire is heavy-handed and often sado-masochistic. The film was independently produced and for years was not screened in Mexico; however, it proved a great success on the underground film circuit in the United States and Europe. Jodorowski himself is Chilean by birth and has been better known in Mexico for his work in experimental theater.[56] In 1967 he had made *Fando y Lis*, his first film, based on a work of the same name by Fernando Arrabal. With his cameraman, Rafael Corkidi, Jodorowski filled the screen with images of sado-masochistic and deviant sexual symbolism in an attempt to express his personal view of the universe. *Fando y Lis, El topo*, and *La montaña sagrada* proved heavy for popular tastes, but the possibilities that they illustrated of making a filmic statement through the combined use of realism and surrealism was not lost on other cineasts. True, the

Alfonso Arau (center) starred in and directed *Calzonzín inspector* (1973). (Azteca Films)

Carmen Salinas and Alfonso Arau in *Calzonzín inspector*. (Azteca Films)

technique was hardly new: Buñuel had experimented with it in *Un Chien andalou*, as had many French avant-gardists and German expressionists in the 1920s. But Jodorowski's films showed how such techniques could be used to interpret the tensions and malaise of contemporary Mexican society, something that had not even been attempted since Bustillo Oro's rather timid experiment in *Dos monjes* (1934) or De Fuentes's *El fantasma del convento* (1934).[57]

If a summarization can be made of the direction taken by Mexican cinema in the 1970s, it is that the new directors—Isaac, Cazals, Fons, Arau, Corkidi, Leduc, and many others—were allowed the freedom to interpret controversial political and social themes. Some established directors like Galindo and Alcoriza took advantage of this climate to also make their own statements. In this they were assured by President Echeverría that they were ''at liberty to bring whatever theme they wished to the screen, be it social or political.''[58] There was disagreement whether a ''new'' Mexican cinema in reality existed. Alcoriza compared his colleagues with the initiators of the Brazilian Cine Novo and concluded that no such movement existed in Mexico.[59] Eduardo Maldonado, an independent filmmaker, opined: "None of the films which have been made within the new Mexican cinema truly respond to the necessity of analysis and critical interpretation that is required by the current social reality of Mexico."[60]

Any attempt here to analyze meaningfully all the important Mexican films made in 1971–1976 is impossible. The choice of the few films discussed is dictated entirely by the fact that this writer happens to be familiar with them and does not imply that, in his judgment, they were superior to others. Also, to discuss thoroughly the complex cinematic, cultural, and literary influences operative on Mexican filmmakers is too extensive an undertaking for this brief survey.[61]

*Mecánica nacional* (1971) was Luis Alcoriza's most popular film, and his most outspoken.[62] Focusing on the urban lower middle class and their uncertain suspension between traditional, rural values and the anomie of a rapidly growing, modern metropolis, Alcoriza aimed devastating barbs at this group. He employed a number of well-known performers in roles that were veritable antitheses of their

Manolo Fábregas in Luis Alcoriza's *Mecánica nacional* (1971). (Pelmex)

popular images. Manolo Fábregas, grandson of the famed Virginia Fábregas, and one of Mexico's best-known actor-producer-directors, played the role of Eufemio, a crude, stupidly *macho* garage owner.[63] The popular *ranchera* songstress Lucha Villa was Chabela, his equally crude wife, and the quintessential mother-figure, Sara García, did a grotesque parody of herself as Eufemio's mother.

Eufemio, his wife, mother, family, and friends set out in a holiday mood to catch the end of an Acapulco-to-Mexico City auto race. The women prepare vast quantities of food since the plan is to spend the night at an area near the finish line so as to observe the end of the race early in the morning. They set out in a caravan through huge traffic jams; a lot of horn-blowing and insults are exchanged with other drivers. The mass of cars finally arrives at an open spot and jams itself into the area so tightly as to make further movement impossible. The occupants of the automobiles, joined by swaggering motorcyclists, proceed to await the dawn by eating, drinking, and indulging in as much sex as possible. Eufemio's mother gorges herself all night long until she is stricken by a massive attack of indigestion. The cars are so packed in that it is impossible to go for a doctor; finally one

Another scene from *Mecánica nacional*. (Pelmex)

motorcyclist volunteers to go, but too late to save granny. She is laid out as if at a wake with her family and friends grieving around her. However, the announcement that the race cars are nearing the finish line draws the mourners away, including Eufemio and his family; granny's corpse is left alone in the midst of a sea of autos and refuse, with just a dog picking at the garbage for company. The final indignity occurs as the weary racing fans start for home. Eufemio props his mother up on the front seat. When he gets caught in the middle of the inevitable traffic jam, word gets out that there is a corpse in Eufemio's car and soon hundreds of people leave their cars to gape at the body. A high-angle panoramic shot recedes from the mass of cars and people to the strains of a lusty *ranchera*.

Alcoriza has a Buñuelian disdain for bourgeois society in general and in *Mecánica nacional* he ruthlessly satirizes the new Mexican middle class, those people who have recently begun to share in the country's economic "miracle" but in the process lost whatever cultural integrity they once had. To emphasize this, he shows two American girls who somehow joined the unruly group, exclaiming in English, "Why, there's nothing *Mexican* here!" Throughout the film, a young couple in white sports outfits and driving a white sports car is repeatedly shown in brief segments. All they do is gorge themselves with paella, omelets, and various other dishes of Spanish cuisine until their at first spotless white outfits and car become a multicolored mosaic of food stains. *Mecánica nacional* was Alcoriza's interpretation of the structure of contemporary Mexican society—materialistic, uncultured, irrational, while responding in a semiconscious way to certain half-remembered folkways. A searing commentary, but evidently a popular one since the Mexican public flocked to the movie.[64]

Alcoriza's depiction of the "common man" was a far cry from the affectionate paternalism of Rodríguez in *Nosotros los pobres* and *Ustedes los ricos*, or even Galindo's expressions of working-class solidarity in *¡Esquina bajan!* of some twenty-odd years before. While Rodríguez idealized the poor in a static social system and Galindo showed the working class as intelligent and motivated if not radical, Alcoriza sees the children of the *lumpenproletariat* of the 1940s as being completely coopted by the worst of petty bourgeois values. Clearly no new Mexican revolution is possible from such as Eufemio or, even more tellingly, from the shallow, sybaritic young people of *Mecánica nacional*. Alcoriza seems to be saying that it was people such as these that looked unemotionally upon the Tlatelolco massacre and quickly shrugged it off. Fifty years of the official Revolution had succeeded admirably in depoliticizing an entire generation and convincing it that the consumer society was its inevitable destiny.

The theme of disillusion with Mexican society in the wake of Tlatelolco was continued in Alfredo Joscowics's *Crates* (1970), produced by CUEC, and *El cambio* (1971), produced by UNAM's Department of Cinematic Activities. The former dealt with the difficulties that the militant students of 1968 had in trying to pick up the pieces of their lives in the face of government repression and society's indifference.[65] In *El cambio*, "dropping out" is what its young protagonists, an artist and a photographer, opt for. Disgusted by the materialism of urban life, the two young men escape to an unspecified seacoast. They build a shack on the beach and are soon joined by their girl friends. For a while they enjoy a simple, bucolic existence, but soon the real world intrudes upon their reverie. Waste from a local factory is poisoning the fish in the surrounding waters, threatening the fishermen's livelihood. When the company's bulldozer flattens their shack, the young men decide to take up the local people's fight. They collect the sludge from the factory in pails and, at a banquet in honor of the company representative, hurl the liquid waste all over him and the local dignitaries. The youths run from the banquet laughing hysterically, näively seeing their act as no more harmful than a prank, albeit politically significant. The local lawman sees it quite differently—he hunts down the two city youths and shoots them down in cold blood. Clearly an allegory of Tlatelolco, *El cambio* is also a bitter commentary on the futility of meaningful change in Mexico.[66]

The most powerful and unsettling statement on the bloody repression of 1968 was to come in the 1975 CONACINE-produced *Canoa* directed by Felipe Cazals. The title refers to the village of San Miguel Canoa, a small community of seven thousand inhabitants twelve kilometers from Puebla. On September 14, 1968, five young employees of the University of Puebla arrived in Canoa intending to climb the nearby Malinche peak, a dormant volcano. A downpour forced them to seek

Felipe Cazals's *Canoa* (1975). (Cineteca)

lodging in the town. They were turned away everywhere by the hostile villagers until Lúcas García offered them his hospitality. During the night a mob of over a thousand townspeople formed, went to Lúcas's house, killed him, and dragged away the five young Puebla men. Two were murdered and the remaining three were savagely beaten, one having three fingers cut off by a machete blow. The mob was about to pour gasoline on the three remaining men and burn them alive when the army and Red Cross intervened. These events occurred in the tension-filled days preceding the Tlatelolco killings and they became the basis for a powerful film by Felipe Cazals, one of the new young directors who was able to work thanks to the Echeverría regime.[67]

Cazals structured *Canoa* in a documentary style with titles giving the dates, and then hours, of the events about to be depicted. In addition, a villager speaks directly to the audience giving socioeconomic data on the town. Thus the film provides a background and attempts an explication of the townspeople's behavior. Economic hardship, illiteracy, a lack of skills necessary in the increasingly technological Mexican economy, ancient superstitions, and official indifference all served to make San Miguel Canoa an isolated community, even though it was but a short distance from Puebla, one of the largest and most heavily industrialized

Scene from *Canoa*.

cities in the country. An autocratic and obscurantist priest, aided by a fanatical lay organization, maintained strict control over most of the town, including the constabulary. The priest had convinced the townspeople that they were threatened by Communist revolutionaries from outside, and in fact shortly before the events described in the film a group of militant students from Puebla had been in the town trying to politicize the people. Thus when the five unsuspecting and completely apolitical university employees arrived in the town with nothing more in mind than an innocent weekend outing, it was a simple matter for the townspeople to suspect them of being Communist agitators "who are trying to place a black and red flag in the church."

Cazals develops his film against the backdrop of the momentous demonstrations in Mexico City. While the five university employees are making plans for their mountaineering outing, a radio commentator attacks the student movement, declaring "peace and progress means the Olympics." One of the employees feels that they should show solidarity with the students; his friend dismisses the idea, saying that they, as workers, have nothing to do with the movement.

*Canoa* is a skillfully crafted film, as well as a remarkable one in the Mexican context. It is nothing short of miraculous that the regime would permit, much less produce, such a statement on the events of 1968, especially so since at the time the incumbent president was widely thought to have been directly responsible for the army's attack on the demonstrators. Of all the "new" Mexican cinema, *Canoa* is perhaps the finest example of the government's commitment—for whatever political reasons—to greater freedom for artists and intellectuals.

In 1975, Cazals also made *El apando* adapted from a novella by José Revueltas on prison life, which the latter based on observations he made during his own imprisonment. This is also a powerful, brutal film although not as well structured as *Canoa*. Nonetheless it is a compelling account of the degradation wrought by an unfeeling penal system. Three prisoners use their wives and the aged mother of one of them to smuggle drugs into the penitentiary. They are caught and the men placed in solitary confinement. At the end, they turn on their captors and are finally subdued in an extremely brutal sequence. *El apando* is most impressive in its images of prison life—the hopelessness, the corruption, the brutality—all presented in a starkly realistic manner.[68]

Although young directors like Cazals were experimenting with topics and techniques new to Mexican cinema, it should not be forgotten that the old directors were still around. Emilio "El Indio" Fernández, his most creative days long past, overcame a boycott against him by most producers to make a few films like *La Choca* (1973) and *Zona roja (Red Zone)* (1975). A shooting on a film location in Coahuila which resulted in the death of a young man for a time seemed to jeopardize what remained of his career.[69]

By the 1970s, Alejandro Galindo was the most respected of the old generation of cineasts. His populist films of the 1940s and 1950s were still admired by the younger critics and filmmakers as being the most socially relevant cinema of the "old" Mexican film industry. But times changed for Galindo as they did for Fernández, Ismael Rodríguez, Gavaldón, and all the other veteran directors. The

Felipe Cazals's *El apando* (1975). (Cineteca)

Emilio "El Indio" Fernández
in 1976. (CONACINE and
Procinemex)

necessity of earning a living had obliged him to direct adaptations of television
soap operas like *Simplemente vivir (Simply to Live)* (1970) or children's movies
like *Pepito y la lámpara maravillosa (Little Joe and the Marvelous Lamp)* (1971).
He made a populist comedy in his old style, *Tacos al carbón (Barbecued Tacos)*
(1971), which was generally considered anachronistic. In 1973 Galindo made two
films of which he was especially proud even though the critics did not share his
opinion—*El juicio de Martín Cortés (The Trial of Martín Cortés)* and *Ante el
cadaver de un líder (Before the Corpse of a Leader)*. The latter was a black comedy
in which the chief protagonist is the corpse of a labor leader discovered in a cheap

A scene from José Estrada's *Maten al león* (1975), a satire about a Caribbean dictatorship. (Procinemex)

hotel. His death is due to natural causes, but once the news gets out, the room becomes a gathering point for the labor leader's friends, associates, and two women each claiming to be his legitimate wife. The official investigation of the death is complicated by union delegations accompanied by brass bands paying their final respects in the midst of much speech-making, a rival union official making political capital of the situation, and a taco vendor setting up shop in the hotel room.

More interesting is Galindo's *El juicio de Martín Cortés*, a subject he had been considering for some years. Martín Cortés was the illegitimate mestizo son of Hernando Cortés, conqueror of the Aztecs, by Malinche, the Indian woman who was his invaluable interpreter as well as mistress. There was also a *don* Martín, Cortés's legitimate son by a well-born Spanish woman. In the mestizo Martín's story, Galindo saw the fundamental dilemma of Mexican society: half Indian and half European, Martín was suspended between two worlds, neither belonging fully to nor being accepted by either.

In *El juicio de Martín Cortés*, the action unfolds on a theater stage where a play on Martín Cortés had been presented. It seems that the actor who was playing Martín (Gonzalo Vega) identified so completely with his role that during the premiere performance he actually killed the actor playing don Martín. The police arrive at the theater with ''Martín'' to conduct the investigation. It is decided to perform the play for the police investigator's (David Reynoso) benefit. The film thus proceeds as a ''play within a play'' with the play's director and the playwright describing the historical background of each scene about to be performed. As the play progresses the tragedy of Martín Cortés, the mestizo, has a deep effect on the spectators. It is clear, at least according to Galindo, that deep racial antagonisms still tear at Mexican society. Even the police inspector, who at the beginning had declared that racial feeling could not be acceptable as a motive because ''In Mexico there is no prejudice,'' becomes so emotionally involved with the play that by the time the pivotal scene comes up—in which Martín attacks his half-

Alejandro Galindo's *El juicio de Martín Cortés* (1973). Gonzalo Vega (center) and David Reynoso (right). (Azteca Films)

brother—he leaps to his feet yelling ''Kill him! Kill him!'' The police inspector is so shaken by his own display of a racial hatred he had not thought existed within him that he disqualifies himself from the case on ''the grounds of being a mestizo.'' In Galindo's final, sardonic comment, a mestizo reporter in the audience is wakened at play's end—he had slept through the entire performance.

The film was not well received and was panned by some critics.[70] Galindo insists that Mexicans, though professing officially to be proud of their origins, really look upon themselves as the bastard off-spring of a symbolic rape. Some students in Veracruz, the director relates, upon being told that the film was the story of the ''first Mexican in history,'' responded ''Ah . . . then he was the first son of a bitch.''[71] Whatever the truth behind the nonacceptance of *El juicio de Martín Cortés*, it is a provocative and well-made, albeit somewhat complicated, work, possibly the only Mexican film that has attempted to explore the complex emotions underlying Mexico's racial composition. It might be that Galindo is right: perhaps Mexicans by and large do not wish to reflect on the problem, or even to admit that one may exist. If so, it is no surprise that *El juicio de Martín Cortés* was a commercial and critical failure. It may very well remain the only Mexican film to ever deal at length with the country's racism.

Although the racial prejudice among Mexicans dealt with in *El juicio de Martín Cortés* did not have box-office appeal, films concerned with other types of social

Hernando Cortés's funeral in *El juicio de Martín Cortés*. (Cineteca)

and political themes continued to be favored by the public. Gustavo Alatriste scored a resounding success with *México, México, ra, ra, ra* (1974), an outrageous satire of Mexican society that was enjoying a successful revival in late 1977.[72] Alberto Isaac dealt with censorship and the unfettered developmentalism of the 1950s in *Tívoli* (1974), which concerns the closing down by the Federal District authorities of a popular burlesque theater.[73]

*Tívoli* may be placed in the genre of *cabaretera* films although the action unfolds in a burlesque theater. The main thrust of the plot deals with a city administration working hand-in-glove with developers seeking to profit from Mexico City's rapid growth. The Tívoli Theater lies in the path of a grandiose urban renewal project and the authorities decide to close it down. The main protagonist is a burlesque comic, played by Alfonso Arau, who leads his fellow performers in a futile struggle to save their theater. The film is also an exercise in nostalgia, since all the musical and comic routines are faithful recreations of those popular in the 1950s, and many of them had been performed by Arau when he worked in burlesque at that time.

Gonzalo Vega and Mercedes Pascual in *El juicio de Martín Cortés*. (Cineteca)

Alejandro Galindo in 1976.
(Cineteca)

A scene from Alberto Isaac's *Tívoli* (1974). (Cineteca)

From left to right, Lyn May, Pancho Córdova, and Alfonso Arau in *Tívoli*. (Azteca Films)

*Tívoli* sparked a new generation of the *cabaretera* films, according to Arau. Among these movies are *Las ficheras (The B Girls)* (1976) and *Muñecas de media noche (Midnight Dolls)* (1979) which featured physically attractive but superficial performers such as Sasha Montenegro and Jorge Rivero. These films demonstrate the utter decadence of the genre: while Alberto Gout's *Aventurera* (1949) was imbued with both eroticism and social commentary, the new crop of cabareteras featured female nudity, soft-core sex, and puerile music-hall jokes. In spite of such flaws, these movies were immensely popular and garnered handsome profits; for instance, *Las ficheras* was being shown simultaneously in twelve first-run movie houses in Mexico City in the summer of 1977.

However, the cabaretera/prostitute genre in the 1970s was not all cheap eroticism. Felipe Cazals combined social commentary with realism in *Las Poquianchis* (1977), a disturbing film dealing with a true-life incident. Three sisters, "Las Poquianchis," kidnapped or bought young girls from poverty-stricken rural families to stock their brothel. Worse still, they resorted to murder to maintain control over the unfortunate women. In the late 1960s, the authorities finally broke up the notorious prostitution ring, although too late for the many girls who had been murdered—or others who had been forced to become killers.[74]

*Actas de Marusia (Letters from Marusia)* (1975), a major CONACINE production, received favorable attention from European critics, partly as a result of extensive international promotion, and was the only recent Mexican film to

A scene from *Las ficheras* (1977)—at the center is Jorge Rivero with his arm around Sasha Montenegro. Lyn May is to the right. (Azteca Films)

generate significant foreign interest.[75] The widely favorable response was also elicited by the fact that the director of the film was Miguel Littín, the famous Chilean cineast, creator of *El chacal de Nahueltoro* (1969) and *La tierra prometida* (1973), who had fled for his life from the bloody coup that took the life of President Salvador Allende on September 11, 1973. Since President Echeverría was a close personal friend of the Marxist Chilean chief executive, Mexico generously opened its doors to many refugees from the Pinochet junta.[76] Littín was a prize catch for the Mexican movie industry, since he was internationally known and admired, especially in Europe where a good many cineasts and critics are leftist. Associated with Littín's name, a Mexican film would be more likely to be noticed. And it was. *Actas de Marusia* was entered at the Cannes Film Festival where, Littín claimed, it came within one vote of being named best film.[77] It was also Mexico's entry for best foreign film in Hollywood's Academy Awards presentations, but it received scant notice from American critics. *Actas de Marusia* did well in Mexico, setting box-office records for a Mexican film.[78] The motion picture tells of a strike in Chile in 1907 against a European-owned mine. The army was called in to quell the strike and the entire town of Marusia was massacred with

A scene from Miguel Littín's *Actas de Marusia* (1975). (Azteca Films)

the exception of two miners who escaped to tell the tale. It was filmed in northern Mexico with six hundred extras, many of them nonprofessionals.[79]

The Echeverría government's identification with international radical causes facilitated the resumption of coproductions with Cuba. *Mina: Viento de libertad (Mina: Wind of Liberty)* (1976) was a CONACITE I/ICAIC coproduction directed by the Spaniard Antonio Eceiza. However, *Caribe, estrella y águila (The Caribbean, Star and Eagle)*, a documentary that Alfonso Arau made to coincide with Echeverría's state visit to Cuba in 1975, has not yet been released. The Dirección General de Cinematografía, the censoring agency, apparently felt that it would exacerbate political divisions within Mexico, where there was already much criticism of Echeverría's policies. Of course, since the Dirección General was unlikely to act on its own authority on such a politically sensitive issue, it was evident that the government wished to limit the degree to which it was identified with the international left.[80]

The Chicano movement in the United States was another subject seen as profitable by Mexican filmmakers in the 1970s. Mexican-American characters had occasionally appeared in Mexican films throughout the industry's history, albeit generally in secondary roles. Surprisingly, in view of the large Mexican-American moviegoing public, films dealing with subjects directly relating to their experience had been few and far between. Galindo, in *Espaldas mojadas*, was one of the first directors to deal at length and sensitively with the problems of Mexican Americans, but other filmmakers showed scant interest in the subject. The reason seems to be many-sided. There was the traditional Mexican disdain for *pochos* and the very real danger that a movie entirely devoted to Mexican Americans would not be commercially successful in Mexico and certainly not so in the rest of Latin America.

As a result of the black civil rights movement in the United States, ethnic and racial pride spread to other groups including Mexican Americans, some of whom, usually the younger and more militant ones, adopted the label of "Chicano." The Chicano movement gained strength first in the universities and then among some of the general Mexican-American populace. News of this new militancy on the part of Mexican Americans filtered back to Mexico and aroused some sympathy on the part of leftist activists, since many Chicano militants also professed radical ideas. In time, some producers felt that commercial exploitation of the subject would be feasible. Pepito Romay directed the first "Chicano" film, *De sangre chicana (Of Chicano Blood)* (1973), which he claimed did very well in Los Angeles.[81] A few other movies followed: *Soy chicano y mexicano (I Am Chicano and Mexican)* (1974), *Soy chicano y justiciero (I Am Chicano and a Seeker of Justice)* (1974), *Chicano grueso calibre (Chicano Heavy Caliber)* (1975), and *Chicano* (1975). Their small number indicates that they did not prove to be quite as popular with Mexican-American audiences as their producers expected they would be. Perhaps Mexican filmmakers had little understanding of the nature of the Mexican-American population in the United States.[82] Carlos Monsiváis characterizes these films as a "series of catastrophes" motivated by the "growing importance and prosperity of the Chicano public."[83]

In spite of the opportunistic approach to the subject of Chicanos or Mexican Americans in general by the state-controlled Mexican cinema, the Chicano films suggested a type of coproducing with U.S. filmmakers in which Mexicans could eventually make a real contribution. In late 1977 and early 1978 Alfonso Arau was in the United States shooting *The Promised Dream*, a film on Mexican illegal workers.[84] A distinguished precedent was the 1953 independent film, *The Salt of the Earth*, produced by the Mineworkers' Union, which concerned a strike in Silver City, New Mexico. The cast included a Mexican actress, Rosaura Revueltas, who was deported from the United States for her association with the controversial film.[85]

Actually, there had always been some cooperation between the American and Mexican film industries. The fad for Mexico that lingered on for a few years after World War II resulted in a spate of mostly terrible Hollywood movies filmed in Mexico in the late 1940s and 1950s like *Sombrero, The Bullfighter and the Lady*, and the crowning disaster, *Pepe* (1960), Cantinflas's only starring role in a Hollywood movie.[86] Yet such foreign filming in Mexico provided much-needed work for Mexican technicians and extras, especially in the 1960s and 1970s when

Mexican production fell off so sharply.[87] In the 1980s serious overpopulation and economic pressures have driven millions of Mexicans to the United States. Cooperation between Mexican and American filmmakers could result in motion pictures that would fulfill a vital educational role in informing the citizens of both countries of the mutual responsibility they share in solving these and other problems. To this end, perhaps the "Chicano" films, as well as Hollywood westerns made in Mexico and showing it as a perennially undeveloped and violent land, have performed a valuable service in demonstrating the need for something better. Perhaps Arau is making a start toward providing this and it is to be hoped that others—from both countries—will follow suit.

Interestingly, the one "Chicano" film that did have artistic merit was written and directed by an American of Mexican descent—Jesús Salvador Treviño. The film was *Raíces de sangre (Roots of Blood)* (1976) produced by CONACINE and filmed on location in Mexicali. It relates the efforts of Mexican Americans and Mexicana to form an international labor union to represent workers employed in *maquiladoras*, the largely American-owned assembly plants along the border. The film is well-made with realistically drawn characters and the case includes both Mexican-American and Mexican performers. However, since *Raíces de sangre* reflects Treviño's militant Chicano philosophy, commercial distributors have shied away from the film and it is generally screened only within the university circuits in both Mexico and the United States.[88]

By the middle of the 1970s the Mexican film industry was in a precarious but still promising condition. The policies of Luis and Rodolfo Echeverría had brought mixed blessings. On the negative side, production of feature-length films was down to the lowest point since the 1930s. The frantic scrambling for the little work available had perpetuated the rivalry between the Churubusco and América studios even though both were government owned. This rivalry was fueled by the old bitter competition between the two cinema workers' unions—the STPC and the STIC—which continued unabated.[89] In the first half of the 1970s the industry was nationalized,[90] and among the most positive results of this was that the directors' ranks were opened to new talent, and films dealing with heretofore prohibited social and political themes were made. For many of these achievements, Rodolfo Echeverría, as director of the Banco Nacional Cinematográfico, was responsible. In addition to opening new directions for the industry, Echeverría traveled widely in the United States and Europe promoting his country's films and succeeding in awakening some international interest in Mexican motion pictures.[91]

The new administration of José López Portillo (1976–1982) reversed the cinematic policies of the Echeverría *sexenio*, although some films like Julián Pastor's *La casta divina (The Divine Caste)* (1977) overlapped into the new administration. The transfer of power began, innocuously enough, with the customary resignations of Echeverría appointees; thus Rodolfo Echeverría handed over his post as head of the Banco Cinematográfico to Hiram García Borja.[92].

López Portillo named his sister, Margarita López Portillo, as head of the Directorate of Radio, Television, and Cinema (DRTC), a newly formed agency for the coordination of all government-owned production activities in the elec-

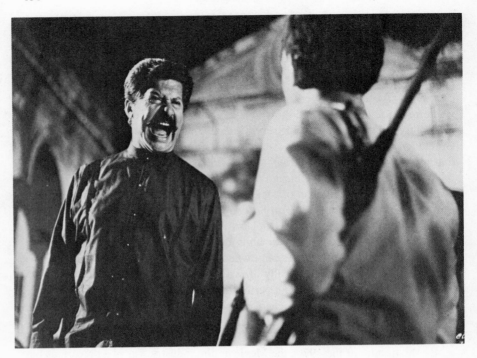

Ignacio López Tarso sounds off in Julián Pastor's *La casta divina* (1977). The film depicts the Yucatecan aristocracy on the eve of the 1910 Revolution. (Azteca Films)

tronic mass media.[93] As regarded the film industry, this was the first step in the implementation of López Portillo's overall economic program to encourage private enterprise and discard government-owned enterprises that were wasteful and inefficient. In the movie industry this meant the retreat of the State from direct participation in filmmaking and the return of private producers.

Shortly after Ramón Charles, a self-declared enemy of official filmmaking, was made the DRTC's chief counsel in early 1979, the Banco Cinematográfico was dissolved, its functions transferred to the DRTC, and its top officers, including García Borja, charged with fraud and corruption. Reflecting the new state of affairs, the Centro de Capacitación Cinematográfica (CCC) seemed to be facing imminent demise as an independent film school.[94] Murky, semiofficial statements threatened the CCC with merger with Churubusco studios or CUEC. In the midst of all this, Bosco Arochi, head of Churubusco, was jailed on charges of fraud as were Fernando Macotela, the studio's Director of Cinematography, and Jorge Hernández Campos of CONACINE, among others.[95] And in July 1979 CONACITE I was dissolved.[96]

These moves were the result of a sweeping reorganization of the film industry in favor of the private sector initiated by Margarita López Portillo as early as July 1977. Her policies naturally caused alarm and resentment among those filmmakers who favored a state-financed cinema of leftist-oriented social commentary—

García Riera reportedly called for a directors' strike to force the government to "respect...freedom of expression."[97] But such militancy aroused little support from filmmakers who depended on the film bureaucracy for whatever work opportunities existed.

Regarding the above problems, Margarita López Portillo stated: "Any line of social films is acceptable if they are made with talent. There exists a group of young directors who work in cooperatives producing good things that debate problems of political or bourgeois life—they do it well. I have faith in them, I am moved that they want to change the world. Who has not dreamed of doing that at the age of 25 or 30?"[98] A propos censorship—"I detest the word 'censorship'— why not say 'supervision'?"[99] And continuing: "We will avoid the presentation of coarse themes that poison the mind.... The people have the right to be respected."[100] And on official filmmaking: "The State will not retreat from pro- duction because it will meet its responsibility of producing a cinema that orients, educates, and entertains."[101]

Although such statements were hardly reassuring to antiestablishment filmmakers, it must be pointed out that the Mexican film industry has always been a business that had to make money to survive. When the State has stepped in, as in the Echeverría years, it was to try to revive a faltering industry as much as to use it to bolster the regime. Luis and Rodolfo Echeverría encouraged a franker and more committed cinema because they believed that in this way Mexican films could find new international markets. However, leftists apparently were neither a profitable nor numerous movie audience and by 1976 Mexican production was at its lowest point since the mid-1930s.

After 1977 the financial health of the film industry improved, even though the organizational problems of 1977–1978 caused a 13% drop in production.[102] How- ever, the outgoing president of the National Chamber of the Cinematic Industry, Manuel Ampudia Girón, reported that "since 1977, average production has increased to 86 films per year...an average rate of increase of 32.7% compared with the 1971–1976 period." As a result, from a total of 20,602 workers in the film industry in 1977, "there was a 5% increase in 1978 [and in 1979], 18.2%— in only two years the number of workers has increased to 25,600.... The fastest growing sector was exhibition, accounting in 1979 for 75.4% of total industry employment; production employed 20.9% and distribution 3.7%. In 1978 private investment increased by 58%; in production this translated to an increase of 84%. By 1979, total investment in the movie industry amounted to almost 69 million dollars. Foreign receipts increased in 1977–1980 by 35.6%, from 10.4 to 14.1 million dollars. In the meantime real production costs, taking inflation into account, decreased by 60% in state-financed films in comparison with 1975 costs; private producers reduced their costs by 35% in this same period."[103]

This improvement in the film industry's financial ledger was achieved by a commercialist thrust that exploited traditional genres, soft-core sex, and whatever timely topics could be quickly taken advantage of. There was also a renewed emphasis on coproducing, a system that lessens somewhat the financial risk for the individual producer and assures distribution in the coproducing countries.

Illustrative of the direction of Mexican cinema at the time was the election in 1980 of Guillermo Calderón Stell as president of the National Chamber of the Cinematic Industry, an association of private producers founded in 1942 which became considerably more visible after 1977; Calderón Stell was the producer of successful cabaretera movies such as *Las ficheras* and *Muñecas de media noche*.

RE-AL Productions was described by *Variety* as "about the biggest Mexican producer making a product geared to the world market." René Cardona, Jr. wrote and directed *Guyana, The Crime of the Century* (1979) as well as an earlier film, *Survival* (1975), based on the crash in the Andes of a Uruguayan plane whose survivors, a rugby team originally headed for a match in Chile, had to resort to cannibalism while waiting to be rescued. *Hostages* (1980) was loosely based on the American hostage situation in Iran. Both *Guyana* and *Hostages* used recognized American actors well past their prime to ensure the widest international distribution. *Guyana*, for instance, starred Stuart Whitman, Joseph Cotten, and Yvonne de Carlo along with an international cast.[104]

Another significant development was the entrance of the giant conglomerate Televisa, S.A. into the film arena. Already exercising a near-monopoly on Mexican commercial television, Televisa initiated the television Spanish International Network (SIN) in the United States and and retained a 75% controlling interest. In 1980, its film production and distribution subsidiary, Televicine Distribution International Corporation, bought out the Spanish Theatrical Division of Columbia Pictures. Columbia's disposal of this operation, which held 40% of the United States Spanish-language market, signaled a new domination of the American Spanish-language movie and television market by Mexican interests. (Azteca Films, a Los Angeles-based distribution firm owned by the Mexican government, already had some 50% of the market.) Columbia turned over its entire Spanish-language film library of five hundred motion pictures to Televicine, as well as licensing its United States subdistrict rights to Cantinflas comedies which it produced and distributed worldwide.[105]

Televicine apparently was convinced of the market potential of the United States market by the box-office success of such movies as *El changle* (*changle* is Mexican slang for "shoe"; the reference here is to the footwear used by soccer players) and *La ilegal* (*The Illegal Alien Woman*) (both 1980), which took in receipts of more than one million dollars apiece shortly after being released in this country. The United States Hispanic market was estimated at 25 million people and represented 40% of Mexico's film export sales. There were about 450 Spanish-language theaters in the United States that brought in $45 million a year.[106] These figures attracted the giant Televisa, through its filmmaking arm, Televicine, to the American scene in production and distribution for both theaters and television.[107]

The administration of José López Portillo played itself out amidst charges of gross mismanagement of the economy and unprecedented corruption.[108] As is well known, when Mexico's vast oil reserves were announced to the world at the beginning of the López Portillo *sexenio*, the country entered a period of such economic expansion that many Mexicans and foreigners felt that Mexico might finally join the ranks of developed nations. Foreign bankers backed up their confidence in the country's future with billions of dollars worth of loans, both to the Mexican government and to private firms. The dream burst with the collapse of oil prices in 1982. Mexico announced it could not service its foreign debt, thereby initiating an international financial crisis.

For the film industry, the national economic disaster led to further retrenching by the remaining state production companies although, as has been described above, Margarita López Portillo's reorganization of the film industry was initiated while the country was still riding the oil boom. The economic setback simply gave greater impetus to the ascendancy of private producers, one of whom implied the irrelevance of quality films to Mexican audiences thus: "The so-called art cinema is accepted and supposedly enjoyed by a select minority or elite, whose capacity to judge and profoundly analyze a film in all its different phases is the result of a long process of culturization, of refined taste, and a sophisticated mentality."[109]

The mass audience within Mexico (and the Mexican-Americans in the United States) had not yet developed such a capacity to enjoy quality cinema, or at least in the judgment of the businessmen who ran the movie industry it had not. If, as Marxists say, film can be used as a weapon to awaken the progressive instincts of a people and mobilize them toward meaningful social change or even revolution, a commercial movie industry was not about to knowingly encourage such a cinema. Margarita López Portillo's patronizing remarks about idealistic young filmmakers were ample evidence of official thinking regarding such a cinema and a reflection of the bitter taste that the Echeverría experiment left in much of the film community. The auteur cinema was left to the young filmmakers in the universities and film clubs during the López Portillo *sexenio*.

The figurative disaster that the López Portillo policies represented for quality filmmaking turned into a literal one with a tragic event: the destruction of the Cineteca Nacional on March 24, 1982. A fire believed to have started with an explosion in the Wings Restaurant located on the ground floor of the Cineteca completely gutted the three-story building with the loss of six lives and the destruction of over 6000 films and two cinemas. A specialized library of film books, thousands of documents, film records, scripts, and photographs were all consumed in the flames. (See p. 114 for a description of the Cineteca's facilities).

Although the fire was most probably of accidental origin, under the prevailing bitterness accusations of sabotage were inevitable. Margarita López Portillo defensively stated that "for two years I had been warning of the danger that the stored filmic materials represented."[110] She said she had asked that the storage vaults be lined with fireproof materials but that her request for 25 million pesos (about one million dollars) was denied by "high authorities" because of the country's precarious economic situation.

A chorus of indignation greeted her statement. Film scholar Jorge Ayala Blanco, director Marcela Fernández Violante, and historian Emilio García Riera among others decried the government's lack of interest in preserving the precious

Alejandro Parodi and Sasha Montenegro in Alfredo Gurrola's *Llámenme Mike*. (Estudio Cinematográfico América)

national heritage represented by the Cineteca. "How could they say there was no money while 40 million pesos [$1,600,000] was spent on a coproduction like *Campanas rojas [The Red Bells]*," exclaimed filmmaker Matilde Landeta.

Landeta's allusion was to an 80-million-peso Mexican-Soviet coproduction premiered with much fanfare on March 19, 1982, in twenty-five theaters of the Federal District. Directed by Sergei Bondarchuk (*War and Peace, Waterloo*) with his usual emphasis on epic battle scenes, the film itself was "pure and simple, an average motion picture, which barely manages to be decorous and acceptable, but are these sufficient reasons to justify the investment of millions?"[111] *Campanas rojas* is "allegedly about U.S. journalist John Reed's experiences during the Mexican Revolution" commented scholar/critic John Mosier. Referring to Salvador Toscano's footage which was collected by his daughter Carmen into a significant documentary and to Paul Leduc's low-budget but excellent *Reed: México insurgente*, Mosier noted that "Bondarchuk does not seem to have seen any of these films.... Any resemblance between his Mexico and the real one appears purely accidental...[and] marred by the presence of contemporary power lines and beer bottles."[112]

In spite of a litany of disasters and failed attempts, some filmmakers doggedly kept alive the tradition of good cinema in Mexico even though their efforts were hard put to compete against domestic *churros* and foreign, principally American, films.

*Llámenme Mike* (*Call Me Mike*, 1979) was finally premiered in the otherwise dismal month of March, albeit in few and hard-to- find theaters "on the periphery"

Alejandro Parodi in *Llámenme Mike* (Pel-Mex)

of Mexico City. Despite the niggardly distribution and promotion, the quality of this film by Alfredo Gurrola soon transcended its unfavorable exhibition conditions. It was an unusual case, "not only because it was a good Mexican film, released three years after it was made, but because it was also an excellent example of what can be done with a foreign genre—in this case the thriller —whose elements cannot be incorporated but still utilized in an intelligent way to make a good parody."[113]

There was never really a Mexican *film noir* although some laudable attempts had been made, notably Alejandro Galindo's *Mientras México duerme* (*While Mexico Sleeps*, 1938), Julio Bracho's *Distinto amanecer* (*A Different Dawn*, 1943), and José Bohr's *Mariguana, el mónstruo verde* (*Marijuana, the Green Monster*, 1935). But *Llámenme Mike* had some characteristics of the genre. The main character Miguelito (Alejandro Parodi), a narcotics cop, is an avid reader of Mickey Spillane's Mike Hammer novels. As a hapless victim of circumstances in a corrupt agency, Miguelito is thrown into a jail cell full of drug traffickers he had jailed himself. Beaten to the point of death, he is miraculously saved by a team of doctors. During the surgery, Miguelito undergoes a transformation becoming, in his own mind, his idol Mike Hammer. "*Llámenme Mike*," he insists to everyone, until he's committed to a mental hospital from which he eventually escapes. Thinking himself the victim of an international Communist conspiracy, "Mike" embarks on a one-man crusade to destroy a gang of drug dealers against whom the police are helpless. Tellingly, they are headed by a character very similar to "Negro" Durazo, the spectacularly corrupt Mexico City police chief appointed by José López Portillo. The principal virtue of director Alfredo Gurrola and his screenwriter Jorge Patiño is that they transcend the Hammer mystique with a healthy dose of humor.

Gurrola and Patiño followed their artistic if not commercial success *Llámenme Mike* with *Días de combate* (*Days of Combat*, 1979), also released three years after its completion. Based on a novel of the same title by Paco Ignacio Taibo II, the film introduces Hector Belascoarán Shayne (Pedro Armendáriz, Jr.), an engineer who abandons his profession to become a private detective. A plumber with whom he shares an office exclaims incredulously, "A private eye? In Mexico? You're crazy—I, on the other hand, *have* work."

Belascoarán is obsessed with capturing a strangler who is causing panic in Mexico City. Thanks to his detailed knowledge of famous stranglers of history, he is invited to appear on a television quiz show, and from that moment on he establishes a strange rapport with the murderer who writes him, "... without me you're nothing, nothing, Belascoarán Shayne."

*Cosa fácil* (*Easy Thing*, 1982), the second adventure of Hector Belascoarán Shayne, again played by Pedro Armendáriz, Jr., combines three distinct cases and plays with them in an intelligent manner. "Within the detective novel, "explains Shayne, "every time that three cases were combined they would blend together until, at a certain instant as if by magic, when one was solved, the other two were also. I wanted to demonstrate the absurdity of the statement, what possible links could possibly exist between the death of Emiliano Zapata, the murder of a homosexual engineer, and the kidnapping of a showgirl's daughter?"[114] And, true, there is no apparent connection aside from the fact that all three incidents occurred in Mexico. As in the best detective fiction, Gurrola uses the genre to reveal the grave ills of society, its violence, corruption, and injustice.

A series in quick succession of three such outstanding state-financed films— *Llámenme Mike*, *Días de combate*, and *Cosa fácil*—by a talented director-writer team struck a bright note in an otherwise discouraging cinematic scene, particularly since both were graduates of the Centro Universitario de Estudios Cinematográficos (CUEC), UNAM's distinguished film school giving proof that some of the country's best young talent was being developed and given an opportunity to make films by the State.

Another bright spot on the cinematic scene was the independent filmmaker Jaime Humberto Hermosillo with his tenth feature film *María de mi corazón* (*Maria My Love*, 1982), adapted from a story by Gabriel García Márquez.[115] Filmed in 16mm, the film tells the bittersweet love story of a novice thief, Hector (Héctor Bonilla) and his former lover, María (María Rojo). Returning from a burglary, he finds María asleep in his apartment. She had just been stood up at her wedding and Hector was the only person she could think of going to. They fall in love again and marry. María uses her skills in magic to form an act with Hector as her assistant. María is a free and carefree soul who overwhelms Hector with her optimism and love of life. One day, however, María's van breaks down

From right to left, María Rojo and Héctor Bonilla in Jaime Humberto Hermosillo's *María de mi corazón*. (Estudio Cinematográfico América)

on the highway while she's on her way to join Hector in Veracruz for a performance. It is the middle of the night in a torrential rain; finally a bus stops for her. It carries a strangely silent and sullen load of passengers. When the bus stops and the passengers get off, María realizes it has arrived at a mental hospital. She tries to use a phone but the nurses think she is one of the patients. The more María protests her sanity and insists on using a phone, the more obsessive she appears. One night she finally gets a call through to Hector but he hangs up on her, thinking she had walked out on him again as she had once before.

Hector, in the meantime, had sought out María's ex-fiance who tells him of her erratic behavior. When a staff member from the hospital finds him, Hector thinks that María is really mentally ill. He visits her (dressed in his magician's tuxedo, as she had imagined he would) but makes no attempt to have her released. María becomes hysterical when he leaves. Is María really insane or has her unconventional and independent behavior been misinterpreted by society and by Hector? Or are the lovers being manipulated by a fate totally beyond their control? In this film, as Tomás Pérez-Turrent wrote, Hermosillo "once again ... demonstrates his unique powers of observation of the [behavior], customs, myths and values of the Mexican middle class, caught in their everyday moods. ... at the same time, while appraising this seemingly banal everydayness, Hermosillo is also capable of penetrating beyond it to the fantastic, without any barrier to separate it from reality."[116]

María Rojo and Héctor Bonilla in another scene from *María de mi corazón* (Clasa Films Mundiales)

Toward the end of 1982, a uniquely Mexican film tradition came to an end. "El Santo," the gold-masked wrestler who always kept his true identity secret, announced his retirement from the screen with his last film, *El Santo contra el asesino de la televisión* (*Santo Versus the Television Assassin*). Santo was the Mexican superhero *par excellence* and his filmography exceeded by far that of Tarzan, James Bond, or Superman—more than fifty films in twenty-four years. "Symbol of justice, tireless collaborator with the well-meaning but inept metropolitan police, Interpol's agent in Mexico, sometime inventor of simple but effective crime-fighting devices, virtuous sportsman (he doesn't drink or smoke), a gentleman admired by the so-called weaker sex to whom he never submits, Santo is that and much more."[117]

Throughout his film career, Santo would combat all manner of monsters, vampires, werewolves, witches, newly resuscitated vampires, mummies (preferably from Guanajuato); he would struggle against extraterrestrials (Martians or assassins from other worlds) or against mad scientists, maniacal stranglers, evil geniuses, graverobbers, international smugglers, kidnappers, secret bands of assassins, the underworld, and other unusual delinquents. Santo was lord and master of all the cardboard sets through which he battled assorted villains, using the latest plastic toys with flashing lights as if they were ultramodern devices. The king of kitsch and unintentional humor, Santo became a wholesome camp figure with a huge following among both adults and children. His films reinforced each other over the years, amounting to a single Mexican-style fairy tale of good versus evil played out on the wrestling mat.[118]

Santo inspired a multitude of other wrestling superheroes who never quite gained the public's acceptance as he did. No sooner had Santo's retirement been announced than a film tribute to him apppeared: José Buil's *Adiós, adiós ídolo mío* (*Farewell, Farewell My Idol*). An aging and arthritic Santo lives on his pension with his faithful servant and her little girl who dresses as Batman. The producers who grew rich from his films disdain him because he's "old and fat." The public, which once adored him, now prefers Superman, Wonder Woman, and the other transnational superheroes that infest the media.[119]

Nonetheless Mexican film production in the closing days of Margarita López Portillo's tenure was in a sorry state. So troubling was the situation that the great photographer Gabriel Figueroa spoke out bitterly during an awards ceremony for independent filmmakers: "The cinema of B-girls, prostitutes, and obscene language should be exhibited only after midnight. The current *sexenio* has been the most disastrous for the national film industry, because all the themes were oriented toward that type of story. Undoubtedly, the future of the commercial Mexican cinema has to take more positive directions, since it is not possible to continue any longer with such themes, which have only succeeded in further reducing the markets for our films."[120]

Tomás Pérez-Turrent echoed Figueroa's statements: "Mexican cinema has not reached such a low level in several decades. Cheap cinema, with no artistic or cultural ambitions, a repetition of the oldest and most time-worn formulas, subpornography, facile folklore, routine melodramas, films aimed at manipulating the emotions and frustrations of the lower strata of the population and the nostalgia of Mexicans and of those of Mexican descent in the United States (presently the so-called Spanish markets of the United States are fundamental to the financial stability of the film industry." And Pérez-Turrent concludes, echoing the director Antonio Bardem's famous phrase about Spanish cinema at the Salamanca talks of 1955, "The resulting cinema is industrially feeble, socially useless, culturally nil, and aesthetically impoverished."[121]

It was apparent to all that the cinema industry was aesthetically very ill and there was no shortage of physicians offering remedies to the patient.[122] However, close to one hundred films were made in 1982 providing steady employment for studio workers. The role of the state as a cultural arbiter was much discussed: what type of official intervention would be prudent in a situation like that existing in 1982 when "quality" state-sponsored film production was practically nil and movies of abysmal quality made by private producers were thriving? The advice was of course being proferred for the incoming administration of Miguel de la Madrid, but the film industry had a low priority in the agenda of a government that faced the most acute economic crisis in fifty years. The State, ideally, should guarantee jobs for workers in the industry and, at the same time, exert a counterinfluence when commercialism and popular fads result in a surplus of undesirable film topics. It was proposed that legislation should also guarantee work for filmmakers trained in the State's own training centers such as CUEC and the Centro de Capacitación Cinematográfica (CCC). "Training a filmmaker is more costly than training a cardiologist and all the money spent on this training will be thrown out the window if the filmmaker cannot find work in the industry."[123]

These were some of the sweeping proposals for a new cinematic law that many thought was long overdue and should be enacted under the new administration. The existing cinematic law dated from 1949 and its most famous provision, that theaters throughout Mexico should screen national films 50 percent of the time, had been almost wholly ignored from the moment it became law. A new law (never legislated under De la Madrid) would seemingly provide "cradle to grave" security for Mexican filmmakers; censorship would protect public morals and family values but not arbitrarily prohibit themes of political or social criticism; clean, comfortable theaters would be guaranteed for the showing of Mexican films as well as adequate promotion.[124]

Other ideas that began to surface at this time were how to utilize television and the mass audience it commanded as a medium for disseminating the cinema. Related to this was the unanticipated videocassette revolution which in the coming years spread throughout Mexico as it would in many other countries.[125] Another idea advanced at this time was to create a secretariat or ministry of culture under which all cinematic activities would be placed.

As the inauguration of Miguel de la Madrid approached, there was apprehension at the uncertain future faced by a nation in financial crisis. But in the film community there was hope—as there always is at the beginning of a new *sexenio*—for new policies, new ideas, and perhaps new opportunities.

Lamented Salomón Laiter, as so many others had, "We are a people rich in cultural traditions. Why are they not reflected in our film theaters?"[126]

# 6

# "... To Rebuild a Ruined Cinema in a Ruined Country": 1981–1989

Alberto Isaac uttered those unsettling words on what was actually a rather optimistic occasion: his appointment on March 25, 1983, as director of the newly created Mexican Cinema Institute (Instituto Mexicano de Cinematografía—IMCINE). Isaac's assumption of the post struck a hopeful chord in a largely disillusioned film community which hoped that, by turning over the reins of the official film agency to one of Mexico's most respected directors instead of to a career bureaucrat, a sea change had occurred in the official attitude toward the film industry. Coming on the heels of Margarita López Portillo's disastrous tenure during the previous administration, it was hoped that the new *sexenio* of Miguel de la Madrid would open the way to the long-awaited resurgence of quality cinema.

Isaac, director of over fifty short features and eight full-length films, among the latter *Tívoli* and *El rincón de las vírgenes*, had been blacklisted by the previous administration for publicly criticizing the investment of half a million dollars in the U.S. production of *Superman*. An infuriated Margarita López Portillo forced him out of his post as director of the Organización Editorial Mexicana. "I paid dearly ... I was totally boycotted," explained Isaac. "They threw me out in the street, I lost two films, one already under contract and the other verbally agreed to; I lost my jobs on *El Sol* and *Esto*."[1]

Isaac's experience was the most extreme instance of what other directors who had established distinguished reputations between 1970 and 1976 had had to go through in the post-Echeverría period. Only Arturo Ripstein managed to continue making films with some regularity while others, such as Felipe Cazals, "[had] been obliged to make films in three weeks, productions of no interest, dedicated to some singing idol; others [worked] for television; and others [made television commercials]."[2]

The new Mexican Cinema Institute brought under its fold the State production companies CONACINE and CONACITE II, the documentary film center, the Churubusco-Azteca and América studios, the State-owned promotion, distribution, and exhibition companies, and the film school, CCC. At the time of his appointment, Isaac was optimistic that this reorganization signaled the beginning of renewed official support for the film industry. However, within a year, Isaac had resigned to return to what he liked to do best—directing films, but the frustration of dealing with a bureaucracy in the throes of economic crisis was also a contributing factor. His principal achievement was to organize the Third Contest of Experimental Cinema in 1985[3] which served to reveal the talents of Alberto Cortés with *Amor a la vuelta de la esquina* (*Love Around the Corner*) in which he demythifies the genre of the cinema of prostitutes, and Diego López's political melodrama *Crónica de familia* (*Family Chronicle*). Shortly after this event, Isaac resigned over a jurisdictional conflict with the State exhibition agency COTSA (Compañía Operadora de Teatros, S.A.), and his successor Enrique Soto Izquierdo failed to continue Isaac's policy of seeking new avenues of dissemination for the cinema.[4]

Still, some filmmakers expressed optimism for the new *sexenio*, even if only because the film industry's condition had deteriorated to such an extent that any change had to be for the better. Said Sergio Olhovich: "The economic crisis should have a favorable effect on the film industry. We have first-class . . . directors, writers, actors—we have an impressive capability for exhibition, over 2500 theaters throughout the country, both commercial and art houses, in addition to excellent laboratories."[5]

Another director, José Estrada, was more guarded: "I think the panorama is quite bleak. . . . I suspect there won't be much funds to play around with for cinema. . . . Therefore we filmmakers will have to dream up new projects involving novel production schemes."[6] Olhovich stated, "A strong nation should not fear creative works. One film is not going to cause a revolution. . . . Another important goal is to decentralize production; films should be made all over the country so new filmmakers can be trained outside of the capital." But the most important goal, continued Olhovich, was to "consolidate a cinematic policy that would be independent of political changes every six years."[7] One way of achieving this, according to Estrada, was to remove the film industry from under the jurisdiction of the Secretaría de Gobernación (equivalent to the U.S. Department of the Interior). "The very fact that the cinema is governed by that ministry, which is charged with internal security, means that they approach filmmaking as a potentially subversive activity, converting Gobernación into a police agency . . . We'll have to lobby to have the Dirección de Cinematografía transferred to the Ministry of Education so that the cinema can finally be administered as a cultural activity."[8] Although this was not to occur under the administration of Miguel de la Madrid, IMCINE, charged with fomenting quality cinema, was finally to be merged in early 1989 with a newly created Council for Culture and the Arts under the Ministry of Public Education.

Symbolizing the gap between the present state of Mexican cinema and what it had once been was the loss of two of its most distinguished figures. On April 11, 1983, Dolores del Río died in La Jolla, California, of chronic hepatitis. Although only 19 of her 56 films were Mexican, Dolores del Río's collaboration with Emilio "El Indio" Fernández, Gabriel Figueroa, and Pedro Armendáriz resulted in two classic works of Mexican cinema, *Flor silvestre* and *María Candelaria* (both 1943), and a long list of distinguished subsequent films. Her influence was "very great and much time would pass before another star of her magnitude would arise. Her death [deprived] Mexican cinema of one of the great figures that gave it an international reputation during its golden age." Her last film was *The Children of Sanchez* (1978) in which she costarred with Anthony Quinn; afterward she dedicated all her time to working with disadvantaged children.[9]

The second great loss to the Mexican and international film world was the death at the age of 83 of Luis Buñuel on July 29 in Mexico City. Buñuel's Mexican films have been discussed earlier and in many other books and articles, and certainly no final assessment is called for here. More appropriate, perhaps, would be some thoughts on the relationship between Buñuel and his adoptive country. According to American critic Michael Wood, Buñuel, in spite of his Mexican citizenship, was "not really a Mexican . . . one cannot *become* a Mexican . . . [it] is a shy, secret country, and even the eloquent diagnoses of its quirks and ills by gifted natives like Octavio Paz and Carlos Fuentes tend to deepen the mystery rather than abolish it. For this reason it is essential to avoid all bland conclusions on the subject."

As Wood wrote:

Mexico gave Buñuel a home when he needed one, reunited him with friends, returned him to his language, and offered him more of those stark, dry landscapes which are so much a part of his visual kingdom. The rocks of Majorca modulate into Mexican boulders; the aridity of *Land Without Bread* stalks the villages of *Nazarín*. But above all, perhaps, Mexico [allowed] Buñuel to practice being *no one*, like Odysseus, and nourished his secret personality and his ability to be everywhere, like those nameless streets. Mexico represents neither a displaced Spain nor a cozy cosmopolitanism. It is the perfect, strenuous, uninvaded exile which opens out on to nothing less than the infinite particulars of the world.[10]

And Buñuel himself commented:

It must also be said that Mexico is a genuine country whose inhabitants are animated by one impulse, a desire for learning and to better themselves, that is rarely encountered elsewhere. Add to that an extreme amiability, friendship, and hospitality that have made of Mexico, from the Spanish Civil War to Pinochet's coup d'etat in Chile, a country of safe haven.[11]

It is perhaps these qualities of the Mexican people, which have not always gone unnoticed by foreign observers, that will enable the society to ameliorate if not totally solve its numerous problems. And the film community, as a microcosm of the attitudes, opinions, ideologies, and problems facing the nation as a whole, continued to vigorously debate questions of national identity, morality, and purpose in the pages of periodicals, in assorted gatherings, and through films themselves. As one observer commented, "The situation of Mexican cinema is similar to that which exists in the country, and we will extricate ourselves from that trap only on the basis of work and the cooperation of everyone."[12]

State production, which had been reduced to just four films in 1982, the last year of the López Portillo administration, showed an encouraging increase in 1983-84. Still, the attempt to gain international prestige and commercial success remained elusive: *Antonieta*, coproduced with Spain and directed by Carlos Saura, "failed completely"[13] just as *Campanas rojas* had in 1982.

Independent filmmaking, however, increased: thirteen films were made in 1982, among them *El día que murió Pedro Infante* (*The Day Pedro Infante Died*) by Claudio Isaac (Alberto Isaac's son) and *Nocaut* (*Knockout*) by José Luis García Agraz. Although the State produced little, "partly because of the country's economic crisis, and partly as a continuation of the tendencies of the previous administration," it was showing an inclination to sponsor films produced outside of the industry such as *Nocaut* and the highly praised *Vidas errantes* (*Wandering Lives*, 1983) by CCC graduate Juan de la Riva.[14]

Claudio Isaac's loosely biographical and intensely personal *El día que murió Pedro Infante* is an unpretentious but well-crafted film that follows the personal and professional frustrations of a young writer. The title stems from the fact that the principal character, Pablo (Humberto Zurita), was born in 1957 on the day that Pedro Infante, the popular movie and singing idol, was killed in a plane crash. Reportedly, the title attracted many people who were then disappointed to discover that the story had nothing to do with Pedro Infante (except for a few brief newsreel sequences of his funeral, in the film's last scene). The film is about Pablo's efforts to publish his second novel while attempting to rekindle a love affair with Teresita (Beatriz Marín). In neither endeavor is he successful. The State-supported firm which had published his first novel now has a new management emplaced by the new government; the editor (Pedro Armendáriz, Jr.) is a bureaucrat incapable of understanding the novel's philosophical implications. Instead he suggests that the writer produce a work based on a theme and outline provided by the editor—a proposal that is contemptuously rejected by the young writer. This simple yet sensitively done film manages to express the frustrations and ennui of educated middle-class youths in a society that offers them few choices.

*Nocaut* was a promising first effort that told the story of Rodrigo (Gonzalo Vega), a boxer who murders his promoter, a notorious drug dealer. At the urging of Beltrán (Wolf Ruvinskis), the promoter/gangster, he had given up a slot on the Olympic squad to turn professional. Rodrigo's resentment is more than justified. Beltrán's insistence that Rodrigo fight without allowing an eye injury to heal effectively ruins the young pugilist's career and he is then reduced to throwing fights. Done in *film noir* technique, the film unfolds in two temporal currents: in the present, as Rodrigo tries to elude pursuing thugs and police, and in the past, reconstructing in flashbacks the events that have led to his present predicament.

For forty-eight hours, he desperately seeks to lose himself in Mexico City, managing to avoid assorted dangers and betrayals. Rodrigo's luck finally runs out, and he is cornered by the murderous thugs—the final, and deadliest, "*nocaut*."

García Agraz "demonstrates an ability to tell a story with verve, to create an atmosphere, enabling Mexico City, especially the city at night, to become an important character in the film... [He] constructs solid, life-like characters and establishes relations between them with a few strokes."[15] If any criticism can be leveled at the film it is that it is probably longer than it need be, and the flashbacks at times become confusing. However, for a first effort the film was impressive and again demonstrated the caliber of training being offered in the publicly supported film schools, in this case the CUEC.

*Vidas errantes* (*Wandering Lives*) was also a highly praised first effort by a graduate of the CCC. Although this writer was unable to view the film, the favorable reactions it has received from many quarters place *Vidas errantes* among the finest examples of recent Mexican cinema. Although completed in 1984, it was not released commercially until the following year. A joint production between CONACINE and a private cooperative, it was one of the first accomplishments of IMCINE. "A reflection of the cinema, within the cinema," this film relates the life of Francisco (José Carlos Ruiz) and his young assistant, Guillermo (Ignacio Guadalupe). Francisco is a peripatetic film exhibitor who travels the Durango countryside in his van, setting up screenings in the most remote villages. *Vidas errantes* is a tribute to the old Mexican cinema, "considerably superior to the average film of today." Fernando has a deep love for movies and he represents those dedicated souls who disseminated Mexican films to the farthest corners of the country. The tragic scene of the fire that destroys Francisco's impromptu theater "can be considered an allegory of the tragedy of the Cineteca, and a moral that even if the dreams and hopes of an entire life are lost because of one person's carelessness, one always has to rise again and continue the struggle for a better life, and a better cinema."[16]

On January 27, 1984, the new home of the Cineteca Nacional was inaugurated. The attractive facility, formerly a small shopping center with four theaters, was purchased from the Society of Composers and Writers and is located on México-Coyoacán Avenue just north of Río Churubusco. Situated around an inner courtyard that insulates it from the noise, pollution, and traffic of the busy thoroughfare outside, the Cineteca complex consists of the administrative offices of the Dirección de Cinematografía, a library, a bookstore, an archive of photographs (many rescued from the old Cineteca and still bearing burn marks), a gallery for cinema-related exhibits, the Documentation and Research Department, and the four theaters: "Jorge Stahl," for double features and children's programs; "Salvador Toscano," for international film weeks and film retrospectives based on different themes—directors, subjects, actors, and others; "Fernando de Fuentes," for foreign films; and "Arcady Boytler," for advance screenings and revivals of Mexican films.[17]

On January 16, 1987, financial administration of the Cineteca was transferred from the Banco Cinematográfico (itself in the process of being dissolved) to the Banco Nacional de Obras y Servicios (BANOBRAS) in keeping with President de la Madrid's instructions for "maintaining Mexican cinema as a living testament of quality of the national culture, and also as a source of employment that

Ofelia Medina as *Frida*, directed by Paul Leduc. (Estudio Cinematográfico América)

can expand and increase its productivity." At that time, the Cineteca had in its archive 2,968 films in both 35mm and 16mm of which 60 percent, or 1770, were Mexican. The library had more than seven thousand volumes and six thousand film periodicals. The four theaters had projected, since 1984, an annual average of 4,700 screenings. The Cineteca had also published fourteen monographs and owned some 1800 videos.[18]

Such tangible developments seemed to indicate the beginnings of greater, though still far from copious, official support for a revitalization of the film industry. Earlier, in four conferences held from August 6 to 13 in the Secretaría de Gobernación, all sectors of the industry presented their suggestions and wish lists. Churubusco studios said it needed funds to modernize and maintain its equipment; STPC and STIC pledged to support private producers committed to quality; the producers and distributors complained that their product was screened in the less desirable theaters while foreign films enjoyed the first-class houses; and the cooperatives insisted (again!) that 50 percent of screen time be reserved for national films in all the country's theaters.[19]

In 1985 four films were released that seemed to highlight both the potential of Mexican cinema and the commercialist tradition of profitable *churros* (low-quality potboilers) that showed no sign of going away.

Paul Leduc's *Frida*, produced by Manuel Barbachano Ponce, was a serendipit-

A Scene from *Frida* (Clasa Films Mundiales)

ous combination of accomplished filmmaking with a topic that could readily appeal to sophisticated foreign audiences.

As Joan and Dennis West described her in *Cineaste*:

Frida Kahlo was the intelligent, spirited, and sexy Mexican beauty whose scandalous bisexual love life included the conquest of Trotsky. The flamboyantly dressed, on-again-off-again wife of the legendary Diego Rivera, the extravagant giant of the Mexican muralist movement. A leftist and revolutionary committed to *Mexicanidad*...and the Mexican Revolution. The heroic survivor of polio, miscarriages and abortions, a crippling and nearly fatal traffic accident, and dozens of surgical operations, who spent much of her life in pain confined to wheelchair or bed. And Latin America's greatest woman artist who, when she died in 1954 at age forty-seven, left a legacy of some two hundred extraordinary paintings including scores of haunting self-portraits.[20]

Certainly a life ready-made for a sensationalized screen adaptation that could very well have been flawed in less capable hands by melodramatic excesses of all kinds. But Paul Leduc used an approach emphasizing images over dialogue, and each scene is as lovingly elaborated as any of Frida's paintings. Leduc does not pretend to provide a linear, structured biography of the artist, employing instead impressionistic images to focus on some of the principal themes and events of Frida's life: childhood memories of her father (Claudio Brook) entertaining the young Frida (Valentina Leduc) and her sister (Cecilia Toussaint) with a puppet show; Frida being carried back from the bus accident that nearly killed her and

A Scene from *Frida* (Clasa Films Mundiales)

left her crippled; a nighttime political rally punctuated by *zapatista* songs; a melancholy New Year's Eve party with couples dancing a charming but sombre *danzón*; the adult Frida (Ofelia Medina) in her wheelchair bringing a meal to Diego Rivera (Juan José Gurrola) as he works on a mural, and they both burst out in good-natured but very bad operatic singing. One lively scene (most traditional in terms of sustained dialogue) involves Frida, Diego Rivera, and David Alfaro Siqueiros (Salvador Sánchez) heatedly discussing Trotsky in the lush garden of the Kahlo home in Coyoacán. Siqueiros, just returned from the Spanish Civil War, melodramatically describes a terrible battle in which he participated. The horribly wounded Spanish soldiers "looked up at their Mexican commander" and somewhat incongruously "demanded to know why Mexico had broken ranks with international socialist solidarity and granted asylum to Leon Trotsky [Max Kerlow]," which is really too much for Rivera who tells his fellow artist to stop spouting such *pendejadas* ("bullshit"). With the exception of this scene and others involving Trotsky, in which more French and Russian are spoken than Spanish, dialogue is nonexistent or kept to a bare minimum.

Throughout the film, Angel Goded's camera moves constantly but unobtrusively, making the viewer feel like an unnoticed spectator in the characters' most intimate moments. Originally filmed in 16mm, the film was expertly blown up to 35mm and retains Goded's sharp, clear cinematography. Inexplicably, *Frida* was not entered in the Academy Award nominations for best foreign-language film

Juan José Gurrola as Diego Rivera in *Frida*. (Alejandro Pelayo)

because when Academy representatives arrived in Mexico to screen the film, some bureaucratic bungling prevented it from being projected for them.[21]

*Frida* represented Manuel Barbachano Ponce's greatest success since *Nazarín* and other Buñuel films. "It gave me great satisfaction because it was like a dream come true," he exclaimed. "To capture and recreate that marvelous atmosphere of Mexico in the 1930s was Paul Leduc's greatest achievement."[22]

In addition to portraying internationally renowned artists and political figures, *Frida* also benefitted from the publication of an important biography of Frida Kahlo[23] and a major exhibition of her work in the National Gallery in Washington, D.C. This was a rather rare confluence of factors that enhanced the international marketability of a Mexican film, but another film received a warm reception because it tapped quite another kind of transnational interest.

Jaime Humberto Hermosillo's *Doña Herlinda y su hijo* (*Doña Herlinda and Her Son*), also produced by Barbachano Ponce, concerns the desire of Rodrigo (Marco Antonio Treviño), a successful Guadalajara doctor, to pursue a passionate love affair with Ramón (Gustavo Meza), a young music student. Having trouble finding privacy for their encounters, Rodrigo even schedules an "examination" for Ramón at his office. Rodrigo's mother, Doña Herlinda (Guadalupe del Toro) is fond of Ramón although she does not let on that she is quite aware of the exact nature of her son's relationship with him. Doña Herlinda, as the matron of an ultrarespectable and prominent family, goes about implementing an elaborate

Marco Antonio Treviño and Gustavo Meza in Jaime Humberto Hermosillo's *Doña Herlinda y su hijo*. (Clasa Films Mundiales)

Another scene from *Doña Herlinda y su hijo*—Guadalupe del Toro is at right (Clasa Films Mundiales)

scheme to protect her son from scandal while at the same time getting what she wants—marrying him to a socially acceptable girl and getting a grandchild (to which Ramón is the godfather). Herlinda deftly accomplishes her goals by film's end—she is proudly showing her family the plans for a new house with a separate wing for Rodrigo and his wife, a nursery for the baby and, in the other wing, a studio and apartment for Ramón. "[Doña Herlinda] is an ace manipulator, but in the context of a repressive society her string-pulling seems a sane, humane, and efficient means of spreading happiness. The result is a jolly *ménage à cinq* in which everyone gets a piece of the best of possible worlds."[24]

In fact, Doña Herlinda's achievement of reconciling radically different life-styles and philosophies and convincing them to coexist under one roof might be seen as a metaphor for the manipulative manner in which the PRI has governed Mexico for much of the last fifty years. In any event, this gentle, humorous story in which gay love is treated with sensitivity and acceptance seems to have found an audience well beyond its borders. Still, the steamy love scenes between Rodrigo and Ramón were somewhat surprising coming from a "shy, secret country" and invited comparison with the Spaniard Pedro Almodóvar's *Ley del deseo* (*Law of Desire*, 1987), a not-so-gentle examination of the obsessiveness of physical desire.

In stark contrast to *Frida* and *Doña Herlinda y su hijo* was *Lola la trailera* (*Lola the Truck Driver*) directed by Raúl Fernández. With wooden acting, atrocious dialogue, amateurish photography, and spotty direction, the film nonetheless was a box-office success in both Mexico and the United States: it made $3.5 million ($2.5 million in the United States and "only" $1 million in Mexico) profit on an investment of $150,000—a powerful rationale to continue making *churros* for the Southwest U.S. Spanish-speaking market.[25]

The statuesque Rosa Gloria Chagoyan stars as Lola who becomes a truckdriver (*trailera*) so her murdered father's truck won't be repossessed by his employer, a notorious drug trafficker. Lola falls in love with an undercover cop and together they wipe out the gang (which has gotten the upper hand over the police in a climactic full-fledged battle complete with grenades and helicopter gunships). In the midst of all this is Amapola (Vitola) and her ambulatory brothel—an eighteen-wheeler that converts to a sleazy night club whose star attraction is another under-cover (in both senses) agent, policewoman Alondra, played by an aging and expanding Irma Serrano. *Lola la trailera* merged the *fichera* movies with the action genre, usually cops versus drug dealers (*narcotraficantes*). In fact it spelled the end of the former and the beginning of the latter, reflecting the expansion of the drug traffic in Mexico.[26] The film, in spite of its low quality, has some elements atypical of the genre (or several genres it encompasses). Lola does enter the extremely macho world of truckdrivers. She succeeds not only professionally (even if she is unable to change a tire and the undercover cop has to do it for her; this can be dismissed as a plot device since the incident leads to their romantic involvement), but also in assisting in the destruction of the drug dealers. Although Alondra is discovered and brutally murdered, Lola herself is never the object of physical or sexual violence (she does come out second best in a fight with a hooker). She seems to continue the María Félix tradition of the "macho

Rosa Gloria Chagoyan as *Lola la trailera* (Pel-Mex)

woman"—the female who competes with men and excels, manipulating them in the process.

Of much better quality but entirely derivative was *El maleficio 2* (*The Curse 2*). Based on a popular *telenovela* (prime-time TV soap), this slick, expensive Televicine production was inspired by the "satanic" genre of horror films like *The Omen* and *Damian*. It starred the respected actor Ernesto Alonso (who had appeared in Luis Buñuel's *Ensayo de un crimen*) and the singing and *telenovela* star Lucía Méndez. The opening scenes were filmed in New York and other scenes in Venice. The confused plot has Enrique de Martino (Alonso) as an immortal (or at least very long-lived) servant of Satan who seeks a boy whose face he has seen in a painting. The trail leads from New York to Venice and thence back to Mexico City and ends with Gabriel (Eduardo Yáñez), an arrogant, brilliant, and disturbed youth with formidable kinetic powers. (After a quarrel with his sister Marcela

Lola and her undercover cop (Pel-Mex)

[Méndez], he causes part of their house to collapse.) Martino falls in love with Marcela and ponders giving up his power and immortality. However, Gabriel, who is in love with his own sister, is becoming increasingly surly and dangerous, which sets the stage for a confrontation between the two evil, supernatural forces. *El maleficio 2* is interesting as an example of the type of film that some Mexican producers feel they must make to compete with U.S. products. It has good special effects, excellent cinematography, and good production values. It was a profitable film and is doing well in videocassette rentals, both in Mexico and the United States.[27]

It is also representative of the type of vehicle used by Televicine (Televisa's filmmaking operation) to promote television performers to movie "stardom." Lucía Méndez is only one such example; another is Roberto Gómez Bolaños, "Chespirito," star of a puerile television program of the same name. But the most resounding success of this TV-to-the-big-screen transition has been María Elena Velasco, "La India María." Her 1987 film *Ni de aquí, ni de allá (Neither From Here nor From There)* was that year's top box-office success.

The character of La India María originally appeared in the early 1970s on Televisa's marathon television variety show "Siempre en Domingo ("Always on Sunday")—a sort of extended Ed Sullivan show where she played brief sketches as host Raúl Velasco's "country cousin," a Mexican version of Minnie Pearl. But her popularity took a quantum leap after she began appearing in films. The character is basically that of a bumpkin, an Indian from a remote village who is naive, illiterate, and unsophisticated but who possesses a shrewd native intelligence that enables her to win out over an assortment of socially advantaged types like "haughty employers, corrupt politicians, incompetent policemen, smugglers and American tourists," the latter usually a Mr. Peppermint (Pancho Córdova), a trusting soul to whom María sells phony pre-Hispanic curios.[28]

La India María's first film was *Tonta tonta pero no tanto (Foolish But Not Too Much,* 1971) followed by other successes: *Pobre pero honrada (Poor But Honest,* 1972), *La madrecita (The Little Mother,* 1973), *La presidenta municipal (The Municipal President,* 1974), and *El miedo no anda en burro (Fear Does Not Ride a Donkey,* 197?).

In *Ni de aquí, ni de allá,* La India María shares the experiences of millions of her countrymen when she emigrates to Los Angeles to work as a domestic. Shot on location in eight weeks for $175,000, the film, which made over one million dollars, was "a tremendous success, even intellectuals went to see it."[29] What these intellectuals saw was an uneven collection of puns, sight gags, and slapstick loosely connected to a story line involving María being hired without proper papers by an American couple and flying to Los Angeles where, in the confusion of the L.A. airport, she is immediately separated from her employers and becomes involved with a remarkably incompetent spy, presumably Russian. He chases her (because she's the only witness to a murder he committed), and the FBI chases both of them thinking that María is another agent "disguised as a Mexican." Then ensues a confusing series of chases, jobs, and occasionally wry observations of American life. She is finally caught and deported, and the film imparts the "message" that poverty ín one's own country is preferable to earning dollars in the United States. Directed by Velasco herself, the film displayed greater cinematic skills than *Lola la trailera,* faint praise though that be.

The popularity of La India María, who may be considered to have replaced Cantinflas as Mexico's favorite comic figure, has been the cause of polemical exchanges. Intellectuals on the left consider the portrayal of the character to be racist—a perpetuation of the stereotype of the socially and mentally retarded Indian which has been a staple of Mexican popular culture since the colonial era.[30] Other observers, on the other hand, interpret her popularity as a reaction against the preponderance of *güeros* (i.e., blondes, fair-complexioned types) in the Mexican media, a phenomenon that rarely escapes the notice of many foreign visitors. Most of the latter—especially those from the United States, who carry their own cultural baggage in these matters—will generally conclude that the ex-

María Elena Velasco as La India María in *Ni de aquí, ni de allá*. (Alejandro Pelayo)

planation is due simply to racism, and this is partly but not entirely true. Alfredo Crevenna, a German-born director who arrived in Mexico in the mid-1930s and was honored in August 1988 as the most prolific filmmaker in the history of Mexican cinema (well over 100 films), opined that the *güeros* (both Mexicans and foreigners) who proliferate on television and in print advertisements symbolize that better, and/or more fashionable, life to which many of the people emerging into or struggling to maintain middle-class living standards aspire to; but, said Crevenna, "... you should ask that question of the advertising agencies."[31]

It is also apparent that the question does not seem to be an issue among the great majority of genetically Indian and mestizo Mexicans (it seems to bother some foreigners more). In any event, the film industry has always done a better job of reflecting Mexican social reality than the more recent television, which, like many others around the world, is probably simply trying to look "American," a not inconsequential influence considering Mexico's geographical location.

Whatever the explanation for mass tastes, the success of films like *Ni de aquí, ni de allá* and *Lola la trailera* points up the eternal problem of Mexican and any other cinema—commercial success is predicated on tapping mass tastes, also referred to as "the lowest common denominator." In this chapter, and indeed throughout this book, the emphasis has been on the somewhat subjective term of "quality" filmmaking. Motion pictures like those of La India María, *Lola la trailera*, and Crevenna's own highly successful *5 nacos asaltan Las Vegas* (*Five Nerds*

*Take Las Vegas*, 1986) offer the majority of viewers—who are working-class people with an average of three to eight years of elementary-school education—escapist entertainment that enables them to forget for an hour and a half their economic and other personal problems. La India María might tangentially reference deeper social problems, but she also makes audiences laugh, either at her or with her.

The Mexican middle class has by and large given up on Mexican cinema—these spectators flock to see Rambo and Star Trek movies and other popular American imports, just like their European and Asian counterparts.[32] A minority with more refined tastes prefer quality American (e.g., Woody Allen films), European, and Japanese cinema. How to win back these middle-class viewers is the dilemma of the Mexican film industry; the "80 percent trash"[33] movies that generate profits for the private producers reflect the majority tastes: *narcotraficante* pictures, often set near the U.S. border, e.g., *El secuestro de Camarena* (*The Abduction of Camarena*, 198?), a sensationalist treatment of the infamous case of the American drug agent murdered in Guadalajara by drug dealers with alleged collaboration by corrupt police officers; an incident that strained United States-Mexican relations; *Rosa de la frontera* (*Rose of the Border*, 1985); sex comedies relating to certain professions, e.g., *Un macho en el salón de belleza* (*A Man in the Hairdressing Salon*, 1987); *Los mecánicos ardientes* (*The Passionate Mechanics*, 1987), and on and on.

One strategy being employed by some Mexican producers is to make films in English, not only to penetrate English-speaking markets (especially the United States), but also to win back Mexican middle-class viewers. One interesting effort along these lines was *Gaby* (1987), the story of a Jewish European refugee who arrived in Mexico as a child. Directed by a Mexican, Luis Malroki, and starring Liv Ullmann as the adult Gaby and Norma Leandro, the Argentine actress who starred in *La historia oficial* (*The Official Story*, 1986), as Gaby's Indian nanny. What is evident from the casting is that such films seem to provide few important roles for Mexican actors simply because very few, if any, are internationally recognized names. Nonetheless, Luciana Cabarga, the film's executive producer, insisted that *Gaby* "is a Mexican film because Mexican money was involved."[34] However, according to Juan López Moctezuma, even though "it was shot in Mexico by a Mexican director, it was done with North American money, but didn't find an audience." In his own effort to tap the most responsive segment of the complex and elusive American market, López Moctezuma in 1987 completed *Welcome María,* coproduced with Mario Moreno, Jr. and starring María Victoria. Bilingual and shot in the streets of Los Angeles, it is about María coming to the United States to find her wetback husband who has stopped writing and sending her money.[35]

Coproductions with the Soviet Union continued, in spite of the resounding failure of *Campanas rojas*. Sergio Olhovich wrote and directed *Esperanza* (*Hope*, 1987), the story of a Russian youth who emigrates to Mexico during a period when both countries are experiencing revolutionary upheaval. *Esperanza* took eight weeks of shooting in Mexico and fourteen in the U.S.S.R. Early reports indicated the film was promising; it was entered in the Rio de Janeiro and Havana film festivals.[36]

A particularly violent genre of recent vintage is the "punk" action movies inspired by foreign models, especially the Australian "Mad Max" films. In *Siete en la mira II: La furia de la venganza* (*Seven in the Rifle Sight II: The Fury of Revenge*, 1986), a bizarre gang of long-haired punks roams a contemporary Mexican countryside seeking a lawman who had killed the gang chief's brother (who rides his motorcycle down from his luxurious Denver home to reassume leadership of his old gang; the source of his wealth is never explained although drug trafficking is likely); they utilize an odd assortment of vehicles, including a pink Cadillac convertible of 1960s vintage. They take over a town in the manner of *The Wild One*, with the difference that they bloodily massacre police and townspeople. Films of this type are a specialty of Producciones Galindo (Pedro Galindo III and Jesús A. Galindo).[37]

This type of movie angers Blanca Guerra, an actress "who is forced to straddle the two extremes of Mexican cinema." She describes her reaction every time she visits the United States: "I see the movie posters at the Spanish-language theaters, showing Mexican films, and I realize that there's literally zero respect for the Mexican audience. I think they would go see better films if better films were offered. This is my long-standing complaint with the producers. The least we can expect is that the films have quality, which they usually don't."[38]

Blanca Guerra appeared in *Nocaut* and in Arturo Ripstein's *El imperio de la fortuna* (*Empire of Fortune*, 1986), the latter a three-hour-and-forty-minute remake of Roberto Gavaldón's *El gallo de oro* (*The Golden Cock*, 1964). One of the major productions of the late 1980s, it is based on a story by Juan Rulfo. Dionisio Pinzón (Ernesto Gómez Cruz) is a humble news hawker in a provincial town. As the film opens, he is announcing that evening's movie (*Santo vs. el Espectro*, or *Santo versus the Specter*) and a lost cow belonging to the church. That night at a fair, Dionisio witnesses a cock fight; taking pity on the losing rooster, he convinces the owner not to kill the badly wounded creature but to give it to him. Dionisio takes the bird home and nurses it back to health by burying it up to its neck—so preoccupied is he with the animal all night that he does not notice his mother dying of a heart attack. In the morning, he discovers her body on the floor of their ramshackle house. Poignant scenes follow of Dionisio dragging around his mother's corpse wrapped in wood and straw fruitlessly trying to raise money for her burial. He finally buries her in a cornfield. In such scenes does Ripstein provide glimpses of the stark poverty of some rural villages. Wryly, he shows the consequences: Dionisio returning the lost cow to the priest who, instead of a cash reward, blesses him without taking his eyes off a television program. In another scene, the priest announces at mass that he's rented out the church during the fair; then we see gaming tables set up in the parish and the pulpit converted to a lighted stage—from which an untalented singer, "La Caponera" (Blanca Guerra), does painfully bad interpretations of popular songs.

Dionisio's rooster recovers and goes on to win a few fights, enough to catch the attention of Lorenzo Benavídez (Alejandro Parodi), a successful breeder, who is

Blanca Guerra and Ernesto Gómez Cruz in Arturo Ripstein's *El imperio de la fortuna*. (Estudio Cinematográfico América)

also La Caponera's lover. Dionisio's rooster is finally killed and he buries the bird in a cemetery (in contrast with his mother). He goes to work for Benavídez picking and training roosters. Benavídez, in turn, teaches Dionisio how to play cards. By this time, Dionisio is relatively affluent so he buys a coffin and hires a man to carry it around for him in his village to show off his new prosperity. Unfortunately he is unable to locate his mother's burial place. Dionisio runs into La Caponera who has left Benavídez; she's impressed by Dionisio's prosperous appearance. They marry and in time a baby girl is born. They return to Benavídez's hacienda and Dionisio challenges his erstwhile employer and teacher to a card game in which the latter loses everything, including his house. From this point, Dionisio enjoys his greatest success which he believes is due to La Caponera who he insists must be at his side during his all-night gambling sessions. Dionisio's obsession changes him—he treats his wife harshly, as an object, a good-luck charm. She flees with their now teenage daughter, "La Pinzona" (Zaide Silva Gutiérrez), and tries to rejoin her old troupe, but they have a new—and equally untalented—singer. La Caponera offers them her daughter but the girl is just as bad. The two women return to Dionisio's house. During a gambling session, he loses everything, including the house; La Caponera dies in a corner of the room where Dionisio still keeps the coffin he had bought for his mother years before. He goes off to another room and puts a bullet through his head. The last

Blanca Guerra in *El imperio de la fortuna* (IMCINE)

scene shows La Pinzona doing an off-key rendition of a song at another dreary rural fair.

Ripstein seemed to have fallen into a decline after his principal works, *Tiempo de morir* (*A Time to Die*, 1965), *El castillo de la pureza* (1972), *El Santo Oficio* (*The Holy Office*, 1973), *El lugar sin límites* (*The Place Without Limits*, 1977), *La viuda negra* (*The Black Widow*, 1977), and *Cadena perpétua* (*Vicious Circle*, 1978), followed by disappointing efforts like *La seducción* (*The Seduction*, 1979), *Rastro de muerte* (*Trace of Death*, 1981) and *El otro* (*The Other*, 1984).[39] "In Mexico there is no such thing as a cinematic career," said Ripstein. "For one to exist it would be necessary to make forty to fifty films as in the past, and of those ten should be exceptional. At the present time, we can only expect to make four or five films, which eliminates the possibility of a career."[40]

*El imperio de la fortuna* marked a revitalization of Ripstein's talent, and a return to his thematic constant—"the tragic framework, the trajectory of the main character toward an ineluctable destiny which we share as witnesses . . ." Dionisio sets in motion the plot's dramatic structure: a man to whom the power represented by money disturbs his primitive simplicity converting it into a pride and arrogance that destroy those around him.[41]

Felipe Cazals is another director who made a number of important films in the 1970s—*Canoa*, *El apando* (both 1975), *Las Poquiánchis* (1976)—who was obliged to retreat from the politically and socially oriented cinema he favored. A flawed yet highly significant film made early during the López Portillo period was *El año de la peste* (*Year of the Plague*, 1978), in which Cazals deals with the political and economic consequences of an ecological disaster. Freely adapted from Daniel Defoe's *Diary of a Plague Year*, Cazals's film unfolds in a large, unidentified city (though it is obviously Mexico City). A mysterious ailment appears among the population, initially as a bronchial infection among children. A courageous doctor wants to issue a public warning but he is vetoed by the hospital administrator and city and federal authorities who want to avert a panic, particularly so as not to discourage investment and scare away tourists. With the connivance of the media, the plague is covered up; municipal garbage trucks collect the dead at night and dispose of the bodies in mass burial sites (a modern version of the way in which the dead were collected during medieval pestilences). Some prophetic touches to the film are its warnings of the disastrous ecological consequences of pollution and unrestricted urban growth—especially vis-à-vis Mexico City. At one point in the film, the authorities extend the school winter vacations to minimize the spread of contagion, a step that was actually taken in January 1989 in Mexico City in an attempt to reduce pollution levels.

The plague disappears as mysteriously as it appeared and the authorities issue their official finding: the illness was caused by a stock of toothpaste illegally sold after its expiration date—a touch of Cazals's irony. *El año de la peste* is also significant in that it is the only science-fiction film made in Mexico to date (Santo movies in which he battles invaders from outer space are *not* science-fiction). Cazals was unhappy with the film because, first, it was made in the América studios which at the time were technically inferior to the Churubusco facilities and, second, due to union problems he was forced to start filming anew after two weeks with an entirely new cast.[42]

In the next few years Cazals was obliged to make purely commercial vehicles. In 1982, however, he returned to making films of social and political content with the highly praised *Bajo la metralla* (*Under Fire*, 1982). In 1985, he returned to the documentary style he had employed so successfully in *Canoa* with *Los motivos de Luz* (*Luz's Motives*). Based on a real-life incident, the film analyzes the life of Luz (Patricia Reyes Spindola), a slum-dweller who has strangled her four children. At the beginning of the film, Luz is being interrogated by an off-camera male voice; she remembers nothing of her children's deaths, in fact she thinks that her boyfriend Sebastián (Alonso Echanove) and his mother (Ana Ofelia Murguía) are responsible because the latter hated Luz.

A lawyer (Martha Aura) and a psychologist (Delia Casanova) take an interest in Luz's case. What they discover is that Luz is a product of an environment of poverty in which women are abused and exploited. As a girl in her village, she had been seduced by the priest; later she moved to Mexico City where she had a baby by the chauffeur in the house where she worked as a servant; afterward she lived with a policeman who beat her and gave her three more sons. Finally she meets Sebastián during a land takeover action by activists. She becomes obsessed with him to the point of resenting her own children—at one point her oldest boy

Patricia Reyes Spindola and Alonso Echanove in *Los motivos de Luz*, written and directed by Felipe Cazals. (Estudio Cinematográfico América)

interrupts Luz while she's trying to have sex with Sebastián; she becomes furious and beats the boy.

Is Luz retarded? (She has visions and hears voices.) Or is she a product of her brutal environment? The psychologist concludes that Luz does not fit the psychological and social profiles of classical theory as developed in Europe and the United States—she decides that Luz lives in a different reality from the rest of us and withdraws from the case. In sum, "the story of Luz is as tragic as that of millions of Mexican women, condemned to subordination, ignorance, and religious fanaticism by a male-dominated society in which the male is worshipped like a god."[43]

In *El tres de copas* (*Three of Hearts*, 1986), Felipe Cazals completely changes pace in relating the story of two drifters and soldiers of fortune who are "closer than brothers," Pedro (Alejandro Camacho) and Damián (Humberto Zurita), sons of Irishmen from the San Patricio Battalion during the United States-Mexican War. They are ex-guerrilla fighters in Benito Juárez's forces that have been resisting the French-supported regime of Maximilian. On their way back to Nochistlán, they stop off at the Lagos de Moreno fair where they meet a gambler accompanied by his beautiful young mistress Casilda (Gabriela Roel). Both fall in love with her but it is Damián who wins Casilda in a card game and presents her to Pedro. They all return to Nochistlán where they start a successful business. However, Damián is obsessed by his passion for Casilda. He spends his time gambling and one day kills a man who mocks him about the woman. Soon after Casilda leaves town with all their money. The dead man's relatives, the Sánchez clan, attempt to avenge him, but Pedro and Damián kill several of them in a shootout and hurriedly leave town.

They encounter a band of highwaymen, also veterans of the war, led by Cipriano Melquisidor (Pedro Armendáriz, Jr.) and join them. When Pedro and Damián discover a buried cache of Winchester rifles hidden during the war against the French, they double-cross Cipriano and run off with the arms. In a whorehouse, they encounter Casilda, but this time she offers herself to Damián whereupon they run off together after a fight with Cipriano in which they shoot out his eye. Casilda once more robs Pedro and Damián and escapes. When they return to Nochistlán, they find Casilda living in their house and running the business. Pedro and Damián sell the property to an ambitious neighbor, Ponciano Méndez (Enrique Lucero), including Casilda's share. Furious, she tries to provoke a fight between Pedro and Damián. However, she is shot in the leg during the altercation, and as Pedro and Damián ride off they are ambushed by the surviving Sánchez brothers. Pedro dies in the fight, and a badly wounded Damián rides back into town where a Sánchez widow kills him with a pair of sewing scissors. The film ends with Casilda marrying Ponciano; she lived a long life, the narrator tells us, and left everything to her twin sons, Pedro and Damián, who became important figures in the region.

*Tres de copas*, unlike most of Cazals's work, is a funny film. He intimates that some of Mexico's most respectable families had similar disreputable beginnings. The narrator (José Carlos Ruiz) is a 1930s *campesino*, presumably an employee of Casilda's sons, Pedro and Damián, but he constantly intrudes into scenes he is narrating; for instance, in the whorehouse scene he comes through a door and bumps into Cipriano. In the final scene where a pregnant Casilda and Ponciano are walking away from the camera, when the narrator says that the twins are not Ponciano's, the latter angrily shuts the gate on the narrator. Zurita and Camacho dress alike in attire reminiscent of Clint Eastwood in a Sergio Leone spaghetti western; they maintain dead-pan expressions most of the time. They don't act their roles, rather they model their way through the film. Only Pedro Armendáriz turns in a lusty, spirited performance. Another joke by Cazals is the unexplained presence of a boy in twentieth century attire; when the Sánchez brothers assault Pedro and Damián, it is this boy who shoots down the remaining ones before they can kill Damián. Is it perhaps his grandson who moves through time to try to save his ancestor? Cazals offers no explanation; the boy's presence is simply an amusing incongruity. And of course, when Damián rides by the woman who is calmly crocheting, she suddenly leaps up and kills him with her sewing scissors. In addition, the film is beautifully photographed by Angel Goded (who also shot *Frida*) on location in Tres Marías just outside Mexico City.

Cazals's next film was *La furia de un dios (Lo del César) (The Fury of a God [Render Unto Caesar]*, 1987), as different from *Tres de copas* as the latter was from *Los motivos de Luz*. The screenplay was adapted by Tomás Pérez Turrent

Alejandro Camacho and Humberto Zurita in Cazals's *El tres de copas*. (Estudio Cinematográfico América)

Felipe Cazals (center) directing Alejandro Camacho and Humberto Zurita in *El tres de copas* (IMCINE)

Gabriela Roel and Humberto Zurita in *El tres de copas* (IMCINE)

from the Albert Camus story, *Caligula*, but here the power-mad and sex-obsessed Roman emperor becomes a ruthless capitalist, Claudio O'Reilly (Humberto Zurita), who inherits an important fish-processing company. He is obsessed with dominating others, economically and sexually (it is suggested that Claudio had incestuous relations with his sister who has died prior to the events of the film).

Claudio tries to break a fishermen's cooperative with the connivance of a federal bureaucrat (Fernando Balzaretti), and monopolize the fishing industry in that part of the country. He berates his board of directors and business partners, characterizing them as weak, greedy fools who leave their money "invested safely in Houston banks and condos in Florida." But Claudio is slipping steadily into madness as he accrues more power; finally the directors arrange to have him murdered and, with the assistance of a corrupt police chief, frame the two leaders of the fishing cooperative with the murder. Again, Angel Goded's masterful photography renders the Yucatán settings in brilliant tones for this tale of corruption among the powerful. *La furia de un dios* was coproduced with Spain's TVE (Televisión Española) which explains the presence of the Spanish actress, Assumpta Serna, in the role of Cecilia, Claudio's wife.

Certainly Felipe Cazals is one of the most creative and interesting Mexican directors working today. He is preoccupied with expanding the thematic possibilities of his country's cinema, as have been other directors, but he seems to be the filmmaker most intent on offering in each of his films "A story totally different from the previous one, and much less with any resemblance to the tired old formulas."[44]

A scene from Felipe Cazals's *La furia de un dios*. (Estudio Cinematográfico América)

On August 6, 1986, Emilio "El Indio" Fernández died of heart failure at the age of 82. The foremost exponent of a nationalist and "Indianist" genre, Fernández was Mexico's most internationally known and honored director (as noted above, Luis Buñuel, was not really a Mexican director). At the time of his physical death, Fernández had been cinematically dead for three decades, since his nationalistic message formed in the postrevolutionary era of the 1940s was considered anachronistic by the younger generation and therefore devoid of commercial possibilities. In recent years, his economic situation worsened to the extent that he was forced to accept small roles in films like *Lola la trailera* (as a narcotics cop) and as a villain in *telenovelas* like "La traición" ("The Betrayal"), in addition to the roles given him by American friends like Sam Peckinpah *(The Wild Bunch, Bring Me the Head of Alfredo Garcia)* and John Huston *(Under the Volcano)*. Fernández's legend surpassed the reality and he was its most fervent believer—a cultured, dynamic, yet crude and violent personality, he was a proud and unique man "...unable to adapt to changing times, preferring to die faithful to his ideals, always expecting to direct 'one more great film,' something he never achieved."[45]

But the "golden age" that Fernández personified was just that—a period in the past that came about from the particular historical and social conditions of the time. Mexico in the 1980s was a totally different society with a dynamic, growing population ever more exposed to international currents in culture, technology, economics, and politics. Its people faced a severe economic crisis which also posed additional challenges because the winds of change were blowing through the country's anachronistic political and economic structure. The PRI's formula for economic development and social stability, which had served it and the country well enough for forty years, was foundering.

The population of Mexico City was approaching 20 million— the largest city in the world—and projections placed its growth, if present trends continued, at 32 million by the year 2000. It was also the most polluted city in the world, with serious consequences for the health of its residents as Cazals's 1978 film *El año de la peste* grimly foretold—an ecological disaster waiting to happen. And as if this were not enough misfortune, a disastrous earthquake struck the sprawling metropolis in October 1985, causing a still undetermined number of deaths (the official count was about seven thousand; many residents scoff at this figure, insisting the tally was much higher) and billions of dollars in reconstruction costs. The collapse of the oil boom plunged Mexico into an economic depression that it still had not overcome on the eve of the decade of the 1990s. Yet in response to these and other pressures the government was taking the first, tentative steps to modernize the economy and diminish dependence on oil exports. In response to public outcry, the authorities were beginning to deal with Mexico City's pollution, although a satisfactory solution is distant. In July 1988 Mexicans went to the polls to elect a new president after the most dramatic campaign in post-revolutionary history; two strong opposition challengers ran energetically against the PRI candidate, Carlos Salinas de Gortari, who finally won with barely 51 percent of the vote.[46]

The runner-up was Cuauhtémoc Cárdenas, candidate of the FDN (Frente Democrático Nacional—a coalition of leftist parties), PRI-renegade, and son of the revered Lázaro Cárdenas; the other candidate was Manuel Clouthier of the conservative PAN (Partido Acción Nacional).

One 1987 film that tried to deal with contemporary problems of economic crisis, corruption, pollution, and terrorism was Alejandro Pelayo's *Días difíciles (Difficult Days)*. The setting is Ciudad Leyva, a fictional city in the north (the film was shot on location in the city of Chihuahua). The Castelar family controls the region's most powerful industrial holding company, but their firms are grappling with the financial problems besetting the country as a whole. In addition, one of their still profitable operations, a chemical plant, accidentally releases a cloud of toxic gas that drifts over to a nearby school, necessitating the hospitalization of many children and the evacuation of nearby neighborhoods. Now the Castelar family faces the wrath of the citizens, many of whom are their employees. The labor union demands that pollution-control devices be installed in the plant, a step that the firm is reluctant to take because of the cost involved and the negative effect it would have on the plant's profitability.

Complications mount. The Castelar brothers, Edmundo (Alejandro Parodi) and Ricardo (Fernando Balzaretti), assume management of the firm after the death of their father (the film begins with his funeral) but disagree on how to approach their myriad problems. Edmundo favors a conciliatory approach while Ricardo, pushed on by the hard-line Ezequiel Rodríguez (Luis Manuel Pelayo, the director's father), who heads the association of industrialists, opposes any conces-

The opening scene from Alejandro Pelayo's *Días difíciles*. To the priest's left is Alejandro Parodi. Right to left, Blanca Guerra and Fernando Balzaretti, (Alejandro Pelayo).

sions. Demonstrations break out and a strike is called at the plant. The federal government becomes involved—a senator proposes legislation to force a cleanup of the Castelar plant. In the midst of all this, Edmundo is kidnapped one afternoon. The family endures days of anxiety as they await the kidnappers' demands. Ricardo, now temporarily heading the enterprise, at the urging of Ezequiel refuses to pay ransom. Edmundo's wife, Luisa (Blanca Guerra), goes on television to plead with the kidnappers that they contact her directly; Ricardo, however, calls the station to say that Luisa has no authority to deal with the kidnappers. This in effect seals Edmundo's fate; the kidnappers uncover their faces to him (one is a Castelar employee), thereby passing a death sentence on him. The film ends as it began, with a funeral—this time Edmundo's. But now the family is irrevocably split—Luisa takes her children and leaves Ciudad Leyva abandoning Castelar industries to an uncertain future.

*Días difíciles* was Pelayo's second film in a trilogy that has as its overall theme the problem of *cacicazgo*—political and/or economic bossism. The first in the trilogy (and his first film) was *La víspera* (*The Prelude*, 1982) about an ex-government minister who has been waiting twelve years for another appointment. As a new government is being inaugurated, he waits for the call that never comes. In

Another scene from *Días difíciles*. (Alejandro Pelayo)

post-production as of February 1989 was the third in the trilogy, *Morir en el golfo (To Die in the Gulf)*—an alternate title also under consideration was *Muertes fértiles (Fertile Deaths)*—about a powerful rural landowner.

Other noteworthy films released in 1987 were Servando González's *El último túnel (The Last Tunnel)*, Luis Alcoriza's *Lo que importa es vivir (Living is What Matters)*, and Alberto Isaac's *Mariana, Mariana,* the last two "worthy of being taken seriously," according to Juan López Moctezuma.[47]

*El último túnel* is a rather standard story of father-son conflict, but set in the spectacular Tarahumara country of Chihuahua and dealing with Mexican social complexities. It is also a fictionalized account of the construction of the railroad that connects Chihuahua City with Los Mochis on the Pacific coast and crosses the Sierra Madre Occidental in which the Barranca del Cobre (Copper Canyon) is located. Manuel Iglesias (David Reynoso) is a hard-working, hard-driving railroad construction foreman whose son, Julián (Gerardo Zepeda), has just received an engineering degree. Manuel is called upon to oversee the laying of the rails connecting the mountains with the sea—the last segment of the Chihuahua-al-Pacifico railroad. He looks forward to having Julián work at his side but the young man is not pleased at the prospect; he prefers to stay in Mexico City and open a night club with his friends. Another interesting plot element that is never

David Reynoso (right) in Servando González's *El último túnel*. (Estudio Cinematográfico América)

developed is that Julián is not Manuel's natural son; not only is he adopted but he is also a Tarahumara Indian. Although Julián seems anxious to deny his background, he speaks fluent Tarahumaran (unusual in that he was raised by a non-Indian father, but he might have grown up in the Tarahumara mountains thus maintaining cultural links with his people—again, a loose end in a vital part of the plot that would do much to explain the relationship between father and son). In any event, Manuel forces Julián to sign on as a construction engineer for the railroad. The work crews come in contact with the Tarahumaras who live in the region (in fact, two work for Manuel). This leads to Julián being smitten by Anarica (Holda Ramírez), a beautiful young Tarahumaran girl, whom he seduces and impregnates but refuses to marry. When Manuel learns of this, he protects and helps her at childbirth. In the meantime, two work teams have been formed: one, with Manuel in charge, to complete the line through the mountains, and the other under Julián's supervision to lay track through the desert, with both lines to meet at the "last tunnel" before the sea. When Manuel's team is trapped in a cave-in, Julián takes charge of the rescue effort. Predictably, Julián reaches his father in time to effect a reconciliation; he agrees to marry Anarica, thus openly accepting his Indian roots which he had been denying since his student days in Mexico City. *El último túnel* does raise some potentially fascinating issues dealing with assimilation; unfortunately, the film never picks up on these topics but prefers instead a melodramatic solution to the conflict between Manuel and Julián. The Tarahumara characters are stereotyped "wise" Indians straight out of stock Hollywood westerns, and shed no light on the complex relations between these reclu-

Gerardo Zepeda and Holda Ramírez in *El último túnel* (IMCINE)

sive, shy people and the Mexican population that ever more encroaches on their mountain domains. The railroad itself is a dramatic metaphor for the end of centuries of self-imposed isolation, first from the Spanish and then from the Mexican authorities.[48]

Luis Alcoriza's *Lo que importa es vivir* is a well-made film about Candelario (Gonzalo Vega), a handsome young drifter who arrives at a run-down hacienda asking for room and board in exchange for work. The owner, *don* Lázaro (Ernesto Gómez Cruz), is wary of Candelario at first, but eventually the charismatic young man wins his boss's confidence by advising him on improved techniques for taking care of the livestock and working the land. Soon the hacienda is enjoying an unaccustomed prosperity, just as *don* Lázaro's wife Chabela (María Rojo) breaks out of the dullness of her isolated, rural life by initiating an affair with the handsome Candelario. Other ranchers become frightened at the "progressive" ideas that Candelario is imparting to the peasants and insinuate to *don* Lázaro that his wife is cheating on him. When he rushes out, rifle in hand, to kill Candelario, *don*

Gonzalo Vega and Ernesto Gómez Cruz in Luis Alcoriza's *Lo que importa es vivir* (IMCINE)

Lázaro accidentally falls down a cliff, suffering a head injury which leaves him brain-damaged. Eventually Chabela gives birth to Candelario's son, and she and Candelario, who is now running the hacienda, raise their baby and *don* Lázaro as if they were brothers (due to his injury, Lázaro has to be taught everything again, like a child). The film's most charming scenes are those where *don* Lázaro and his "brother" stand contrite while Candelario chastises them for some youthful transgression. When *don* Lázaro is killed in an accident, Candelario demonstrates sincere grief at the funeral. *Don* Lázaro's death leaves the way open for Candelario and Chabela to marry and acceptance by the town's society. However, Candelario balks at the structured, restraining life that marriage and "respectability" portend, especially having to deal with people who not long before had resented and humiliated him and now look upon him as a potential political and economic asset. While Chabela is in town enjoying a party in their honor, Candelario abandons the ranch with their son "to see the sea," promising to return the boy safely some day.

*Mariana, Mariana,* directed by Alberto Isaac who took over after José Estrada's untimely death, is an evocative piece about first love and coming of age in a Mexico City very different from the polluted megalopolis of today. At a funeral Carlos (Pedro Armendáriz, Jr.) meets Rosales, whom he has not seen in many years. On the drive back they reminisce about their school days in the 1940s. The film then becomes a long flashback centering around Carlitos (Luis Mario

Elizabeth Aguilar and Luis Mario Quiroz in Alberto Isaac's *Mariana, Mariana*. (Estudio Cinematográfico América)

Quiroz) and his infatuation with his best friend Jim's mother, Mariana (Elizabeth Aguilar). It is also about his own family, dominated by his mother (Saby Kamalich), a woman constantly concerned about morals and etiquette who has to cope with Carlitos's older brother's sexual escapades and her husband's extramarital affairs. But Mariana becomes an obsession for him, until one day he runs away from school to declare his love for her; she gently explains the impossibility of his love and gives him his very chaste, first kiss. In the meantime, Rosales has tattled on Carlitos to the school principal, who goes to his home to tell his mother. Aghast, his parents send him to a psychiatrist (actually two, who spout Freudian babblings and end up arguing with each other), then a priest, and finally oblige him to change schools. Carlitos loses contact with Jim and Mariana, and later he hears from Rosales that she had committed suicide. Mariana was the mistress of an important politician, and after she denounced a group of his corrupt friends at a party, she and her protector fought bitterly after which she killed herself. The bittersweet memory still haunts the adult Carlos even though Rosales insists that those times belong in the past. Carlos agrees, even though he thinks that just as he and Rosales exist now, so did Mariana and Jim, intensely for him.

Angel Goded's photography enhances Isaac's nostalgic recreation of a Mexico that is also very much in the past. The scenes in the school are of interest for the class differences they demonstrate. The school was obviously a rather exclusive private institution whose student body came from upper-middle-class families.

Apparently in response to the social and political milieu of the time, a few mestizo and Indian students had been admitted on scholarships, Rosales among them. When they are the objects of some mild racial epithets, the teacher explains to the *ninōs bien* ("privileged" or "socially advantaged"), Carlitos and Jim, why it is wrong to harbor such feelings. Otherwise, *Mariana, Mariana* is not socially meaningful; it is principally a nostalgic evocation of a lost childhood and the first manifestations of puberty.

Other noteworthy recent films are *Thanatos* (1984) and *Polvo de luz* (*Dust of Light*, 1988) by another new director, Cristián González, who was appointed in January 1989 as head of the Subdirección de Autorizaciones (censorship office) of the Dirección de Cinematografía—in itself an unusual step since never before had a filmmaker been placed in charge of that critical office.

González, who entered CUEC at the age of 20 (and left it a year later), spent three years writing *Thanatos*. The story is based on an escape artist named Sobec who was popular on "Siempre en Domingo." González changed the character to a woman, a divorced mother who runs a pastry shop with her partner, another single woman. She is discovered by a television producer whose career is threatened by low ratings; he names her Thanatos, symbolizing death in Greek mythology, and puts her on television where she becomes a huge hit. However, in her final escape routine she disappears inexplicably. The film, which was produced by STPC, was, in González's words, "more of a teenager picture, of the imagination—in it I wanted to express everything I knew about making a movie." *Thanatos*, while interesting, does not succeed as either a fantasy or a parody, but it must have been a valuable exercise for González, because his second film, *Polvo de luz*, is an impressive achievement.

The film has just three characters, none of whom are given names. A young married couple, Alejandro Camacho and Rebecca Jones (married in real life), arrive by motorboat (the boatman is Agustín Yáñez, who doesn't utter a word in the entire film) at a breathtakingly beautiful island, the setting for an attractive home. (The interiors were filmed in Emilio Fernández's home in Coyoacán; the exteriors at Lake Valsequillo in the State of Puebla.) We soon learn that the man is dying of an incurable disease and the couple have gone to this lovely, isolated spot to spend their last days together. She is an artist and he is a filmmaker, intending to record the remaining days of his life. The deep love he has for his wife causes him anguish when he reflects on the unfairness of his early death, and he lashes out in despair at her in apparent cruelty. Idyllic happiness is punctuated by moments of bitterness until death finally comes and he is put to rest in the lake that surrounds the house.

*Polvo de luz* is characterized by slow pacing and scenes of great beauty. It was shot by Jośe Ortiz Ramos, a veteran cinematographer (*Nosotros los pobres, Ustedes los ricos*) and the haunting music score, played by a cello, was written by Emiliano Marentes Martínez, a young composer. The film was shot in three and a half weeks for $150,000 (*Thanatos* took nine weeks and cost $50,000).

González's views on his own work are illuminating: "The critics don't like me—they say I'm not Mexican. Somebody told me that *Thanatos* was a cold film because I didn't show feeling but I think it had some good things about Mexican mythology; in *Polvo de luz* I tried to change my technique. I wanted to deal with loneliness and tenderness. I learned while doing it—making a film is a magic thing. One can have the best camera and photographer, but the magic moment cannot be repeated. I don't know if it's a good film, but it is unique. I had to work with feelings, so I didn't improvise too much. I discussed the scenes with the actors, and they expressed their views. The crew is also making the same picture and they are very sensitive to how the shooting is progressing. At the end of the first week they were very happy—in fact they continued working even though I was unable to pay them that week's salary."

González's views are typical of Mexico's young filmmakers, perhaps imbued with greater significance in view of the crucial position that he holds in the State film bureaucracy. He is concerned with recapturing the Mexican middle-class audience and he feels that the "only solution is to make movies in English, with American actors" because that is what these viewers are accustomed to seeing. On commercial films: "These films touch the real feelings of people who can't afford other types of entertainment. They have no access to culture, these are people who can't read, who don't wear shoes. They watch movies about violence, drugs, sex comedies—80 percent of Mexican movies are like this. If a woman is not a prostitute, she's being raped, or willing to have sex on the spur of the moment. Our policy is to try to influence the commercial producers to return to family entertainment."[49]

González's comments point up the dilemma of Mexican cinema. From the 1930s through the 1950s, the middle class went to see Mexican films and the generally higher caliber of motion pictures made in that era reflected in part the more elevated culture of their audiences. The deterioration in quality of Mexican films beginning in the late 1950s coincided with the loss of this audience. At that time also Mexican middle-class audiences were discovering an improved Hollywood product and more innovative European films. For whatever the myriad contributory reasons—the death and retirement of the the great stars, the change in government policies every six years, a basic cultural transformation of Mexican society (e.g., the youth could not relate to film themes of the 1940s and 1950s and looked to foreign models), economic realities of moviemaking—the commercial product markedly declined in quality. Most quality films of today are State-supported and made for a tiny minority of the intellectual class who attend films by Cazals, Ripstein, Alcoriza, Isaac, and others.

Alejandro Pelayo also addressed these issues, but foresaw a brighter future for Mexican cinema:

I'm very optimistic—for the first time in our history there are three generations of film-makers, each one with something different to say with its own style. Alcoriza is the last of the directors who began their careers in the 1960s, but the CONACINE directors—Cazals, Ripstein, Leduc, Fernández Violante [*Amor nocturno que te vas* (*Evening Love That Fades Away*, 1987)]—who started in the 1970s are all still quite active. Then there's the group ranging from thirty to forty years old—Diego López, Alberto Cortés, myself, Busi Cortés

[*El secreto de Romelia* (*Romelia's Secret*, 1988)]. We generally work through producers' cooperatives, in which we own the films we make. And finally there's an under-thirty group, people who entered the business about ten years ago. Among these are Luis Estrada, son of the late José Estrada, and María Novarro, who has just completed a film, *Lola*, about women which has nothing in common with any previous feminine or feminist cinema.

I'm speaking of Mexican quality cinema, not the other kind. For the latter, it is a problem of demand—while it exists, it'll continue to be made. But as far as quality cinema is concerned, I'm optimistic because a Council for Culture and the Arts has just been formed [January 1989], under the Ministry of Education, which will encompass the cinema for the first time. It will have the same status as the Institute of Fine Arts [Bellas Artes] and the Anthropological Institute. With this development, Mexico will finally have a cultural policy, which we've never had before. With this new organization, I think about ten to twelve quality films a year will be produced, and of these, three or four might be extraordinary, another three of good quality, and the rest less so. Coproducing will figure prominently— for instance Spain's national television network is strongly supporting Mexican and other Latin American cinema.

"The problem is that I can exhibit a film like *Días difíciles*, but the public doesn't go to see it. It's not a problem of exhibition, because my film was premiered in five theaters. The public is simply not interested in the theme. There are two kinds of viewers: the mass working-class public that goes to see comedies, action, violence, drug smugglers. It coincides somewhat with the undocumented Mexicans in the United States, among whom the most popular stars are La India María and the Almada brothers. The middle-class public, to which my movie is directed, doesn't come—they prefer to see *Rambo* and other American movies. Thus we have a serious problem, we don't have a public. And if a film doesn't reach a weekly *tope*, a minimum number of ticket sales, then it's withdrawn. Our only hope then is to try to break even in the art circuit, like the Cineteca theaters. That's why official support is very important—the role of IMCINE and the public television channel in promoting our films on television, radio, and in the press. It happened once, under Echeverria —I remember seeing *Canoa* in packed movie houses.

Pelayo also stressed the importance of international promotion, with a strong Mexican presence at film festivals. The Argentine and Brazilian cinemas have established a foothold in the United States and European art house circuits which is the market that Pelayo thinks that Mexican filmmakers should set their sights on. "We'll never have a mass public as long as our pictures are in Spanish, but we want that 'art house' public. I'm optimistic that we'll arrive in the decade of the 1990s because we'll have the cinematic product that'll enable us to reach out to an international public. For a film industry to have this appeal, it has to be profoundly national, like *Babette's Feast*. The only quality Mexican film that's been successful internationally in the last fifty years has been *Frida*. The film has its flaws, it's really just a series of sketches—but it is uniquely Mexican. Even though Mexico is one of the few countries in which really cheap films can be still be made, we still cannot recover our production costs domestically, so we have to export. And we're talking about production costs of $150,000 to $300,000, not millions of dollars. We're experimenting with novel production arrangements—cooperatives, coproductions, television, videocassettes, cable, satellite transmission. In coming years the Argentine and Brazilian cinemas will undergo crises due to inflation and unsettled politics; they don't have younger generations of directors to replace the current ones. And much of their best talent emigrates, to Europe, the United

States, and even to Mexico. So, I'm optimistic—I think all of these factors will come together by the middle 1990s, and Mexican cinema will be once again, as it was in the 1940s and the 1970s, the predominant one in Latin America."[50]

Another view, more representative of the filmmakers from the "middle generation," is expressed by Felipe Cazals:

Predictions are difficult because the future is complex. There is a generational problem because the young directors who are on their way up also have a right to their space. Since the economic space of Mexican filmmaking is very small, the picture for me is very problematic. This is the moment in my professional life in which I best know my craft. Thus I see many complications. My projects, as always, are many—although not one is yet finalized. At present, deciding on a film project is much more difficult for me. I think more about it—much more than in the past. I'm more self-critical now. At the same time, the economic circumstances surrounding film production are much more adverse. One can count on less money, fewer facilities.

Mexican cinema has lost much ground. The situation is most worrisome. We are in a period of reorganization being initiated with a certain amount of good will. But cinema is much more than good will—it needs a lot of support and enthusiasm. To make films, or to help in the making of films, is very difficult from the State's viewpoint. It needs faith and a willingness to spend. There is no norm of action because talent is the only limitation, there's no other. One has to act in good faith, there must be trust, a willingness to take chances. No one can write a predetermined novel, or paint a predetermined picture— similarly one cannot make film 'X' because, on that basis, no creativity is possible. And in Mexico, the film industry is not a priority—well, it is from a cultural point of view. But given the current priorities in this country, cinema is not among the most important.

Therefore the future is very uncertain. I wish I were an incurable optimist. But unfortunately I've been in this business too many years and I know that there is no cinema possible without a constant struggle—one must struggle every day, as if it were the first day. But the moment comes when one is overtaken by fatigue. But I can agree with Pelayo that there is a continuity, that there will be new filmmakers and that Mexican cinema will always exist. But what I would want is an informative and assertive cinema, especially outside of Mexico.[51]

The views set forth by González, Pelayo, and Cazals are generally representative of the majority of serious Mexican filmmakers; such concerns, however, are not shared by the commercial producers who feel that "quality" cinema is a luxury they cannot afford and therefore should be the financial responsibility of the State.

Ignacio Durán, the new director of IMCINE as of January 1989, concurred that a new generation of filmmakers has emerged from television, the industry itself, and the State schools:

Talented people in their twenties and early thirties, such as Arturo Velasco, Diego López, and others. The film market in the United States is quite competitive, and we want to penetrate the American market, especially the East, with films for the general public, and not only in theaters but also cable TV and videocassettes. What has happened with television in Spain, France, and Germany, in which the state-owned networks finance films which are first released in theaters and then shown on television, should also be done in Mexico. It is something that would be beneficial for both mediums, and I see it happening in Mexico, not perhaps in the short run but possibly in a few years.

One of the objectives of the industry will be to promote, encourage, and sponsor well-made films, and not just cultural ones, but also those with commercial appeal. It's an endless discussion, but I think that little by little the film producers are coming to terms with the fact that they should change their emphasis. The general public is becoming much more demanding, and wants better material, so the film producer will have to find new ways to combine the two aspects—it has been done in the past, and I don't see why it cannot be done again.[52]

"The Mexican cinema is dying,"[53] glumly declares Jorge Ayala Blanco in the conclusion to his masterful study, *La condición del cine mexicano*. But perhaps the reports of its death have been greatly exaggerated. In the words of the late Manuel Michel, "... never had a patient survived so robustly such a long illness."[54] This writer would cautiously advance the proposition that Mexican cinema is changing rather than dying. It is changing in response to innumerable and complex social, economic, cultural, and political currents both within Mexico and from without. With so many good people concerned about it, it is unlikely to wither away. First of all, the cinema in Mexico, as in all other countries, expresses the national heritage and the cultural fiber of a people. Alejandro Galindo, the venerable patriarch of Mexican cinema, stated that "... in those images up there on the screen is where Mexicans can find their identity."[55] Film industries are changing and in the process undergoing their own crises in France, Italy, Spain, Britain, Eastern Europe, the Soviet Union, China, and almost anywhere else that comes to mind. Alarums have been sounded that "... even the larger cinemas in Europe are today dominated by American films...[and] the film industry in Europe is facing its most serious economic crisis ever....There is a warning, too, that the abolition of national aid would amount to the complete disappearance of the European film industry."[56] In Mexico there are many bright, capable, creative, and motivated people seeking to resuscitate the cinema in the face of bureaucratic timidity, political pressures, and, as in the rest of the world, the pervasive cultural influence of American films.

The great filmmakers and performers who created Mexican cinema—Salvador Toscano, Fernando de Fuentes, Emilio Fernández, Dolores del Rio, Pedro Armendáriz, Gabriel Figueroa, Alejandro Galindo and so many others—molded a great tradition that contemporary filmmakers seek to build on. The filmmakers of the past examined and interpreted a Mexican society recently emerged from revolution and fratricidal warfare. Today's filmmakers have no such recent dramatic events on which to focus their creative talents—just the experience of a nation seeking to modernize while coping with the burdens of the past: poverty, exploitation, and ignorance.

National cinematic revivals, the explosion of new talents who reinterpret a people's historical experience, have often occurred after great national traumas. German expressionism was a reaction to the disastrous defeat in World War I. The great Soviet cinema of the 1920s and early 1930s was a product of revolutionary upheaval. Italian neorealism arose from the ashes of fascism and the French *nouvelle vague* from World War II. The new Spanish cinema surged during and after forty years of Francoist repression; and even Hollywood, which is like no other film industry in the world, has reacted to domestic and foreign events. Argentine, Brazilian, Chilean, Cuban, and other Latin American filmmakers have often worked under great personal peril to make socially oriented, committed, and above all, honest cinema.

The Mexico of the 1980s has not experienced trauma greater than seeing its currency on the verge of collapse and its foreign debt balloon. Disconcerting certainly, but hardly comparable to Argentina's "dirty war"—and fortunate because as Cristián González commented, "If it takes military dictatorship and mass torture to inspire a good cinema, then I'm glad we don't have it."[57]

To paraphrase Alberto Isaac's statement at the beginning of this chapter, Mexican cinema is not in ruins, and neither is Mexico. As Gabriel Figueroa stated: "The new filmmakers will have to work very hard to achieve an image of Mexico worthy of showing to the world."[58] The road ahead is difficult and uncertain, of that there is no doubt, but if the commitment, creativity, and dedication of Mexico's filmmakers, both old and new, are any reflection of the larger society, then both Mexico and its cinema have a promising and perhaps even exciting future.

# Appendix 1

## SELECTED FILMOGRAPHIES

FERNANDO DE FUENTES
Born December 13, 1894, in Veracruz; died July 4, 1958, in Mexico City.

*El anónimo* (1932)
*El prisionero trece* (1933)
*La Calandria* (1933)
*El Tigre de Yautepec* (1933)
*El compadre Mendoza* (1933)
*Cruz Diablo* (1934)
*El fantasma del convento* (1934)
*!Vámonos con Pancho Villa!* (1935)
*La familia Dressel* (1935)
*Las mujeres mandan* (1936)
*Allá en el Rancho Grande* (1936)
*Bajo el cielo de México* (1937)
*La Zandunga* (1937)
*La casa del ogro* (1938)
*Papacito lindo* (1939)
*Allá en el trópico* (1940)
*El jefe máximo* (1940)
*Creo en Dios* (1940)
*La gallina clueca* (1941)

*Así se quiere en Jalisco* (1942)
*Doña Bárbara* (1943)
*La mujer sin alma* (1943)
*El rey se divierte* (1944)
*Hasta que perdió Jalisco* (1945)
*La selva de fuego* (1945)
*La devoradora* (1946)
*Allá en el Rancho Grande*
    (1948, second version)
*Jalisco canta en Sevilla* (1948)
*Hipólito el de Santa* (1949)
*Por la puerta falsa* (1950)
*Crimen y castigo* (1950)
*Los hijos de María Morales* (1952)
*Canción de cuna* (1952)
*Tres citas con el destino* (1953) (Mexican
    episode, coproduction with Spain and
    Argentina; other two segments directed
    by Florián Rey and León Klimovsky)

LUIS BUÑUEL
Born February 22, 1900, in Calanda, Spain; died July 29, 1983, in Mexico City. The
filmography lists Buñuel's Mexican films only.

*Gran Casino* (1946)
*El gran calavera* (1949)
*Los olvidados* (1950)
*Susana (carne y demonio)* (1950)
*La hija del engaño* (1951)
*Una mujer sin amor* (1951)

*El bruto* (1952)
*Robinson Crusoe* (1952)
*El* (1952)
*Abismos de pasión* (1953)
*La ilusión viaja en tranvía* (1953)
*El río y la muerte* (1954)

*Ensayo de un crimen* (1955)
*La muerte en este jardín /*
    *La Mort en ça Jardin* (1956)
*Nazarín* (1958)
Los ambiciosos / La Fièvre
    Monte a El Pao (1960)

*Viridiana* (1961)
*El ángel exterminador* (1962)
Simón del desierto (1964)


EMILIO FERNANDEZ
Born March 27, 1904, El Hondo, Coahuila; died in Mexico City on August 6, 1986.

*La isla de la pasión (Clipperton)* (1941)
*Soy puro mexicano* (1942)
*Flor silvestre* (1943)
*María Candelaria* (1943)
*Las abandonadas* (1944)
*Bugambilia* (1944)
*Pepita Jiménez* (1945)
*La perla* (1945)
*Enamorada* (1946)
*Río Escondido* (1947)
*Maclovia* (1948)
*Salón México* (1948)
*Pueblerina* (1948)
*La malquerida* (1949)
*Duelo en las montañas* (1949)
*Del odio nació el amor (The Torch,*
    English-language version of
    *Enamorada* (1949)
*Un día de vida* (1950)
*Víctimas del pecado* (1950)
*Islas Marías* (1950)
*Siempre tuya* (1950)
*La bienamada* (1951)
*Acapulco* (1951)

*El mar y tu* (1951)
*Cuando levanta la niebla* (1952)
*La red* (1953)
*Reportaje* (1953)
*El rapto* (1953)
*La rosa blanca* (coproduction with
    Cuba) (1953)
*La rebelión de los colgados*, codirector
    Alfredo Crevenna (1954)
*Nosotros dos* (coproduction with
    Spain) (1954)
*La tierra de fuego se apaga,*
    in Argentina (1955)
*Una cita de amor* (1956)
*El impostor* (1956)
*Pueblito* (1961)
*Paloma herida* (coproduction with
    Guatemala) (1962)
*Un dorado de Pancho Villa* (1966)
*El crepúsculo de un dios* (1968)
*La Choca* (1973)
*Zona roja* (1975)
*México norte* (1977)
*Erótica* (1978)


ALEJANDRO GALINDO
Born January 14, 1906, in Monterrey, Nuevo León

*Almas rebeldes* (1937)
*Refugiados en Madrid* (1938)
*Mientras México duerme* (1938)
*El muerto murió* (1939)
*Corazón de niño* (1939)
*El monje loco* (1940)
*Ni sangre ni arena* (1941)
*El rápido de las 9:15* (1941)
*Vírgen de medianoche* (1941)
*Konga roja* (1943)
*Divorciadas* (1943)
*Tribunal de justicia* (1943)

*La sombra de Chucho el Roto* (1944)
*Tu eres la luz* (1945)
*Campeón sin corona* (1945)
*Los que volvieron* (1946)
*Hermoso ideal* (1947)
*El muchacho alegre* (1947)
*¡Esquina bajan!* (1948)
*Una familia de tantas* (1948)
*Hay lugar para dos* (1948)
*Confidencias de un ruletero* (1949)
*Cuatro contra el mundo* (1949)
*Capitán de rurales* (1950)

Doña Perfecta (1950)
Dicen que soy comunista (1951)
El último round (1952)
Los dineros del diablo (1952)
Por el mismo camino (1952)
Sucedió en Acapulco (1952
Las infieles (1953)
Espaldas mojadas (1953; released 1955)
Los Fernández de Peralvillo (1953)
La duda (1953)
¡ . . . Y mañana serán mujeres! (1954)
Historia de un marido infiel (1954)
Tres melodías de amor (1955)
Hora y media de balazos (1956)
Policías y ladrones (1956)
Tu hijo debe nacer (1956)
Esposa te doy (1956)
Piernas de oro (1957)
Te vi en TV (1957)
Manos arriba (1957)
Echenme al gato (1957)
Raffles (1958)
La edad de la tentación (1958)
El supermacho (1958)
México nunca duerme (1958)
La vida de Agustín Lara (1958)
¡Ni hablar del peluquin! (1959)

Ellas también son rebeldes (1959)
Mañana serán hombres (1960)
La muerte y el crimen (1961)
Corona de lágrimas (1967)
Remolino de pasiones (1968)
Cristo 70 (1969)
Verano ardiente (1970)
Simplemente vivir (1970)
Tacos al carbón (1971)
Pepito y la lámpara maravillosa (1971)
Triángulo (1971)
San Simón de los magüeyes (1972)
El juicio de Martín Cortés (Los hijos de
    La Malinche) (1973)
Ante el cadáver de un líder (1973)
Y la mujer hizo al hombre (1974)
Las del talón (1977)
Que te vaya bonito (1977)
Mojados (Wetbacks) (1977)
El milagro en el circo (1978)
Dimas el león (1979)
Cruz de olvido (1980)
El sexo de los pobres (1981)
El color de nuestra piel (1982)
Lázaro Cárdenas (1985)
¡México grita! (1986)

## LUIS ALCORIZA
Born September 5, 1921, Badajoz, Spain. Family emigrated to Mexico during Spanish Civil War.

Los jóvenes (1960)
Tlayucan (1961)
Tiburoneros (1962)
Amor y sexo (1963)
El gángster (1964)
Tarahumara (1964)
Divertimento (one part of Juego peligroso;
    the other part directed by Arturo
    Ripstein) (1966)
El oficio más antiguo del mundo (1968)
Paraíso (1961)
Mecánica nacional (1971)
El muro del silencio (1971)

Esperanza (one part of Fe, esperanza y
    caridad; directors of other two parts:
    Alberto Bojórquez and Jorge Fons)
Presagio (1974)
Las fuerzas vivas (1975)
A paso de cojo (1978)
Viacrucis nacional (Semana Santa
    en Acapulco) (1980)
Han violado a una mujer (In Spain,
    Tac Tac) (1981)
El amor es un juego extraño (1983)
Terror y encajes negros (1984)
Lo que importa es vivir (1985)

## ALBERTO ISAAC
Born 1923, Mexico

En este pueblo no hay ladrones (1965)

Las visitaciones del diablo (1967)

*Olimpiada en México* (1968)
*Futbol México 70* (1970)
*Los días del amor* (1971)
*El rincón de las vírgenes* (1972)
*Tívoli* (1974)

*Cuartelazo* (1976)
*Los noches de Paloma* (1977)
*Tiemp de lobos* (1981)
*Mariana, Mariana* (1986)
*Navidad en la sangre* (1988)

## FELIPE CAZALS

Born June 27, 1937, in Guetari, Spain. Family emigrated to Zapotec, Jalisco four months later. Raised in Mexico City.

*La manzana de la discordia* (1968)
*Familiaridades* (1969)
*Emiliano Zapata* (1970)
*El jardín de tía Isabel* (1971)
*Aquellos años* (1972)
*Los que viven donde sopla el viento suave*
   (documentary) (1973)
*Canoa* (1975)
*El apando* (1975)
*Las Poquiánchis* (1976)

*La güera Rodríguez* (1977)
*El año de la peste* (1978)
*Rigo es amor* (1980)
*El gran triunfo* (1980)
*Las siete Cucas* (1980)
*Bajo la metralla* (1982)
*Los motivos de Luz* (1985)
*El tres de copas* (1986)
*Las inocentes* (1986)
*La furia de un dios* (Lo de César) (1987)

## ARTURO RIPSTEIN

Born December 13, 1943, in Mexico City.

*Tiempo de morir* (1965)
*HO* (first part of *Juego peligroso*;
   Luis Alcoriza directed other part) (1966)
*Los recuerdos del porvenir* (1968)
*El castillo de la pureza* (1972)
*El santo oficio* (1973)
*Foxtrot* (1979)
*Lecumberri* (1976)
*El lugar sin límites* (1977)

*La viuda negra* (1977)
*Cadena perpétua* (1978)
*La tía Alejandra* (1978)
*La ilegal* (1979)
*La seducción* (1980)
*Rastro de muerte* (1981)
*El otro* (1984)
*El imperio de la fortuna* (1986)
*Mentiras piadosas* (1988)

# Appendix 2

## USEFUL ADDRESSES

Cineteca Nacional
Avenida México-Coyoacán No. 389
Colonia Xoco
03330 México, D.F.

Director: Lic. Mercedes Certucha
Subdirección de Autorizaciones:
   Lic. Cristián González
Director, Documentación e Investigación:
   Lic. Antonio Bautista

Telephones: 6-88-88-64, 5-84-46-40

Instituto Mexicano de Cinematografía
   (IMCINE)
Avenida México-Coyoacán No. 340
Esq. Carrillo Puerto
Col. General Anaya
03340 México, D.F.

Director: Lic. Ignacio Durán
Telephones: 6-88-60-67, 6-88-58-52

Corporación Nacional Cinematográfica,
   S.A. de C.V. (CONACINE)
Atletas No. 2
Col. Country Club
04220 México, D.F.

Director: Lic. Fernando Macotela
Telephones: 5-49-62-03
           5-49-07-32

Películas Mexicanas, S.A. de C.V.
Avenida División del Norte 246
5° piso
03300 México, D.F.
Director: Lic. Francisco Gómez

Telephones: 6-88-78-76, 6-88-09-70

Estudios Churubusco-Azteca, S.A.
Atletas No. 2
Col. Country Club
04220 México, D.F.

Telephone: 5-49-30-60

Estudios América, S.A.
Calzada de Tlalpan, No. 2818
04220 México, D.F.

Telephone: 5-77-81-22

Consejo Estatal de Cine,
   Teatro y Televisión
Rufino Tamayo 4
Apdo. Postal 39-C
Col. Acapantzingo
Cuernavaca, Mor.
México

Luciana Cabarga, Coordinadora General
Lic. Alma Rossbach Suárez,
   Subcoordinadora
Telephone: (73) 12-92-15, 12-92-16

Alejandro Pelayo
Soc. Cop. José Revueltas
Atletas 39
Col. Country Club
Deleg. Coyoacán
04220 México, D.F.

Telephone: 5-49-16-21, 5-44-69-69

U.S. representative:
Jorge Penichet
Bilingual Educational Services, Inc.,
2514 South Grand Ave.,
Los Angeles, CA 90007-9979,
Telephone: (213) 749-6213.

# Notes

PREFACE

1. Vincent Canby, "Uncovering Luis Bunuel's [sic] Mexican Treasures," *New York Times*, 18 January 1976, p. D-13.

INTRODUCTION

1. See Erich Keel, "From Militant Cinema to Neo-Realism: The Example of *Pueblo Chico*," *Film Quarterly* 24 (Summer 1976): 17−24.
2. Albert Johnson, "Journals," *Film Comment*, May−June 1980, pp. 2, 4.
3. For an assessment of Argentine cinema in the mid-seventies, see Steven Kovács, "Screening the Movies in Argentina," *New Boston Review*, December 1977, pp. 19−21.
4. Julianne Burton, "The Hour of the Embers: On the Current Situation of Latin American Cinema," *Film Quarterly* 30 (Fall 1976): 33−44; Peter Biskind, "In Latin America They Shoot Filmmakers," *Sight and Sound* (Summer 1976), pp. 160−61.
5. "Una entrevista con Fernando Birri," *Cine cubano*, no. 42/43/44 (1967), pp. 13−21.
6. Siegfried Kracauer, *From Caligari to Hitler: A Psychological History of the German Film* (New York: The Noonday Press, 1960), pp. 4, 6.
7. Paul Smith, ed., *The Historian and Film* (Cambridge: At the University Press, 1976), p. 7.
8. This author knew Antonio Eguino at the City College of New York in 1962−1967. Eguino had a great liking for Mexican *ranchera* music, a taste he acquired from Mexican films. Arau, whom the author met in Los Angeles in 1978, had been a member of a popular song and dance duo, "Arau and Corona," in Mexico in the late 1950s, which performed in films and on the stage. He was in Cuba in 1959 when Fulgencio Batista was overthrown and stayed on for several years, causing him political problems on his return to Mexico.
9. These and other aspects of the influence of Mexican cinema, especially among Colombia's urban poor, are discussed by Gloria Cecilia Gómez in "El cine mejicano en Colombia," *Cromos* (Bogotá), no. 3094, 4 May 1977, pp. 74−77. The New York-based Peruvian novelist and poet Isaac Goldemberg told this writer in August 1980 that Mexican films "had a tremendous influence on the popular classes in Peru—Mexican slang, clothing styles, attitudes toward *machismo*, and music were all enthusiastically emulated by the Peruvian lower classes."

CHAPTER 1

1. Agustín Mahieu, *Breve historia del cine nacional, 1896−1974* (Buenos Aires: Alzamor Editores, 1976), pp. 7−24.
2. Geraldo Santos Pereira, *Plano Geral do Cinema Brasileiro: História, Cultura, Economia e Legislação* (Benfica, Guanabara: Editor Borsoi, 1973), pp. 61−62.
3. Georges Sadoul, *Histoire du Cinéma Mondial des Origines à nos Jours* (Paris: Flammarion Editeur, 1949), pp. 7−18.
4. He comments: "Malamente puede escribirse la historia de esta etapa [muda] cuando solo se ha logrado ver *una* cinta muda nacional, El automóvil gris; tal es mi caso y el de casi todos los demás estudiosos del cine del país." Emilio García Riera, *Historia documental del cine mexicano*, 10 vols. to date (Mexico City: Ediciones Era, 1969−   ), 1: 7; hereinafter referred to as *Historia*.
5. *Salón Rojo (programas y crónicas del cine mudo en México), vol. 1 (1895−1920)*, Cuadernos de

193

Cine #16 (Mexico City: Dirección General de Difusión Cultural, UNAM, 1968), hereinafter referred to as *Salón Rojo*.

6. Ibid., pp. 7 – 8.
7. Both the *Enciclopedia de México*, 10 vols. (Mexico City: Instituto de la Enciclopedia de México, 1968), 2: 540 and the *Diccionario Porrúa: Historia, Biografía y Geografía de México*, 2 vols., 3d ed. (Mexico City: Editorial Porrúa, 1970), 1: 435 attribute the establishment of this theater to Salvador Toscano. The confusion seems to stem from the fact that in 1897 Toscano opened his *second* theater, also on Plateros Street (his first locale had been on No. 17 Jesús María Street in early 1897). *Salón Rojo*, p. 17.
8. Quoted in *Salón Rojo*, pp. 9, 11, 14. Unless otherwise noted, all translations are author's.
9. Quoted in ibid., p. 15.
10. *Enciclopedia de México*, 2: 540; *Diccionario Porrúa*, 1: 435.
11. *Salón Rojo*, p. 17.
12. Ibid., p. 18.
13. Ibid., pp. 19 – 20; Sadoul, *Histoire du Cinéma Mondial*, p. 25.
14. *Salón Rojo*, p. 20.
15. Ibid., pp. 20 – 21.
16. Ibid., pp. 22 – 23.
17. Ibid., pp. 25 – 26.
18. Ibid., pp. 26 – 27.
19. Ibid., p. 28.
20. Eugenia Meyer, coordinator, *Cuadernos de la Cineteca Nacional: Testimonios para la historia del cine mexicano*, 8 vols. (Mexico City: Dirección de Cinematografía de la Secretaría de Gobernación, 1976), 1: 13.
21. These were as follows: Teatro Riva Palacio, Teatro Apolo, Sala Pathé, Gran Salón Mexicano, Academia Metropolitana, Salón High Life, Salón Art Noveau, Salón de Moda, Salón Verde, Spectatorium, Salón Monte Carlo, El Molino Blanco, Salón Music Hall, Pabellón Morisco, and Salón Cinematográfico (which after November 1906 was renamed Salón Rojo). *Salón Rojo*, p. 35.
22. Quoted in ibid., pp. 35, 37. Eric Rhode observes: "We may find it ironic that a class only recently touched by the hope of literacy should have been the first to give itself over to moving images; but the truth is that the cinema was to be a desperately needed consolation and source of knowledge to the poor, the illiterate and to immigrant communities (as in America) unable to speak the native language." *A History of the Cinema from its Origins to 1970* (New York: Hill and Wang, 1976), p. 21.
23. Moisés González Navarro, *Población y sociedad en México (1900 – 1970)*, 2 vols. (Mexico City: UNAM, 1974), 1: 43.
24. *Salón Rojo*, p. 45.
25. Meyer, *Cuadernos*, 1: 13. Also see Alejandro Sorondo, "Jorge Stahl Inició de Niño una Carrera Cinematográfica que ha Durado 82 Años," *Excélsior*, 22 September 1976, pp. 9 – B, 10 – B; and Agustín Gurezpe, "Hoy es el Homenaje a Jorge Stahl [*sic*] Frente al Monumento del 'Ariel' ", *Excélsior*, 8 October 1976, Section Cine, Teatro, Radio y TV, p. 1.
26. *Salón Rojo*, p. 31.
27. Ibid. Film runs through the projector at the rate of 10.98 meters a minute.
28. Ibid., pp. 32 – 33.
29. Ibid., p. 34.
30. The first had been Salvador Toscano's *Don Juan Tenorio* (1898).
31. Emilio García Riera, *El cine mexicano* (Mexico City: Ediciones Era, 1963), p. 14.
32. *Salón Rojo*, pp. 52 – 53; although Toscano was not responsible for the making of this film, a scene from it can be seen briefly in *Memorias de un mexicano*.
33. Rodolfo Usigli, *Mexico in the Theater*, translated with an introduction by Wilder P. Scott (University, Miss.: Romance Monographs, Inc., 1976), p. 114.
34. Ibid., p. 110.
35. "Una Gran Dama," *Tiempo*, 26 October 1945, p. 30; Daniel Cosío Villegas, gen. ed., *Historia moderna de México*, 8 vols. (Mexico City: Editorial Hermes, 1955 – 1972), vol. 4, *El Porfiriato—La vida social* by Moisés González Navarro (1957), pp. 801 – 12.
36. Carlos Monsiváis, "Junto contigo le doy un aplauso al placer y al amor," *Textos* (Guadalajara), año 2, no. 9 – 10 (1975), p. 39; Ruth S. Lamb, *Mexican Theater of the Twentieth Century: Bibliography and Study* (Claremont, Calif.: Ocelot Press, 1975), p. 7.

37. Raoul Fournier Villada, "He Makes Mexico Laugh," *Américas*, March 1953, pp. 6–8.
38. Ibid., p. 7.
39. *Salón Rojo*, p. 58.
40. Ibid., pp. 58–59.
41. Ibid., pp. 63–65.
42. Ibid., p. 65.
43. Oscar Valdés and Miguel Torres, "En compañía de Max Linder," *Cine cubano* 6, no. 35 (1966): 45–49; *Salón Rojo*, pp. 66–67; D. J. Wenden, *The Birth of the Movies* (London: Macdonald and Co., 1975), p. 28.
44. Pierre Leprohon, *The Italian Cinema*, translated from the French by Roger Greaves and Oliver Stallybrass (New York and Washington, D.C.: Praeger Publishers, 1972), pp. 24–25.
45. "Temporada Dramática," *Tiempo*, 16 March 1945, p. 46.
46. A similar cinema fire in Paris at the Bazar de la Charité in May 1897 took a heavy toll of life, mostly aristocrats. Rhode, *A History of the Cinema*, p. 19.
47. *Salón Rojo*, pp. 59–60, 113–14. The truth of the matter is that the era's nitro cellulose stock was highly flammable and the movie "salons," which were often nothing more than wooden shacks, added to the danger. A fireproof film was not to be available until 1952 with the introduction of acetate-based film stock. Clive Coultass, "Film Preservation: The Archives," in Smith, *The Historian and Film*, p. 35.
48. As is the case with the United States, Mexico does not date its independence from the actual date of administrative separation from Spain. This occurred with the signing of the Treaty of Córdoba on August 24, 1821, by Agustín Iturbide and the last viceroy, Juan Odonojú. A provisional government was set up in Mexico City on September 28. The date that Mexicans observe as independence day is September 16, 1810, which commemorates Father Miguel Hidalgo y Costilla's abortive *jacquerie*.
49. E. Bradford Burns, *Latin American Cinema: Film and History* (Los Angeles: UCLA Latin American Center, 1975), p. 18. Even though Burns erroneously dates the film in 1918, his comments acquire greater significance when it is realized that such a film was produced under an officially anti-indigenous regime, and that it might have reflected an already strong prerevolutionary current of interest in Mexico's Indian past—and present.
50. Howard F. Cline, *The United States and Mexico* (New York: Atheneum, 1963), p. 122.
51. Ibid., p. 121.
52. *Salón Rojo*, p. 77.
53. Ibid.
54. Ibid., p. 79.
55. Ibid. The tone of this advertisement is not surprising in view of the campaign of vilification at this time against Madero's provisional government and against him personally. Porfirian elements nostalgic for the "good old days" were still plentiful, and presumably these were the people who responded with their "enthusiastic applause" to the sight of Porfirio Díaz on the screen. For a representative sample of films exhibited in 1912, including comedy shorts by Max Linder and Rabinet, and American westerns, see ibid., pp. 79–80.
56. Quoted from the Salón Rojo's advertisement for *La revolución en Chihuahua*, ibid., p. 82. Rare films of the campaign against Pascual Orozco can be seen in *Memorias de un mexicano*, including shots of General Victoriano Huerta in the field directing the federal forces. These are among the earliest films taken of combat.
57. Cosío Villegas, *Historia moderna de México*, p. 791.
58. Ibid.
59. Ibid., p. 790.
60. *Salón Rojo*, pp. 54–56.
61. Ibid., pp. 95–96.
62. Leprohon, *The Italian Cinema*, p. 28.
63. *Salón Rojo*, pp. 100–101.
64. Ibid., p. 104.
65. Ibid., pp. 112–13.
66. Ibid., p. 125.
67. Ibid., pp. 125–26.
68. Ibid., p. 139.
69. Actually "whistled"—in Mexico an audience generally displays its displeasure not by hissing but by whistling.

70. From *El águila y la serpiente*, quoted in Monsiváis, "Junto contigo le doy un aplauso al placer y al amor," p. 43.
71. Federico Heuer, *La industria cinematográfica mexicana* (Mexico City: n.p., 1964), p. 6; Francisco A. Gómezjara and Delia Selene de Dios, *Sociología del cine* (Mexico City: Sep/Setentas, 1973), p. 48.
72. From E. Bradford Burns's introduction to Beatriz Reyes Nevares, *The Mexican Cinema: Interviews with Thirteen Directors*, trans. Carl J. Mora and Elizabeth Gard (Albuquerque: University of New Mexico Press, 1976), p. xii.
73. John Womack, Jr., *Zapata and the Mexican Revolution* (New York: Vintage Books, 1970), pp. 319, 322–23, 324, 327, 329, 339. Pablo González was a partner in the film company, Azteca Films; the other two were the actress Mimí Derba and the director and producer, Enrique Rosas. García Riera, *El cine mexicano*, p. 16.
74. *Salón Rojo*, p. 144.
75. Ibid., pp. 153, 155.
76. Ibid., pp. 157–58. A list of the players provides what is probably a fairly complete picture of Mexico's film actors at this time.
77. Ibid., pp. 158, 186–87.
78. Ibid., pp. 170–75; *Diccionario Porrúa*, 1: 1146; García Riera, *El cine mexicano*, pp. 14–15.
79. Leprohon, *The Italian Cinema*, p.45.
80. *Salón Rojo*, pp. 179–80.
81. Leprohon, *The Italian Cinema*, p. 50; García Riera, *El cine mexicano*, p. 12.
82. *Salón Rojo*, p. 185. See also on pages 106–108 the discussion on national traits in films.
83. *Diccionario Porrúa*, 1: 435.
84. For instance in Argentina, along with Brazil, the other major Latin American film-producing country, production consistently lagged behind Mexico's, and the initiatives seemed to be largely in the hands of immigrants. For example, Eugenio Py, a French photographer, was the "Salvador Toscano" of Argentina, installing the first Lumière projector and filming the first footage of public events and street scenes. His first effort was a 17-meter film, *La bandera argentina* (1900), followed by *Visita del Dr. Campos Salles a Buenos Aires* (1900) and *Visita del General Mitre al Museo Nacional*. Eugenio Cardini (1880–1962), a native Argentinian, made *Escenas callejeras* (1902) after constructing, in 1896, the first movie camera ever made in Argentina and "almost undoubtedly in South America." An Italian immigrant, Mario Gallo, who arrived in Argentina in 1905, made *Fusilamiento de Dorrego* in 1908, the first Argentine film made from a script. The Uruguayan Julio R. Alsina (1883–1944) produced a film on Argentina's centennial, *La revista del centenario* (1910). Another Italian, Federico Valle, who had studied with Méliès, arrived in 1911, and until 1930 produced a newsreel, *Film Revista*. In 1915 Humberto Cairo wrote and directed *Nobleza gaucha*, the greatest success of the Argentine film industry to that time. In 1916 Alcides Greca, a Santa Fean, produced *El último malón*. Other notable films of the period were José Agustín Ferreyra's *El tango de la muerte* (1917) and Roberto Guidi's *El mentir de los demás* (1919). Mahieu, *Breve historia*, pp. 11–21. Brazilian production was practically nonexistent prior to 1920, although screenings of foreign films followed the pattern established in the rest of the hemisphere. The period 1913–1922 is referred to as the "*Fase Artesanal*, que inclui as primeiras tentativas de produção organizada, devida mais ao esforco pessoal de pioneiros de que a una estrutura industrial mais consistente." Santos Pereira, *Plano Geral do Cinema Brasileiro*, p. 36.
85. For instance, beginning in 1918 the Guanajuatan Indalecio de Noriega Colombres made the following films: *Carros alegóricos de Chapultepec*, *Madero en Guanajuato*, *Corrida de toros*, *Fuerzas zapatistas*, *Llegada de don Francisco I. Madero a México*, *El terrible Pérez*, *Juegos de beisbol en Guanajuato*, *La oración de la noche*, *El molinito*, *Revista histórica nacional*, *Caballos de la calle*, *Pieza teatral*, *Por ahí viene ya*, *Madame Butterfly*, *El año pasado por agua*, *El bateo*, *Modelo parisiense*, *Discurso de Vale Coyote*, and others. His daughter, María Teresa Noriega, sold them in 1972 to the Centro Universitario de Estudios Cinematográficos for 20,000 pesos. In 1976 she accused its director, Manuel González Casanova, of losing 39 rolls of the "first sound films." González Casanova gave assurances that the films were in the UNAM Filmoteca but that Ms. Noriega had not included the records when delivering the films. See Ricardo Perete, "Desaparecen 39 Rollos con las Primeras Películas Sonoras," *Excélsior*, 11 June 1976, p. C–1 and 15 June 1976, p. B–13.
86. Maria Rita Eliezer Galvão, *Crônica do Cinema Paulistano* (São Paulo: Editora Ática, 1975).
87. García Riera, *El cine mexicano*, p. 13.

88. Meyer, *Cuadernos*, 1: 14.
89. Cline, *The United States and Mexico*, p. 191.
90. Ibid., pp. 192—93.
91. Jesús Abitia was also a friend of General Obregón; in fact, he filmed many of the latter's military campaigns. Reyes Nevares, *The Mexican Cinema*, p. 23.
92. García Riera, *El cine mexicano*, p. 19.
93. Ibid., p. 13.
94. Yet many voices were raised against the film's blatant racism, including those of the NAACP and the president of Harvard University. Wenden, *The Birth of the Movies*, p. 54.
95. Blaine P. Lamb, "The Convenient Villain: The Early Cinema Views the Mexican-American," *Journal of the West* 14 (October 1975): 75.
96. W. A. Swanberg, *Citizen Hearst* (New York: Charles Scribner's Sons, 1961), pp. 296—97. Judging from some typical comments in U.S. newspapers on the eve of our entrance into the war, the nation was on the verge of hysteria over the situation in Mexico. The Buffalo *Express* visualized "hordes of Mexicans under German officers, sweeping into Texas, New Mexico and Arizona." *The New York American* (a Hearst paper) stated: "Mexico . . . would retake the Southwest and restore it to barbarism; Japan would take the Far West and 'orientalize' it; Germany and Russia would enslave generations of Americans in the payment of vast war indemnities." Barbara W. Tuchman, *The Zimmerman Telegram* (New York: Dell Publishing Co., 1958), p. 187. The "Plan of San Diego"—a vast Texas-based plot to wrench the former Mexican territories of California, New Mexico, Nevada, Colorado, Arizona, and Oklahoma back from the United States and establish an independent republic affiliated with Mexico— surfaced at this time. Of doubtful authenticity—or perhaps concocted by disgruntled Mexican-Americans working with Mexican and German *provocateurs*—it fed American paranoia. Tuchman speculates that a report of this "conspiracy" reached the German foreign minister, Arthur Zimmerman, and might have inspired his offer to Mexico of an alliance and return of the territories lost in 1848 if it declared war on the United States. Ibid., p. 97. The "Plan" was ostensibly suggested by one F. de P. González, editor of the newspaper *La libertad* in San Diego, Texas. Juan Gómez-Quiñones, "Piedras contra la Luna, México en Aztlán y Aztlán en México: Chicano-Mexican Relations and the Mexican Consulates, 1900—1920," in James W. Wilkie, Michael C. Meyer, Edna Monzón de Wilkie, eds., *Contemporary Mexico: Papers of the IV International Congress of Mexican History* (Berkeley, Los Angeles, London: University of California Press; and Mexico City: El Colegio de México, 1976), p. 518. Another writer states: "Most authorities, later, suspected the Plan of San Diego was devised either by a German agent to stir up trouble at the United States' back door or by one of the many wealthy American landowners who were being dispossessed in Mexico at this time." T. R. Fehrenbach, *Lone Star: A History of Texas and the Texans* (New York: Macmillan Publishing Co., 1968), p. 691. The Plan of San Diego is available as Senate Document 285, 66th Congress, U.S. Govt. Printing Office and is reprinted in, The Editors of Winston Press, *Viewpoints: Red & Yellow, Black & Brown* (Minneapolis, Minn.: Winston Press, 1972), pp. 257—58.
97. Lamb, "The Convenient Villain," p. 76.
98. *Salón Rojo*, pp. 227—28.
99. Ibid., p. 205.
100. George A. Huaco, *The Sociology of Film Art* (New York: Basic Books, 1965), pp. 25—151.
101. Itzhak Bar-Lewaw, *Introducción crítico-biográfica a José Vasconcelos (1882—1959)* (Madrid: Ediciones Latinoamericanas, 1965), pp. 107—24; José Vasconcelos, *Indología, una interpretación de la cultura iberoamericana* (Barcelona: Agencia Mundial de Librería, 1926), pp. 139—91.
102. Cline, *The United States and Mexico*, p. 203.
103. In 1919 the Ministry of War produced three films, *El Block-house de alta luz, Honor militar*, and *El precio de la gloria*—all directed by Fernando Orozco Berra. These apparently were semi-documentary movies extolling the virtues of the revolutionary soldier. In 1925 Jorge Stahl produced *La linterna de Diógenes*, described by García Riera as propaganda for President Plutarco Elías Calles. These films seem to be the extent to which the Mexican cinema was utilized for political purposes prior to 1930.
104. *Salón Rojo*, pp. 225—26.
105. De Witt Bodeen, "Ramón Novarro," *Films in Review* 18 (November 1967): 528—47.
106. Since Al Jolson's *The Jazz Singer* was released just before *Evangeline*, United Artists had Dolores del Río sing three songs in French, a language in which she was quite proficient, and

hurriedly incorporated these scenes into the movie before releasing it.

107. José Gómez Sicre, "Dolores del Río," *Américas,* 19 December 1967, pp. 8—17; De Witt Bodeen, "Dolores del Rio," *Films in Review* 18 (May 1967): 266—83.

108. Mahieu, *Breve historia del cine nacional,* p. 23.

109. García Riera, *El cine mexicano,* p. 20.

## CHAPTER 2

1. *Salón Rojo,* p. 14.
2. Luis Reyes de la Maza, *El cine sonoro en México* (Mexico City: UNAM, Instituto de Investigaciones Estéticas, 1973), p. 11, hereafter *Cine sonoro.* Gaumont personally tested his *cronophone* at the 1920 Paris Universal Exposition. See also Perete, "Desaparecen 39 Rollos," for an account of Indalecio de Noriega Colombres's efforts with a similar sound system in 1918.
3. Rhode, *A History of the Cinema,* p. 269.
4. Ibid., pp. 79—85.
5. Kracauer, *From Caligari to Hitler,* p. 67.
6. Rhode, *A History of the Cinema,* p. 119.
7. Ibid., p. 124.
8. Ibid., p. 154.
9. Ibid.
10. Germán Arciniegas, *Latin America: A Cultural History,* trans. Joan MacLean (New York: Alfred A. Knopf, 1967), p. 495.
11. *Cine sonoro,* p. 13.
12. Ibid., and pp. 107—10.
13. Wenden, *The Birth of the Movies,* pp. 178, 179.
14. Alfonso Pintó, "Hollywood's Spanish-Language Films," *Films in Review* 24 (October 1973): 474—83, 487.
15. Joaquín de la Horia, "Fotofónicas en español," *Cinelandia* (December 1929) outlined in *Historia,* 1: 9. Manuel Michel makes the same point about subtitles in "Mexican Cinema: A Panoramic View," *Film Quarterly* 18 (Summer 1965): 48.
16. De la Horia, "Fotofónicas en español," p. 9.
17. One hundred thirteen of these Spanish-language films made by fourteen companies between 1930 and 1935 are listed in Pintó, "Hollywood's Spanish-Language Films," pp. 476—83, 487. The companies were Sono Art—World Wide, Chris Phillips Prods., Hollywood Spanish Pictures Co., Ci-Ti-Go, MGM, First National, Warner Brothers, Universal, Columbia, Paramount (U.S. and Joinville, France), Exito Corp., Inc./Paramount, Fox, 20th Century Fox, RNS Ltd., and Metropolitan Pictures Corp. Among other films made after 1935 and available in the UCLA Film Archive are *La vida bohemia* (1937), Columbia-Cantabria Films starring Gilbert Roland and Rosita Díaz and directed by Joseph Berne; and *Verbena trágica* (1938), Columbia-Cantabria Films, starring Fernando Soler and directed by Charles Lamont.
18. Pintó, "Hollywood's Spanish-Language Films," p. 475; see also idem, "Cuando Hollywood Habló en Español," *Américas,* October 1980, pp. 3—8.
19. The Spanish word here would be *castizo,* "pure," or "correct" as in the Castilian spoken in Castile. In Spanish-American usage, the terms "*castellano*" and "*español*" are employed interchangeably; in Spain, however, a regional nationalist would take exception to "Castilian" being characterized as *the* Spanish language since technically Castilian, Galician, Catalan, Basque, and Valencian are *all* "Spanish" languages. Fortunately, the latter Iberian distinctions have no bearing on the matter of the Spanish variant employed in Latin-American films.

      The 1944 Mexican film *La barraca* was dubbed in the Valencian dialect. Jorge Ayala Blanco, *La aventura del cine mexicano* (Mexico City: Ediciones Era, 1968), p. 244 fn. Recently there have been more Catalan movies made, an important example being Antonio Ribas's *La ciutat cremada* (1977). Roger Mortimore, "Spain," in Peter Cowie, ed., *International Film Guide 1977* (London: Tantivy Press, 1978), p. 253. The Xornadas do Cine Ourense, a Galician film festival, was held in 1977 for the fifth straight year. Ibid. See also Stanley Meisler, "In Spain It's Great to Be a Polyglot," *Los Angeles Times,* 27 April 1977, p. I—10.
20. *Cine sonoro,* p. 23; see also *Historia,* 1: 20.
21. *Cine sonoro,* p. 22.
22. *Historia,* 1: 20.
23. The influence of the Hollywood movie has been consistently denounced by Marxist film historians, especially with regard to the Latin American film industries. Yet it is interesting to note that up to 1972, Chiang Ch'ing, Mao Tse-tung's widow, lovingly viewed again and again

Greta Garbo's *Queen Christina* (1933). "The Rise and Fall of Mao's Empress," *Time*, 21 March 1977, p. 59.

24. Viewed at UCLA Film Archive, December 1976. Columbia-Cantabria Films (1938). Directed by Charles Lamont, produced by Jaime del Amo. With Fernando Soler, Luana de Alcañiz, Juan Torena, Pilar Arcos, Cecilia Callejo, Jorge Mari, Carlos Villarias, Romualdo Tirado, Sergio de Karlo, and Leonor Turich.

25. In 1937, 38 full-length features were produced in Mexico. Garcia Riera, *El cine mexicano*, p. 25.

26. By 1950 it was estimated that 300 theaters in the United States ran exclusively Spanish-language programs and another 100 theaters ran Spanish-language showings once or twice a week. William D. Allen, "Spanish-Language Films in the U.S.," *Films in Review* 1 (July-August 1950): 1, 42—45.

27. Meyer, *Cuadernos*, 1: 66.

28. *Cine sonoro*, pp. 78—79.

29. Ayala Blanco, *La aventura*, pp. 291—92. Cube Bonifant had been a silent film actress; two of her films were Carlos Noriega Hope's *Los chicos de la prensa* (1921) and *La gran noticia* (same year). García Riera, *El cine mexicano*, p. 21.

30. *Cine sonoro*, pp. 132—33; see also Xavier Villaurrutia, *Crítica cinematográfica*, Cuadernos de Cine #18 (Mexico City: UNAM, Dirección General de Difusión Cultural, 1970).

31. The first Mexican sound film was actually Raphael J. Sevilla's *Más fuerte que el deber* (Films Tenoch, 1930). It apparently was fairly well received by the Mexican public and demonstrated the feasibility of a national industry based on sound movies. However, the film has been relegated to limbo by most Mexican cineasts who prefer to date the beginning of the sound era with the more commercially successful *Santa* (*Historia*, 1: 17).

Joselito Rodríguez mentions another film, *Sangre mexicana*, for which he had invented a portable, inexpensive sound system. In 1930 he was in Los Angeles exhibiting this movie when representatives of the *Santa* production company arrived seeking to purchase an American sound recording system. Rodríguez says he approached his countrymen to offer his sound system, but when they learned it was invented by a Mexican they ignored him. Finally, the high cost of the U.S.-made systems and Rodríguez's persistence persuaded the *Santa* producers to purchase his system. Martha Aurora Espinosa, "El cine sonoro fue un auténtico invento mío: Joselito Rodríguez," *Uno Más Uno*, 27 January 1981, p. 22.

32. Ibid., p. 27.

33. Salvador Elizondo, "Moral sexual y moraleja en el cine mexicano," *Nuevo Cine*, no. 1 (April 1961), quoted in *Historia*, 1: 27. See also ibid., pp. 25—27; Ayala Blanco, *La aventura*, pp. 128—30; and *Cine sonoro*, pp. 28—29, 259, 264—69.

34. For leftist attacks on Sinclair and *Thunder Over Mexico* see "Thunder Over Mexico" [poster and text], p. 69; "To Upton Sinclair" [poster and text], p. 70; and P. Lorentz, "Thunder Over Mexico" [review], *Film Culture*, nos. 48—49 (Winter-Spring 1970). For other sources on Eisenstein and his stay in Mexico see Marie Seton, *Eisenstein* (Paris: Editions du Seuil, 1967); Gabriel Ramírez, ed., *¡Que viva México!* (Mexico City: Ediciones Era, 1964); Harry M. Geduld and Ronald Gottesman, eds., *Sergei Eisenstein and Upton Sinclair: The Making and Unmaking of ¡Que Viva Mexico!* (Bloomington and London: Indiana University Press, 1970); Jean Mitry, *S. M. Eisenstein* (Paris: Editions Universitaires, 1962); Jay Leyda, *Kino, A History of the Russian and Soviet Film* (London: Allen and Unwin, 1960); Sadoul, *Histoire du Cinéma*, pp. 425—30; Rhode, *A History of the Cinema*, pp. 108, 289; Marie Seton, "Vignettes of Eisenstein," *Films in Review* 2 (April 1951): 29—31; synopsis of *¡Que Viva Mexico!* in *Experimental Cinema*, no. 5 (1934). This summary of Eisenstein's activities in Mexico is largely based on Alfonso Reyes's account as quoted in *Historia*, 1: 18—19. See also *Cine sonoro*, pp. 236—43 for Adolfo Fernández Bustamante's remarks in *El Ilustrado*, 11, 18, and 25 June and 16 July 1931.

35. For discussions of different national styles in filmmaking see Leprohon, *The Italian Cinema*, p. 20, and for the silent French and German cinemas of the 1920s see Paul Monaco, *Cinema and Society: France and Germany During the Twenties* (New York: Elsevier, 1976), passim but especially chapter 3, "The Film as National Folklore," pp. 68—79. Regarding Eisenstein's influence on Mexican cinema see Glauber Rocha's denunciation in *Cahiers du Cinéma*, no. 195 (November 1967) as quoted in *Historia*, 1: 19—20.

36. Ibid., p. 19.

37. García Riera, *El cine mexicano*, pp. 31—34.

38. Ibid., pp. 37—39.

39. Meyer, *Cuadernos*, 1: 21—29.

40. *Historia*, 1: 38.
41. All these quotes are found in ibid., p. 54. See also Ayala Blanco's analysis in *La aventura*, pp. 131–33.
42. *Historia*, 1: 53.
43. Ibid., pp. 57–58.
44. Ibid., p. 59; see also Philippe Pilard's remarks in ibid. For García Riera's commentary see ibid., p. 58 and also idem, *El cine mexicano*, pp. 31–32; Ayala Blanco, *La aventura*, pp. 16–22. A retrospective of De Fuentes's work was held in 1976 in Venice. Agustín Gurezpe, "Homenaje a Fernando de Fuentes en la 'Mostra' de Venecia 1976," *Excélsior*, 7 May 1976, p. C–1.
45. *Historia*, 1: 70. The account of the making of *Redes* is taken from ibid., pp. 69–72.
46. Ayala Blanco, *La aventura*, p. 194.
47. Ibid.
48. *Historia*, 1: 84–86. A similar theme was used in *La vida bohemia* (1937). In this Columbia-Cantabria production—one of the last of Hollywood's efforts at Hispanic moviemaking—Gilbert Roland portrayed a Parisian writer in love with Rosita Díaz, who eventually dies of tuberculosis. Viewed at UCLA Film Archive, December 1976.
49. Catherine Macotela, "El sindicalismo en el cine (primera parte)," *Otrocine* no. 2 (April-June 1975), pp. 60–61. What later would become the STIC (Sindicato de Trabajadores de la Industria Cinematográfica) was founded in 1919 under the name of Unión de Empleados Confederados del Cinematógrafo (UECC) during a period of intense anarcho-syndicalist activity in Mexico. The Carranza government at this time was also taking steps to regulate the infant film industry; this caused alarm among exhibitors and distributors and led to the organization in 1920 of the Unión de Alquiladores Mexicanos. The first strike called by UECC was in 1925 against the Tampico theaterowners who were forced to yield to the strikers' demands and sign collective contracts. Another important strike occurred in 1927 when the advent of sound caused the dismissal of many musicians. Ibid., pp. 60–61.
50. For details on this aspect of the film industries of the Soviet Union and Japan, see Rhode, *A History of the Cinema*, pp. 79–116 and Joseph L. Anderson and Donald Richie, *The Japanese Film: Art and Industry*, foreword by Akira Kurosawa (New York: Grove Press, 1960), pp. 128–30.
51. *Historia*, 1: 90–91, 111.
52. Although there is no evidence that De Fuentes intended these three films as a trilogy, for purposes of analysis they are being considered as such here.
53. *Historia*, 1: 92.
54. José Bohr corroborates this: "Y jamás el gobierno de Cárdenas influyó en la tónica de las producciones; nunca manejó censura de contracensura. Lo único que este hombre buscó fue dar sindicatos para que los trabajadores, artistas, etcétera estuvieran protegidos. Ni una vez rechazaron alguna cinta mía por contener una cosa en pro o en contra." Meyer, *Cuadernos*, 1: 40.
55. For production details, plot outline, and additional comments by Salvador Elizondo, José de la Colina, and Carlos Monsiváis see *Historia*, 1: 91–97. See also García Riera, *El cine mexicano*, pp. 32–34; Ayala Blanco, *La aventura*, pp. 23–31.
56. *Historia*, 1: 112.
57. Ibid.
58. Fehrenbach, *Lone Star*, p. 75.
59. The surface aspects of the plot are not of major importance since they principally involve the rivalry of two friends for the love of the same girl and the way in which the resulting tensions and misunderstandings are cleared up. For details see *Historia*, 1: 128; for Luz Alba's comments see ibid., pp. 131–32; for Carlos Monsiváis's and Tomás Pérez Turrent's comments see ibid., p. 132. Ayala Blanco has an interesting discussion of the literary origins of *Allá en el Rancho Grande*: it is a free adaptation of a turn-of-the-century Spanish play by Joaquín Dicenta. The *comedia ranchera*'s inspiration from the Spanish *sainete* (one-act comedy) and *zarzuela* (operetta) is also apparent. From the former, it takes the humorous situation and comedy of errors; from the latter, the interludes of gay music. A native source is the Mexico City burlesque or music hall of the 1920s, an observation also made by Luz Alba above. Ayala Blanco, *La aventura*, pp. 64–66. See also García Riera, *El cine mexicano*, p. 34; Reyes Nevares, *The Mexican Cinema*, pp. 1–2; and Alejandro Galindo, *Una radiografía histórica del cine mexicano* (Mexico City: Fondo de Cultura Popular, 1968), p. 133.
60. Tito Guízar was mentioned in a Spanish exercise book used by this author in a New York high school circa 1953 as the best-known "Latin-American troubador." By that time, however,

Guízar was quite passé south of the border and had long since been supplanted in popularity by both Jorge Negrete and Pedro Infante.

61. Claes af Geijerstam, *Popular Music in Mexico* (Albuquerque: University of New Mexico Press, 1976), pp. 41–45.

62. See Monsiváis, ''Junto contigo le doy un aplauso al placer y al amor,'' pp. 39–56, and idem, ''The Culture of the Frontier: The Mexican Side,'' in Stanley R. Ross, ed., *Views Across the Border: The United States and Mexico* (Albuquerque: University of New Mexico Press, 1978), pp. 50–67.

63. *Historia*, 1: 140.

64. Mahieu, *Breve historia*, p. 31.

65. *Historia*, 1: 117–18.

66. Ibid., p. 146.

67. Ibid., p. 147.

68. Ibid., p. 151.

69. Ibid., p. 135.

70. Ibid., pp. 167–68. See also Bambi, ''Lupe Vélez Tuvo Mucha Suerte en su Carrera, Pero no en sus Amores: Edelmira Zúñiga,'' *Excélsior*, 14 December 1976, pp. 1–B, 2–B, 10B.

71. *Historia*, 1: 172. See also Gómez Sicre, ''Dolores del Río,'' pp. 15–16 and Reyes Nevares, *The Mexican Cinema*, p. 18.

72. Since 1931, when *Santa* was released, a little over 15 million pesos had been invested in the movie industry. The majority of the profits from this capital were obviously not reinvested in the industry, since by 1939 the economic base of the cinema was as unstable as it had been in 1931. *Historia*, 1: 230.

73. See for instance, Emilio Fernández's account of how he and David Silva obtained financial backing for their first film, *La isla de la pasión*, from General Juan F. Azcárate. Reyes Nevares, *The Mexican Cinema*, p. 15.

74. Monaco, *Cinema and Society*, p. 33.

75. *Historia*, 1: 230–31.

76. Román Gubern, *Cine español en el exilio, 1936–1939* (Barcelona: Editorial Lumen, 1976), pp. 13–17.

77. ''Muerte del Actor Angel Garasa,'' *Mañana*, 4 September 1976, p. 62.

78. John Aldape, ''In 'mean, sexy' roles Emilia Guiu was a superstar,'' *The Arizona Republic*, 18 February 1973, p. L–2.

79. Reyes Nevares, *The Mexican Cinema*, p. 66.

80. Ibid., p. 31.

81. *Historia*, 1: 179–80.

82. Ibid., pp. 192–93.

83. Ibid., pp. 202–204. See also Reyes Nevares, *The Mexican Cinema*, pp. 21–42; Meyer, *Cuadernos*, 1: 93–108; García Riera, *El cine mexicano*, p. 63.

84. *Historia*, 1: 254–57; Ayala Blanco, *La aventura*, pp. 40–47.

85. *Historia*, 1: 260.

86. Ibid.

87. Ibid.

88. Ibid., pp. 260–61; Allen L. Woll, ''Hollywood's Good Neighbor Policy: The Latin Image in American Film, 1939–1946,'' *Journal of Popular Film* 3 (Fall 1974): 278–91; Paul J. Vanderwood, ''Images of Mexican Heroes in American Films'' (presented at the annual meeting of the American Historical Association, Washington, D.C., 28–30 December 1976), pp. 4–11.


CHAPTER 3

1. Cline, *The United States and Mexico*, p. 263.

2. *Historia*, 1: 264.

3. Miguel Ãngelo, ''Brasil: 75 anos de cinema,'' *O Cruzeiro*, 15 September 1971, pp. 158–62.

4. *Historia*, 2: 48.

5. Ibid., p. 10.

6. E. Bradford Burns, ''National Identity in Argentine Films,'' *Américas*, November–December 1975, p. 10. See also Raymond del Castillo, ''The Cinema in Argentina,'' *The Penguin Film Review*, no. 4 (1947), p. 101; Mahieu, *Breve historia*, pp. 46–47.

7. *Historia*, 2: 21.

8. Ibid., 1: 274.

9. For an approximation of *cantinflismo,* see *Enciclopedia de México,* 2:139–40. See also Marie Rose Oliver, "Cantinflas," *Hollywood Quarterly* 2 (1946–1947): 252–56.

10. *Historia,* 2: 12.

11. Ibid.

12. García Riera, *El cine mexicano,* pp. 77–78. See also Dr. Raúl Fournier's analysis of Cantinflas's humor in "Necesidad de reir," *Hispanoamericano,* 2 June 1950, p. 28; and E. R. E., "El gran éxito de papá Cantinflas," *Contenido* (Mexico City), July 1979, pp. 33–36.

13. *Historia,* 2: 15–16.

14. Ayala Blanco, *La aventura,* p. 52.

15. Francisco Pineda Alcalá, *La verídica historia del cine mexicano,* prologue by Fernando Morales Ortiz (Mexico City: n.p., 1965), pp. 49–51.

16. Galindo, *Una radiografía histórica,* photograph caption between pages 64 and 65.

17. Reyes Nevares, *The Mexican Cinema,* p. 15.

18. For instance, one million pesos was spent on *Simón Bolívar.* It was filmed at the CLASA studios with 10 days on location in the state of Veracruz. *Historia,* 2:24.

19. A 1953 Cuban–Mexican coproduction, *La rosa blanca,* with the Mexican actor Roberto Cañedo, was disappointing in its portrayal of José Martí. José Antonio González, "Apuntes para la historia de un cine sin historia," *Cine cubano,* no. 86/87/88 (1973 or 1974), p. 42.

20. Regarding a recent Cantinflas film, *El ministro y yo,* one critic said: "His decadence is complete: the same jokes, exact gestures, identical situations. Naturally, their effectiveness is lessened: the people laugh less, we might even say very little." Miguel Donoso Parejo, "CINE: El ministro y yo," *Mañana,* 24 July 1976, p. 10.

21. Enrique Colina and Daniel Díaz Torres, "Ideología del melodrama en el viejo cine latinoamericano," *Cine cubano,* no. 73/74/75 (1972), p. 19. This is an interesting Marxist analysis of the ideological bases of the commercial Mexican and Argentine cinemas. Predictably, the authors consider the principal themes and values expressed in many films to be "reactionary" and part of a bourgeois "plot" to suppress progressive cultural currents among the people. Many Mexican films have undoubtedly reflected and espoused middle-class values, but it could hardly be otherwise since filmmaking in Mexico (and all other countries) from the beginning was a bourgeois activity for a bourgeois audience. That many of these films might have inculcated middle-class values in the lower-class audiences that flocked to see them is also quite likely, but this was simply a natural process and hardly the result of sinister machinations. Mexico and Argentina to date have not had totalitarian governments that could mobilize cultural activities to reflect "official" values, even if the middle sectors in these countries could ever have agreed on what their "official" values should be. Colina and Díaz Torres, naturally enough since they are Marxists, fail to see that the Cuban cinema is the only one in Latin America that truly and consciously espouses an official viewpoint. This is not meant to deride Cuban films either in their content or technical quality. A Marxist viewpoint is as valid as any other but it does stem, in Cuba, from an absolute centralization of decision making. In Mexico in the 1970s, even though the industry had in effect been nationalized through the centralization of credit facilities in the Banco Nacional Cinematográfico, and content of both scripts and completed films was scrutinized by the Dirección de Cinematografía (as is still done), a wider range of ideas, from conservative to socialist, have been expressed in Mexican films than in those of revolutionary Cuba.

The theoretical basis for Colina and Díaz Torres is the "hypodermic model and mass society thesis" (Andrew Tudor, *Image and Influence: Studies in the Sociology of Film* [London: George Allen and Unwin, 1974]) which Tudor calls "deeply misleading" (p. 30). He says that this model suggests "people are the passive recipients of whatever the communicators care to 'inject'. . . . Some versions of the general thesis even go so far as implying conspiracy; media men as manipulators of society" (p. 31). Tudor goes on to say that "We see what we wish to see, and we twist messages around"—a process called "selective perception" (p. 35). He cites the "Mr. Biggott" studies—a series of antiprejudice cartoons shown to a test audience; about two-thirds of the sample "clearly misunderstood" the cartoons' intentions. Observers in this country have noticed a similar reaction to the character of Archie Bunker in the "All in the Family" television series: viewers of similar opinions have tended to identify with Bunker rather than "learn" that bigotry is negative and antisocial.

22. This film, as will be explained in chapter 4, was hardly a standard melodrama. On the contrary, it was an insightful social statement.

23. Meyer, *Cuadernos,* 2: 18; see also pp. 11–23 for Sara García's account of her career. For

additional comments on the self-sacrificing yet tyrannical mother image, as visualized in Mexican popular culture, see Aurelio de los Reyes et al., *80 años de cine en México,* Serie Imágenes 2 (Mexico City: UNAM, Difusión Cultural, 1977), pp. 110–11. The image is not that uniquely Mexican, of course; in the United States it is readily recognizable as the "Jewish mother" syndrome, especially in Philip Roth's novel, *Portnoy's Complaint.*

24. However, in *Maria Candelaria* (1943), Fernández, immediately after the opening credits, juxtaposes a girl's head with pre-Columbian sculptures to emphasize the racial links—a technique directly borrowed from Eisenstein. For additional comments on the Fernández-Figueroa style, see Ayala Blanco, *La aventura,* pp. 35–39, 92.

25. By way of clarification, both these films were produced in English and Spanish-language versions. In Spanish, *The Pearl* (based on a story by John Steinbeck) was, of course, *La perla* (*Historia,* 3: 15); *The Torch* (1949), costarring Paulette Goddard, was *Enamorada* in its Spanish-language version, with María Félix in the title role. Ibid., pp. 129–34. The dates in the text for both films correspond to the Spanish-language versions. See also Reyes Nevares, *The Mexican Cinema,* pp. 11–19.

26. Carlos Perea in *México Cinema,* 1 July 1942, as quoted in *Historia,* 2: 53.

27. "Balance Cinematográfico," *Tiempo,* 22 January 1943, p. 36.

28. According to its first director, Lic. Carlos Carriedo Galván, in an interview published in *Cinema Reporter,* 1 July 1942, and reprinted in *Historia,* 2: 53–54.

29. For a complete list of board members, see *Historia,* 2: 54, n. 3.

30. "Balance Cinematográfico," p. 36.

31. *Historia,* 2: 54.

32. As García Riera refers to it. Ibid., p. 111.

33. Both García Riera (ibid.) and Mahieu (*Breve historia,* pp. 44–45) attribute this to formula films which appealed to the least demanding and most unsophisticated segments of the Latin American publics.

34. *Historia,* 2: 111. However, toward the end of the war Argentina reversed its policy and declared war on Germany. Raw film stock from the U.S. again became available for Argentine filmmakers; this caused a small panic in Mexican film circles since they realized that this would make Argentine films competitive once again. "Peligro para México," *Hispanoamericano,* 19 April 1946, p. 39. This does not mean that Hollywood movies were completely edged out of the Latin American market during World War II. For instance, in November 1942, box-office receipts in the Federal District were broken down as follows: Mexican films, 636,839 (pesos); U.S., 1,253,110; and Argentine, 63,042. "Balance Cinematográfico," p. 37.

35. "Tres Veces 'Santa'," *Tiempo,* 26 March 1943, p. 39.

36. *Historia,* 2: 111–12.

37. Ibid., pp. 113–14.

38. Ibid., and Reyes Nevares, *The Mexican Cinema,* p. 18. See also "Sin Prejuicios," *Tiempo,* 25 April 1943, p. 59.

39. See Raymond Borde's comments in *Historia,* 2: 169; see also Ayala Blanco, *La aventura,* pp. 195–96.

40. Reyes Nevares, *The Mexican Cinema,* pp. 18–19.

41. Ibid., p. 19.

42. Label applied to a genre of postwar gangster movies set in shabby urban environments and featuring cynical, alienated "antiheroes." Also called "underground movies" by Manny Farber. Howard Hawks's *The Big Sleep* (1946) is considered one of the most important examples of the *film noir* style. Penelope Houston, *The Contemporary Cinema* (Baltimore: Penguin Books, 1966), pp. 65–67. See also John S. Whitney, "A Filmography of Film Noir," *The Journal of Popular Film* 5 (1976): 321–57.

43. *Historia,* 2: 156.

44. "Moral sexual y moraleja en el cine mexicano," *Nuevo Cine,* no. 1 (April 1961) as quoted in *Historia,* 2: 156–57. For a discussion of Fernández and Bracho see Natalia Askenazy, "The Two Kinds of Mexican Movies," *Films in Review* 2 (May 1951): 35–39.

45. CLASA had 10 sound stages and Azteca 18. H. H. Wollenberg, "Round the World's Studios," *The Penguin Film Review,* no. 1 (1946), p. 53.

46. "Nuevos Estudios," *Tiempo,* 12 March 1943, p. 45.

47. RKO did eventually buy into the Churubusco studios. H. H. Wollenberg, "Round the World's Studios," *The Penguin Film Review,* no. 3 (1947), pp. 39–40. According to Catherine Macotela, RKO and Universal tried to buy the CLASA studios. "El sindicalismo en el cine (primera parte)," *Otrocine,* no. 2 (April–June 1975), p. 65.

48. "Ofensiva Frustrada," *Tiempo*, 17 September 1943, pp. 48, 50.
49. *Historia*, 1: 206 and 2: 90; Macotela, "El sindicalismo en el cine," p. 66. A total of five articles by Macotela traces the complicated unionization process. The first article appears in *Otrocine*, no. 2 (April—June 1975), pp. 60—67. The subsequent articles appear as follows: "(segunda parte)," ibid., no. 3 (July—September 1975), pp. 57—63; "(tercera parte)," ibid., no. 4 (October—December 1975), pp. 65—69; "(cuarta parte)," ibid., no. 5 (January—March 1976), pp. 59—65; and "(quinta parte)," ibid., no. 6 (April—June 1976), pp. 46—48. Henceforth, references to any of the above articles will be " '(tercera parte),' p. 66," etc.
50. "(segunda parte)," p. 60. In 1934 it was renamed "Unión de Trabajadores de los Estudios Cinematográficos de México" (UTECM). On occasion this name was still being used for STIC until 1944. "Sección 7 vs. Solís," *Tiempo*, 14 April 1944, p. 50. See also "Aniversario Sindical," ibid., 30 April 1943, p. 42.
51. *Historia*, 2: 207.
52. Ibid.
53. "(primera parte)," p. 65.
54. Ibid., p. 64.
55. "(segunda parte)," p. 57.
56. Ibid., p. 61. The STPC had at its inception 2,192 members.
57. *Historia*, 3:14. For a complete account of this complex affair see the series of articles by Catherine Macotela in *Otrocine*, cited above. See also "Ultimo Episodio," *Tiempo*, 14 September 1945, p. 5; and "Alma de España," *Tiempo*, 22 February 1946, p. 35, on the STIC/STPC dispute which was preventing Miguel de Molina, a Spanish dancer, from performing. For additional details on the organization of both STPC and STIC, see Heuer, *La industria cinematográfica mexicana*, p. 121.
58. *Historia*, 2: 286.
59. For elaborations on this, see ibid. and Ayala Blanco, *La aventura*, pp. 241—46. For an interesting view of the Mexican cinema from the other side, that is, from a pro-Franco Spaniard, see Ernesto Giménez Caballero, *Amor a Méjico (A través de su cine)*, Cuadernos de Monografías no. 5 (Madrid: Seminario de Problemas Hispanoamericanos, April 1948). The author attempts to establish that Mexico through its cinema preserves the best of traditional Spanish values. First, the Catholic religion, through such films as *San Francisco de Asís* and *María Candelaria*; second, the Spanish knightly tradition in the films of Jorge Negrete and *Enamorada*; and finally, the picaresque genre in Cantinflas's movies. The work is an attempt to emphasize that Spain and Mexico remain closely tied by cultural and religious bonds in spite of the Mexican government's hostility to Franco and its support of the Spanish Republic's government-in-exile headquartered in Mexico City.
60. Ayala Blanco, *La aventura*, p. 244. A footnote on this page states that copies of the film were dubbed in the Valencian dialect. There were also plans to have Orson Welles narrate the film for English-speaking audiences. " La Barraca' en Norteamérica," *Tiempo*, 2 November 1945, p. 41.
61. Galindo, *Una radiografía histórica*, pp. 143—44.
62. "Caja de Sorpresas," *Tiempo*, 30 March 1945, p. 39.
63. Christopher Finch, *The Art of Walt Disney: From Mickey Mouse to the Magic Kingdom* (New York: Harry N. Abrams, Publisher, 1975), pp. 113—14.
64. This in spite of the fact that the project had some powerful backing. William Jenkins's daughter, Elisabeth, was ready to support it at the urging of producer Alfonso Sánchez Tello and journalist Isaac Díaz. In addition, Nelson Rockefeller delayed Robert Trasker's induction into the army until 1943 so he could go to Mexico and work on the script. "'Potrero del Llano'," *Tiempo*, 20 November 1942, p. 47. Another film, *Espionaje en el golfo*, was made in which the sinking of the *Potrero del Llano* is an incident. "'Charro' Patriótico," *Tiempo*, 6 November 1942, p. 37.
65. Ibid.
66. Mexico was the only Spanish-speaking Latin American country to contribute a combat unit to the Allied war effort (Brazil also sent a substantial force to the European theater of war). This was Expeditionary Squadron 201 made up of 300 volunteers from the Mexican air force. It was formed in July 1944 and saw action in the Philippines and Formosa (Taiwan). Cline, *The United States and Mexico*, p. 278.

## CHAPTER 4

1. For a detailed account of these years see Francisco Aranda, *Luis Buñuel: A Critical Biography*, trans. David Robinson (London: Seeker and Warburg, 1975), pp. 116—30.

2. Libertad Lamarque's only recorded comment concerning *Gran Casino* and Buñuel: "En fin, lamento que nunca más, despues de tantos años, volví a filmar con él." Meyer, *Cuadernos*, 6: 71.
3. *Historia*, 3: 163.
4. José Luis Ceceña, *Siempre*, 6 August 1969, as quoted in *Historia*, 3: 95—96 fn.
5. Ibid., p. 95.
6. Miguel Contreras Torres, *El libro negro del cine mexicano* (Mexico City: Editora Hispano—Continental Films, 1960), p. 53. See also Joel Edelstein's comments in "Official Statement by the University of the Americas Concerning the Conflict of 1976 and Its Consequences," Santa Catarina Mártir, Puebla, 1 July 1977, Appendix A, p. 23.
7. Contreras Torres, *El libro negro*, p. 55.
8. Ibid., p. 51; Geijerstam, *Popular Music in Mexico*, p. 109. O'Farrill was the owner of XHTV, the first television station in the country; Azcárraga owned XEWTV. Contreras Torres might have meant that Jenkins money was also invested in XEW instead of Azcárraga being associated with XHTV. An interesting note is that Ing. Guillermo González Camarena in 1939 patented a color television system in Mexico and in 1940 registered it in the United States. His system was later adopted by CBS and RCA Victor. "La Televisión en México," *Hispanoamericano*, 17 August 1951, pp. 3—6.
9. *Historia*, 3: 173—74.
10. "Contra un Monopolio," *Hispanoamericano*, 13 February 1953, p. 45. See also "Contra un Monopolio (2)," ibid., 27 February 1953, p. 42.
11. Felipe Mier Miranda, "La industria nacional cinematográfica mexicana," (Licenciate thesis, UNAM, 1963), p. 32.
12. See *Historia*, 3: 203—207 and Ayala Blanco, *La aventura*, pp. 81—97.
13. Ayala Blanco, *La aventura*, p. 92.
14. *Historia*, 3: 176.
15. Reyes Nevares, *The Mexican Cinema*, pp. 50—51.
16. For the extensive summary on this film see *Historia*, 3: 217—22; Ayala Blanco, *La aventura*, pp. 113—19.
17. *Historia*, 3: 272, 275.
18. For an extensive commentary on this film see ibid., pp. 309—14. Ayala Blanco dedicates a long analysis to *Una familia de tantas* in *La aventura*, pp. 54—63. See also "Sainete Mexicano," *Hispanoamericano*, 29 July 1949, p. 29.
19. Galindo did not get any more specific than this. Personal interview, Mexico City, 7 July 1977.
20. Ibid. Galindo had been thinking of making *El juicio de Martín Cortés* for some time. See Galindo, *Una radiografía histórica*, pp. 55—83. See also Reyes Nevares, *The Mexican Cinema*, pp. 29—30; Meyer, *Cuadernos*, 1: 93—108; Alejandro Galindo, *¿Qué es el cine?* (Mexico City: Editorial Nuestro Tiempo, 1975); idem, *El cine, genocidio espiritual: De 1900 al "crash" de 29* (Mexico City: Editorial Nuestro Tiempo, 1971).
21. Personal interview, Mexico City, 7 July 1977.
22. The writer remembers seeing Tin-Tan in just such a costume on the stage of the Alameda Theater in the early 1940s. For biographical details see, *Historia*, 3: 48.
23. "El fabuloso 'Tin-Tan'," *Mañana*, 29 May 1976, p. 56. For Mexican attitudes toward pachucos see Octavio Paz, *The Labyrinth of Solitude*, trans. Lysander Kemp (New York: Grove Press, 1961), pp. 12—18. For a discussion of Tin-Tan's pachuco character and its metamorphosis see Monsiváis, "The Culture of the Frontier," pp. 63—64. See also "Authentic Pachuco," *Time*, 10 July 1944, p. 72. Tin-Tan appeared briefly in at least one American film, *Song of Mexico* (1945), a Republic picture. See advertisement in *Hispanoamericano*, 30 November 1945, p. 15.
24. For an assessment of the social significance of popular dances see Carlos Monsiváis, "Es el baile del pingüino un baile elegante y fino," *Diálogos* (Colegio de México) 13 (September—October 1977): 11—14.
25. *Historia*, 4: 133. See also ibid., pp. 132—34 for comments from *Cahiers du Cinéma* on Ninón Sevilla, and Ayala Blanco, *La aventura*, pp. 145—52. For comments on *Sensualidad* (1950) see ibid., pp. 152—54.
26. For an interesting discussion of the genre in relation to culture see Tudor, *Image and Influence*, pp. 223—31.
27. *Historia*, 4: 286, 289.
28. Interview, Mexico City, 7 July 1977.
29. *Historia*, 4: 68—73.
30. Ibid., p. 143; for commentary on *Los olvidados* see pp. 156—76.

31. "El Drama del Pueblo," *Hispanoamericano*, 22 September 1950, p. 24; "'Los Olvidados' y la Critica," ibid., 7 March 1952, p. 52. See also Daniel Díaz Torres, "Los Olvidados," *Cine cubano*, no. 78/79/80 (1972), pp. 134–35.

32. Vincent Canby, "Uncovering Luis Bunuel's [sic] Mexican Treasures," p. D–13.

33. *Historia*, 6: 25–39.

34. Buñuel's Mexican films are discussed by Aranda in his *Luis Buñuel*, pp. 128–69. See also Freddy Buache, *The Cinema of Luis Buñuel*, trans. Peter Graham (London: The Tantivy Press, 1973), pp. 42–95, 117–37. For a discussion of Buñuel's adaptations of the Mexican melodrama to his own ends, see Daniel Díaz Torres and Enrique Colina, "El melodrama en la obra de Luis Buñuel," *Cine cubano*, no. 78/79/80 (1972), pp. 156–64. For additional data see: Daniel Aubry and J. M. Lacor, "Luis Buñuel," *Film Quarterly* 12 (Winter 1958): 7–9; Emilio García Riera, "La eterna rebelión de Luis Buñuel," *Tiempo de cine*, no. 13 (March 1963), pp. 8–13, 64; idem, "Viridiana," *Film Culture*, no. 24 (1962), p. 74; idem, "The Eternal Rebellion of Luis Buñuel," ibid., no. 21 (1960), p. 42; idem, "The Films of Luis Buñuel," ibid., p. 58; Peter Harcourt, "Luis Buñuel: Spaniard and Surrealist," *Film Quarterly* 20 (Spring 1967): 2–19; Kenji Kanesaka, "A Visit to Luis Buñuel," *Film Culture*, no. 41 (1966), p. 60, reprinted in Andrew Sarris, ed., *Interviews with Film Directors* (New York: Avon Books, 1967), pp. 65–74; "Luis Buñuel hace la anatomía del churro cinematográfico," *Cine cubano*, no. 78/79/80 (1972), pp. 112–13; "Filmografía Luis Buñuel," ibid., pp. 166–75; Emir Rodríguez Monegal, "El mito Buñuel," *Tiempo de cine*, no. 14/15 (July 1963), pp. 7–10; "Entretien avec Luis Buñuel," *Cahiers du Cinéma*, no. 191 (June 1967), pp. 14–18; Fernando Pérez, "Nazarín," *Cine cubano*, no. 78/79/80 (1972), pp. 136–37; Fernando Césarman, *El ojo de Buñuel: Psicoanálisis desde una butaca*, prologue by Carlos Fuentes (Barcelona: Anagrama, 1976); Carol Miller, "El Precio de la Experiencia," *Hispanoamericano*, 11 April 1977, p. 50; Penelope Gilliatt, "Profiles: Long Live the Living!" *The New Yorker*, 5 December 1977, pp. 53–72; Randall Conrad, "'I Am Not a Producer!'—Working with Buñuel," *Film Quarterly* 23 (Fall 1979): 2–11; Ado Kyrou, *Luis Buñuel* (Paris: Editions Seghers, 1970); and Carol Miller, "Luis Buñuel: El Ojo de la Libertad," *Hispanoamericano*, 12 January 1981, pp. 54–57.

35. *Historia*, 5: 145–52; Ayala Blanco, *La aventura*, p. 197; "Misterio y Claridad," *Hispanoamericano*, 20 September 1954, pp. 41–43.

36. *Historia*, 5: 7.

37. See Santiago Reachi's remarks in "A la Conquista del Interés Mundial," *Hispanoamericano*, 27 December 1954, pp. 46–47. See also "Otra Operación de Cimex," ibid., 9 August 1954, p. 41 for details on how the firm bought up the distributors in the U.S. (Azteca Films) and Cuba (Manuel Espinosa Iglesias's Distribuidora de Películas Continental). Clasa-Mohme remained the independent U.S. distributor.

38. "Premios a la moral," *Hispanoamericano*, 18 January 1953, p. 39.

39. *Historia*, 5: 235–38; "En México se Filmará a Colores," *Hispanoamericano*, 7 December 1953, p. 50; "Películas en Colores," ibid., 8 February 1954, p. 46. The average cost of a film went from 750,200 pesos in 1954 to 936,300 in 1955. *Historia*, 6: 8.

40. "Emigran Productores a Cuba," *Hispanoamericano*, 29 March 1954, p. 55. However, Cuban actors and technicians protested the "Mexicanization" of moviemaking on the island. "Martí Ganó la Batalla," ibid., 9 November 1953, p. 47. See also "Actividad Mexicana en el Extranjero," ibid., 24 May 1954, p. 60; "Pacto con Cuba," ibid., 14 June 1954, p. 47. For additional background on Cuban cinema and its relation to Mexico in the prerevolutionary period, see Nestor Almendros, "The Cinema in Cuba," *Film Culture* no. 3 (1956), p. 21 and González, "Apuntes para la historia," pp. 37–45.

41. Another method of ensuring at least some distribution of Mexican films abroad was by requiring reciprocity, that is, if foreign films were to be shown in Mexico, the other country had to accept a like number of Mexican films in exchange. Such arrangements existed with Spain, Britain, Argentina, Italy, and Japan. "Intercambio con España," *Hispanoamericano*, 2 November 1953, p. 44.

42. "Películas de 2 Semanas," ibid., 28 June 1954, p. 58.

43. *Historia*, 7: 8.

44. See Manuel González Casanova, *¿Qué es un Cine-Club?* (Mexico City: Dirección General de Difusión Cultural, Sección de Actividades Cinematográficas, UNAM, 1961), pp. 11–16; "El CCM," *Hispanoamericano*, 13 July 1951, pp. 42–43; "9 Programas del Cine Club," ibid., 28 September 1951, p. 48; "3 Grandes Obras," ibid., 7 December 1951, p. 44; "El Pasado

Vuelve,'' ibid., 16 May 1952, p. 60; ''Labor Fructuosa,'' ibid., 11 November 1952, p. 48; and ''Exitos del Pasado,'' ibid., 3 April 1953, p. 45. The charter of the Federación Mexicana de Cine Clubs is reprinted in *Historia*, 6: 15–19.

## CHAPTER 5

1. Heuer, *La industria cinematográfica*, p. 179.
2. *Historia*, 6: 132; ''Acusaciones del 'Indio','' *Hispanoamericano*, 27 September 1954, p. 47.
3. For a detailed analysis of the Mexican political system and its role in economic development see Roger D. Hansen, *The Politics of Mexican Development* (Baltimore: Johns Hopkins University Press, 1971). See also Pablo González Casanova, *Democracy in Mexico*, trans. Danielle Salti (New York: Oxford University Press, 1972). For a more up-to-date assessment see ''Mexico's Reluctant Oil Boom,'' *Business Week*, 15 January 1979, pp. 64–74; James Flanigan, ''Mexican Oil: The U.S. Is Most definitely *Not* in the Driver's Seat,'' *Forbes*, 22 January 1979, pp. 29–32; idem, ''Why Won't the Mexicans Sell Us More Oil?'', *Forbes.*, 29 October 1979, pp. 41–52.
4. *Historia*, 8: 195.
5. Ibid., p. 194.
6. Ibid., p. 10. The ''Santo'' series may have been of bad quality but it was remarkably enduring nonetheless as well as continuously profitable. See Agustín Gurezpe, '''Rencor y Envidia Porque mis Películas Siempre Ganan Dinero,' Dice El Santo,'' *Excélsior*, 6 April 1977, Section Cine, Teatro, Radio y TV, p. 1; and Jorge Ayala Blanco, *La búsqueda del cine mexicano (1968–1972)*, 2 vols., Cuadernos de Cine #22 (Mexico City: UNAM, Dirección General de Difusión Cultural, 1974), 1: 295–304.
7. *Historia*, 7: 389.
8. Ibid., 8: 436.
9. Ibid., 7: 321–22.
10. Ibid., pp. 459–60.
11. Ibid., 8: 11–26.
12. Ibid., pp. 358, 361–62.
13. Ibid., p. 354.
14. Jomi García Ascot, ''El cine y el escritor,'' *Cine cubano*, no. 31/32/33 (1966), p. 104.
15. See ibid., pp. 104–105 and *Historia*, 8: 114–36 for an extensive recapitulation of the commentary on this film.
16. See *Historia*, 8: 139–86 for an extensive commentary. See also García Riera, ''Viridiana,'' p. 74; David Stewart Hull, ''Viridiana,'' *Film Quarterly* 15 (Winter 1961/62): 55–56; Buache, *The Cinema of Luis Buñuel*, pp. 117–27; and Aranda, *Luis Buñuel*, pp. 190–205.
17. *Historia*, 8: 292–96. See also Ayala Blanco, *La aventura*, pp. 284–88.
18. See Reyes Nevares, *The Mexican Cinema*, pp. 63–76 and Alberto Isaac, ''Cine latinoamericano: reportaje a Luis Alcoriza,'' *Tiempo de cine*, año 5, no. 20/21 (Spring–Summer 1965), pp. 38–40, 80.
19. Ayala Blanco, *La aventura*, p. 304.
20. Vivian Lash, ''Experimenting with Freedom in Mexico,'' *Film Quarterly* 19 (Summer 1966): 19. Lash writes that 18 films were completed while Ayala Blanco specifies and lists 12. For a complete listing of the films entered in the competition, see Ayala Blanco, *La aventura*, pp. 3–5 and Appendix above, pp. 223–24.
21. Ayala Blanco, *La aventura*, p. 306.
22. Ibid., pp. 308–10. An interesting footnote to the film is that Luis Buñuel appeared in a cameo role.
23. With the exception of Miguel Barbachano Ponce, already well established in film circles as a producer of ''quality'' cinema.
24. Ayala Blanco, *La aventura*, p. 305.
25. Tomás Pérez-Turrent and Gillian Turner, ''Mexico,'' in Peter Cowie, ed., *International Film Guide 1976* (London: Tantivy Press, 1977), p. 207.
26. Ayala Blanco, *La búsqueda*, 1: 13. *En el balcón vacío* was premiered at the French Institute and later shown at UNAM. Apparently it has never been shown commercially in Mexico. García Ascot, ''El cine y el escritor,'' p. 104. The film is easily available at the Cineteca Nacional. Also included in the STPC's 1965 awards was distribution of the prize-winning film through the state channels. Independent filmmaking is not any easier in other countries, including the U.S. See for

example Janet Stevenson, "Why So Few Independent Feature Films?" *In These Times,* 6–12 December 1977, p. 22.

27. Pérez-Turrent and Turner, "Mexico," in Cowie, ed., *International Film Guide 1974*, p. 237.

28. Ayala Blanco, *La búsqueda*, 1: 11.

29. See Elena Poniatowska's comments in *Historia*, 8: 200 and the *Visión* article quoted in ibid., pp. 202–203.

30. Alan Riding, "Mexico Elects a Symbol," *The New York Times Magazine,* 13 June 1976, p. 14; see also Sergio Zermeño, *México: Una democracia utópica: El movimiento estudiantil del 68,* prologue by Carlos Monsiváis (Mexico City: Siglo Veintiuno Editores, 1978).

31. Much more extensive coverage was given by the U.S. press to the American black athletes who gave a "black power" salute during the playing of the "Star-Spangled Banner" after being awarded their gold medals.

32. See also Elena Poniatowska, *Massacre in Mexico*, trans. Helen R. Lane (New York: Viking Press, 1975), originally published as *La noche de Tlatelolco: Testimonios de historia* (Mexico City: Ediciones Era, 1971).

33. Ayala Blanco, *La búsqueda*, 1: 13.

34. Ibid., 2: 333.

35. Ibid. For a discussion of the film, see pp. 332–37.

36. Ibid., pp. 339–40. For a discussion of *El grito*, see pp. 337–48.

37. Díaz Ordaz was quoted as saying, "If what you desire is to bury the cinema industry, I will preside over the funeral. The government is not interested in that industry." Galindo, *¿Qué es el cine?*, p. 129. Luis Echeverría had been appointed to the governing board of the Banco Cinematográfico in 1963. *Historia*, 8: 351.

38. Rodolfo Echeverría's professional name was Rodolfo Landa. He had been politically active as well as having been a performer; in 1952 he was elected a deputy to congress. "La Probable XLII Legislatura," *Hispanoamericano*, 13 June 1952, p. 9.

39. Cárdenas is considered by some to have been Marxist; Echeverría was nothing of the kind. Many observers looked upon the latter's wooing of the international left as little more than political opportunism.

40. For an assessment of the Echeverría presidency, see Riding, "Mexico Elects a Symbol," pp. 14–15, 19, 22.

41. *Informe general sobre la actividad cinematográfica en el año 1976 relativo al Banco Nacional Cinematográfico, S.A. y sus filiales* (Mexico City: Banco Nacional Cinematográfico, 26 November 1976), p. 11.

42. Ibid., p. 13.

43. Ibid., pp. 11–12.

44. Manuel Michel, "CCC: Un retrato escrito," *Otrocine*, no. 1 (January–March 1975), pp. 62–68.

45. "Edificio," *Cineteca Nacional 1974* (compiled for in-house reference), pp. 30–31.

46. "Acervo," ibid., pp. 35–38; *Informe general*, p. 408.

47. *Informe general*, p. 16.

48. Ibid., pp. 159–60. For more information on CONACINE see ibid., pp. 159–68; for CONACITE I, see pp. 187–91; and for CONACITE II, see pp. 201–204.

49. *Anuario de la producción cinematográfica mexicana, 1970/Mexican Film Production, 1970/ Production cinématographique mexicaine, 1970* (Mexico City: Procinemex, n.d.)

50. *Anuario . . ., 1971.*

51. *Anuario . . ., 1972.*

52. Alejandro Galindo characterized Alcoriza's *Mecánica nacional* as falsely portraying the way Mexicans behave, and bitterly attacked the Echeverría brothers for their policies toward the film industry. This writer suspects that Galindo's resentment was occasioned by the favoritism shown to young directors like Cazals. Galindo's own pet projects were realized in 1973: *El juicio de Martín Cortés* and *Ante el cadáver de un líder* (the latter his personal favorite), but they were not given the distribution or promotion he felt they deserved. Personal interview, Mexico City, 5 July 1977.

53. There are discrepancies between the Banco's figures and those from Procinemex's *Anuario*. For instance, the latter shows 72 full-length features and 8 independent films for 1971 for a total of 80 films, while the Banco indicates a total of 75. However, the *Informe general* also lists 7 films made by foreign companies in Mexico for a total of 82, a figure not reflected in the table.

54. Interview with Sigifredo García Sanz, Mexico City, 15 July 1977. García Sanz was associated with the film industry from 1947 to the early 1970s, principally in accounting but often becoming

involved in other areas of filmmaking. In July 1977, Margarita López Portillo, in her capacity as General Director of Radio, Television, and Cinema—a post created especially for her—ordered a thoroughgoing reorganization of the film industry's financial structure and García Sanz was designated as a consultant to coordinate the project. At the time, he was hopeful that this meant a retreat from state participation in filmmaking.

55. However, it is true that the lowest yearly number of films made up to that time in the decade—42 films—was made in 1976. "México y Argentina Dominados por el Sexo en su Cinematografía," *Excélsior,* 19 January 1977, Section Cine, Teatro, Radio y TV, p. 5.

56. See Sergio Guzik, "A Mass Changes Me More: An Interview with Alexandro [*sic*] Jodorowski," *The Drama Review* 14 (Winter 1970): 70–76. In the same issue, see also "The Mole: Excerpts from a Film Script," pp. 57–69.

57. For more on Jodorowski, see Miguel Barbachano Ponce, "Crítica de Cine: La Montaña Sagrada," *Excélsior,* 6 October 1976, Section Cine, Teatro, Radio y TV, p. 1. Jodorowski expressed impatience with the Mexican public's reception of his films. Complaining about censorship and the cuts he was obliged to make, Jodorowski said that "here in Mexico they are afraid of me, others are not censored." "La Gente de Mexico no Está Preparada Para ver mis Películas: Jodorowski," *Excélsior,* 1 October 1976, Section Cine, Teatro, Radio y TV, p. 1. For commentary on *Fando y Lis* and *El topo,* see Ayala Blanco, *La búsqueda,* 2: 407–15.

58. "Reitera LE que hay Libertad Para Tratarlo Todo en Cine," *Excélsior,* 28 June 1976, p. A–29. See also 'El Gobierno Mexicano Nacionalizó la Industria del Cine y Ahora se Producen Películas que antes se Consideraban 'Tabúes'," *Excélsior,* 26 October 1976, Section Cine, Teatro, Radio y TV, p. 1.

59. Reyes Nevares, *The Mexican Cinema,* pp. 67–68.

60. Agustín Gurezpe, "Ninguna Película del Nuevo Cine Mexicano Responde a la Necesidad Crítica de la Realidad Actual de Nuestro País," *Excélsior,* 22 July 1976, Section Cine, Teatro, Radio y TV, p. 1.

61. For this, the reader may consult Ayala Blanco's two invaluable works, already extensively cited here: *La aventura del cine mexicano* and *La búsqueda del cine mexicano,* 2 vols.

62. Its gross receipts up to January 1974 were second only to *The Godfather*—7,558,000 pesos. Sam Askinazy, "Mexico's Own Film $600,000 Behind 'Godpop,'" *Variety,* 9 January 1974, p. 10.

63. Manolo Fábregas has produced, directed, and acted in Spanish-language versions of *Life with Father, My Fair Lady,* and *Fiddler on the Roof,* as well as many other adaptations of hit American shows. Marvin Alisky, "Fábregas's Broadway-to-Mexico Theater," *The Christian Science Monitor,* 2 October 1970, p. 4.

64. See Ayala Blanco, *La búsqueda,* 1: 164–69; Reyes Nevares, *The Mexican Cinema,* pp. 63, 69; Marvin Alisky, "Mexico versus Malthus: National Trends," *Current History* 66 (May 1974): 229–30; "Lo Mejor de los Estrenos en 1972," *Hispanoamericano,* 15 January 1973, p. 56; and Angel A. Pérez Gómez, "Luis Alcoriza: Mecánica nacional," *Reseña* (Madrid), año 14, no. 103 (March 1977), p. 29.

65. Ayala Blanco, *La búsqueda,* 2: 503.

66. Ibid., pp. 503–506. See also Alvaro Uribe, "Entrevista a Alfredo Joskowicz," *Otrocine,* no. 3 (July–September 1975), pp. 64–67; José Luis Peralta, "El cambio," ibid., pp. 68–70.

67. For an account of the town and the actual events, see Elsa R. de Estrada, "Ecos de un linchamiento en el pueblo de las bocinas," *Contenido* (Mexico City), June 1976, pp. 72–82. For a description of how the screenplay was written see Tomás Pérez-Turrent, "Una experiencia alrededor de Canoa," *Otrocine,* no. 2 (April–June 1975), pp. 8–12. See also Fernando Gaxiola, "Canoa, memoria de un hecho vergonzante," *Otrocine,* no. 1 (January–March 1975), p. 10; "Reportaje y Denuncia," *Hispanoamericano,* 16 February 1976, p. 59; Antonia Landa G., "Canoa," *Otrocine,* no. 4 (October–December 1975), pp. 14–15; and Martha L. Sepúlveda, "Sobre Canoa," ibid., pp. 16–18.

68. Poli Délano, "El apando," *Otrocine,* no. 6 (April–June 1976), p. 33; Douglas Sánchez, "El apando," ibid., pp. 34–35; Jaime A. Shelley, "Conversación con Felipe Cazals," ibid., no. 3 (July–September 1975), pp. 34–43.

69. Agustín Gurezpe, "'Nunca más Traeré Pistola al Cinto,' Prometió el 'Indio' Fernández ayer en los Churubusco," *Excélsior,* 14 December 1976, Section Cine, Teatro, Radio y TV, pp. 1, 5; Juan de Ayala, "A Ultima Hora el 'Indio' Fernández Tuvo que Pagar $150,000 de Fianza," ibid., 11 December 1976, p. 1; Ayala Blanco, *La búsqueda,* 1: 19–39.

70. See Luis Reyes de la Maza, "De cómo el papá de Martin Cortés se fue mucho para el Tívoli," *Otrocine,* no. 1 (January–March 1975), pp. 33–39.

71. Reyes Nevares, *The Mexican Cinema,* p. 29.

72. Letter from Christon I. Archer, 1 December 1977. See also Stanley Meisler, "Is This Democracy?" *Los Angeles Times*, 7 March 1976, p. IX–4.

73. Francisco Sánchez, "Tívoli," *Otrocine*, no. 1 (January–March 1975), pp. 19–22; Jaime A. Shelley, "Entrevista con Alberto Isaac," ibid., pp. 23–32.

74. Jesús Salvador Treviño, "The New Mexican Cinema," *Film Quarterly* 34 (Spring 1980): 30–31.

75. There has been scant attention paid to recent Mexican films by American critics. *Canoa*, which won a "Silver Bear" at the 1976 Berlin Film Festival (Ricardo Perete, "¡Corte!" *Excélsior*, 1 October 1976, Section Cine, Teatro, Radio y TV, p. 1) apparently has never been released to general audiences in the United States. However, the Museum of Modern Art in 1977 did acquire for its permanent holdings eight recent Mexican films including *Actas de Marusia (The New Yorker*, 17 January 1977, p. 18). The series was sent on tour around the country and reviewed by Dennis West ("Mexican Cinema in 1977: A Commentary on the Mexican Film Festival Presently Touring the U.S.," *The American Hispanist* 2 [May 1977]: 6–7, 13–14). For reviews of Paul Leduc's *Reed: México insurgente* see Lewis H. Diuguid, "AFI's Latin American Film Festival," *The Washington Post*, 17 March 1974, p. E4; Kevin Thomas, " 'Reed' Treats Mexico Revolt," *Los Angeles Times*, 9 March 1976, p. IV–8; and Michael Goodwin, "'Reed: Insurgent Mexico," *Take One* 4 (December 1974): 31. Rafael Corkidi's *Pafnucio Santo* (1976) was shown at the 15th New York Film Festival—the first Mexican film ever included—and reviewed by Lawrence van Gelder, "Film Festival: Pafnucio Santo," *New York Times*, 27 September 1977. See also Carl Mora, "Let's Screen More Latin Films," *Nuestro*, October 1977, p. 59; and idem, "Mexico's Commercial Films: Sources for the Study of Social History," *PCCLAS Proceedings* 6 (1977–1979): 205–15.

76. Pedro Chaskel, another exiled Chilean cineast, praised Mexico for the support it had given Littín: "it represents not only a courtesy, but also backing for the Chilean resistance which struggles for the liberation of our country." He also said that the cameraman Jorge Muller and the actress Carmen Bueno had last been reported in "a concentration camp where they had been tortured." Agustín Gurezpe, "Habla Pedro Chaskel, Chileno en el Exilio—Tarea de Cineastas Latinoamericanos: Luchar por Descolonización Cultural," *Excélsior*, 29 May 1976, p. 30–A.

77. He singled out Tennessee Williams, one of the jurors, as being responsible for the negative vote. Williams had attacked violence in films, presumably with *Actas de Marusia* in mind. Agustín Gurezpe, "Littín Afirma que Perdió en Cannes por un Voto," *Excélsior*, 18 June 1976, p. C–1.

78. It opened at 14 theaters in the Federal District and took in 668,767 pesos in one day's receipts. Miguel Pareja Donoso, "Actas de Marusia," *Mañana*, 24 April 1976, p. 10.

79. Betty Jeffries Demby, "The 30th Cannes Film Festival," *Filmmakers Newsletter*, October, 1980, pp. 28–33. The special treatment accorded Littín in Mexico did not fail to elicit criticism; he denied that he "ever pretended to leadership or to take the attitude that he was a hero or saviour of the Mexican cinema . . . he received the normal salary of a Mexican film director." "Respuesta de Miguel Littín a Avila Camacho," *Excélsior*, 27 October 1976, Section Cine, Teatro, Radio y TV, p. 1. See also Fernando Gaxiola, " 'Actas de Marusia'—la posibilidad de un cine popular," *Otrocine*, no. 1 (January–March 1975), p. 9; "Actas de Marusia," *La Revue du Cinéma—Image et Son*, no. 306 (May 1976), pp. 66–67; "Film in Chile: An Interview with Miguel Littín," *Cineaste* 4: 4–9; "Nuevo cine, nuevos realizadores, nuevos filmes: Entrevista a Miguel Littín," *Cine cubano*, no. 63–65 (1970), pp. 1–6; "Premios para 'Actas de Marusia' y 'Universidad Comprometida,' en Huelva," *Excélsior*, 14 December 1976, Section Cine, Teatro, Radio y TV, p. 1; "It's Been a Great Year for International Films," *The Hollywood Reporter*, 26 October 1976, p. 18; "Chilean Exile Makes Hit with 'Letters from Marusia,'" ibid., 26 October 1976, p. 61; David Wilson, "Letters from Marusia," *Sight and Sound* (Winter 1976/1977), pp. 60–61.

80. "El Arte Como Función Social," *Hispanoamericano*, 11 April 1977, pp. 41–42. See pages 39–43 for an interview with Arau. See also Agustín Gurezpe, "En 'Suspenso' la Película que Arau Filmó en La Habana," *Excélsior*, 9 October 1976, Section Cine, Teatro, Radio y TV, p. 1.

81. Ricardo Perete, "¡Corte!" *Excélsior*, 29 July 1976, Section Cine, Teatro, Radio y TV, p. 1.

82. From personal observation, it seems apparent to this writer that most young Chicanos have little fluency in Spanish—a disadvantage that would effectively preclude them from being a major audience for Mexican films, "Chicano" or otherwise. For instance, *Chicano* (1975) is purportedly based on the exploits of the New Mexico land grant activist Reies López Tijerina, yet the film apparently has not been shown commercially in New Mexico. At any rate, following the brief spate of publicity on Tijerina as a result of his and his followers' seizure in 1967 of the courthouse at Tierra Amarilla, New Mexico, he retreated into general anonymity with the

exception of a visit to President Echeverría that seems to have been reported only in Albuquerque (Tomas Martinez, "Echeverria Meets Group," *Albuquerque Journal*, 13 June 1976, p. 1). The fact that Jaime Casillas, director of *Chicano*, thought that Tijerina was still a major figure among Mexican-American militants points to the lack of knowledge in Mexico regarding the situation. See Charles R. Garrett II, "El Tigre Revisited," *Nuestro*, August 1977, pp. 16–18, 20. Katy Jurado, a well-known Mexican actress with long experience in Hollywood, voiced criticism of Chicanos saying that she "did not understand" the Chicano movement because they are "North Americans" fighting their own country, an attitude which she found "absurd." "Katy Dijo en París que no Entiende a los Chicanos," *El Sol de México*, 22 July 1977, p. E4.

83. David R. Maciel, ed., *La otra cara de México: el pueblo chicano*, prologue by Carlos Monsiváis (Mexico City: Ediciones "El Caballito," 1977), p. 16. The "Chicano public," it seems, prefers the "traditional" package films. The new Mexican cinema with its slow-paced intellectualizing in the European style did not prove popular among Mexican-American audiences according to Gonzalo Checa, president of the California Association of Spanish Film Exhibitors. Carl Hillos, "Gonzalo Checa Espera el Envío de 'Tradicionales'," *Novedades*, 7 January 1975, Section Novedades en los Espectáculos, pp. 1, 4. See Ayala Blanco's discussion of Mexican Americans in Mexican films and Chicano filmmaking in the United States in *La búsqueda*, 2: 353–58; Carlos Morton, "Why No Chicano Film Makers? Platica con Luis Sedano y Antonio Orgaz," *La Luz*, June 1977, pp. 25–28; Rafael C. Castillo, "Films: Cine Festival," *Nuestro*, December 1979, pp. 51–52; Victor Valle, "Let the Chicano Films Roll," ibid., pp. 51–52; David R. Maciel, "Del pocho, al bracero, al chicano: Perspectives on the Chicano in the Contemporary Mexican Cinema," in Linda B. Hall, ed., *Popular Culture in Mexico and the U.S. Southwest* (San Antonio, Texas: Trinity University Press, forthcoming); and Jesús Salvador Treviño, "Chicano Cinema" (unpublished paper).

84. Letter from Alfonso Arau, 7 November 1977. In 1979 Arau completed *Mojado Power*, a musical comedy filmed in Tijuana and California. It was produced by AMX Productions. "Alfonso Arau's Latest, 'Mojado Power'," *The Hollywood Reporter*, March 1979, p. S–18.

85. "En Defensa de una Actriz," *Hispanoamericano*, 13 March 1953, p. 47. See also Larry Ceplair and Steven Englund, *The Inquisition in Hollywood: Politics in the Film Community, 1930–1960* (Garden City, N.Y.: Anchor Press/Doubleday, 1980), pp. 417–18.

86. *Historia*, 7: 367–71. Cantinflas's debut was in the supporting role of Passepartout in *Around the World in 80 Days*.

87. Wini Scheffler, "Foreign Filming Leaves Below-the-Line Income," *Mex-Am Review* 43 (August 1975): 4–5, 7, 9.

88. Luis Torres, "Raices de sangre: First Feature Film Directed by a Chicano," *Somos*, June/July 1978, pp. 17–19; Jesús Salvador Treviño, "Chicano Cinema," pp. 15–16; Maciel, "Del pocho"; Armando Mora, "Qué Actores Irán con los Chicanos" and idem, "Actores de la Metrópoli Alternarán con Chicanos," *El Sol de México*, 30 August 1976; Agustín Gurezpe, "El Cine Estadounidense Está Cerrado Para los Actores y Realizadores 'Chicanos'," *Excélsior*, 26 August 1976, Section Cine, Teatro, Radio y TV; and Eduardo de la Vega Alfaro, "Butaca: 'Raíces de Sangre'," *Uno Más Uno*, Mexico City, n.d.

89. For instance, CONACINE II lodged a protest in behalf of STIC when the filming of Mariano Azuela's novel, *Los de abajo*, was assigned to Churubusco. "En Octubre se Rodará 'Los de Abajo,' de Mariano Azuela," *Excélsior*, 13 September 1976, Section Cine, Teatro, Radio y TV, p. 1. See also Agustín Gurezpe, "Técnicos y Manuales Contra los Largometrajes en los 'América'," ibid., 21 July 1976, p. 1; idem, "Es Necesario que se Reanude la Comunicación Entre STIC y STPC," ibid., 10 September 1976, p. 1; idem, "Maximino Molina Pide que se Establezca la Competencia Entre Churubusco y América," ibid., 12 October 1976, p. 1; and Beatriz Reyes Nevares, "Entre cretinos y voraces naufraga el cine mexicano," *Siempre*, 3 January 1973, pp. 40–41, 70.

90. "El Gobierno Mexicano Nacionalizó," p. 1; Gregg Kilday, "Mexico's Revolution in Film-Making," *Los Angeles Times*, 24 March 1976, p. IV–14.

91. Sam Askinazy, "Echeverria Exit: His Film Reforms Open Up Mexico," *Variety*, 5 January 1977, pp. 16, 56; Agustín Gurezpe, "RE Acabo con el Cine Vacío de 30 Años: que Continúe de Director del Banco," *Excélsior*, 22 May 1976, p. 24–A; Wilson McKinney, "Mexican Film Industry Improving Its Quality," *San Antonio Express-News*, 5 October 1975, p. 8–A; Louis Margorelles, "Le Renoveau Mexicain," *La Revue du Cinéma—Image et Son*, no. 280 (January 1974), pp. 72–90; "Cinéma Mexicain," ibid., no. 295 (April 1975), pp. 20–28; Beatriz Reyes Nevares, "El cine mexicano es hoy de mejor calidad," *Siempre*, 27 December 1972, pp. 42–43; Martha Naranjo, "Echeverria—Giant of Mexican Filmmaking," *The Hollywood Reporter*, 26

October 1976, pp. 1, 64; "Mexico Carves Out Share of World Film Market," ibid., p. 9.

For additional readings on the Echeverría *sexenio* and its impact on films see Alberto Ruy Sánchez, "Cine mexicano: producción social de una estética, *"Historia y Sociedad*, no. 18 (Summer 1978), pp. 71–83; Javier Solórzano, "El nuevo cine en México: Entrevista a Emilio García Riera, *"Comunicación y cultura* 5 (March 1978), pp. 7–18; David Ramón, "Un sexenio de cine en México," *Comunicación* 21 (March 1977), pp. 24–33; Emilio García Riera, "Seis años de cine mexicano (1)," *Proceso*, 6 November 1976, pp. 68–69; idem, "Del cine mercantil al cine de autor," ibid., 13 November 1976, pp. 72–73; idem, "El choque con la censura hipócrita," ibid., 20 November 1976, pp. 72–73; Cristina Pacheco, "El Cine, Su Vicio" [interview with Emilio García Riera], *Siempre*, 1 November 1978, pp. 32–34, 70.

92. Agustin Gurezpe, "Reyes Heroles dió Posesión a García Borja en el Banco Cinematográfico," *Excélsior*, 9 December 1976, Section Cine, Teatro, Radio y TV, p. 1.

93. Rubén Torres, "Crean la Productora Nacional de Radio y Televisión, Dependiente de la Sría de Gobernación," *El Heraldo de México*, 5 July 1977, p. 1D.

94. In a letter received by this writer dated 23 July 1980 from Humberto Enríque Hernández, an official of the Secretaría de Gobernación, the CCC is mentioned as being headed by Alfredo Joscowicz. In the same letter it is stated that Benito Alazraki is director of CONACINE and Carlos Ortiz Tejeda is head of CONACITE II. A subsequent description of CUEC as "the only advanced school of cinema in the country" indicated that the CCC was no more. Germán Ramos Navas, "de todos modos CUEC te llamas," *Excélsior: Diorama de la Cultura*, 7 September 1980, p. 3. However, as of early January 1981, the film school was still in operation, with Joscowicz in charge. Martha Aurora Espinosa, "Actualización técnica, temática, de exhibición, y distribución, necesidades del cine nacional," *Uno Más Uno*, 13 January 1981, p. 22. See also Pérez Turrent and Turner, "Mexico," *International Film Guide 1981*, pp. 218–21.

95. "Cabos sueltos: Víctimas del pecado: el fin del Centro de Capacitación Cinematográfica," *Nexos* 24 (December 1979), pp. 4–5, 9, 11.

96. According to Ying Ying Wu, "Trying Times in Mexico," *Nuestro*, May 1980, p. 27.

97. Ibid.

98. Luis Suárez, "Habla Margarita López Portillo," *Siempre*, 11 July 1979, p. 29.

99. Ibid.

100. "Pido buena fe y sentido de responsabilidad para afrontar la crisis del cine mexicano, dice Margarita López Portillo," *Siempre*, 13 June 1979, p. 58.

101. Ibid.

102. Wu, "Trying Times in Mexico," p. 27; "Margarita López Portillo Hails Impact of Revitalization of Film Production," *The Hollywood Reporter*, March 1979, p. S–3 (this issue contained a special section on Mexican cinema).

103. "Informe de labores del periodo lectivo del Sr. Manuel Ampudia Girón," *Organo Informativo de la Cámara Nacional de la Industria Cinematográfica*, 10 March 1980, pp. 12–19.

104. *Guyana* was a Mexican-Spanish coproduction with Izaro Films; CONACINE financed 20% of the total production costs which were almost 2,600,000 dollars. *Variety*, 19 March 1980, p. 39. This was a special issue devoted to Latin American filmmaking. The Mexican section begins on p. 65. See also Alejandro Sigler M.'s interview with René Cardona, Jr. in *Organo Informativo*. January 1980, p. 11.

105. Stephen Klein, "Televicine Rolls Yank Hispanic Link," *Variety*, 28 May 1980, p. 3; "'Televisa' Moves Ahead," *The Hollywood Reporter*, March 1979, p. 5–4.

106. "Mexican Conglom in U.S. Toehold," *Variety*, 26 March 1980, pp. 1, 99.

107. Televisa's operation prompted a charge by the Spanish Broadcasters of America that the Mexican corporation was monopolizing Spanish-language television broadcasting in the United States. Specific allegations were that Televisa-controlled SIN illegally owned five of its affiliated stations and that it also owned a sales firm which sold advertising to its own network affiliates. In 1980, SIN claimed to have 57 affiliates; in 1988 the number had risen to over 400. Paul R. Wieck, "FCC Investigates Spanish TV Network," *Albuquerque Journal*, 13 September 1980, p. B-8. See also Anne Bagamery, "SIN, the original," *Forbes*, 22 November 1982, pp. 96-99. A controversy arose in 1986 when Jacobo Zabludovsky, the anchor for Televisa's evening news program, "24 Horas," announced he would take over "Noticiero Nacional SIN" originating in Miami. (A specially edited version of "24 Horas" anchored by Zabludovsky was carried by SIN [later Univisión] stations until about 1987.) SIN's news executives, accusing him of being a propagandist for the Mexican government, strongly opposed the move—obliging Zabludovsky to change his plans and remain in Mexico. Carlos Marín, "A Zabludovsky no se le cree por considerarlo vocero del gobierno,"

*Proceso*, 27 October 1986, pp. 20–25. See also idem, "Alemán reconoce que en información Televisa se autocensura," ibid, 15 September 1986, pp. 6–8. In 1988, the now Univisión network was bought by Hallmark Cards Incorporated after a court ruling that Televisa's ownership of the Spanish-language network constituted an illegal monopoly as well as a violation of U.S. law which prohibits foreign ownership of communications media. In 1987 Telemundo, a competing Spanish-language network, was formed by Henry Silverman of New York; the CEO is Carlos Barra, a Cuban-American. Ignacio González Janzen, "Empresarios estadunidenses desbancan a Televisa en el control de la televisión en español en EU," *Uno Más Uno*, 26 July 1988, p. 24. See also Adolfo Aguilar Zinser, "Mexico's Acrimonious TV Network Loses Its Sting," *Wall Street Journal*, 19 August 1988, p. 17 and Marshall Ingwerson, "Spanish-Language TV Now Taps Growing U.S. Hispanic Market," *Albuquerque Journal Entertainer*, 31 March 1989, p. F33 (reprinted from *Christian Science Monitor*).

108. Larry Rohter, "From Reviled Ex-Leader, a Double-Barreled Blast," *New York Times*, 11 November 1988, p. A-4; Matt Moffett, "Mexico's Most-Vilified Former President Writes Best-Seller to Defend His Actions," *Wall Street Journal*, 29 November 1988, p. A14.

109. Ignacio Rodríguez C., "El cine comercial no puede ser elitista," *Organo Informativo*, 10 March 1980, p. 31.

110. Jorge Carrasco, "Luto Nacional," *Hispanoamericano*, 5 April 1982, p. 61.

111. Idem, "Campanas Rojas," *Hispanoamericano*, 29 March 1982, p. 58.

112. John Mosier, "Ambitious Epics: *Cecilia* and *The Red Bells*," *Americas*, Jan-Feb 1983, p. 59.

113. Jorge Carrasco, "Una Buena Película," *Hispanoamericano*, 15 March 1982; see also Julio J. Etienne, "El Buen Cine Mexicano," ibid., 25 August 1987, p. 59.

114. Jorge Carrasco, "Desprecio Malinchista," ibid., 27 Dec. 1982, p. 59.

115. For an interview with Hermosillo and a partial filmography, see Emilio García Riera, "Conversación con Jaime Humberto Hermosillo," *Primer Plano (Revista de la Cineteca Nacional)*, no. 1 (November–December 1981): 3–30.

116. Tomás Pérez-Turrent, "María de mi corazón," in Peter Cowie, ed., *International Film Guide 1982*, p. 205; see also Jorge Carrasco, "Una Buena Muestra de Cine Independiente," *Hispanoamericano*, 18 June 1985, n.p.

117. Jorge Carrasco, "Superhéroe a la Medida," ibid., 20 September 1982, p. 56.

118. For a Santo filmography, see José Xavier Navar, "Imágenes: Las estrellas del colchón," *Su otro yo*, vol. 9, no. 4 (April 1982): 40–41; see also Nelson Carro, *El cine de luchadores* (Mexico City: Filmoteca de la UNAM, 1984.)

119. Jorge Carrasco, "Nuevo Cine Mexicano," *Hispanoamericano*, 11 October 1982, p. 55. A classic example of life imitating art is the phenomenon of "Super Barrio," a masked champion of the poor who appeared after the 1985 Mexico City earthquake. "Dressed in red tights, gold cape, face mask and a shirt emblazoned with the letters SB, Mexico's homegrown superhero leads the fight for fair housing, electricity and sewers here. All it takes is a call to his telephone hotline, and Super Barrio will arrive at the scene of injustice in his Barriomobile, accompanied by lawyers, militants of the Assembly of Barrios and often the press." This real-life superhero keeps his identity a secret and has gained admittance to meetings and public hearings at the Ministries of the Interior (*Gobernación*) and Urban Development and even los Pinos, the presidential residence. An ex-professional wrestler, he has received film and comic book offers, and even offers to return to the ring, all of which Super Barrio has refused: "My struggle is a social struggle, not a commercial one," he says. "We are not confronting Martians, but landlords. Our enemies are not imaginary, but real." Larry Rohter, "The Poor Man's Superman, Scourge of Landlords," *New York Times*, 15 August 1988, n.p. Super Barrio also extended his activities to Mexican communities in the United States. Arturo Gonzalez, Jr., "Not To be Confused with Bird or Plane, Mexico's Caped Crusader Packs a Political Paunch," *People Weekly*, 10 April 1989, pp. 114–115.

120. Carlos Loret de Mola, "Desacato a Gabriel Figueroa: El Cine Desperdiciado," *Siempre*, 24 Nov. 1982, p. 41.

121. Tomás Pérez-Turrent and Gillian Turner, "Mexico," in Peter Cowie, ed., *International Film Guide 1982*, p. 201; for background on Bardem's comment see Carl J. Mora, "The Odyssey of Spanish Cinema," *New Orleans Review* 14, no. 1 (Spring 1987): 13.

122. It seemed that the Mexican cinema had been in a permanent crisis since the 1950s, and even prior to that. "Like a festering wound eating away at the cinematic structure is the famous crisis. Never had a word been uttered so often, manipulated, and exploited as that permanent crisis of our cinema. Nonetheless, never had a patient survived so robustly such a

long illness." Manuel Michel, "Cine mexicano: utopía y realidad," *Plural*, vol. 11–7, no. 127 (April 1982): 67.

123. Carlos Crespo Aragón and Erika Domínguez Cervantes, "José Estrada: Crisis del cine mexicano," *Plural*, vol. 11–9, no. 129 (June 1982): 73.

124. Ibid., p. 74

125. Erika Domínguez, "Emilio García Riera: Un sexenio de cine mexicano," *Plural*, vol. 12–3, no. 135 (Dec. 1982)

126. "Una Cinematografía Planificada," *Hispanoamericano*, 8 March 1982, p. 57.

CHAPTER 6

1. Héctor Rivera, "Isaac cree posible levantar un cine en ruinas en un país arruinado," *Proceso*, no. 336, 11 April 1983, p. 50.

2. Tomás Pérez-Turrent and Gillian Turner, "Mexico," in Peter Cowie, ed., *International Film Guide 1982* (London: Tantivy Press, 1983), p. 202.

3. The first was in 1964 (see pp. 107–109), and the second in 1971. The latter was called National Contest of Independent Cinema in Super 8, and resulted in an ideological controversy between proponents of a political cinema led by Paco Ignacio Taibo II and others whose spokesman was Gabriel Retes who favored a more traditional "aesthetic" cinema. Moisés Viñas, *Historia del cine mexicano* (Mexico City: UNAM-UNESCO, 1987), p. 266.

4. Ibid., p. 277.

5. Erika Domínguez, "Direccion del cine mexicano," *Plural*, vol. 12–7, no. 139, April 1983, p. 54.

6. Ibid.

7. Ibid., p. 55.

8. Ibid., p. 55-56.

9. Jorge Carrasco, "Luto en el Cine Mexicano," *Hispanoamericano*, 25 April 1983, pp. 44–47. See also Archibaldo Burns, "Dolores del Río: de sus cenizas, la leyenda," *Proceso*, no. 337, 18 April 1983, pp. 50–53.

10. Michael Wood, "The Discreet Charm of Luis Buñuel," *American Film*, September 1982, p. 38. See also, idem, "Buñuel was always ready for death . . . from the moment he was born," *The Listener*, 9 February 1984, pp. 10–12 and Jorge Carrasco, "Un Artista Integro," *Hispanoamericano*, 8 August 1983, pp. 58–59.

11. Luis Buñuel, *Mi último suspiro* (Mexico City: Plaza & Janes, 1982), p. 206.

12. Jorge Carrasco, "Perspectivas Sobre la Cinematografía Nacional," *Hispanoamericano*, 25 July 1983, p. 59.

13. Ibid.

14. Tomás Pérez-Turrent and Gillian Turner, "Mexico," in Peter Cowie, ed., *International Film Guide 1985* (London: Tantivy Press, 1986), p. 213.

15. Tomás Pérez-Turrent, "Nocaut (Knockout)," *International Film Guide 1984*, p. 215.

16. Jorge Carrasco, "Vidas Errantes," *Hispanoamericano*, 24 September 1985, p. 46.

17. "Qué es la Cineteca Nacional" [brochure] (Mexico City: Cineteca Nacional, January 1986).

18. "Se Dinamiza la Cineteca Nacional," *Hispanoamericano*, 28 July 1987, p. 65.

19. Jorge Carrasco, "Plan de Recuperación Cinematográfica," ibid., 19 August 1986, p. 68; see also "Piden Acciones Concretas Para Salvar al Cine," ibid., 26 August 1986, p. 64.

20. Joan M. West and Dennis West, "Frida," *Cineaste* 16, no. 4 (1988): 54. In 1971 Marcela Fernández Violante made a much-praised short feature entitled *Frida Kahlo*. Moisés Viñas, *Historia del cine mexicano*, p. 268; see also " 'We are Losing Our Identity': An Interview with Mexican Director Marcela Fernández Violante," *Film/Literature Quarterly* 15, no. 1 (1987): 3.

21. Jorge Carrasco, "Una Biografía Poco Convencional," *Hispanoamericano*, 1 April 1986, p. 19.

22. Hortensia Caymares and Luciano Castillo, "Barbachano o la pasión de crear," *Cine cubano* #118 (1987): 60. Not all critics were as enthusiastic about the film—Jorge Ayala Blanco fumed: "Such pathetic boring intellectuals. Any vacuity enthuses them, any childish vision of Frida Kahlo interpreted by an awful actress, with no script, without character development, with no film." *La condición del cine mexicano (1973–1985)* (Mexico City: Editorial Posada, 1986), p. 254.

23. Hayden Herrera, *Frida: A Biography of Frida Kahlo* (New York: Harper & Row, 1983).

24. Elliott Stein, "Don Hermosillo and the Sun," *Film Comment*, June 1986, p. 54.

25. Greg Goldin and Marc Cooper, "Mexico's Movies: Now Playing at a Theater Near You," *Southwest Airlines Spirit*, July 1986, p. 54.

26. Interview, Mario Aguiñada, Cineteca Nacional, Mexico City, 30 January 1989.

27. Interview, Marco Bracamonte, marketing manager, VideoVisa, Inc., Los Angeles, CA, 25 October 1988. The United States videocassette market for Spanish-language films, 80% Mexican but also including some Argentine, Venezuelan, and Spanish features, has expanded dramatically in the last few years. VideoVisa is among the largest firms with about 300 titles (as of October 1988 and with four or five new titles every month). Others are: Million Dollar Video, Mexcinema, Filmex, and Mexvideo. Some smaller companies are American General Film, Isela Vega Video, Escomex, Pantera Video, and Madera Video. California represents 50% of the American market for Mexican films, both for theatrical showings and videocassette rentals with Texas the second largest followed by Arizona, New Mexico, and Colorado. New York and south Florida are "difficult" because of their overwhelmingly non-Mexican Hispanic populations which are generally not receptive to most Mexican film genres. However, musicals featuring *música tropical* do well in Miami. The videos do not have English subtitles. The majority are commercial, low-budget films although VideoVisa has a "Linea Connoisseur" featuring art films; other companies have similar lines. The immigration law of 1986 apparently has also been a factor in the expansion of the Mexican video market in the U.S. Southwest, because Spanish-language movie theaters have been targets for sweeps by INS agents. The resulting drop in attendance has forced many of these theaters to close because their former patrons (the undocumented ones) have resorted to the much safer renting of movies for home viewing.

    In Mexico, 30% of the country's approximately 16 million households have VCRs which works out to about 4,850,000 sets, the majority in Beta format although VHS has been gaining ground since 1980. Bracamonte explained the reason for the predominance of Beta in Mexico: "The smaller videocassettes were easier to smuggle—a truck could be loaded with one hundred Beta cassettes instead of fifty VHS. But with the opening up of the Mexican economy this will change." Video rentals have proliferated throughout Mexico (and into Central and South America), outlets include specialized shops and video rental sections in department stores, supermarkets, and other businesses. As elsewhere, renting a video is more economical than going to a theater—luxury theaters in Mexico charge 15,000 pesos ($6.60) admission for foreign films and important premieres. By contrast, admission at the Cineteca theaters is 1600 pesos (80 cents), about the same as commercial theaters that show Mexican films. See also Jorge Isaac, "El video ¿complemento o rivalidad con el cine?," *Cámara*, año VII, no. 54 (June–July 1988), pp. 45–48.

28. Larry Rohter, "Film Version of Everyman Wins Mexico," New York Times, 6 November 1988, p. 6.

29. Interview, Mario Bracamonte, Los Angeles, 25 October 1988.

30. Ayala Blanco, *La condición del cine mexicano*, pp. 89–94.

31. Interview, Alfredo Crevenna, Mexico City, 7 February 1989. In Japan, it is common to employ Western Caucasian (and occasionally non-Caucasians such as Sammy Davis, Jr.) to promote products in television and print commercials, perhaps a more curious phenomenon; Mexico at least was the colony of a European power which imparted to it a legacy of cultural values that emphasize the European ideal—and of course, unlike the Japanese, many Mexicans are entirely or partly of European descent. Some explanations for the use of foreign models in Japanese advertising were advanced by George Fields in *From Bonsai to Levi's, When West Meets East: An Insider's Surprising Account of How the Japanese Live* (New York and Scarborough, Ontario: Mentor Books, New American Library), 1985. "Loveable and 'tame' foreigners who are kept by Japanese brands help greatly to alleviate the national inferiority complex and create gratitude toward the brands that were able to hire them." (p. 118) "The use of [Western] stars coincides with the ascension of Japan as an economic colossus." (p. 118) "All these companies were *nonverbally* communicating the fact that they were of international status." (p. 119) And perhaps as a corollary to Mexico: "Foreign stars flood the Japanese screen, but now only newly arrived foreigners are surprised and ask why," (p. 120).

32. Many foreign filmmakers complain about the "dumping" of American films in their countries, which has an inhibiting effect on local production; in effect, expensive Hollywood productions make their profit in the United States and are then made available in Latin America and Europe for extremely low quantities—$25,000 to $30,000 for films that cost up to forty million to produce. Interview, Juan López Moctezuma, Azteca Films, Los Angeles, 26 October 1988; see also Rose Doyle, "U.S. Films Capture European Market," *Europe*, May/June 1984, pp. 44–45; Michael Chanan, *Twenty-Five Years of the New Latin American Cinema*, (London: Channel 4; BFI Books, 1983), p. 3.

33. Interview, Cristián González, Cineteca Nacional, 10 February 1989.

34. Interview, Luciana Cabarga, Mexico City, 8 February 1989. Ms. Cabarga is director of the Morelos State Commission of Film, Theater, and Television, whose purpose is to attract filmmakers to Morelos. (See Appendix 2 for address).

35. Interview, Los Angeles, 26 October 1988. López Moctezuma has had extensive experience in making films for non-Mexican audiences. He is best-known for his horror films like *La mansión de la locura* (1971), *Alucarda, Daughter of Darkness* (1975), and *To Kill a Stranger* (1983) with Dean Stockwell, Donald Pleasance, and Aldo Ray. López Moctezuma, together with Alejandro Jodorowski, Rafael Corkidi, and José Antonio Alcaraz formed the Mexican surrealist film movement of the 1970s. See Phil Hardy, *Encyclopedia of Horror Movies* (New York: Harper & Row, 1987).

36. "Malo, el cine comercial mexicano: Sergio Olhovich," *Uno Más Uno*, 9 April 1988, p. 28; "Exhibirán en los Festivales de Rio de Janeiro y La Habana, la Película Mexicana-Soviética Esperanza," *Excélsior*, 4 September 1988, p. 4-B.

37. José Felipe Coria, "La furia de lo irracional," *Uno Más Uno*, 20 July 1988, p. 28.

38. Goldin and Cooper, "Mexico's Movies . . . ," p. 95.

39. Julio J. Etienne, "El Imperio de la Fortuna," *Hispanoamericano*, 19 May 1987, p. 65; see also Frédéric Sabourad, "Féstivals: 9° Féstival des trois continents à Nantes: La carte de l'identité," *Cahiers du Cinéma*, no. 404 (February 1988): *Le Journaldes*, no. 80, p. VIII and Nelson Carro, "El imperio de la fortuna," *Dicine*, no. 20 (July–August 1987), p. 24.

40. Ayala Blanco, *La condición del cine mexicano*, pp. 375–87; Viñas, *Historia del cine mexicano*, pp. 277–78. For a psycho-politico-social interpretation of *Cadena perpétua*, see Charles Ramírez Berg, "Cracks in the *Macho* Monolith: *Machismo*, Man, and Mexico in Recent Mexican Cinema," *New Orleans Review* 16, no. 1 (Spring 1989): 67–74.

41. Verónica Espinosa, "En México no existe la carrera cinematográfica," *Uno Más Uno*, 23 June 1988, p. 23.

42. Interview, Felipe Cazals, Churubusco studios, Mexico City, 9 February 1989.

43. "Un Brillante Cierre de la Muestra," *Hispanoamericano*, 17 December 1985, p. 46.

44. Mauricio Peña, *El Heraldo*, 20 October 1988, quoted in *Cineteca Nacional*, año 6, no. 62, February 1989, p. 19.

45. Jorge Carrasco, "Adiós a Uno de los Grandes del Cine," *Hispanoamericano*, 19 August 1986, p. 66; see also Héctor Rivera, "El Indio, tan intenso en la furia como en la ternura," *Proceso*, 11 August 1986, pp. 42–49: the article also contains pieces by Armando Ponce, "En los últimos años el 'Indio' se dejó arrastrar por la leyenda en la soledad de su casona descuidada," pp. 44–47 and Carlos Monsiváis, "Notas sobre un personaje y una obra, " pp. 48–49; the article summarizes his daughter's memoirs of growing up with him, Adela Fernández, *El Indio Fernández, vida y mito* (Mexico City: Panorama Editorial, 1986; a major critical study published just before Fernández's death is Paco Ignacio Taibo I, *El Indio Fernández: El cine por mis pistolas*, Serie Genio y Figura" (Mexico City: Joaquín Mortiz/Planeta, 1986). See also Emilio García Riera, "Emilio Fernández," *Dicine*, no. 22 (November–December 1987), pp. 2–3 and Alejandro Rozado, "Lo trágico en el cine de Emilio Fernández," ibid., pp. 4–6; part two appears in ibid., no. 23 (January–February 1988), pp. 10–12. A belated tribute in the United States was given Fernández at the Telluride Festival with a screening of *The Pearl* and clips from other of his films. See M. S. Mason, "Old Mining Town Screens Some Shining Film Nuggets, *The Christian Science Monitor*, 15 October 1985, p. 33.

46. It is beyond the scope of this study to attempt analyses, much less predictions, of the Mexican political situation. Following the election of Carlos Salinas de Gortari on July 1, 1988, the opposition charged fraud and challenged the results in the courts and by means of demonstrations. For instance, opposition delegates jeered Miguel de la Madrid's last State of the Union speech and walked out waving ballots—unheard-of behavior in the Mexican Congress; similar demonstrations broke out at Salinas's inauguration. Accusations of electoral fraud have been common in Mexico; the difference this time was that some in the PRI, starting with Salinas himself, tacitly acknowledged the truth of the accusations. At this writing, Salinas seems to have asserted himself by moving against corrupt officials of the oil workers union and stock manipulators, inspiring an incipient acceptance among the largely skeptical Mexican public which initially saw him as a weak technocrat. Following are some comprehensive early accounts, but for generally reliable reporting on the developing political and economic situation in Mexico, the *Wall Street Journal*, the *New York Times*, and *The Economist* are among the best sources. Matt Moffett, "New Mexican President Is In Political Jeopardy Before Taking Office," *Wall Street Journal*, 31 August 1988, pp. 1, 17; Larry Rohter, "Mexico

City Journal: Now, the Urban Sprawl Wonder Diet," *New York Times*, 24 December 1988, p. 4; idem, "Can He Save Mexico?" *New York Times Magazine*, 20 November 1988, pp. 34–37, 84, 92–93; idem, "Mexicans Hoping for 'Salinastroika'," *New York Times*, 5 January 1989, p. A10; Matt Moffett, "Mexico City's Subsidies Present Stiff Challenges to President Salinas," *Wall Street Journal*, 10 January 1989, pp. A1, A14; Brian O'Reilly, "Doing Business on Mexico's Volcano," *Fortune*, 29 August 1986, pp. 72– 74.

47. Interview, Juan López Moctezuma, Los Angeles, 26 October 1988.

48. It is a common sight to see Tarahumara families on the streets of Chihuahua, and others come into contact with the modern world in communities like Divisadero and Creel. Eduardo Benítez, professor of electrical engineering at the Instituto Tecnológico de Chihuahua, told this writer in 1984 that there was just one Tarahumara enrolled in the school in spite of outreach programs to encourage young Indians to assimilate into the mainstream culture.

49. Interviews, Cineteca Nacional, Mexico City, 7 and 10 February 1989.

50. Interview, Mexico City, 8 February 1989. See also Antonio Berruti, "Pelayo habla de Días Difíciles," *Dicine*, no. 25 (May– June 1988), pp. 12–13.

51. Interview, Mexico City, 10 February 1989.

52. Interview, Mexico City, 2 February 1989.

53. P. 625.

54. "Cine mexicano: utopía y realidad," *Plural*, vol. 11–7, no. 127 (April 1982): 67. A more recent assessment concludes: "In effect, there has always been talk of a crisis of our cinema, but this referred to content, subject matter, and other artistic matters, but almost never to economic aspects, which in large part influence the others: due to the way in which cinematic policies and the industry are developing, the Mexican cinema has been relegated to being, first, a commercial product, leaving aside its artistic and social aspects, which explains why it fails to reflect Mexican reality." Colectivo Alejandro Galindo, "El cine mexicano y sus crisis," *Dicine*, no. 19 (May–June 1987), pp. 12–13. See also ibid., part two in no. 20 (July– August 1987), pp. 12–15 and part 3 in no. 21 (September– October 1987), pp. 16–18.

55. J.L. Espinosa, "Al finalizar este sexenio terminan para el cine mexicano 12 años de 'inversión térmica,'" *Uno Más Uno*, 9 August 1988, p. 24.

56. Doyle, "U.S. Films Capture European Market," pp. 44–45.

57. Interview, Mexico City, 10 February 1989.

58. Verónica Espinosa, "Mucho deberán trabajar los nuevos cineastas para mostrar al mundo otra imágen de nuestro cine," *Uno Más Uno*, 28 April 1988, p. 24. For a broad assessment of the difficulties and challenges facing Latin American filmmakers in the face of decreasing audiences, new technologies, increasing costs, and other factors see Paul Leduc, "Nuevo cine latinoamericano," *Dicine*, no. 24 (March–April 1988), pp. 2–5. Leduc also mentions the proposal of Columbia Pictures' David Picker to have the "major studios," in view of the success of *La Bamba*, make films in Spanish, or at least in dual versions, to reach the "enormous Spanish-speaking public in the United States and throughout the world." Leduc's reaction: "Thus while our audacious producers start to make *churritos* in English, the majors study the possibility of making films in Spanish. *No comments* [sic]." (pp. 3–4)

# A Note on Sources

The primary sources for a study of Mexican films are, of course, the films themselves. Although they are distributed widely throughout the United States, such movies are almost always restricted to the Spanish-language theater circuits and screened without English subtitles. Azteca Films, which for many years was the United States distributor for Mexican motion pictures, was closed at the beginning of 1989, and its functions taken over by the parent company, Películas Mexicanas, S.A. de C.V. (Pelmex).

Mexican films with subtitles and in 16mm are of limited availability. Films Incorporated, 5547 N. Ravenswood Ave., Chicago, Illinois 60640-1199, offers a small selection. The latest catalogue available in early 1989 (and dated 1987) listed the following films: Luis Buñuel's *The Criminal Life of Archibaldo de la Cruz* (*Ensayo de un crimen* 1955), *Nazarín* (1958), *Viridiana* (1961), *The Exterminating Angel* (*El ángel exterminador*, 1962), and *This Strange Passion* (*El*, 1952); *The Olympics in Mexico* (1970, Alberto Isaac, dir.); *The Pearl* (1947, Emilio Fernández, dir.—English version); *Time in the Sun* (1939, Eisenstein's footage from *Que Viva México*); and *¡Torero!* (1957, Carlos Velo, dir.).

New Yorker Films, 16 West 61st St., New York, NY 10023 lists the following films in their 1989 catalogue: Paul Leduc's *Frida* (1987); Buñuel's *Viridiana*, *Susana* (1951), *A Woman without Love* (*Una mujer sin amor*, 1951), *El bruto* (1952), *Wuthering Heights*, (*Abismos de pasión*, 1953), *Viridiana*, and *Simon of the Desert* (*Simón del desierto*, 1965); Ruy Guerra's *Eréndira* (1983), Leduc's *Reed: Insurgent Mexico* (*Reed: México insurgente*, 1971); and Arturo Ripstein's *Castle of Purity* (*La mansión de la locura*, 1972).

In cities that have television stations affiliated with the Univisión (formerly Spanish International Network—SIN) and Telemundo networks, a steady fare of old Mexican films is available as well as other Latin American and Spanish films. In most of these cities, a pay-TV service called Galavisión transmits newer Mexican films.

In the last six years, the videocassette "revolution" has also encompassed Mexican films. A brief description of American video companies specializing in Mexican films is given in Chapter 6, note 27, pp. 214–15. Although the majority selections available are commercial movies, the patient seeker will come across many quality films, from the classics of the 1940s and 1950s to the new Mexican cinema of the 1970s to the present.

For researchers interested in going to the source, the Cineteca Nacional is the obvious destination. As described in Chapter 6, p. 153, the original Cineteca was destroyed by fire on March 24, 1982, and the new Cineteca was inaugurated on January 27, 1984, in its new quarters on México-Coyoacán Avenue (see Appendix 2 for addresses of the Cineteca and other film organizations.) . Its attentive staff can assist with specific research interests, arrange for screening of films, and try to put you in touch with directors, performers, and other film people. It is of course best to contact the Cineteca management ahead of time and not just drop in with no advance notice and ask for screenings to be scheduled.

Just across the street from the Cineteca is IMCINE, the Mexican Cinema Institute (see Appendix 2 for address). And a pleasant stroll further east (staying north of Río Churubusco Avenue) through quiet residential neighborhoods will take you to División del Norte Avenue where the "Producers' Condominium" is located (see address for Películas Mexicanas, Appendix 2). Here are the headquarters of Pel-Mex and the offices of the commercial producers—those oft-condemned creators of the tacky yet profitable *churros*. Continuing east through more attractive residential areas, you will arrive at Tlalpan Avenue and the Churubusco-Azteca studios on the south side of Río Churubusco Avenue. If you prefer not to walk, taxis are plentiful and buses run on Río Churubusco (see Appendix 2 for address).

As to published sources, Emilio García Riera's exhaustive *Historia documental del cine mexicano* (9 volumes) is the indispensable work. As of this writing, volume 10 was scheduled for publication in 1989. Other volumes on Mexican cinema by Mexican publishers are hard to obtain, even in Mexico. Such books are rarely printed in quantities greater than two thousand copies and are usually soon out of print.

Among specialized film journals, *Dicine*, edited by Emilio García Riera, is excellent. The monthly program and bulletin issued by the Cineteca Nacional is useful as are its other publications.

The only other sources of information on Mexican filmmaking are the Mexico City print media. The best newspaper sources are *Excélsior, El Heraldo, El Sol, and Uno Más Uno*. The weekly magazines *Siempre* and *Tiempo* (in the United States, *Hispanoamericano*) are good sources. The latter has a regular cinema section which usually reviews foreign films, but does cover major developments in the domestic film industry. In the United States, *Variety* occasionally carries reviews of major new Mexican films as well as news of Mexican and other Latin American film industries; so does *The Hollywood Reporter*.

At this writing, Dana Evans Balibrera's documentary, *The Golden Age of Mexican Cinema*, is in post-production. The only film treatment in English on the subject, it contains historic interviews with Emilio Fernández, Alejandro Galindo, Gabriel Figueroa, Roberto Rodríguez, and Lupita Tovar. Dana Evans Balibrera and Mario Balibrera are coproducers of *El Indio—una leyenda del cine*, also in post-production. This documentary is based on interviews in Spanish with Emilio Fernández taped in 1983 (for more information, contact Danamar Productions, 4751 Heatherwood Drive, Tuscaloosa, AL 35405; telephone [205] 556-5847). Alejandro Pelayo produced a documentary for Mexican television entitled *Los que hicieron nuestro cine*, which is available by arrangement with him or his U.S. representative (see Appendix 2 for address).

Ever since Emilio García Riera, together with Jaime Humberto Hermosillo, established a film studies center (Centro de Investigaciones y Enseñanza Cinematográficas) at the University of Guadalajara, this institution has been enhancing its reputation in cinematic activities. In 1986, the Center initiated a film festival dedicated to showcasing the best of each year's Mexican film production in addition to retrospectives on genres and directors. The university's publishing program has also begun to emphasize cinema studies.

The author welcomes queries on any of the above items or regarding any aspect of Mexican cinema. You may write to Carl J. Mora, 8 Canyon Lane, Cedar Crest, NM 87008.

The bibliography following contains the principal books and articles in Spanish, English, and French on Mexican cinema as well as a basic selection of works on other Latin American countries. Some works on Spanish film are included because of the continual interaction between Mexican and Spanish filmmakers both in the past and at the present time.

# BIBLIOGRAPHY

## A. ARCHIVES AND LIBRARIES CONSULTED:

American Film Institute, Beverly Hills, California
Cineteca Nacional, Mexico City, Mexico
Cinema-Television Library, University of Southern California, Los Angeles, California
UCLA Film Archive, Los Angeles, California
UCLA Theater Arts Library, Los Angeles, California
Zimmerman Library, University of New Mexico, Albuquerque, New Mexico

## B. MAGAZINES AND JOURNALS:

*Cahiers du Cinéma*, Paris
*Cámara*, Mexico City (1981–1989)
*Cartel*, Mexico City (1947–1948)
*Celuloide*, Mexico City (1946)
*Cine*, Mexico City (1938)
*Cine al Día*, Caracas
*Cine-Arte*, Mexico City (1986– )
*Cineaste*, New York
*Cine-Club*, Mexico City (1955)
*Cine cubano*, Havana (1960–1988)
*Cinelandia*, New York (1929–1930)
*Cinema Reporter*, Mexico City (1938–1951)
*Cine Mexicano*, Mexico City (1944–1958)
*Cineteca Nacional*, Mexico City (1983–1989)
*Cuadernos de Cine*, Bogotá
*Dicine*, Mexico City (1984–1988)
*Film Culture*, New York
*Film Quarterly*, Berkeley, California (volumes 1–5 [1947–1951] were entitled *Hollywood Quarterly*; volumes 6–11 [1952

–1957] were entitled *Quarterly of Film, Radio, and Television*)
*Films in Review*, Somerville, New Jersey
*Hablemos de Cine*, Lima
*Hollywood Reporter, The*, Los Angeles
*Ilustrado*, Mexico City (1933–1935)
*La Revue du Cinéma—Image et Son*, Paris
*Mañana*, Mexico City
*México Cinema*, Mexico City (1942–1955)
*Nuevo Cine*, Mexico City (1961)
*Ojo al Cine*, Cali, Colombia
*Organo Informativo de la Cámara Nacional de la Industria Cinematográfica*, Mexico City (1979– )
*Otrocine*, Mexico City (1975–1976)
*Penguin Film Review, The*, London
*Reseña*, Madrid
*Siempre*, Mexico City
*Tiempo* (distributed in the United States under the title of *Hispanoamericano)*
*Tiempo de Cine*, Montevideo

## C. NEWSPAPERS

*Cine Mundial*, Mexico City
*Diario Fílmico Mexicano*, Mexico City (1943–1944)
*Excélsior*, Mexico City
*Heraldo, El*, Mexico City
*Novedades*, Mexico City; see also supple-
   ment *México en la Cultura*
*Sol de México, El*, Mexico City
*Uno Más Uno*, Mexico City
*Variety*, New York


## D. BOOKS

Abellán, José Luis, ed. *El exilio español de 1939*. 6 vols. Madrid: Taurus Ediciones, S.A.,
   1976. Vol. 1, *La emigración republicana*, by Vicente Llorens.
Adelman, Alan, editor. *A Guide to Cuban Cinema*. Latin American Monograph and
   Document Series 4. Pittsburgh: Center for Latin American Studies, University of
   Pittsburgh, 1981.
Agramonte, Arturo. *Cronología del cine cubano*. Havana: ICAIC, 1966.
Alcalá, Manuel. *Buñuel (Cine e Ideología)*. Madrid: Editorial Cuadernos para el Diálogo,
   1973.
Almendros, Nestor. *A Man with a Camera*. Translated from the Spanish by Rachel Phillips
   Belash. New York: Farrar, Strauss, Giroux, 1984.
_____ . *Conducta impropia (Un filme de Néstor Alméndros)*. Madrid: Playor, 1984.
Almoina, Helena. *Bibliografía del cine mexicano, 1960–1985*. Mexico City: Filmoteca
   UNAM, 1985.
_____ . *Notas para la historia del cine en México*. 2 vols. Mexico City: Filmoteca
   UNAM, 1980.
Amo, Alvaro del. *Comedia cinematográfica española*. Madrid: Editorial Cuadernos para
   el Diálogo, 1975.
Anderson, Joseph L. , and Richie, Donald. *The Japanese Film: Art and Industry*. Foreword
   by Akira Kurosawa. New York: Grove Press, 1960.
Aranda, Francisco. *Luis Buñuel: A Critical Biography*. Translated by David Robinson.
   London: Secker and Warburg, 1975.
Arciniégas, Germán. *Latin America: A Cultural History*. Translated by Joan MacLean.
   New York: Alfred A. Knopf, 1967.
Armes, Roy. *Third World Filmmaking and the West*. Berkeley, Los Angeles, London: Uni-
   versity of California Press, 1987.
*Anuario de la producción cinematográfica mexicana, 1970*. Mexico City: Procinemex,
   n.d. Also see *Anuarios* for 1971–1974.
Ayala Blanco, Jorge. *La aventura del cine mexicano*. Mexico City: Ediciones Era, 1968.
_____ . *La búsqueda del cine mexicano (1968–1972)*. 2 vols. Cuadernos de Cine #22.
   Mexico City: UNAM, Dirección General de Difusión Cultural, 1974.
_____ . *La condición del cine mexicano (1973–1985)*. Mexico City: Editorial Posada,
   1986.
Bardèche, Maurice, and Brasillach, Robert. *Histoire du Cinéma*. 10 vols. Paris: André
   Martel, 1954. Vol. 2, *Le cinéma parlant*, pp. 430–36.

Bawden, Liz-Anne, ed. *The Oxford Companion to Film*. New York and London: Oxford University Press, 1976.

Besas, Peter. *Behind the Spanish Lens: Spanish Cinema Under Fascism and Democracy*. Denver: Arden Press, 1985.

Blanco, Carlos. *Don Quijote cabalga de nuevo*. Madrid: Editorial Fragua, 1973.

Buache, Freddy. *The Cinema of Luis Buñuel*. Translated by Peter Graham. London: The Tantivy Press, and New York: A.S. Barnes, 1973.

Bukalski, Peter J. *Film Research: A Critical Bibliography with Annotations and Essays*. Boston: G.K. Hall and Co., n.d.

Buñuel, Luis. *Mi último suspiro (memorias)*. Mexico City: Plaza & Janes, 1982.

_____ . *Mon Dernier Soupir*. Paris: Editions Robert Laffont, 1982.

_____ . *My Last Sigh*. New York: Alfred A. Knopf. 1983.

Burns, E. Bradford. *Latin American Cinema: Film and History*. Los Angeles: UCLA Latin American Center, 1975.

Burton, Julianne, editor. *Cinema and Social Change in Latin America: Conversations with Filmmakers*. Austin: University of Texas Press, 1986.

_____ . *The New Latin American Cinema: An Annotated Bibliography of English-Language Sources, 1960–1976*. Cineaste Pamphlet no. 4. New York: Cineaste, 1976.

Bustillo Oro, Juan. *Vientos de los veintes*. Mexico City: Sep/Setentas, n.d.

Campbell, Leon G.; Cortés, Carlos E.; and Pinger, Robert. *Latin America: A Filmic Approach*. Film Series no. 1. Riverside: University of California, Latin American Studies Program, October 1975.

Caparrós Lera, José María and Rafael de España. *The Spanish Cinema: An Historical Approach*. Translated by Carl J. Mora. Barcelona: Centre for Cinematic Research "Film-Historia," 1987.

Careaga, Gabriel. *Erotismo, violencia y política en el cine*. Mexico City: Cuadernos de Joaquín Mortiz, 1981, pp. 86–99 on Pedro Infante.

Carr, Larry. *More Fabulous Faces: The Evolution and Metamorphosis of Dolores del Rio, Myrna Loy, Carole Lombard, Bette Davis, and Katherine Hepburn*. Garden City, NY: Doubleday, 1979, pp. 1–51.

Carro, Nelson. *El cine de luchadores*. Mexico City: Filmoteca de la UNAM, 1984.

Castro, Antonio. *El cine español en el banquillo*. Valencia, Spain: Fernando Torres Editor, 1974.

Cawkwell, Tim and Smith, John M. *The World Encyclopedia of the Film*. n.p.: A&W Visual Library, November Books, 1972.

Ceplair, Larry and Englund, Steven. *The Inquisition in Hollywood: Politics in the Film Community, 1930–1960*. Berkeley, Los Angeles, London: University of California Press, 1983.

Césarman, Fernando. *El ojo de Buñuel: Psicoanálisis desde una butaca*. Prologue by Carlos Fuentes. Barcelona: Anagrama, 1976.

Chanan, Michael. *The Cuban Image: Cinema and Cultural Politics in Cuba*. London: BFI Publishing; Bloomington: Indiana University Press, 1985.

_____ , editor. *Twenty-Five Years of the New Latin American Cinema*. London: Channel 4 Television; BFI Books, 1983.

*Cine y revolución en Cuba*. Prologue by Miquel Porter. Barcelona: Editorial Fontamara, 1975.

*Cineteca Nacional*, 1974. Mexico City: n.p., n.d.

*Cineteca Nacional*, 1975. Mexico City: n.p., n.d.

*Cineteca Nacional, Memoria 1976*. Mexico City: Cineteca Nacional, 1976, 102 pp.

*Cineteca Nacional, Memoria 1977.* Mexico City: Cineteca Nacional 1977, 155 pp.
*Cineteca Nacional, Memoria 1978.* Mexico City: Cineteca Nacional, 1978, 132 pp.
*Cineteca Nacional, Memoria 1979.* Mexico City: Cineteca Nacional, 1979, 51 pp
*Cineteca Nacional, Memoria 1980.* Mexico City: Cineteca Nacional, 1980, 69 pp
*Cineteca Nacional, Memoria 1981.* Mexico City: Cineteca Nacional, 1981, 63 pp.
*Cineteca Nacional, Memoria 1982.* Mexico City: Cineteca Nacional, 1982, 47 pp.
*Cineteca Nacional, Memoria 1983.* Mexico City: Cineteca Nacional, 1983, 36 pp
*Cineteca Nacional, Memoria 1984.* Mexico City: Cineteca Nacional, 1984, 80 pp.
*Cineteca Nacional, Memoria 1985.* Mexico City: Cineteca Nacional, 1985, 64 pp.
*Cineteca Nacional, Memoria 1986.* Mexico City: Cineteca Nacional, 1986, 70 pp.
*Cineteca Nacional, Memoria 1987.* Mexico City: Cineteca Nacional, 1987, 70 pp.
*Cineteca Nacional, Memoria 1988.* Mexico City: Cineteca Nacional, 1988, 63 pp.
Colina, José de la. *Miradas al cine.* Mexico City: Sep/Setentas, 1972.
_____ and Pérez-Turrent, Tomás. *Luis Buñuel: Prohibido asomarse al interior.* Colección Genio y Figura. Mexico City: Joaquín Mortiz/Planeta, 1986.
Comisión Nacional de Cinematografía. *El libro de oro del cine mexicano, 1949.* Mexico City, 1949.
Contreras Torres, Miguel. *El libro negro del cine mexicano.* Mexico City: Editora Hispano-Continental Films, 1960.
Contreras y Espinosa, Fernando. *La producción, sector primario de la industria cinematográfica.* Textos de Cine #4. Mexico City: UNAM, 1973.
Cortés, Carlos E.; Campbell, Leon G.; and Curl, Alan. *A Filmic Approach to the Study of Historical Dilemmas.* Film Series no. 2. Riverside: University of California, Latin American Studies Program, October 1976.
Cosío Villegas, Daniel. *Historia moderna de México.* 8 vols. Mexico City: Editorial Hermes, 1955–1972. Vol. 4, *El Porfiriato—La vida social,* by Moisés González Navarro, 1957.
Cowie, Peter, ed. *International Film Guide.* 21 editions to date. London: The Tantivy Press, 1968– .
_____ , gen. ed. *World Filmography.* London: The Tantivy Press; South Brunswick, NJ and New York: A.S. Barnes and Co., 1977, pp. 439–56.
Cremoux, Raúl. *La televisión y el alumno de secundaria del Distrito Federal.* Mexico City: Centro de Estudios Educativos, A.C., February 1968.
*Cronología de la cultura cinematográfica (1849-1986), Serie: Historia del cine en El Ecuador.* Quito: Nueva Editorial, 1987.
*Diccionario Porrúa: Historia, Biografía y Geografía de México.* 2 vols. 3d ed. Mexico City: Editorial Porrúa, 1970. Vol. 1, A-LL.
Eisenstein, S.M. *¡Que viva México!* Prologue by José de la Colina. Mexico City: Ediciones Era, 1971.
*El automóvil gris.* Introduction by Federico Serrano y Fernando del Moral G. Cuadernos de la Cineteca Nacional #10. Serie Guiones Clásicos del Cine Mexicano. Mexico City: Cineteca Nacional, 1972.
*El cine: Desde Lumière hasta el Cinerama.* 2 vols. Barcelona: Libreria Editorial Argos, 1965.
Eliezer Galvão, Maria Rita. *Crônica do Cinema Paulistano.* São Paulo: Editora Ática, 1975.
*El Topo: A Book of the Film by Alejandro Jodorowski.* New York and London: Douglas Links, 1971.
*Enciclopedia de México.* 10 vols. Mexico City: Instituto de la Enciclopedia de Mexico, 1968. Vol. 2.

*Enciclopedia ilustrada del cine*. Barcelona: Editorial Labor, 1969.

Equipo "Cartelera Turia." *Cine español, cine de subgéneros*. Valencia, Spain: Fernando Torres, Editor, 1974.

Feldman, Simón. *El director de cine: mitos y sometimientos*. Buenos Aires: Granica Editor, 1974.

Fernańdez, Adela. *El Indio Fernández: Vida y mito*. Mexico City: Panorama Editorial, 1986.

Flores García, Alejandro. *Cinecompendio, 1971 / 1972*. Mexico City: Editorial A. Posta, 1973.

_____ . *Cinecompendio, 1972 / 1973*. Mexico City: Editorial A. Posta, 1974.

_____ . *Cinecompendio, 1973 / 1974*. Mexico City: Editorial A. Posta, 1975.

_____ . *Cinecompendio, 1974 / 1975*. Mexico City: Editorial A. Posta, 1976.

Font, Domènec. *Del azul al verde: el cine español durante el franquismo*. Barcelona: Editorial Avance, 1976.

Ford, Charles. *Historia popular del cine*. Translated from the French by Leoncio Sureda Guyto. *Barcelona: Editorial AHR, 1956*.

*40 aniversario cine sonoro mexicano*. Mexico City: Comisión Organizadora de los Actos Conmemoratorios del 40 Aniversario del Cine Sonoro Mexicano, November 1971.

Furhammer, Leif and Isaksson, Folke. *Politics and Film*. Translated by Kersti French. New York and Washington, D.C.: Praeger Publishers, 1971.

Galindo, Alejandro. *El cine, genocidio espiritual: De 1900 al "crash" de 29*. Mexico City: Editorial Nuestro Tiempo, 1971.

_____ . *¿Que es el cine?* Mexico City: Editorial Nuestro Tiempo, 1975.

_____ . *Una radiografía histórica del cine mexicano*. Mexico City: Fondo de Cultura Popular, 1968.

_____ . *Verdad y mentira del cine mexicano*. Mexico City: Aconcagua Ediciones y Publicaciones, 1981.

García Márquez, Gabriel. *La aventura de Miguel Littín clandestino en Chile*. Mexico City: Editorial Diana, 1986.

García Riera, Emilio. *Arturo Ripstein habla de su cine*. Colección Testimonios del Cine Mexicano. Guadalajara: Universidad de Guadalajara, Centro de Investigación y Enseñanza Cinematográficas, 1988.

_____ . *El cine mexicano*. Mexico City: Ediciones Era, 1963.

_____ . El cine y su público. Coleccion Testimonios del Fondo #1. Mexico City: Fondo de Cultura Económica, 1974.

_____ . *Historia documental del cine mexicano*. 9 vols. to date. Mexico City: Ediciones Era, 1969–.

_____ . *Julio Bracho: 1909–1978*. Coleccion Cineastas de México. Guadalajara: Universidad de Guadalajara, Centro de Investigación y Enseñanza Cinematográficas, 1987.

_____ . *México visto por el cine extranjero*. 4 vols. Mexico City: Ediciones Era and Guadalajara: Universidad de Guadalajara, 1987–1988.

Geduld, Harry M. and Gottesman, Ronald, eds. *Sergei Eisenstein and Upton Sinclair: The Making and Unmaking of Que Viva Mexico!* Bloomington and London: Indiana University Press, 1970.

Geijerstam, Claes af. *Popular Music in Mexico*. Albuquerque: University of New Mexico Press, 1976.

Gertner, Richard. *International Motion Picture Almanac 1976*. New York, Hollywood, and London: Quigley Publishing Co., 1976, pp. 695–96.

Giménez Caballero, Ernesto. *Amor a Méjico (A través de su cine)*. Cuadernos de Monografías no. 5. Madrid: Seminario de Problemas Hispanoamericanos, April 5, 1948.

Gomezjara, Francisco A. and Selene de Dios, Delia. *Sociología del cine*. Mexico City: Sep/Setentas, 1973.

González Casanova, Manuel. *¿Que es un cine-club?* Mexico City: Dirección de Difusión Cultural, Seccion de Actividades Cinematográficas, UNAM, 1961.

González Navarro, Moisés. *Población y sociedad en México (1900–1970)*. 2 vols. Serie Estudios 42. Mexico City: UNAM, Facultad de Ciencias Políticas y Sociales, 1974.

Gubern, Román. *Cine español en el exilio, 1936–1939*. Barcelona: Editorial Lumen, 1976.

_____. *El cine sonoro en la República 1929–1936. Historia del cine español II*. Barcelona: Editorial Lumen, 1977.

Guerrero Suárez, Jorge. *Dolores del Río*. Mexico City: By the Author, 1979.

_____. *El Cine Sonoro Mexicano: sus inicios, 1930–1937*. Cuadernos de la Cineteca Nacional #8. Serie Ensayos, Investigaciones y Biografías. Mexico City: Cineteca Nacional, 1987.

Gumucio Dagrón, Alfonso. *Historia del cine boliviano*. Mexico City: Filmoteca UNAM, 1983.

Hennebele, Guy and Gumucio-Dagrón, Alfonso, eds. *Les Cinémas de L'Amérique Latine*. Paris: Lherminier, 1981.

Heuer, Federico. *La industria cinematográfica mexicana*. Mexico City: By the Author, 1964.

Higginbotham, Virginia. *Spanish Film Under Franco*. Austin: University of Texas Press, 1988.

*Homenaje a los iniciadores del cine en Mexico (1896–1938)*. Cuadernos de la Cineteca Nacional #9. Mexico City: Cineteca Nacional, 1979.

Hopewell, John. *Out of the Past: Spanish Cinema After Franco*. London: BFI Books, 1986.

Hijar, Alberto, ed. *Hacia un tercer cine*. Cuadernos de Cine #20. Mexico City: UNAM, 1972.

Huaco, George A. *The Sociology of Film Art*. New York: Basic Books, 1965.

Huss, Roy and Silverstein, Norman. *The Film Experience: Elements of Motion Picture Art*. New York, Evanston, and London: Harper and Row, 1968.

*Informe general sobre la actividad cinematográfica en el año 1971 relativo al Banco Nacional Cinematográfico, S.A.* Mexico City: Banco Nacional Cinematográfico, January 21, 1972.

*Informe general...en el año 1972...* Mexico City: January 23, 1973.

*Informe general...en el año 1973...* Mexico City: January 22, 1974.

*Informe general...en el año 1974...* Mexico City: January 21, 1975.

*Informe general...en el año 1976...* Mexico City: November 26, 1976.

Izaguirre, Rodolfo. *El cine en Venezuela*. Temas Culturales Venezolanos, Serie I. Caracas: n.p., n.d.

Jacobs, Lewis. *The Emergence of Film Art: The Evolution and Development of the Motion Picture as an Art, from 1900 to the Present*. New York: Hopkinson and Blake, Publishers, 1974.

Jarvie, I.C. *Movies and Society*. New York: Basic Books, Inc. 1970.

Jeanne, Rene and Ford, Charley. *Historia ilustrada del cine*. 3 vols. Madrid: Alianza Editorial, 1974.

Johnson, Randal and Stam, Robert. *Brazilian Cinema*. Rutherford, Madison, Teaneck, N.J.: Fairleigh Dickinson University Press; London and Toronto: Associated University Press, 1982.

Keller, Gary D., editor. *Chicano Cinema: Research, Reviews and Resources*. Binghamton, N.Y.: Bilingual Review Press, 1985.

Kracauer, Siegfried. *From Caligari to Hitler: A Psychological History of the German Film*. 2d ed. New York: The Noonday Press, 1960.

Kyrou, Ado. *Luis Buñuel*. Paris: Editions Seghers, 1970.

*La fábrica de sueños: Estudios Churubusco 1945–1985*. Mexico City: Instituto Mexicano de Cinematografía, 1985.

La Fuente, María Isabel de. *Indice bibliográfico del cine mexicano (1930–1965)*. Mexico City: n.p., 1967.

———. *Indice bibliográfico del cine mexicano (1966–1967)*. Vol. 2. Mexico City: Editorial América, 1968.

Lamb, Ruth S. *Mexican Theater of the Twentieth Century: Bibliography and Study*. Claremont, Calif.: Ocelot Press, 1975.

León Frías, Isaac. *Los años de la conmoción, 1967–1973: Entrevistas con realizadores sudamericanos*. Mexico City: Dirección General de Difusión Cultural, UNAM, 1979.

Leprohon, Pierre. *The Italian Cinema*. Translated from the French by Roger Greaves and Oliver Stallybrass. New York and Washington, D.C.: Praeger Publishers, 1972.

*Libertad Lamarque, autobiografía*. Buenos Aires, Madrid, Mexico City and Santiago de Chile: Javier Vergara Editor, 1986.

Littín, Miguel. *El chacal de Nahueltoro, La tierra prometida*. Textos de Cine #5, Serie Guiones 1. Mexico City: UNAM, Direccion General de Difusión Cultural, 1977.

Lizalde, Eduardo. *Luis Buñuel*. Cuadernos de Cine #2. Mexico City: UNAM, Dirección General de Difusión Cultural, 1962.

MacBean, James Roy. *Film and Revolution*. Bloomington and London: Indiana University Press, 1975.

Madrid, Francisco. *Cincuenta años de cine: Crónica del séptimo arte*. Buenos Aires: Ediciones del Tridente, 1964.

Magaña Esquivel, Antonio. *Los teatros en la ciudad de Mexico*. Mexico City: Colección Popular Ciudad de México, Departamento del Distrito Federal, 1974.

Mahieu, Agustín. *Breve historia del cine nacional, 1896–1974*. Buenos Aires: Alzamor Editores, 1976.

Manchel, Frank. *Film Study: A Resource Guide*. Rutherford, N.J.: Fairleigh Dickinson University Press, 1973.

Manvell, Roger and Fraenkel, Heinrich. *The German Cinema*. New York and Washington, D.C.: Praeger Publishers, 1971.

Martínez Pardo, Hernando. *Historia del cine colombiano*. Bogotá: Editorial America Latina, 1978.

Martínez Torres, Augusto and Pérez Estremera, Manuel. *Nuevo cine latinoamericano*. Barcelona: Editorial Anagrama, 1973.

Méndez Berman, León and Mar, Santos. *El embrollo cinematográfico*. Mexico City: Editorial Cooperación, 1953.

Méndez Leite, Fernando. *Historia del cine español*. Madrid: Ediciones Rialp, 1965.

Meyer, Eugenia, coordinator. *Cuadernos de la Cineteca Nacional: Testimonios para la historia del cine mexicano*. 8 vols. Mexico City: Dirección de Cinematografía de la Secretaría de Gobernación, 1976.

Michel, Manuel. *Al pie de la imágen: Críticas y ensayos*. Cuadernos de Cine #15. Mexico City: UNAM, Dirección General de Difusión Cultural, 1968.

———. *El cine y el hombre contemporáneo*. Prologue by Carlos Fuentes. Cuadernos de la Facultad de Filosofía, Letras y Ciencias #14. Xalapa, Ver.: Universidad Veracruzana, 1962.

Millingham, F. *Por qué nació el cine*. Buenos Aires: Editorial Nova, 1954.

Mitry, Jean. *Histoire du Cinéma: Art et Industrie*. 3 vols. Paris: Editions Universitaires, 1967.
_____. *S.M. Eisenstein*. Paris: Editions Universitaires, 1962.
Monaco, Paul. *Cinema and Society: France and Germany During the Twenties*. New York, Oxford, Amsterdam: Elsevier, 1976.
Morales, María Luz. *El cine: Historia ilustrada del séptimo arte*. 3 vols. Barcelona, Madrid, Buenos Aires, Mexico City, Rio de Janeiro: n.p., 1950.
Montalbán, Ricardo with Thomas, Bob. *Reflections: A Life in Two Worlds*. New York: Doubleday and Co., 1980.
Myerson, Michael, ed. *Memories of Underdevelopment: The Revolutionary Films of Cuba*. New York: Grossman Publishers, 1973.
Nacional Financiera, S.A. *Statistics on the Mexican Economy*. Mexico City: Nacional Financiera, S.A., 1966.
Nubila, Domingo di. *Historia del cine argentino*. Buenos Aires: Edicion Cruz de Malta, 1959.
O'Connor, John E., and Jackson, Martin A., eds. *American History / American Film: Interpreting the Hollywood Image*. Foreword by Arthur M. Schlesinger, Jr. New York: Frederick Ungar Publishing Co., 1979.
Palacios More, René and Pires Mateus, Daniel. *El cine latinoamericano: O por una estética de la ferocidad, la magia y la violencia*. Madrid: Sedmay Ediciones, 1976.
Pastor Legnani, Margarita and Vico de Peña, Rosario. *Filmografía uruguaya*. Montevideo: Cinemateca Uruguaya, 1973.
Pereyra, Miguel. *El lenguaje del cine: Su técnica, su estilo, su arte*. Madrid: Aguilar, 1956.
Pérez, Ismael Diego. *"Cantinflas," genio del humor y del absurdo*. Mexico City: Editorial Indo-Hispana, 1954.
Pineda Alcalá, Francisco. *La verídica historia del cine mexicano*. Prologue by Fernando Morales Ortiz. Mexico City: n.p., 1965.
Portas, Rafael E. and Rangel, Ricardo E. *Enciclopedia cinematográfica mexicana, 1897–1955*. Mexico City: Publicaciones Cinematografistas, n.d.
Ramírez, Gabriel. *El cine yucateco*. Mexico City: Filmoteca UNAM, 1980.
Reyes de la Maza, Luis. *Cien años de teatro en México (1810–1910)*. Mexico City: Sep/Setentas, 1972.
_____. *El cine sonoro en Mexico*. Mexico City: UNAM, Instituto de Investigaciones Estéticas, 1973.
_____. *El teatro en México durante el porfirismo, tomo III (1900–1910)*. Mexico City: UNAM, 1968.
_____. *Salón rojo (programas y crónicas del cine mudo en México), vol. 1 (1895–1920)*. Mexico City: UNAM, Dirección General de Difusión Cultural, 1968.
Reyes, Alfonso; Guzmán, Martín Luis; and Onís, Federico de. *Frente a la pantalla*. Cuadernos de cine #6. Mexico City: UNAM, Dirección General de Difusión Cultural, 1963.
Reyes, Aurelio de los. *Cine y sociedad en México 1896–1930. Volume 1: Vivir de sueños (1896–1920)*. Mexico City: UNAM and Cineteca Nacional, 1981.
_____. *Los orígenes del cine en México (1896–1900)*. Mexico City: UNAM, Dirección General de Difusión Cultural, 1973.
_____; Ramón, David; Amador, María Luisa; and Rivera, Rodolfo. *80 años de cine en México*. Serie Imágenes #2. Mexico City: UNAM, Dirección General de Difusión Cultural, 1977.
Reyes Nevares, Beatriz. *Trece directores del cine mexicano*. Mexico City: Sep/Setentas, 1973.

———. *The Mexican Cinema: Interviews with Thirteen Directors*. Translated by Carl J. Mora and Elizabeth Gard. Albuquerque: University of New Mexico Press, 1976.

Rhode, Eric. *A History of the Cinema from Its Origins to 1970*. New York: Hill and Wang, 1976.

Riding, Alan. *Distant Neighbors: A Portrait of the Mexicans*. New York: Alfred A. Knopf, 1985, pp. 309–311.

Roberts, John Storm. *Salsa! The Latin Dimension in Popular Music*. New York: BMI, The Many Worlds of Music, issue 3, 1976.

———. *The Latin Tinge: The Impact of Latin American Music on the United States*. New York: Oxford University Press, 1979.

Román, Ernesto and Figueroa Perea, MariCarmen. *Premios y distinciones otorgados al cine mexicano [en] festivales internacionales 1938–1984*. Mexico City: Cineteca Nacional, Departamento de Documentación e Investigación, 1986.

Ross, Stanley R., ed. *Views Across the Border: The United States and Mexico*. Albuquerque: University of New Mexico Press, 1978.

Rovirosa, José. *Cine-Club*. Mexico City: Instituto Mexicano del Seguro Social, 1970.

Rulfo, Juan. *El gallo de oro y otros textos para cine*. Prologue and notes by Jorge Ayala Blanco. Madrid: Ediciones Era and Alianza Editorial, 1980.

Sadoul, Georges. *El cine: Su historia y su técnica*. Translated by Juan José Arreola. Mexico City: Fondo de Cultura Económica, 1952.

———. *Histoire du Cinéma Mondial des Origines a nos Jours*. Paris: Flammarion Editeur, 1949.

Salcedo Silva, Hernando. *Crónicas del cine colombiano 1897–1950*. Bogotá: Carlos Valencia Editores, 1981.

*Salt of the Earth*. Screenplay by Michael Wilson. Commentary by Deborah Silverton Rosenfelt. Old Westbury, NY: The Feminist Press, 1978.

Sanjinés, Jorge y Grupo Ukamau. *Teoría y práctica de un cine junto al pueblo*. Mexico City: Siglo Veintiuno Editores, 1979.

Santillán, Antonio. *El cine*. Barcelona, Buenos Aires, Bogotá: Editorial Bruguera, 1962.

Santos Pereira, Geraldo. *Plano Geral do Cinema Brasileiro: História, Cultura, Economia, e Legislação*. Benfica, Guanabara: Editor Borsoi, 1973.

Saragoza, Alex M. *Mexican Cinema in Cold War America, 1940–1958: An Inquiry into the Interface Between Mexico and Mexicans in the United States*. ChPEC Working Paper Series. Berkeley: University of California, 1983.

Sarris, Andrew, ed. *Interviews with Film Directors*. New York: Avon Books, 1967.

Silva, Alberto. *Cinema e humanismo*. Rio de Janeiro: Pallas, 1975.

Schnitman, Jorge A. *Film Industries in Latin America: Dependency and Development*. Norwood, NJ: Ablex Publishing Co., 1984.

Smith, Paul, ed. *The Historian and Film*. Cambridge: At the University Press, 1976.

Solanas, Fernando E. and Getino, Octavio. *Cine, cultura, y descolonización*. Buenos Aires: Siglo XXI, 1973.

Taibo I, Paco Ignacio. *El indio Fernández: el cine por mis pistolas*. Colección Genio y Figura. Mexico City: Joaquín Mortiz/Planeta, 1986.

———. *María Felix: 47 pasos por el cine*. Colección Genio y Figura. Mexico City: Joaquín Mortiz/Planeta, 1985.

Taylor, John Russell. *Cinema Eye, Cinema Ear*. New York: Hill and Wang, 1974.

Tigler, Parker. *Classics of the Foreign Film: A Pictorial Treasury*. New York: The Citadel Press, 1962.

Torres, Augusto M. *Cine español, años sesenta*. Barcelona: Editorial Anagrama, 1973.

Trelles Plazaola, Luis. *El cine visto en Puerto Rico (1962-1973)*. Colección Uprex. Río Piedras: Editorial Universitaria, Universidad de Puerto Rico, 1975.

Tudor, Andrew. *Image and Influence: Studies in the Sociology of Film*. London: George Allen and Unwin, 1974.

Usigli, Rodolfo. *Mexico in the Theater*. Translated with an introduction by Wilder P. Scott. University, Miss.: Romance Monographs, Inc., 1976.

Valverde, Umberto. *Reportaje crítico al cine colombiano*. Bogotá and Cali: Editorial Toronuevo Limitada, 1978.

Vasconcelos, José. *Indología, una interpretación de la cultura iberoamericana*. Barcelona: Agencia Mundial de Librería, 1926.

Vega Alfaro, Eduardo de la. *El cine de Juan Orol*. Mexico City: Filmoteca UNAM, 1985.

_____. *Juan Orol: 1897-1988*. Colección Cineastas de México. Guadalajara: Universidad de Guadalajara, Centro de Investigación y Enseñanza Cinematográficas, 1987.

Villaurrutia, Xavier. *Crítica cinematográfica*. Edited by Miguel Capistrán. Cuadernos de Cine #18. Mexico City: UNAM, Dirección General de Difusión Cultural, 1970.

Viñas, Moisés. *Historia del cine mexicano*. Mexico City: UNAM-UNESCO, 1987.

Wenden, D.J. *The Birth of the Movies*. London: MacDonald and Co., 1975.

Wilkie, James W.; Meyer, Michael C.; and Wilkie, Edna Monzón de, eds. *Contemporary Mexico: Papers of the IV International Congress of Mexican History*. Berkeley: University of California Press; and Mexico City: El Colegio de Mexico, 1976.

Woll, Allen L. *The Latin Image in American Film*. Latin American Studies, vol. 39, Los Angeles: UCLA Latin American Center Publications, 1977.

Womack, John, Jr. *Zapata and the Mexican Revolution*. New York: Vintage Books, 1970.

## E. ARTICLES

"Actas de Marusia." [review] *La Revue du Cinéma—Image et Son*, no. 306 (May 1976), pp. 66–67.

Alba, Gustavo A. de. "A propósito de Buñuel." *Otrocine* (Mexico City), no. 3 (July-September 1975), pp. 25–26.

_____. "La otra virginidad." *Otrocine*, no. 1 (January–March 1975), pp. 12-16.

Alcalá, Manuel. "Entrevista con Humberto Solás." *Reseña* (Madrid) (March 1977):26-27.

_____. "Huelva 76: II Semana de Cine Iberoamericano," *Reseña* (February 1977):35–36.

Aldape, John. "In 'mean, sexy' roles Emilia Guiu was superstar." *The Arizona Republic*, 18 February 1973, p. L-2.

Alisky, Marvin. "Mexico's Rural Radio." *Quarterly of Film, Radio & Television* 8 (Winter 1953-1954): 405–17.

_____. "Mexico versus Malthus: National Trends." *Current History* 66 (May 1974): 200–30.

Allen, William D. "Spanish-Language Films in the U.S." *Films in Review* 1 (July–August 1950): 1, 42–45.

Almendros, Nestor. "The Cinema in Cuba." *Film Culture* no. 3 (1956), p. 21.

Amador, Omar G. "Galanes latinos, Lolita y La Bamba. "*Américas*, July–August 1988, pp. 2–9.

Ângelo, Miguel. "Brasil: 75 años de cinema." *O Cruzeiro* (Rio de Janeiro), 15 September 1971, pp. 158–62.

Aragón, Luis. "Libros: el cine mexicano." *Cine cubano*, no. 17 (January 1964), p. 63.

Askenazy, Natalia. "Movieland Stretches Southward: A Newsletter from Mexico City." *Films in Review* 1 (May–June 1950): 14–43.

_____. "The Two Kinds of Mexican Movies." *Films in Review* 2 (May 1951): 35-39.

Aubry, Daniel and Lacor, J.M. "Luis Buñuel." *Film Quarterly* 12 (Winter 1958): 7-9.

"Authentic Pachuco." [on Germán Valdez "Tin-Tan"] *Time*, 10 July 1944, p. 72.

Ayala Blanco, Jorge. "Fuensanta: Que triste será la tarde en que te vayas al cine a ver a López Velarde." (La Cultura en México: Suplemento de Siempre) *Siempre*, 20 December 1972, p. xv.

_____. "Pancho Villa en el jardín de los senderos que se trifurcan." *Siempre*, 15 September 1982, p. XVI.

_____. "Western con vihuela." *Cine cubano*, nos. 71/72 (1971), pp. 126–28.

Azurduy, Victoria. "El cine venezolano: ¿vía crucis?" *Otrocine*, no. 6 (April–June 1976), pp. 4–8.

Beguiristain, Mario E. "Nestor Almendros' Days of Heaven are Finally Here," *Nuestro*, November 1979, pp. 21-22.

Berg, Charles. *"Mexico, Mexico, Ra,Ra,Ra."* [review] *Film Quarterly* 32 (Spring 1979): 49–50.

_____. *"Canoa."* [review] *Film Quarterly* 32 (Spring 1979): 50–52.

Biskind, Peter. "In Latin America They Shoot Filmmakers." *Sight and Sound* (Summer 1976), pp. 160–61.

_____. "Ripping off Zapata: Revolution Hollywood Style." *Cineaste* 7, no. 2, pp. 11–17.

Bodeen, Dewitt. "Dolores del Rio." *Films in Review* 18 (May 1967): 266–83.

_____. "Ramon Novarro." *Films in Review* 18 (November 1967): 528–47.

Buñuel, Juan. "A Letter on *Exterminating Angel*." *Film Culture*, no. 41 (1966), p. 66

Burns, Archibaldo. "Dolores del Río: de sus cenizas, la leyenda." *Proceso*, no. 337, 18 April 1983, pp. 50–53.

Burns, E. Bradford. "Film." In *Handbook of Latin American Studies* 38. Edited by Dolores Moyano Martin and Donald E.J. Stewart. Gainesville: University of Florida Press, 1976, pp. 59–69.

_____. "Films." [review of *Los gauchos judíos*] *The Nation*, 16 August 1975, p. 126.

_____. "National Identity in Argentine Films." *Américas*, November–December 1975, pp. 4–10.

Burton, Julianne. Book review of *Nuevo cine latinoamericano, Hacia un tercer cine*, and *Cine, cultura y descolonización*. *Hispanic American Historical Review* 55 (May 1975): 382–86.

_____. *"Film."* In Handbook of Latin American Studies 40. Edited by Dolores Moyano Martin. Gainesville: University Presses of Florida, 1978, pp. 57-67.

_____. "Pedro and the Captain." *Film Quarterly* 34, no. 1 (Fall 1985): 30–32.

_____. *"The Hour of the Embers:* On the Current Situation of Latin American Cinema." *Film Quarterly* 30 (Fall 1976): 33–44.

_____. *"The Traitors."* [film review] *Film Quarterly* 30 (Fall 1976): 57–59.

Butler, Ron. "Cantinflas: Príncipe mexicano de la comedia." *Américas*, April 1981, pp. 7–9.

Cabada, Juan de la. "Mis pasos en el cine." *Otrocine*, no. 1 (January–March 1975), pp. 40–45.

_____. "Mis pasos en el cine (segunda parte)." *Otrocine*, no. 2 (April–June 1975), pp. 34–40.

Carlesimo, Cheryl. "Painting with Light." [article on Nestor Almendros] *American Film* 6 (April 1981), pp. 30–34, 69–71.

Carrasco, Jorge. "Luto en el Cine Mexicano." [obituary on Dolores del Río] *Hispanoamericano*, 25 April 1983, pp. 44–47.

_____ . "Un Artista Integro." [obituary on Luis Buñuel] *Hispanoamericano*, 8 August 1983, pp. 58–59.

Casal, Lourdes and Surkin, Marvin. "Recent Cuban Cinema." *Cineaste* 6, no. 4, pp. 22, 52.

Castillo, Raymond del. "The Cinema in Argentina." *The Penguin Film Review*, no. 4 (1947), pp. 100–104.

Caymares, Hortensia and Castillo, Luciano. "Barbachano o la pasión de crear." *Cine cubano*, no. 118 (1987), pp. 59–63.

Chávez, Carlos. "Films by American Governments: Mexico." *Films*, no. 3 (Summer 1940), pp. 20–21.

Chiles, Frederic G. and Mraz, J. "The Historical Film Essay: TODO ES MAS SABROSO CON..." *PCCLAS Proceedings* 4 (1975): 183–86.

Chinchilla, Norma and Dietz-Fee, Terry. "Chile with Poems and Guns: A Strong Analytical Tool." *PCCLAS Proceedings* 4 (1975): 191–92.

*Cineaste* 4, no. 3, pp. 1–14. [special issue: Latin American militant cinema].

"Cine cubano entrevista a Pedro Chaskel, nuevo secretario general de la UCAL." *Cine cubano*, nos. 73/74/75 (1972), pp. 117–19.

"Cinéma Anti-imperialiste en Amérique Latine." *Cahiers de Cinéma*, no. 253 (October–November 1974)

"Cinema as a Gun: An Interview with Fernando Solanas." *Cineaste*, no. 2, pp. 18–26.

"Cinéma Mexicain." *La Revue du Cinéma—Image et Son*, no. 295 (April 1975), pp. 20–28.

"Cinema Novo vs. Cultural Colonialism: An Interview with Glauber Rocha." *Cineaste* 4, no. 1, pp. 2–9, 35.

Clark, Jacqueline. "Report from the Argentine: Buenos Aires Prefers U.S. and Italian Films." *Films in Review* 1 (March 1950): 16, 48.

Colectivo Alejandro Galindo. "El cine mexicano y sus crisis." [part one] *Dicine*, no. 19 (May–June 1987), pp. 12–13; [part two] no. 20 (July–August 1987), pp. 12–15; [part three] no. 21 (September-October 1987), pp. 16–18.

Colina, José de la. "En busca de una niñez perdida." *Cine cubano*, no. 14–15 (October–November 1963.), pp. 85–88.

_____ . "Viridiana." Cine cubano, no. 10 (1964), pp. 21–25.

Colina, Enrique and Díaz Torres, Daniel. "Ideología del melodrama en el viejo cine latinoamericano." *Cine cubano*, nos. 73/74/75 (1972), pp. 14–26.

Conrad, Randall. "A Magnificent and Dangerous Weapon: The Politics of Luis Buñuel's Later Films." *Cineaste* 7, no. 4 (1977): 10–18, 51.

Cortés, Carlos E. "The Societal Curriculum and the School Curriculum: Allies or Antagonists?" *Educational Leadership: Journal of the Association for Supervision and Curriculum Development* 36, no. 7 (April 1979): 475–79.

Couselo, Jorge Miguel. "Cine argentino: presente vago y futuro incierto." *Plural*, vol. 12-1, no. 133 (October 1982): 49–53.

Crespo Aragón, Carlos and Erika Domínguez Cervantes. "José Estrada: Crisis del cine mexicano." *Plural*, vol. 11–9, no. 129 (June 1982): 71–75.

Darvell, Michael. "Pan-European: Tapping the Minority Audiences." *Film* (British Federation of Film Societies), series 2, no. 5 (August 1973).

Delpar, Helen. "Mexico, the MPPDA, and Derogatory Films, 1922-1926." *The Journal of Popular Film and Television* 12, no. 1 (Spring 1984): 34–41.

Demby, Betty Jeffries. "The 30th Cannes Film Festival." *Filmmakers Newsletter,* October 1980, pp. 28–33.

Díaz Torres, Daniel. "El cine cubano en América Latina." *Cine cubano*, no. 68 (1971), pp. 67–77.

_____ and Colina, Enrique. "El melodrama en la obra de Luis Buñuel." *Cine cubano*, no. 78/79/80 (1972), pp. 156–59, 162, 164.

Domínguez, Erika. "Disección del cine mexicano." *Plural*, vol. 12–7, no. 139, April 1983, pp. 52–57.

_____ . "Emilio García Riera: Un sexenio de cine mexicano." *Plural*, vol. 12-3, no. 135 (December 1982): 45–48.

Dreifus, Claudia. "Carlos Fuentes: When Eternity Moves." *Film Comment*, June 1986, pp. 48–52.

Duarte, Patricia. "Welcome to Ricardo's Reality." *Nuestro*, October 1979, pp. 24–26.

Eceiza, Antonio. "Sobre el cine y la literatura." *Cine cubano*, no. 39 (1967), pp. 26–28.

Ehrmann, Hans. "Latin American Cinema: Film and History." [review of E. Bradford Burns's book] *Film Quarterly* 24 (Summer 1976): 26–27.

"El Arte Como Función Social." [interview with Alfonso Arau] *Hispanoamericano*, 11 April 1977, pp. 39–42.

Ellis, Kirk. "Stranger than Fiction: Emilio Fernandez' Mexico." *The Journal of Popular Film and Television* 10, no. 1 (Spring 1982): 27–36.

"En la Cumbre de la Fama." [article on María Félix] *Hispanoamericano*, 21 November 1955, pp. 40–45.

"Entretien avec Luis Buñuel." *Cahiers du Cinéma*, no. 191 (June 1967), pp. 14–18.

Espinosa, Martha Aurora. "El cine nacional se ha convertido, durante sus 50 años de vida, en un círculo vicioso: Galindo." *Uno Más Uno*, 12 January 1981, p. 23.

*Experimental Cinema*, no. 5 (1934). [Synopsis for *Que Viva Mexico*].

Falcoff, Mark. "The Uruguay That Never Was: A Historian Looks at Costa-Gavras's State of Siege." *Journal of Latin American Lore* 2 (1976): 239–56.

Fenin, George N. "Perspectivas: Introducción del cine argentino en Estados Unidos." *Tiempo de Cine* (Montevideo), año 11, no. 7 (July–September 1961), p. 13.

Fernández, Carlos. "Nuevamente sobre el cine mexicano." *Cine cubano*, no. 17 (January 1964), pp. 12–14.

_____ . "Unas palabras sobre el cine mexicano." *Cine cubano*, no. 7 (1961), pp. 56–58.

"Film in Chile: An Interview with Miguel Littín." *Cineaste* 4, no. 4, pp. 4–9.

"Filmografía del cine cubano." *Cine cubano*, nos. 23/24/25 (1964), pp. 129–42.

"Filmografía Luis Buñuel." *Cine cubano*, nos. 78/79/80 (1972), pp. 166–75.

"5 Frames are 5 Frames, Not 6, But 5: An Interview with Santiago Alvarez." *Cineaste* 6, no. 4, pp. 17–21.

Flores Márquez, Fortunato. "Lo Mejor de los Estrenos en 1972." *Hispanoamericano*, 15 January 1973, p. 56.

_____ . "Recopilación Contemporánea." *Hispanoamericano*, 20 November 1972, p. 54.

Fournier Villada, Raoul. "He Makes Mexico Laugh." [article on Cantinflas] *Americas*, March 1953, pp. 6–8, 44–46.

"Fruto del Pueblo." [article on Cantinflas] *Tiempo*, 28 June 1971, pp. 19–21.

Fuentes, Carlos. "El cine y el escritor." *Cine cubano*, no. 31/32/33 (1966), pp. 101–102.

García Ascot, Jomi. "El cine y el escritor." *Cine cubano*, no. 31/32/33 (1966), pp. 103–105.

García Ponce, Juan. "El cine y el escritor," *Cine cubano*, no. 31/32/33 (1966), pp. 106–108.

García Riera, Emilio. "Conversación con Jaime Humberto Hermosillo." *Primer Plano (Revista de la Cineteca Nacional)*, no. 1 (November-December 1981): 3–30.

_____ . "La eterna rebelión de Luis Buñuel." *Tiempo de Cine*, no. 13 (March 1963), pp. 8–13, 64.

_____ . "La semana en el cine: Los 50 años de cine nacional." *Uno Más Uno*, 2 January 1981, p. 18; and 3 January 1981, p. 18.

_____ . "Medio siglo de cine mexicano." *Cine cubano*, no. 31/32/33 (1966), pp. 75–97.

_____ . "Seis años de cine mexicano." *Proceso*. 6, 13, and 20 November 1976.

_____ . "The Eternal Rebellion of Luis Buñuel." *Film Culture*, no. 21 (1960), p. 42.

_____ . "The Films of Luis Buñuel." *Film Culture*, no. 21 (1960), p. 58.

_____ . "Viridiana." *Film Culture*, no. 24 (1962), p. 74.

Garner, Van. "Chile with Poems and Guns: A Counterproductive Model." *PCCLAS Proceedings* 4 (1975): 187–89.

Gaxiola, Fernando. " 'Actas de Marusia'—la posibilidad de un cine popular." *Otrocine*, no. 1 (January-March 1975), p. 9.

_____ . "Canoa, memoria de un hecho vergonzante." *Otrocine*, no. 1 (January-March 1975), p. 10.

Gerald, Yvonne. "The Comedy of Cantinflas." *Films in Review* 9 (January 1958): 6–11.

Gillet, John. "The Cinema of Luis Buñuel by Freddy Buache." [book review] *Film*, series 2, no. 5 (August 1973), p. 20.

Gilliatt, Penelope. "Profiles: Long Live the Living!" [interview with Luis Bunuel] *The New Yorker*, 5 December 1977, pp. 53–72.

Goldin, Greg and Marc Cooper. "Mexico's Movies: Now Playing at a Theater Near You." *Southwest Airlines Spirit*, July 1986, pp. 53–54, 87–95.

Gómez, Gloria Cecilia. "El cine mejicano en Colombia." *Cromos* (Bogotá), no. 3094 (4 May 1977), pp. 74–77.

Gómez Sicre, José. "Dolores del Río." *Américas*, December 1967, pp. 8–17.

González, José Antonio. "Apuntes para la historia de un cine sin historia." *Cine cubano*, no. 86/87/88 (1973 or 1974), pp. 37–45.

González Casanova, Manuel. "The Participation of Our Schools in the Defense and Diffusion of National Culture." *The Journal of the University Film Association* 29, no. 2 (Spring 1977): 3–7.

Goytisolo, Juan. "Algunas consideraciones respecto al cine español." *Cine cubano*, no. 10 (1963), pp. 12–15.

Grant, Jacques. "Aprés Royan et à propos du cinéma d'Amérique Latine." *Cinema 74*, no. 187 (May 1974), pp. 40–49.

Green, Marc. "How Much Discipline for the Study of Film?" *The Chronicle of Higher Education*, 15 September 1975.

Greenbaum, Richard. "Luis Buñuel, 1900–1983." *Films in Review* 34, no. 8 (October 1983): 484–86.

Guevara, Alfredo. "IV reseña del cine latinoamericano." *Cine cubano*, no. 12 (July 1963), pp. 54–59.

Gumucio Dagrón, Alfonso. "Cine obrero sandinista." *Plural*, vol. 11–10, no. 130 (July 1982): 35–40.

Haddad García, George. "Dolores de mi Corazón." *Nuestro*, April 1979, pp. 31–33.

Hairston, Florence. "Use with Caution: These Films are Biased." *PCCLAS Proceedings* 4 (1975): 171–77.

Harcourt, Peter. "Luis Buñuel: Spaniard and Surrealist." *Film Quarterly* 20 (Spring 1967): pp. 2–19.

H.H. *"El Topo."* [review] *Films in Review*, no. 10 (December 1971).

Hinojosa, Gerardo. "Auandar Anapu: odres nuevos, vino viejo." *Otrocine*, no. 1 (January–March 1975), pp. 46–48.

Hull, David Stuart. "Viridiana." [review] *Film Quarterly* 15 (Winter 1961/62): 55–56.

Isaac, Alberto. "Cine latinoamericano: reportaje a Luis Alcoriza." *Tiempo de cine*, año 5, no. 20/21 (Spring–Summer 1965), pp. 38–40, 80.

Johansen, Jason C. "A New Wave Cresting." *Nuestro,* May 1980, pp. 24–25, 63.

Johnson, Randal. "Film." In Dolores Moyano Martin, ed., *Handbook of Latin American Studies: No. 48—Humanities,* pp. 59–77. Austin: University of Texas Press, 1986.

Kanesaka, Kenji. "A Visit to Luis Buñuel." Film Culture, no. 41 (1966), p. 60.

Keel, Erich. "From Militant Cinema to Neo-Realism: The Example of *Pueblo Chico.*" *Film Quarterly* 24 (Summer 1976): 17–24.

Konder, Rodolfo. "The Carmen Miranda Museum: Brazilian Bombshell Still Box Office in Rio." *Américas,* September–October 1982 pp. 17–20.

Kovacs, Katherine S. "Miguel Littín's *Recurso del Método*: The Aftermath of Allende." *Film Quarterly* 33 (Spring 1980): 22–29.

Kovacs, Steven. "Las Amazonas de Cine." [article on Venezuelan film board] *Sight and Sound,* Spring 1978, pp. 91–93.

Krohn, Bill. "Brésil, Ma «Fatale Attraction»." *Cahiers du Cinéma,* no. 404 (February 1988), pp. 28–32.

"La Aventura Mexicana." *Hispanoamericano,* 22 March 1976, p. 59.

"La cinematografía mexicana, su historia, su realidad, sus potencialidades." *Militancia: temas del socialismo* 1, no. 1 (September 30, 1974): 55–58.

Lamb, Blaine P. "The Convenient Villain: The Early Cinema Views the Mexican-American." *Journal of the West* 14 (October 1975): 75–81.

Lambert, Gavin. "Nazarin." [review] *Film Quarterly* 13 (Spring 1960): 30–31.

Landa G., Antonio. "Canoa." *Otrocine,* no. 4 (October–December 1975), pp. 14–15.

Lash, Vivian. "Experimenting with Freedom in Mexico." *Film Quarterly* 19 (Summer 1966): 19–24.

"Las Películas Mexicanas en los EE UU." *Tiempo,* 27 April 1945, p. 37.

"La Televisión en Mexico." *Hispanoamericano,* 17 August 1951, pp. 3–6.

"Leopoldo Torre-Nilson Interviewed by Fred Wellington." *Film Culture,* no. 46 (1967), n.p.

Lescale, Aurora. "México Indígena." *Cine cubano,* no. 103 (1982), pp. 108–111.

"Les Jours de L'Amour." [review of Alberto Isaac film] *La Revue du Cinéma—Image et Son,* no. 301 (December 1975), pp. 115–16.

Lintz de Nava, Arlene. "Entrevista con Gabriel Retes." *Otrocine,* no. 1 (January–March 1975), pp. 55–61.

"Los Independientes." *Otrocine,* no. 1 (January–March 1975), p. 54.

"'Los Olvidados' y la Crítica." *Hispanoamericano,* 7 March 1952, p. 52.

"Los Próximos 'Arieles.'" *Hispanoamericano,* 13 February 1953, p. 44.

"Luis Buñuel hace la anatomía del churro cinematográfico." *Cine cubano,* no. 78/79/80 (1972), pp. 112–13.

Luna, Andrés de and Charaund, Susana. "Los independientes: entrevista a Eduardo Maldonado." *Otrocine,* no. 6 (April–June 1976), pp. 29–32.

MacBean, James Roy. "Fernando Solanas, An Interview." *Film Quarterly* 24 (Fall 1970): 37–43.

_____. *"La Hora de los Hornos." Film Quarterly* 24 (Fall 1970): pp. 31–37.

Macotela, Catherine. "El sindicalismo en el cine (primera parte)." *Otrocine,* no. 2 (April–June 1975), pp. 60–67.

_____. "El sindicalismo en el cine (segunda parte)." *Otrocine,* no. 3 (July–September 1975), pp. 57–63.

_____. "El sindicalismo en el cine (tercera parte)." *Otrocine,* no. 4 (October–December 1975), pp. 65–69.

_____. "El sindicalismo en el cine (cuarta parte)." *Otrocine,* no. 5 (January–March 1976), pp. 59–65.

———— . "El sindicalismo en el cine (quinta parte)." *Otrocine*, no. 6 (April–June 1976), pp. 46–48.

Maffer, Sergio. "México en tres niveles." *Cine cubano*, no. 63/65 (1970), pp. 14–16.

Margorelles, Louis. "Le Renouveau Mexicain." *La Revue de Cinéma—Image et Son*, no. 280 (January 1974), pp. 72–90.

Martínez Ortega, Gonzalo. "El encuentro de un hombre solo." *Militancia: temas del socialismo* 1, no. 1 (September 30, 1974): 64–68.

Matas, Julio. "Theater and Cinematography." In *Revolutionary Change in Cuba*, edited by Carmelo Mesa-Lago, pp. 427–45. Pittsburgh: University of Pittsburgh Press, 1971.

Mekas, Adolfas. "A Letter from Mexico." *Film Culture*, no. 20 (1959), p. 72.

Méndez, José Carlos. "Hacia un cine político: la cooperativa de un cine marginal." (La Cultura en México/Suplemento de *Siempre*) Siempre, 1972.

Michel, Manuel. "CCC: Un retrato escrito." *Otrocine*, no. 1 (January–March 1975), pp. 62–68.

———— . "Cine mexicano: utopía y realidad." *Plural*, vol. 11–7, no. 127 (April 1982): 67–70.

———— . "Mexican Cinema: A Panoramic View." *Film Quarterly* 18 (Summer 1965): 46–55.

Miller, Clyde. "Filmmakers of Churubusco." *Américas*, April 1974, pp. 15–20.

Miller, Carol. "Luis Buñuel: El Ojo de la Libertad." *Hispanoamericano*, January 12, 1981, pp. 54–57.

Mistron, Deborah. "A Hybrid Subgenre: The Revolutionary Melodrama in the Mexican Cinema." *Studies in Latin American Popular Culture* 3 (1984): 47–56.

———— . "The Role of Pancho Villa in the Mexican and the American Cinema." *Studies in Latin American Popular Culture* 2 (1983): 1–13.

Monsiváis, Carlos. "Es el baile del pingüino un baile elegante y fino." *Diálogos* (El Colegio de México) 13 (September–October 1977): 11–14.

———— . "Junto contigo le doy un aplauso al placer y al amor." *Textos* (Guadalajara), año 2, no. 9–10 (1975), pp. 39–56.

———— . "Los de atras se quedarán (I) (Notas sobre cultura y sociedad de masas en los setentas)." *Nexos* 26 (February 1980): 35–43.

———— . "Notas sobre la cultura mexicana en el siglo XX: XII. El cine nacional." In *Historia general de Mexico,* vol. 4, pp. 434–59. Mexico City: Centro de Estudios Históricos, El Colegio de México, 1976.

———— . "Proyecto de periodización de historia cultural de México.: *PCCLAS Proceedings* 4 (1975): 39–49.

———— . "The Culture of the Frontier: The Mexican Side." In Stanley R. Ross, ed. *Views Across the Border: The United States and Mexico*. Albuquerque: University of New Mexico Press, 1978, pp. 50–67.

Mora, Carl J. "Alejandro Galindo: Pioneer Mexican Filmmaker." *Journal of Popular Culture* 18, no. 1 (Summer 1984): 101–12.

———— . "Cinema, Spanish." In Robert Kern, ed. *Historical Dictionary of Modern Spain*. Westport, CT: Greenwood Press, forthcoming.

———— . "Introduction," "Feminine Images in Mexican Cinema: The Family Melodrama; Sara García, 'The Mother of Mexico'; and the Prostitute." *Studies in Latin American Popular Culture* 4 (1985): 228–235.

———— . "Let's Screen More Latin Films." *Nuestro*, October 1977, p. 59.

———— . "Mexican Cinema in the 1970s." In Leonard Folgarait, ed., *Mexican Art of the 1970s* (Nashville, Tenn.: Vanderbilt University, Center for Latin American and Iberian Studies, 1984), pp. 37–44.

———. "Mexico's Commercial Films: Sources for the Study of Social History." *PCCLAS Proceedings* 6 (1977–1979): 205–15.

———. "Spain's Cinema of the 'Autonomies.'" *New Orleans Review* 13, no. 2 (Summer 1986): 32–42.

———. "The Odyssey of Spanish Cinema." *New Orleans Review* 14, no. 1 (Spring 1987): 7–20.

Mortimore, Roger. "Buñuel, Sáenz de Heredia and Filmófono." *Sight and Sound* (Summer 1975), pp. 180–82.

Mosier, John. "Actresses and Acting." *Américas*, September–October 1983, pp. 58–59.

———. "Ambitious Epics: *Cecilia* and *The Red Bells*." *Américas*, January–February 1983, p. 59.

———. "El cine mexicano: Raúl Araiza." *Américas*, July–August 1982, pp. 57–58.

———. "Currents in Latin American Film." *Américas*, May 1978, pp. 2–8.

——— and Gonzáles, Alexis. "Marcela Fernández Violante: cineasta singular." *Américas*, January-February 1983, pp. 15-19.

Nicholson, Irene. "Mexican Films: Their Past and Future." *Quarterly of Film, Radio & Television* 10 (1955–56): 248–52.

"Nota de redacción." [review of García Riera's book *El cine mexicano*] *Cine cubano*, no. 31/32/33 (1966), pp. 98–100.

Noyola, Antonio. "Retrospectiva del cine mexicano no industrial." *Otrocine*, no. 6 (April–June 1976), pp. 49–57.

———. "Trece directores del cine mexicano." [book review] *Otrocine*, no. 1 (January–March 1975), pp. 69–71.

"Nuevo cine, nuevos realizadores, nuevos filmes: entrevista a Miguel Littín." *Cine cubano*, no. 63–65 (1970), pp. 1–6.

O'Connor, Chris. "Dolores del Rio: Forever Beautiful." *Modern Maturity*, February–March 1981, pp. 69–71.

Olhovich, Sergio. "Dos directores de cine se critican recíprocamente." *Militancia: temas del socialismo* 1, no. 1 (30 September 1974.): 59–63.

Oliver, Maria Rosa [Marie Rose]. "Cantinflas." *Hollywood Quarterly* 2 (1946–1947): 252–56.

———. "The Native Films of Mexico." *The Penguin Film Review*, pp. 73–79. London and New York: Penguin Books, 1948.

Orme, Jr., William A. "Using TV to Send Social Message." *R&D Mexico*, 16 June 1982, pp. 15–18.

Ostria, Vincent. "L'Enfance de l'Homme." [review of Luis Alcoriza's *Tiburoneros (Pecheurs de Requins)*] *Cahiers du Cinéma*, no. 402 (December 1987), pp. 44–46.

Pacheco, Cristina. "El Cine, Su Vicio." [interview with Emilio García Riera] *Siempre*, 1 November 1978, pp. 32–34, 70.

Paz, Octavio. "Nazarin." [review] *Film Culture*, no. 21 (1960), p. 60.

P.C. "El Topo." [review] *Film*, series 2, no. 9 (December 1973), pp. 18–19.

*Pensamiento crítico* (Havana), no. 42 (July 1970). [Special issue on Cuban cinema.]

Peralta, José Luis. "El cambio." *Otrocine*, no. 3 (July–September 1975), pp. 68–70.

Pérez, Fernando. "Nazarín." *Cine cubano*, no. 78/79/80 (1972), pp. 136–37.

Pérez Gómez, Angel A. "Luis Alcoriza: Mecánica nacional." *Reseña*, año 14, no. 103 (March 1977), pp. 28–29.

Pérez-Turrent, Tomás. "No es lo mismo los tres mosqueteros que cuatro años después." *Otrocine*, no. 4 (October–December 1975), pp. 4–9.

_____ . "Una experiencia alrededor de Canoa." *Otrocine,* no. 2 (April–June 1975), pp. 8–12.

Pierre, Sylvie. "Brésil (suite)—Glauber Rocha pourquoi?" *Cahiers du Cinéma,* no. 393 (March 1971): *Le Journaldes,* no. 71, p. II.

_____ . "Le cinéma brésilien à Beaubourg: Zut aux exoticophiles!" *Cahiers du Cinéma,* no. 393 (March 1971): *Le Journaldes,* no. 71, pp. I-II.

Pinto, Alfonso. "Cuando Hollywood Habló en Español." *Américas,* October 1980, pp. 3–8.

_____ . "Hollywood's Spanish-Language Films." *Films in Review* 24 (October 1973): 474–83, 487.

Portes, Francisco. "Ignacio López Tarso: el actor y el acento." *Mundo Hispánico* (Madrid), March 1977, pp. 57–60.

Quijada, Miguel Angel. "El joven cine español de la época franquista." *Otrocine,* no. 5 (January–March 1976), pp. 12–17.

Ramírez Berg, Charles. "Cracks in the *Macho* Monolith: *Machismo,* Man, and Mexico in Recent Mexican Cinema." *New Orleans Review* 16, no. 1 (Spring 1989): 67–74.

_____ . "Mexican Cinema: A Study in Creative Tension." *New Orleans Review* 10, no. 2 (Summer/Fall 1983): 149–52.

Ramón, David. "Semana del cine mexicano no industrial." *Otrocine,* no. 4 (October–December 1975), pp. 20–22.

_____ . "Un sexenio de cine en México." *Comunicación* 21 (March 1977): 24–33.

Ramos Navas, Germán. "De todos modos CUEC te llamas." *Excélsior: Diorama de Cultura,* 7 September 1980, p. 3.

"Reportaje a Alberto Isaac." *Tiempo de cine,* año 5, no. 21/22 (Spring–Summer 1965), pp. 41–44.

"Responde a Cine cubano: Alberto Isaac." *Cine cubano,* no. 31/32/33 (1966), pp. 115–16.

"Responde a Cine cubano: Emilio García Riera." *Cine cubano,* no. 31/32/33 (1966), pp. 110–11.

"Responde a Cine cubano: Icaro Cisneros." *Cine cubano,* no. 31/32/33 (1966), pp. 113–15.

"Responde a Cine cubano: José Luis Ibáñez." *Cine cubano,* no. 31/32/33 (1966), pp. 111–13.

"Responden a Cine cubano: Oscar Kantor, David José Kohon, Mabel Itzkovich, Rodolfo Kuhn, Leopoldo Torre Nilsson, Saulo Benavente." *Cine cubano,* no. 31/32/33 (1966), pp. 64–74.

Reyes, Aurelio de los. "El cine como indicador entusiasmadó." *Diálogos,* no. 77 (September-October 1977), pp. 30–32.

Reyes de la Maza, Luis. "De como el papá de Martín Cortés se fue mucho para el Tívoli." *Otrocine,* no. 1 (January–March 1975), pp. 33–39.

Reyes Nevares, Beatriz. "Cine mexicano: habla Ricardo Garibay." *Siempre,* 13 December 1972, pp. 40–41.

_____ . "El cine mexicano es hoy de mejor calidad." *Siempre,* 27 December 1972, pp. 42–43.

_____ . "Entre cretinos y voraces naufraga el cine mexicano." *Siempre,* 3 January 1973, pp. 40–41, 70.

_____ . "Salomón Laiter: profeta de un nuevo cine." *Siempre,* 24 January 1973, p. 45.

Rico, María Elena. "Anatomía de un éxito loco: Allá en el Rancho Grande." *Contenido,* June 1976, pp. 20–56.

Rivera, Héctor. "El Indio [Fernández], tan intenso en la furia como en la ternura." *Proceso,* 11 August 1986, pp. 42–48.

———. "[Alberto] Isaac cree posible levantar un cine en ruinas en un país arruinado." *Proceso*, 11 April 1983, pp. 48–51.

Rodríguez, João Carlos. "El indio y el cine brasileño." *Plural*, vol. 11–12, no. 132 (September 1982): 47–53.

Rodríguez Alemán, Mario. "Entrevista con Antonio Eceiza." *Cine cubano*, no. 39 (1967), pp. 15–25.

———. "Bosquejo histórico del cine cubano." *Cine cubano*, no. 23/24/25 (1964), pp. 25–33.

Rodríguez Monegal, Emir. "El mito Buñuel." *Tiempo de cine*, no. 14/15 (July 1963), pp. 7–10.

Rossi, Eduardo A. "Lo que el tiempo se tragó." *Otrocine*, no. 3 (July–September 1975), pp. 4–9.

———. "Veinte años del cine argentino." *Otrocine*, no. 4 (October–December 1975), pp. 44–52.

"Round the World's Studios," *The Penguin Film Review*, no. 1 (1941), pp. 53–54.

Rubia Barcia, J. "Luis Buñuel's *Los Olvidados.*" *Quarterly of Film, Radio & Television* 7 (1952–53): 392–401.

Sabourad, Frédéric. "Festivals: 9° Féstival des trois continents à Nantes: La carte de l'identité." [review of Arturo Ripstein's *Imperio de la fortuna*] *Cahiers du Cinéma*, no. 404 (February 1988): *Le Journaldes*, no. 80, p. VIII.

Saderman, Alejandro. "Cine argentino, o de crisis en crisis." *Cine cubano*, no. 31/32/33 (1966), pp. 51–62.

Sánchez, Alberto Ruy. "Cine mexicano: producción social de una estética." *Historia y Sociedad*, no. 18 (Summer 1978), pp. 71–83.

Sánchez, Francisco. "Miguel Littín: poesía y militancia política." *Otrocine*, no. 4 (October–December 1975), pp. 28–33.

———. "Tívoli." *Otrocine*, no. 1 (January-March 1975), pp. 19–22.

Sanjinés, Jorge. "Cine revolucionario: la experiencia boliviana." *Otrocine*, no. 6 (April–June 1976), pp. 61–70.

Scheffler, Wini. "Foreign Filming Leaves Below-the-Line Income." *Mex-Am Review* 43 (August 1975): 4–5, 7,9.

Schumann, Jochem. "Ten Years of Cuban Films: 1959-1969." *Publik* (Frankfurt), 1 May 1970.

Schumann, Peter B. "El cine de El Salvador." *Plural*, vol. 12–8, no. 140 (May 1983): 46–48.

———. "El cine de Venezuela." *Plural*, vol. 12–6, no. 138 (March 1983): 59–65.

Sepúlveda, Martha L. "Sobre Canoa." *Otrocine*, no. 4 (October–December 1975), pp. 16–18.

Seton, Marie. "Vignettes of Eisenstein." *Films in Review* 2 (April 1951): 29–31.

Shelley, Jaime A. "Conversación con Felipe Cazals." *Otrocine*, no. 3 (July–September 1975), pp. 34–43.

———. "Conversación con Miguel Littín." *Otrocine*, no. 4 (October–December 1975), pp. 34–43.

———. "El cine mexicano, ¿campeón sin corona?" *Otrocine*, no. 1 (January-March 1975), pp. 2–5.

———. "Entrevista con Alberto Isaac." *Otrocine*, no. 1 (January–March 1975), pp. 23–32.

———. "La herencia de los productores, esa ancla enmohecida que puede frenarlo todo." *Otrocine*, no. 2 (April–June 1975), pp.2–3.

"Simón del desierto." *Cine cubano*, no. 78/79/80 (1972), p. 143.

Stam, Robert. "Slow Fade to Afro: The Black Presence in Brazilian Cinema." *Film Quarterly* 36, no. 2 (Winter 1982–83): 16–32.

Stamm [*sic*], Robert and Xavier, Ismael. "Recent Brazilian Cinema: Allegory/ Metacinema/Carnival." *Film Quarterly* 41 (Spring 1988): 15–30.

Stein, Elliott. "Don Hermosillo and the Sun." [on the Third Miami Film Festival and Jaime Humberto Hermosillo's *Doña Herlinda y su hijo* and other of his films] *Film Comment*, June 1986, pp. 53–57.

Sterrit, David. "Puerto Rico: new presence in film." *The Christian Science Monitor*, 21 August 1987, pp. 19–20.

Suárez, Joseantonio. "El cine en Portugal." *Otrocine*, no. 4 (October–December 1975), pp. 10–13.

Sutherland, Elizabeth. "Cinema of Revolution—90 Miles from Home." *Film Quarterly* 15 (Winter 1961/62): 42.

"The Latin-American Film." *The Penguin Film Review*, no. 2 (1947), pp. 34–35.

Toubiana, Serge. "Pour en Réalisme de Rêve." [interview with Ruy Guerra, director of *Eréndira*] *Cahiers du Cinéma*, no. 354 (December 1983): *Le Journal des*, no. 38, pp. III–IV.

Tozzi, R.V. *"Torero!"* [review] *Films in Review* 8 (June–July 1957): 224–25.

Treviño, Jesús Salvador. "The New Mexican Cinema." *Film Quarterly* 32 (Spring 1979): 26–37.

Tuchman, Mitch. *"The Man from Maisinicu."* [review] *Film Quarterly* 30 (Fall 1976): 59–60.

Turner, R.H. *"Macario."* [review] *Film Quarterly* 14 (Winter 1960): 50.

"Una Oportunidad Más." *Hispanoamericano*, 9 February 1976, p. 61.

Uribe, Alvaro. "Entrevista a Alfredo Joskowicz." *Otrocine*, no. 3 (July–September 1975), pp. 64–67.

Valdés, Oscar and Torres, Miguel. "En compañía de Max Linder." *Cine cubano*, no. 35 (1966), pp. 45–49.

Vanderwood, Paul. "An American Cold Warrior: Viva Zapata! (1952)." In *American History/American Film: Interpreting the Hollywood Image*, edited by John E. O'Connor and Martin A. Jackson, pp. 183–201. New York: Frederick Ungar Publishing Co., 1979.

_____ . "Filming History: Promise and Problems." *PCCLAS Proceedings* 4 (1975): 179–82.

"XXV Aniversario de la Muerte de Pedro Infante." *Hispanoamericano*, 26 April 1982, p. 48.

Viany, Alex. "Cine brasileño: lo viejo y lo nuevo." *Cine cubano*, no. 20 (1964), pp. 8–10, 12–29.

_____ . "Production in Brazil." *Films in Review* 2 (February 1951): 28–32.

"Víctimas del pecado: el fin del Centro de Capacitación Cinematográfica." *Nexos* 24 (December 1979): 4–5, 9, 11.

Volman, Dennis. "Brazilian workmen and artists help filmmaker recreate a lost world." [on Carlos Diegues and the making of *Quilombo*] *The Christian Science Monitor*, 23 March 1984, p. 21.

_____ . "Film's New Barbarians: Brazilian Directors Strive to Blend Mass Appeal, Artistic Merit." *The Christian Science Monitor*, 22 March 1984, pp. 16–17.

"'We Are Losing Our Identity': An Interview with Mexican Director Marcela Fernández Violante." *Film Literature Quarterly* 15, no. 1 (1987): 2–7.

Weinberg, Herman G. "Raíces." [review] *Film Culture* 3 (1957): 17–18.

West, Dennis. "Documenting the End of the Chilean Road to Socialism: *La batalla de Chile*." *The American Hispanist* (February 1978), pp. 13–15.

_____ . "Highlights of the First International Festival of New Latin American Cinema." *Review* (Center for Inter-American Relations) 28 (January–April 1981): 53–56.

———— . "Mexican Cinema in 1977: A Commentary on the Mexican Film Festival Presently Touring the U.S." *The American Hispanist* 2 (May 1977): 6–7.

———— . *"One Way or Another (De Cierta Manera)." Caribbean Review* 8 (Summer 1979): 42–44.

———— . "Reconciling Entertainment and Thought: An Interview with Julio García Espinosa." *Cineaste* 16, nos. 1–2 (1987-88): 20–26.

———— . "Slavery and Cinema in Cuba: The Case of Gutiérrez Alea's *The Last Supper." The Western Journal of Black Studies* (Summer 1979): 128–33.

West, Joan M. and West, Dennis. *"Frida."* [film review] *Cineaste* 16, no. 4 (1988): 54, 56.

———— . *"Frida*: An Interview with Paul Leduc." *Cineaste* 16, no. 4 (1988): 55.

White, Arnold. "Films in Focus: Nestor Almendros." *Films in Review* 35, no. 10 (December 1984): 607–609.

Wilson, David. "Letters from Marusia." [review] *Sight and Sound* (Winter 1976/77), pp. 60–61.

Woll, Allen L. "Hollywood's Good Neighbor Policy: The Latin Image in American Film, 1939–1946." *Journal of Popular Film* 3 (Fall 1974): 278–91.

Wollenberg, H.H. "Round the World's Studios." *The Penguin Film Review,* no. 3 (1947), pp. 39–40.

———— . "Round the World's Studios." *The Penguin Film Review,* no. 6 (1948), p. 43.

Wood, Michael. "Buñuel was always ready for death...from the moment he was born." *The Listener,* 9 February 1984, pp. 10–12.

———— . "The Discreet Charm of Luis Buñuel." *American Film,* September 1982, pp. 34–39.

Wu, Ying Ying. "Trying Times in Mexico." *Nuestro,* May 1980, pp. 26–27.

Yakir, Dan. "The Mind of Cinema Novo." *Film Comment,* September-October 1980, pp. 40–44.

Young, Colin. "Letter from Mexico." *Film Quarterly* 14 (Fall 1960): 62–63.

## F. UNPUBLISHED SOURCES

Falcoff, Mark, "Original Sin and Argentine Reality: Peronist History and Myth in *The Traitors*." Paper presented at the Twenty-Second Annual Meeting of the Pacific Coast Council on Latin American Studies, Arizona State University, Tempe, 21-23 October 1976.

Geffner, Daniel I. "Cultural Dependency and Film Industry Development in Latin America, 1900–1970." Paper presented at the Twenty-Third Annual Meeting of the Pacific Coast Council on Latin American Studies, San Jose, California, 20–22 October 1977.

———— . "Film and Revolution in Latin America: Conceptualizing a Structural Framework for Cinema Engagé." Paper presented at the Twenty-Second Annual Meeting of the Pacific Coast Council on Latin American Studies, Arizona State University, Tempe, 21–23 October 1976.

Vanderwood, Paul J. "Images of Mexican Heroes in American Films." Paper presented at the annual meeting of the American Historical Association, Washington, D.C., 28–30 December 1976.

———— . "Response to 'An Overview of Film and Revolution in Latin America.'" Paper presented at the Twenty-Second Annual Meeting of the Pacific Coast Council on Latin American Studies, Arizona State University, Tempe, 21–23 October 1976.

Whittaker, Marsha D. "Socio-political History of the Treatment of Women in Mexican Films, 1930–1975." Paper presented at the Twenty-Third Annual Meeting of the Pacific Coast Council on Latin American Studies, San Jose, California, 20–22 October 1977.

BIBLIOGRAPHY

## G. THESES AND DISSERTATIONS

Amado G., Francisco and Echeverría, Alicia. "El cine mexicano, estudio psicológico." Licenciate thesis, UNAM, 1960.

Bermeo, César Adolfo. "The Political Cinema of Latin America: The Dialectic of Dependency and Revolution." Ph.D. dissertation. University of California, Los Angeles, 1981.

Bixby, Barbara Evans. "The Weave of the Serape: Sergei Eisenstein's 'Que Viva Mexico!' as a Multitext." Ph.D. dissertation, The University of Florida, Gainesville, 1979.

Cisneros, René. "The Comic Verbal and Nonverbal Expression in the Mario Moreno Cantinflas Film: Meaning and Illocutionary Force." Ph.D. dissertation, The University of Texas, Austin, 1978.

Fernández, Henry Cecilio. "The Influence of Galdós on the Films of Luis Buñuel." Ph.D. dissertation, Indiana University, Bloomington, 1976.

Macotela, Fernando. "La industria cinematográfica mexicana. Estudio jurídico y económico." Licenciate thesis, UNAM, 1969.

Mier Miranda, Felipe. "La industria cinematográfica mexicana." Licenciate thesis, UNAM, 1963.

Sandro, Paul Denney. "Assault and Disruption in the Cinema: Four Films by Luis Buñuel." Ph.D. dissertation, Cornell University, Ithaca, N.Y., 1974.

Schnitman, Jorge Alberto. "The Argentine Film Industry: A Contextual Study." Ph.D. dissertation, Stanford University, Palo Alto, California, 1979.

# Index

*Abismos de pasión,* 95, 96
Abitia, Jesús, 22
Academia Mexicana de Ciencias y Artes Cinematográficas, 99
Academy Awards, 134, 156–57
*Actas de Marusia,* 133
*Adiós, adiós ídolo mío,* 147
*Adventures of Robinson Crusoe,* 95, 96
Agüeros, Ernesto, 20
Aguilar, Antonio, 102
Aguilar, Elizabeth, 180
Antonio, Luis, 102
Aherne, Brian, 51
*Ahí está el detalle,* 53
Alarcón, Gabriel, 76–77
Alatriste, Gustavo, 107, 115, 130
Alazraki, Benito, 96
Alba, Luz. *See* Bonifant, Cube
Alcalde, Jorge A., 11
Alcañiz, Luana, 32, 33, 71
Alcoriza, Luis, 49, 91, 105, 106, 107, 115, 116, 117, 120, 121–23, 176, 178, 182
Aldama, Julio, 107
Alemán, Miguel, 75, 76, 77, 78, 84, 87, 114
*alemanismo,* 83, 87
Alexandrov, Grigori, 36
Alfonso XIII, 26
*Allá en el Rancho Grande,* 43, 45, 47–48, 49, 53, 56
Allen, Woody, 164
Allende, Salvador, 1, 134
Almada brothers, 183
*Almas rebeldes,* 48
*Almas tropicales,* 27
Almodóvar, Pedro, 159
Alonso, Ernesto, 92, 160
Alva brothers, 21. *See also* Rosas, Enrique
América studios, 102, 107, 114, 115, 137, 150, 168
*Amok,* 70
*Amor a la vuelta de la esquina,* 150

*Amor nocturno que te vas,* 182
Ampudia Girón, Manuel, 139
ANDA (Asociación Nacional de Actores), 98, 113
Anda, Raúl de, 44, 48, 80
*Angeles y querubines,* 115
*Ante el cadáver de un líder,* 127–28
*Antonieta,* 152
Apollinaire, Guillaume, 30
Aragón Leiva, Agustín, 37
Arau Alfonso, 3, 117, 120, 130, 133, 135, 136, 137
Argentina: alternate cinema in, 2; "dirty war," 185; film production in 1940s compared with Mexico's, 53; U.S. sanctions against, 59; early filmmaking, 262n84; mentioned, 21, 27, 43, 48, 52, 76, 183, 185
Arieles, 99
Armendáriz, Pedro, 58, 59, 63, 66, 70, 95, 151, 185
Armendáriz, Jr., Pedro, 144, 152, 170, 179
Arochi, Fernando, 138
Arrabal, Fernando, 119
*Arrival of a Train,* 6
Asociación de Productores, 102
Asociación Nacional de Actores. See ANDA
Asúnsolo y López Negrete, Dolores. *See* Río, Dolores del
*Atavismo,* 27
*A Trip to the Moon,* 8
Aura, Martha, 168
Autry, Gene, 47
*Aventurera,* 85–87, 133
Avila Camacho, Maximino, 77
Avila Camacho, Miguel, 52, 59, 69, 70, 72, 76
Ayala Blanco, Jorge, 34, 39, 41, 72, 79, 106, 112, 113, 141, 185
*¡Ay Jaliso no te rajes!,* 56, 58
*Ay, qué tiempos, señor don Simón!,* 53, 56, 67

Azcárraga, Emilio, 66, 67
Azteca Films (production company), 20, 21
Azteca Films (U.S. film distributor), 140
Azteca studios, 68

Babette's Feast, 183
Bajo la metralla, 168
Balzaretti, Fernando, 172, 174
Banco de México, 77
Banco Nacional Cinematográfico, 59, 62, 75,
  77, 97, 101, 110, 114, 115, 116, 117, 137,
  138, 153
Banco Nacional de México, 59, 77
BANOBRAS. See Banco Nacional de Obras
  y Servicios
Banco Nacional de Obras y Servicios (BAN-
  OBRAS), 153
Bandera, Manuel de la, 19, 21
Bara, Theda, 25
Barbachano Ponce, Manuel, 96, 103, 154, 157
Bardem, Antonio, 147
Barragán, María. See Fábregas, Virginia
Bassols, Narciso, 41
Batista, Fulgencio, 99
Batman, 147
Baviera, José, 49, 71
Belle de jour, 30, 91–92
belle époque, 5, 29, 53
Beristain, Leopoldo, 13
Bernhardt, Sarah, 15
Best Maugard, Adolfo, 26, 37
Bikinis y rock, 115
biograph, 7
Birth of a Nation, 24
Blanch, Anita, 71
Blasco Ibáñez, Libertad, 70
Blasco Ibáñez, Vicente, 53, 70
Blood and Sand, 53
Blood of the Condor. See Yawar Mallku
Bohemios, 42
Bohr, José, 143
Bojórquez, Alberto, 116
Bolivia, 1
Bolsheviks, 29
Bond, James, 146
Bondarchuk, Sergei, 142
Bonifant, Cube, 34, 39
Bonilla, Héctor, 144
Borges, Jorge Luis, 40
bourgeoisie, attitudes of, 50
Boytler, Arcady, 37, 38
Bracero Program, 73
Bracho, Julio, 53, 60, 62, 66, 74
Brazil: film industry during World War II, 52–
  53; mentioned, 73, 183, 185. See also
  Cinema Novo
Bring Me the Head of Alfredo Garcia, 173

Brook, Claudio, 155
Bugambilia, 70
Buil, José, 147
Buñuel, Luis, 30, 75, 76, 90–96, 99, 101,
  105, 106, 107, 119, 120, 151, 157, 160,
  173
Burón, Leopoldo, 12
Bustillo Oro, Juan, 39, 42, 50, 53, 54, 56,
  59, 60, 81, 106, 120

cabaretera films, 83–87, 97, 130–133
Cabarga, Luciana, 164
cable television, 183, 184
Cadena perpétua, 167
Calabacitas tiernas, 82
Calderón Stell, Guillermo, 140
Caligula, 172
Callejo, Cecilia, 33
Calzonzín inspector, 117
Camacho, Alejandro, 169, 170, 181
Campanas rojas, 142, 152, 164
Campeón sin corona, 80
Camus, Albert, 172
Cannes Film Festival, 40, 62, 134
Canoa, 124–126, 167, 168, 183
Cantinflas. See Moreno, Mario, "Cantinflas"
Capulina vs las momias, 115
Cárdenas, Cuauhtémoc, 174
Cárdenas, Lázaro, 40, 42, 47, 49, 50, 51, 69,
  76, 114, 174
Cardona, René, 106
Cardona, Jr., René, 140
Carewe, Edwin, 26
Caribe, estrella y águila, 135
Carioca, José, 73
Carmina, Rosa, 85
carpa (tent show), 12, 50
Carranza, Venustiano, 17, 18, 19, 20, 21, 106
Carrasco, Ezequiel, 20
Carrillo, Salvador, 69
Cartas del Japón, 115
Casanova, Delia, 168
Castro, Fidel, 103
Catarino, don (music-hall performer), 13
Catholic Church, 52
Cazals, Felipe, 112, 115, 120, 124–26, 133,
  149, 167–68, 169, 170, 172, 174, 182,
  184
CCC (Centro de Capacitación Cinematográf-
  ica), 114, 138, 148, 150, 152
censorship office. See Subdirección de Auto-
  rizaciones
centennial of independence, 11, 14, 15
Centro de Capacitación Cinematográfica, See
  CCC
Centro Universitario de Estudios Cinemato-
  gráficos. See CUEC

"Chaflán," Carlos López, 44
Chagoyan, Rosa Gloria, 159
Chaplin, Charles, 19, 25, 31
Chapultepec studios, 22
Charles, Ramón, 138
charro films, 37, 47. See also ¡Ay Jalisco no te rajes!; comedia ranchera; Mano a mano
Chávez, Carlos, 40
Chevalier, Maurice, 32
Chicano, 136
Chicano films, 136, 137
Chicano grueso calibre, 136
Chicano movement, 135–36
Chicanos, 136. See also Mexican Americans
Chile, 1, 115, 151
chronophone, 28
Chucho el Roto, 42
Churubusco-Azteca studios, 70, 115, 150. See also Churubusco studios
Churubusco studios, 68, 99, 110, 114, 137, 138, 154, 168. See also Churubusco-Azteca studios
Cienfuegos, Jesús, 77
Cimex. See Cinematográfica Mexicana Exportadora
5 nacos asaltan Las Vegas, 163–64
Cinéaste, 155
Cinecitta, 43
Cine Club de México, 99
Cinema Novo: objectives of, 1; mentioned, 111, 120. See also Brazil
Cinemascope, 98, 99
Cinemateca de México, 106
Cinematic Law of 1949, 76, 148
Cinematic Law, new one proposed, 148
Cinematográfica Latino Americana, S.A. See CLASA Films; CLASA studios
Cinematográfica Mexicana Exportadora (Cimex), 98, 114
Cinematógrafo Lumière, first screenings in, 6
Cineteca Nacional, 114, 141–42, 153, 154, 183
CLASA Films, 43, 68
CLASA (Cinematográfica Latino Americana, S.A.) studios, 43, 49, 68
Cline, Howard, summarizes Obregón's administration, 22
Clouthier, Manuel, 174
Colina, José de la, 105
Colombia, 103
color films, 48, 49, 99
Columbia Pictures Spanish Theatrical Division, 140
comedia ranchera, 46, 47, 58, 74, 83, 84, 99, 115
Comisión Nacional de Cinematografía. See National Cinematic Committee

Commedia dell'arte, 14
Communism, 47, 89
Compañero presidente, 115
Compañía Nacional Productora de Películas, 34, 38
CONACINE, 115, 124, 133, 137, 138, 150, 153
CONACITE I, 115, 135, 138
CONACITE II, 115, 150
Confederación de Trabajadores Mexicanos. See CTM
Constitutionalists, 17
Constitution of 1857, 21
Constitution of 1917, 18–19, 21
Constitution of Querétaro, 21. See also Constitution of 1917
Contreras Torres, Miguel, 27, 31, 48, 51, 53, 60, 77
Conventionists, 18
cooperatives, 183
coproductions, 98, 99, 135, 136–37, 139–40, 183
Córdova, Arturo de, 50, 51, 53, 70, 96
Córdova, Pancho, 162
Corkidi, Rafael, 106, 112, 115, 119, 120
Cortés, Alberto, 150, 182
Cortés, Busi, 182
Cortés, Mapy, 53, 102
Cosa fácil, 144
Coss, Joaquín, 21, 22
COTSA (Compañía Operadora de Teatros, S.A.), 150
Cotten, Joseph, 140
Council for Culture and the Arts, 150, 183
Crates, 115, 123
Creo en Dios, 52
creoles, 84
Crespo, José, 32
Crevenna, Alfredo, 163
Crónica de familia, 150
cronófono, 28
Cruz Alarcón, Juan de la, 34
Cruz Diablo, 42
CTM (Confederación de Trabajadores Mexicanos), 42, 69, 70
Cuando los hijos se van, 54, 56, 57, 81
Cuando quiero llorar no lloro, 115
Cuba: new film industry in, 1; prerevolutionary filmmaking, 2; coproductions with Mexico, 99, 135; postrevolutionary cinema, 103; mentioned, 185
Cuba baila, 103
Cubans: in U.S., 34; in Mexican films, 85
CUEC (Centro Universitario de Estudios Cinematográficos), 106, 112–13, 123, 138, 144, 148, 153, 181
Cuevas, José Luis, 105

Cunha, Angela María de, 102
Custodio, Alvaro, 85, 87

Dalí, Salvador, 30
*Damian*, 160
Dancigers, Oscar, 75, 90
Darnell, Linda, 53
Davis, Bette, 51
Davison, Tito, 106
de Carlo, Yvonne, 140
Defoe, Daniel, 168
De Fuentes, Fernando. *See* Fuentes, Fernando de
Delgado, Miguel M., 53, 115
Delluc, Louis, 30
del Río, Dolores. *See* Río, Dolores del
Demare, Lucas, 53
DeMille, Cecil B., 34
*De raza azteca*, 27
Derba, Mimí, 20, 22, 35
*De sangre chicana*, 136
*Diary of a Chambermaid*, 91
*Diary of a Plague Year*, 168
*Días de combate*, 144
*Días difíciles*, 174–75, 183
Díaz, Félix, 16, 21
Díaz, Porfirio: appears in films, 8, 9, 13, 15; economic policies, results of, 10; use of cinema, 13; overthrown, 15; portrayed by John Garfield, 51
Díaz Ordaz, Gustavo, 101, 106, 111, 112, 113
Dictionnaire des Films, 39
Diestro, Alfredo del, 39
Dietrich, Marlene, 32
Dirección de Cinematografía, 88, 102, 135, 150, 153, 181
Directors' Guild, 69, 70, 75, 105
Disney, Walt, 73
*Distinto amanecer*, 60, 66–67, 74, 143
distribution of films: reorganization proposed, 97; reorganization plan announced, 98. *See also* Garduño Plan
*Doña Bárbara*, 60
*Doña Herlinda y su hijo*, 157–59
Donald Duck, 73
*Don Juan Tenorio*, 7, 8
*Don Quijote de la Mancha*, 8
*Dos monjes*, 42, 120
Draper, Jack, 41
Dreiser, Theodore, 36
DRTC (Directorate of Radio, Television, and Cinema), 137–38
Durán, Ignacio, 184
Durazo, "Negro," 144

Eastwood, Clint, 170
Eceiza, Antonio, 135
Echanove, Alonso, 168

Echeverría, Rodolfo, 114, 116, 117, 137, 139, 141. *See also* Landa, Rodolfo
Echeverría Alvarez, Luis, 112, 113, 115, 116, 117, 120, 134, 135, 137, 139, 141, 149, 183
economics of film industry, 19, 38, 48–49, 102–103, 117–19, 139–41
Ecuador, 103
Edison, Thomas A., 6
Eguino, Antonio, 1, 3, 111
*1810 o los libertadores de México. See Mil ochocientos diez*
Eisenstein, Sergei, 25, 31, 36–37, 41, 58
Eisenstinian current in Mexican films, 42, 58, 79–80, 96
*El*, 95, 96
*El ángel exterminador*, 92, 107
*El anónimo*, 37
*El año de la peste*, 168, 174
*El apando*, 126, 167
*El bruto*, 95–96
El Buen Tono, 8
*El cambio*, 115, 123–24
*El castillo de la pureza*, 115
*El caudal de los hijos*, 34, 51
*El chacal de Nahueltoro*, 1, 134
*El changle*, 140
*El compadre Mendoza*, 37, 39–40, 42, 47, 89
*El coraje del pueblo*, 1
*El día que me quieras*, 43
*El día que murió Pedro Infante*, 152
*El fantasma del convento*, 42, 120
*El gallo de oro*, 165
*El gendarme desconocido*, 53, 54, 56
*El gran calavera*, 90–91
*El grito*, 113
*El grito de Dolores* (reviewed by El Imparcial), 11–12, 14
*El hombre sin patria*, 27
*El imperio de la fortuna*, 165–67
*El indio*, 50
Elizondo, Salvador, 35–36, 67, 105–106
*El jardín de tía Isabel*, 115
*El juicio de Martín Cortés*, 82, 127, 128–29
*El lugar sin límites*, 167
*El maleficio*, 2, 160–61
*El miedo no anda en burro*, 162
*El muchacho alegre*, 80
*El otro*, 167
*El precio de la gloria*, 19
*El principio*, 115
*El prisionero trece*, 37
*El profeta Mimí*, 115
*El pulpo humano*, 57
*El rey del barrio*, 82–83
*El rincón de las vírgenes*, 115, 149
El Santo, 102, 146–47, 168, 213n119

*El Santo contra el asesino de la televisión,* 146

*El Santo Oficio,* 167

*El secreto de Romelia,* 183

*El secuestro de Camarena,* 164

*El sueño del caporal,* 27

*El suplicio de Cuauhtémoc,* 14

*El topo,* 119

*El tres de copas,* 169–70

*El último túnel,* 176–78

*Enamorada,* 78, 83

*En defensa propia,* 20

*En el balcón vacío,* 106–107, 109

*En el viejo Tampico. See Gran Casino*

*En este pueblo no hay ladrones,* 108

English-language films, Mexican reaction to, 30–31

*Ensayo de un crimen,* 92–95, 160

*En tiempos de don Porfirio,* 50

Epstein, Jean, 30

*Espaldas mojadas,* 88–89, 102, 136

*Esperanza,* 164–65

Espinosa Iglesias, Manuel, 77

*¡Esquina bajan!,* 80, 123

Estela Pavón, Blanca, 80

Estrada, José, 115, 150, 179, 183

Estrada, Luis, 183

European film industries, crisis of, 185

Fábregas, Manolo, 72, 122

Fábregas, Virginia, 12, 14, 122

Fairbanks, Douglas, 25, 31

Falaci, Oriana, 112

*Fando y Lis,* 119

*Fantômas,* 30

FDN (Frente Democrático Nacional), 174

Federación Mexicana de Cine Clubs, 99

*Fe, esperanza y caridad,* 116

Félix, María, 60, 70, 78, 99, 159

Fellini, Federico, 119

Fernández, Emilio "El Indio," 37, 41, 56, 58–59, 62, 66, 70, 74, 78, 79, 80, 82, 83, 87, 92, 96, 99, 101, 106, 126, 151, 173, 181, 185

Fernández, Fernando, 78

Fernández, Raúl, 159

Fernández, Violante, Marcela, 141, 182

Feuillade, Louis, 30

Feyder, Jacques, 38

*fichera* films, 159. *See also cabaretera* films

Figueroa, Gabriel, 50, 58, 69, 79, 80, 87, 147, 151, 185, 186

*film noir,* 60, 66, 143, 152

Films Mundiales, 59, 62, 68

Fink, Agustín J., 62, 66

fire, in Acapulco movie salon, 14

First Contest of Experimental Cinema, 107–109

Fisher, Ross, 48

Fitzsimmons-Corbett fight, film of, 7

Flaherty, Robert, 41

*Flor silvestre,* 59, 62, 74, 151

Fons, Jorge, 116, 120

Foster, Norman, 60, 70

France, 25, 40, 99, 101, 184, 185

Franco, Francisco, 71

Frausto, Antonio R., 39, 44

French influence: in arts before 1910, 12; on pre-1914 film comedy, 14; new wave, 111; avant-gardists, 120

Frente Democrático Nacional. *See* FDN

*Frida,* 154–57, 170, 183

Fuentes, Carlos, 40, 105, 151

Fuentes, Fernando de, 37, 39, 42, 43, 47, 48, 49, 59, 60, 99, 120, 185

*Fulguración de la raza,* 27

Futurists, 29–30

*Gaby,* 164

Galán, Alberto, 63, 67

Galindo, Alejandro, 48, 50, 53, 56, 57, 60, 69, 80–82, 83, 88, 89, 92, 101, 102, 106, 120, 123, 126–29, 136, 143, 185

Galindo, Jesus A., 165

Galindo III, Pedro, 165

Gallegos, Rómulo, 60

Gamboa, Federico, 34

Gámez, Rubén, 108, 109

Garasa, Angel, 49

Garbo, Greta, 32

García, Sara, 54, 57, 122

García Agraz, José Luis, 152, 153

García Ascot, Jose Miguel (Jomí), 103, 105, 106–107, 109

García Borja, Hiram, 137, 138

García Márquez, Gabriel, 40, 108, 144

García Riera, Emilio: on lack of sources for silent films in Mexico, 5; on Contreras Torres's films, 27; on *Santa,* 35; on Eisenstein, 37; on *El compadre Mendoza,* 39; on *"contenido social,"* 40; on Cantinflas in *El gendarme desconocido,* 53–54; on Galindo dealing with social issues, 81; on *Aventurera,* 87; on editorial board of *Nuevo Cine,* 105; writes script of *En el balcón vacío,* 106; calls for directors' strike, 139; mentioned, 108, 141

Gardel, Carlos, 43

Garduño, Eduardo, 77–78, 97. *See also* Garduño Plan

Garduño Plan, 97

Garfield, John, 51

Gaumont, M. León, 28

Gavaldón, Roberto, 69, 70, 72, 74, 106, 126, 165

Gavilanes, Paco, 7

*género chico*, 12–13
genres, 56, 57, 74, 98, 99
German expressionism, 25, 120, 185
Germany, 25, 40, 43, 59, 184, 185
Getino, Octavio, 2
Glauber, Rocha, 1
Goded, Angel, 156, 170, 172, 180
"Golden Age"; of silent films, 20–21; of
   1946–1952, 75
Gómez Bolaños, Roberto, "Chespirito," 161
Gómez Cruz, Ernesto, 165, 178
González, Cristián, 181–82, 184, 186
González, Gilberto, 41
González, Servando, 176
González Casanova, Manuel, 106
"Good Neighbor" policy, 50
Gout, Alberto, 57, 85, 87, 133
Granat, Jacobo, 14, 15, 17, 18
*Gran Casino*, 76–90, 91
Great Britain, 40, 75, 185
Griffith, D. W., 24
Grovas, Jesús, 59
Grovas, S. A., 59
Guadalupe, Ignacio, 153
*Guanajuato Destroyed*, 8
Guatemala, 103
Guerra, Blanca, 165, 175
Guerrero, Carmen, 39
Guerrero, Juan, 109
Guillén, Ernesto, 35
Guillot, Pascual, 71
Guiú, Emilia, 49
Guízar, Tito, 47–48, 51
Gurrola, Alfredo, 143, 144
Gurrola, Juan José, 109, 156
*Guyana: The Crime of the Century*, 140
Guzmán, Martín Luis, 18

Hammer, Mike (novels), 143
Haro, Felipe de Jesús, 11
Havana Film Festival, 165
Hayworth, Rita, 53
Hearst, William Randolph, 24
Hermosillo, Jaime Humberto, 144, 145, 157
Hernández, Silvio, 41
Hernández Campos, Jorge, 138
Heuer, Federico, 101
Hidalgo y Costilla, Miguel, 11
Hispanic films (Hollywood), 28–29, 31–34,
   43, 45, 75, 106
Hispanics in U.S., 33–34
*Historia del P.R.I.*, 115
Hitler, Adolf, 43, 71
Hollywood films: popularity of, 22; in 1920s,
   25; Mexican actors in, 27; in Spanish,
   French, and German, 32; Hispanic mov-
   ies, 43, 45; Mexican competition with, 49;
   produced in Mexico, 49; effects of World

War II on, 52, 59; implements Good
   Neighbor Policy, 73; distortion of Latin
   American culture in, 74; Luis Buñuel in,
   75; coproductions with Mexico, 136–37;
   mentioned, 53, 101, 134, 185
*Honor militar*, 19
Horton, Edward Everett, 26
*Hostages*, 140
Huerta, Victoriano, 16, 17
Hugo, Victor, 15
Huston, John, 173

ICAIC (Instituto Cubano de Artes e Industrias
   Cinematográficas), 1, 103, 135
Icardo, Rafael, 64
*Il Fuoco*, 20
IMCINE (Instituto Mexicano Cinematográf-
   ico), 149, 150, 153, 183, 184
Inclán, Miguel, 56, 63, 80, 85
independent films, 109–10, 112
"indianist" films, 42
Infante, Pedro, 58, 80, 99, 152
Institute of Fine Art (Belles Artes), 183
Instituto Cubano de Artes e Industrias Cine-
   matográficas. *See* ICAIC
Instituto Mexicano de Cinematografía. *See*
   IMCINE
Interpol, 146
Isaac, Alberto, 108, 109, 112, 115, 117, 120,
   130, 149, 150, 152, 176, 179, 180, 182,
   186
Isaac, Claudio, 152
Italian films: in Mexico, 16, 19; influence on
   Mexican cinema of, 20
Italian neorealists, 36, 111, 185
Italy, 14, 25, 30, 40, 43, 59, 185

Janitzio, 40, 41–42, 62
Jannings, Emil, 31, 32
Japan, 43, 59, 115
*Jengibre contra dinamita*, 50
Jenkins, William O.: U.S. consul in Puebla,
   kidnapped, 21; monopoly over film distri-
   bution, 76–78; mentioned, 97, 110
Jodorowski, Alejandro, 115, 119–20
Jolson, Al, 34
Jones, Rebecca, 181
Joskowics, Alfredo, 112, 115, 123
*Juan Soldado*, 19
*Juarez*, 51
Junco, Tito, 85
Jurado, Katy, 95

Kahlo, Frida, 155, 156, 157
Kamalich, Saby, 180
Kerlow, Max, 156
kinetoscope, 6
Kracauer, Siegfried, 3

Kubin, Alfred, 29
Kuleshov, Lev, 29

L'Age d'or, 30, 75
La banda del automóvil gris, 21, 22
La barraca, 69, 70–72, 74
La casta divina, 137
La Choca, 126
La condición del cine mexicano (book), 185.
    See also Ayala Blanco, Jorge
La Cucaracha, 99
La Decena Trágica (The Tragic Ten), 16
La fórmula secreta, 108
La fuga, 60
La furia de un dios (Lo del César), 170, 171
La guerra gaucha, 53
La historia oficial, 164
La hora de la verdad, 70
La hora de los hornos, 2
La ilegal, 140
La ilusión viaja en tranvía, 95, 96
La India María. See Velasco, María Elena
La isla de la pasión, 56
La víspera, 175
Laiter, Salomón, 106, 109, 148
La linterna de Diógenes, 27
La luz, 20
La madrecita, 162
La madrina del diablo, 48
La mancha de sangre, 84
La mansión de la locura, 115
Lamarque, Libertad, 76
La monja alférez, 70
La montaña sagrada, 115, 119
La mujer del puerto, 37, 38–39, 84
La mujer de nadie, 48
Landa, Rodolfo, 93. See also Echeverría, Ro-
    dolfo
Landeta, Matilde, 142
Land Without Bread, 151. See also Las
    Hurdes—Tierra sin pan
Lang, Fritz, 25
La presidenta municipal, 162
Lara, Agustín, 35
La revolución en Chihuahua, 15
La revolución en Veracruz, 15
Las abandonadas, 70
Las ficheras, 133, 140
La seducción, 167
Las Hurdes—Tierra sin pan, 75. See also Land
    Without Bread
La soñadora, 20
Las Poquiánchis, 133, 167
Last Year at Marienbad, 30
La tierra prometida, 1, 134
"La traición" (telenovela), 173
La viuda negra, 167

Latin America, effects of World War II on,
    52
Latin American culture vis-a-vis mainstream
    Western culture, 40
La vida inútil de Pito Pérez, 60
La Zandunga, 48
Leandro, Norma, 164
Leduc, Paul, 106, 112, 115, 120, 142, 154,
    155, 157, 182
Leduc, Valentina, 155
Lerdo de Tejada, Miguel, 35
Le Silence, 30
Lesser, Sol, 37
Ley del deseo, 159
Linder, Max, 14
Littín, Miguel, 1, 111, 134–35
Llámenme Mike, 142–44
Locarno Film Festival, 62, 107
Lola, 183
Lola la trailera, 159–60, 162, 163, 173
Lombardo Toledano, Vicente, 42, 69
López, Diego, 150, 182, 184
López Aretche, Leobardo, 112
López Mateos, Adolfo, 101, 106
López Moctezuma, Carlos, 54, 78
López Moctezuma, Juan, 115, 164, 176,
    215n35
López Portillo, José, 137, 138, 140, 141, 144,
    152, 168
López Portillo, Margarita, 137, 138, 139, 141,
    147, 149
López, y Fuentes, Gregorio, 50
Lo que importa es vivir, 176, 178–79
Los expatriados, 102
Los Fernández de Peralvillo, 89–90
Los jóvenes, 106
Los mecánicos ardientes, 164
Los motivos de Luz, 168–69, 170
Los olvidados, 91
Los tres García, 80
Lowe, Edmund, 26
Lucero, Enrique, 170
Lucía, 1
Lumière, Louis and Auguste, 2
Lytell, Bert, 26

Macedo, Rita, 93
McLaglen, Victor, 26
Maclovia, 41
Macotela, Fernando, 138
Madero, Francisco, 15, 16, 34
Mad Max films, 165
Madre querida, 45
Madrid Hurtado, Miguel de la, 141, 147, 148,
    149, 150, 153
Magdaleno, Mauricio, 39
Maicon, Boris, 48
Maldonado, Eduardo, 120–21

Malroki, Luis, 164
*Mano a mano*, 37
maquiladoras, 137
Marentes Martínez, Emiliano, 181
*María Candelaria*, 41, 60, 62–66, 74, 151
mariachis, 48
*María de mi corazón*, 144–45
*Mariana, Mariana*, 176, 179–81
*Mariguana, el mónstruo verde*, 143
Marín, Beatriz, 152
Marín, Gloria, 53, 87, 88
Márquez, Luis, 41
Martínez, Adalberto, "Resortes," 90
Martínez Casado, Juan José, 35
Martínez del Río, Jaime, 26
Martínez Ortega, Gonzalo, 115
Marx, Karl, 81
Maupassant, Guy de, 38
*Mecánica nacional*, 115, 117, 121–23
Medina, Ofelia, 156
Méliès, G., 8
melodrama, 57, 74, 83, 99, 115
*Memorias de un mexicano*, 7, 14
*Memories of Underdevelopment*, 1
Méndez, Lucía, 160
Menichelli, Pina, 20
Mexican Americans, 33, 34, 82, 136, 137
Mexican Americans portrayed in Mexican
    films, 80, 88, 135–36, 137
*Mexican Bus Ride*. See *Subida al cielo*
Mexican Cinema Institute, 149, 150. *See also*
    IMCINE
Mexican films in U.S. *See* United States,
    Spanish-language film market in
Mexican image in U.S. films, 24
Mexican Revolution: as model for others, 3;
    films of, 15, 17–18; Díaz resigns, 15; de-
    scribed, 16–17, 18–19; affects Mexican
    image in U.S. films, 24; effects on cin-
    ema, 28; portrayed on film, 43, 44, 47
Mexico: international cultural and political in-
    fluence of, 3; policies under Porfirio Díaz,
    5
Mexico City: 1985 earthquake, 174; pollu-
    tion, 168, 174
*México de mis recuerdos*, 60
México-Films studios, 38, 68
México-Lux production company, 19–20
*México, México, ra, ra, ra*, 130
Meza, Gustavo, 157
Michel, Manuel, 106, 109
*Mientras México duerme*, 50
*1810 o los libertadores de México*, 19
Miller, Paco, 82
*Mina: Viento de libertad*, 135
Ministry of Public Education, 150
*Miracle on Main Street*, 51
Miroslava, 93

Mistral, Gabriela, 40
*Moana*, 41
Modigliani, Amedeo, 30
Monsiváis, Carlos, 38, 48, 106, 136
Montalbán, Ricardo, 70
Montenegro, Sasha, 133
Morales, Roberto A., 48
Moreno, Antonio, 25, 35
Moreno, José Elias, 88
Moreno, Mario, "Cantinflas," 12–13, 48, 50,
    53–54, 56, 68, 69, 70, 82, 97, 136, 140,
    162
Moreno, Mario, Jr., 164
Morillo, Amparo, 72
*Morir en el golfo*, 176
Moscow State School of Cinematography, 29
Mosier, John, 142
*Muertes fértiles*. See *Morir en el golfo*
Muni, Paul, 51
*Muñecas de media noche*, 133, 140
Muñoz, Evita, 80
Muñoz, Rafael F., 44
Murguia, Ana Ofelia, 168
Murnau, F. W., 41
Museum of Modern Art, 67, 75
Mussolini, Benito, 43, 71

Nacional Financiera, 59, 77
National Autonomous University of Mexico.
    *See* UNAM
National Chamber of the Cinematic Industry,
    139, 140
National Cinematic Committee (Comisión
    Nacional de Cinematografía), 77
National Gallery (Washington, D.C.), 157
Nationalist cinema, backed by Banco Cine-
    matográfico, 62
National School for Theatrical Music and Art,
    cinematic school formed as part of, 19
Navarro, Carlos, 41
*Nazarín*, 92, 99, 151
Negrete, Jorge, 48, 56, 58, 69, 70, 76, 87,
    97, 99, 113
Negri, Pola, 31
Neruda, Pablo, 40
New Latin American Cinema: First Interna-
    tional Festival of, 1–2; current status of,
    2; inspirational roots of, 3
newsreels: style of, 14; in 1912, 15; in 1919,
    22; mentioned, 25
New York City, as market for Mexican films,
    34
Nichols, Mike, 90
*Ni de aquí, ni de allá*, 162, 163
*Ni sangre ni arena*, 53, 56
*No basta ser madre*, 57
*Nocaut*, 152–53, 165
Noriega Hope, Carlos, 34

"Northern Dynasty," 21–22
*Nosotros los pobres,* 58, 80, 81, 91, 123, 181
*No te engañes corazón,* 48
*nouvelle vague,* 185
Novarro, Ramón, 26, 27, 32
"Novel of the Mexican Revolution" (literary
    movement), 40
*Novillero,* 48
*Nuevo Cine* (magazine), 105
Nuevo Cine group, 106–106

Obregón, Alvaro, 18, 21, 25
O'Farrill, Rómulo, 77
Office for Coordination of Inter-American Af-
    fairs, 68, 73
Olhovich, Sergio, 150, 164
*Olimpiada en México,* 112
Olympics (1968), 111, 112. *See also* Student
    Movement of 1968
Operadora de Teatros, S. A., 77, 110, 114
Orellana, Carlos, 35
Organización Editorial Mexicana, 149
Orol, Juan, 45
*Oro, sangre y sol,* 27
Orozco, José Clemente, 25, 30
Orozco, María Teresa, 41
Ortiz Ramos, José, 181
Oumansky, Constantin, 66

pachucos, 82
Padilla, Emma, 20, 22
Palma, Andrea, 38, 67, 85
PAN (Partido Acción Nacional), 174
Panchito, 73
Pardavé, Joaquín, 50, 53, 54
Parodi, Alejandro, 165, 174
Parra, Víctor, 80, 88, 89, 90
Partido Accíon Nacional. *See* PAN
Partido Revolucionario Institucional (PRI), 101,
    159, 174
Pascual, el pato (Donald Duck), 73
Pastor, Julián, 108, 137
Pathé Freres, 8, 10, 11
Patiño, Jorge, 144
Paz, Octavio, 151
Peckinpah, Sam, 173
pelado: defined, 43; film portrayals of, 82
Pelayo, Alejandro, 174, 175, 182–84
Pelayo, Luis Manuel, 174
Películas Mexicanas, 98, 114
Películas Nacionales, S.A., 78, 98, 114
Peón Contreras, Arturo, 19
*Pepe,* 136
*Pepito y la lámpara maravillosa,* 127
Pereira, Antonio Carlos, 102
Pérez Turrent, Tomás, 38, 39, 106, 110, 145,
    147, 170
Pershing, John J., 21

Phillips, Alex, 37
Picasso, Pablo, 30
Pickford, Mary, 31, 37
Pinal, Silvia, 107
Pinochet, Augusto, 134
"Plan for the Restructure of the Mexican Film
    Industry," 114
Plan of San Luis Potosí, 15
*Pobre pero honrada,* 162
pochos, 82, 136. *See also* Mexican Ameri-
    cans
"police" films, effects of, 19
*Polvo de luz,* 181, 182
Pons, María Antonieta, 85
popular culture in prerevolutionary period, 13
Posa Films, 50, 53, 68
*Potrero del Llano* (Mexican freighter sunk by
    Germans), 74
Power, Tyrone, 53
PRI. *See* Partido Revolucionario Institucional
Procinemex, 114
Producciones Galindo, 165
production costs, 38
Productora Quetzal. *See* México-Lux
propaganda in films during Revolution, 19
Puerto Ricans, 33–34, 102–103
Puerto Rico, 102, 103
Puig, Manuel, 40
Pulido, Oscar, 89

*¡Que viva Mexico!,* 37, 41, 58
Quinn, Anthony, 151
Quiroz, Luis Mario, 179–80
*QRR (Quién resulta responsable),* 115

racism: in U.S. films, 24; Mexican attitude
    toward, 82; regarding films of La India
    María, 162–63
*Raíces,* 96–97, 103
*Raíces de sangre,* 137
Rambo movies, 164, 183
Ramírez, Holda, 177
*Rastro de muerte,* 167
Rathvon, N. Peter, 68
RE-AL Productions, 140
*Redes,* 40–42, 58
Reed, Donald. *See* Guillén, Ernesto
Reed, John, 142
*Reed: México insurgente,* 115, 142
*Refugiados en Madrid,* 50
regulations on licensing and operation of movie
    salons, 16
Reisman, Phil, 68
Resnais, Alain, 30
Revueltas, José, 126
Revueltas, Rosaura, 136
Rey, Fernando, 92, 107
Reyes, Bernardo, 16

Reyes de la Maza, Luis, 5–6, 11
Reyes Spindola, Patricia, 168
Reynoso, David, 128, 176
Rhode, Eric, 28
Río, Dolores del, 26–27, 31, 32, 37, 48, 58,
    62, 63, 70, 99, 151, 185
*Río Escondido*, 78–80
Ripstein, Arturo, 115, 149, 165, 167
Riva, Juan de la, 152
Rivera, Diego, 25, 30, 36, 78, 155, 156
Rivero, Jorge, 133
RKO Radio Pictures, 68
Rockefeller, Nelson, 68, 73
Rodríguez, Abelardo, 97
Rodríguez, Ismael, 80, 81, 91, 99, 123, 126
Rodríguez, Joselito, 35, 56
Rodríguez, Roberto, 35
Roel, Gabriela, 169
Rogers, Roy, 47
Rojo, María, 144, 178
Rojo, Rubén, 86
Roland, Gilbert, 27
Romay, Pepito, 136
Romero, José Rubén, 60
Roosevelt, Franklin Delano, 50, 72
*Rosa de la frontera*, 164
Rosas, Enrique, 8–9, 13, 14, 20, 21, 22
Roslyn, John R., 6
Roth, Martha, 81
Ruiz, José Carlos, 152, 170
Ruiz Cortines, Adolfo, 97
Rulfo, Juan, 165
*Rumbo a Brasilia*, 102
Ruvinskis, Wolf, 152
Russia, 25, 29, 30, 43, 164

Sadoul, Georges, 38, 39
Saenz de Sicilia, Gustavo, 35
Salamanca talks of 1955 (Spain), 147
Salinas de Gortari, Carlos, 174
Salón Rojo, 10, 14, 15, 17, 18, 20, 24–25
*Saludos Amigos*, 73
Sánchez, Salvador, 156
Sánchez Valenzuela, Elena, 22
*Sangre hermana*, 17
*Sangre y arena* (novel), 53
Sanjines, Jorge, 1, 111
*Santa*, 34–36, 37, 60, 84
Santo. *See* El Santo
*Santo contra el cerébro diabólico*, 102
*Santo contra el Espectro*, 165
*Santo vs la hija de Frankenstein*, 115
satellite transmission, 183
Saura, Carlos, 152
Sbert, José María, 106
Secretaría de Gobernación, 102, 150, 154
*Sensualidad*, 57, 85
Sequeyro, Adela, 48

serials, 19, 22
Serna, Assumpta, 172
Serna, Mauricio de la, 59
Serrano, Irma, 159
Seton, Marie, 37
Sevilla, Ninón, 85, 87
"Siempre en Domingo" (television show),
    162, 181
*Siempre listo en las tinieblas*, 50
*Siempre tuya*, 87
*Siete en la mira II; La furia de la venganza*,
    165
silent films, 5, 16
Silva, David, 80, 81, 88, 89, 90
Silva, Gustavo, 13
Silva Gutiérrez, Zaide, 166
*Simón Bolívar*, 53, 56
*Simón del desierto*, 92, 107
*Simplemente vivir*, 126
Sinclair, Upton, 36, 37
Sindicato de Trabajadores de la Industria Ci-
    nematográfica. *See* STIC
Sindicato de Trabajadores de la Producción
    Cinematográfica. *See* STPC
Siqueiros, David Alfaro, 25, 30, 156
Smith, Paul, 3
social classes, influence of early cinema on,
    19
Society of Composers and Writers, 153
Solanas, Fernando, 2
Soler, Domingo, 38, 44, 71, 79
Soler, Fernando, 33, 50, 54, 81, 85, 90
Solís, Enrique, 42, 69
*Sombrero*, 136
Soto, Roberto, 13
Soto Izquierdo, Enrique, 150
Soto Rangel, Arturo, 78
Soviet Union. *See* Russia
*Soy chicano y justiciero*, 136
*Soy chicano y mexicano*, 136
*Soy puro mexicano*, 74
Spain, 31, 43, 48, 49, 53, 70, 71, 74, 99,
    107, 152, 185
Spanish cinema, 185
Spanish Civil War, 50, 107, 151, 156
Spanish International Network (SIN), 140,
    212n107
Spanish language: silent film titles in, 16; vis-
    a-vis English-language films, 30–31; sub-
    titles in, 32. *See also* Hispanic films
Spanish-language films in U.S. *See* United
    States, Spanish-language film market
Spain's national television network. *See* TVE
    (Televisión Española)
Spanish refugees, 49
Spanish Republic, 72
Spillane, Mickey, 143
Stahl, Carlos, 21, 27

Stahl, Jorge, 9, 10, 21, 27, 31, 38, 68
star system, 57, 75
Star Trek movies, 164
STIC (Sindicato de Trabajadores de la Indus-
tria Cinematográfica), 69, 70, 99, 102,
107, 115, 137, 154
STPC (Sindicato de Trabajadores de la Pro-
ducción Cinematográfica), 69–70, 99, 102,
105, 106, 107, 109, 110, 137, 154, 181.
See also First Contest of Experimental
Cinema
Strand, Paul, 40
student movement of 1968, 111–12
Subdirección de Autorizaciones, 181
Subida al cielo, 95
Superman, 146, 147
Superman, 149
surrealism, 29–30
Survival, 140

Tabu, 41
Tacos al carbón, 127
Taft, William Howard, 13
Taibo II, Paco Ignacio, 144
Tamés, Manuel, 44
Tango Bar, 43
Tarahumara—Drama del pueblo, 115
Tarzan, 146
Técnicos y Manuales, 69. See also STIC;
STPC
Televicine Distribution International Corpora-
tion, 140, 160, 161
Televisa, S.A., 140, 161, 212n107
television, 148, 182
Thanatos, 181, 182
That Obscure Object of Desire, 92
theater, French and Spanish influence on, 12–
13, 14. See also Fábregas, Manolo; Fá-
bregas, Virginia; género chico
The Bullfighter and the Lady, 136
The Cabinet of Dr. Caligari, 29, 42
The Card Players, 6
The Children of Sanchez, 151
The Discreet Charm of the Bourgeoisie, 92
The Graduate, 90
The French Connection, 107
The Great Train Robbery, 8
The Magic Hat, 6
The Milky Way, 92
The Passion of Jesus Christ, 7
The Jazz Singer, 34
The Mad Empress, 51
The North American Invasion, 17
The Pearl, 59
The Promised Dream, 136
The Real Mexico, 24
The Salt of the Earth, 136
The Taming of the Shrew, 78

The Three Caballeros, 73
The Torch, 59
The Wild Bunch, 173
The Wild One, 165
The Young and the Damned. See Los olvida-
dos
Third Contest of Experimental Cinema (1985),
150
Thunder Over Mexico, 37, 41
Tiburón, 21
Tiburoneros, 107
Tiempo de morir, 167
Time in the Sun, 37
Tin-Tan. See Valdez, Germán, "Tin-Tan"
Tissé, Eduard, 36
Tívoli, 117, 130–133
Tlayucan, 107
Tonta tonta pero no tanto, 162
Torena, Juan, 33
Toro, Guadalupe del, 157
Torres, Raquel, 27
Toscano, Carmen, 7, 106, 142
Toscano Barragán, Salvador, 7, 8–9, 14, 142,
185
Toussaint, Cecilia, 155
Tovar, Lupita, 27, 35
Tres hermanos, 74
Treviño, Jesús Salvador, 137
Treviño, Marco Antonio, 157
Tribunal de justicia, 60
Tristana, 92
Trotsky, Leon, 155, 156
Tuero, Emilio, 49, 50, 54
TVE (Televisión Española), 172, 183

Ukamau, 1
UKAMAU Group, 1
Ullmann, Liv, 164
Una familia de tantas, 57, 81–82, 89
UNAM (Universidad Nacional Autónoma de
México), 106, 112
un carbonero en el baño, 8
Un Chien Andalou, 30, 75, 120
Under the Volcano, 173
Un drama en los aires, 8
Uninci Films, 107
Unión de Empleados Confederados del Cine-
matógrafo, 69. See also STIC
Unión de Trabajadores de Estudios Cinema-
tográficos de México. See UTECM
unionization in film industry, 42, 69, 75. See
also STIC; STPC
United States: films of Veracruz occupation,
17–18; tensions with Mexico, 21; movie
production in 1919, compared with Mexico's, 22; Mexico as subject for U.S. films,
22–24; mentioned, 40, 52, 102, 103

United States, Spanish-language film market
  in, 33–34, 140
*Un macho en el salón de belleza,* 164
Urbina, Luis G., 6, 9, 10, 13, 28
*Ustedes los ricos,* 80, 123, 181
UTECM (Unión de Trabajadores de Estudios
  Cinematográficos de México), 42

Valdés, Martha, 89
Valdez, Germán, "Tin-Tan," 82–83
Valentino, Rudolph, 25
Vallarino, Ramón, 44
Valle-González, David, 41
*Vámonos con Pancho Villa,* 43–45, 47, 49,
  89
Vasconcelos, José, 25, 30
Vayre, Gabriel, 6
Vega, Gonzalo, 128, 152
Veidt, Conrad, 31
Velasco, Arturo, 184
Velasco, María Elena, 162, 163, 164, 183
Velasco, Raúl, 162
Velázquez, Agustín, 41
Velázquez, Fidel, 69
Vélez, Lupe, 27, 32, 48
Venezuela, 99, 103
Venice Film Festival, 40
*Verbena trágica,* 33–34
Veriscope, 7
Victoria, María, 164
*Vidas errantes,* 152
videocassettes, 148, 161, 183, 184, 214n27
Villa, Francisco "Pancho," 17, 18, 21, 44
Villa, Lucha, 122
Villaseñor, Isabel, 37

Villaurrutia, Xavier, 34
*Viridiana,* 92, 96, 107
Vitagraph Company, 26, 51
Vitola, 159
*Vuelven los García,* 80

Walerstein, Mauricio, 115
Walsh, Raoul, 26
*War and Peace,* 142
Warner Brothers, 51
*Waterloo,* 142
*Welcome María,* 164
Welles, Orson, 60
Welter, Ariadna, 93
*West Side Story,* 103
Whitman, Stuart, 140
Wiene, Robert, 42
Wilson, Woodrow, 17, 24
Windsor, Claire, 26
Wonder Woman, 147
Wood, Michael, 151
World War I, 2, 18, 21, 43
World War II, effects on Mexico, 72, 73
Wright, Harry, 68, 69
*Wuthering Heights.* See *Abismos de pasión*

Yáñez, Agustin, 181
Yáñez, Eduardo, 160
*Yawar Mallku,* 1

Zapata, Emiliano, 17, 144
Zepeda, Gerardo, 176
Zinnemann, Fred, 41, 58
*Zona roja,* 126
Zurita, Humberto, 152, 169, 170, 172

Compositor: Trend Western Technical Corporation
Text: 10/12 Times Roman
Display: Goudy Extra Bold
Printer: Maple-Vail Book Mfg. Group
Binder: Maple-Vail Book Mfg. Group